TESTAMENTARY CAPACITY

TESTAMENTARY CAPACITY

Law, Practice, and Medicine

Martyn Frost
Stephen Lawson
Robin Jacoby

OXFORD
UNIVERSITY PRESS

OXFORD
UNIVERSITY PRESS

Great Clarendon Street, Oxford, OX2 6DP,
United Kingdom

Oxford University Press is a department of the University of Oxford.
It furthers the University's objective of excellence in research, scholarship,
and education by publishing worldwide. Oxford is a registered trade mark of
Oxford University Press in the UK and in certain other countries

First Edition published in 2015
Impression: 1

Published in the United States of America by Oxford University Press
198 Madison Avenue, New York, NY 10016, United States of America

British Library Cataloguing in Publication Data
Data available

Library of Congress Control Number: 2014959114

ISBN 978–0–19–872752–1

Printed and bound by
Lightning Source UK Ltd

Cover Image: The cover design incorporates the Probate Court certified copy of the will of John Banks, testator in the seminal case of Banks v Goodfellow, 1870.

FOREWORD

Although its title is *Testamentary Capacity*, this book covers a wider range of issues, such as knowledge and approval and undue influence, which are so closely linked that it is essential that they be treated together. On 1 December 2014 I handed down a judgment in a safeguarding case, *The Public Guardian v CT and Another* [2014] EWCOP 51, in which Robin Jacoby had been instructed as the single joint expert. He found that CT had capacity in most of the areas he had been asked to assess, but, as I remarked in the judgment, the most striking feature of the report was 'the repetition of a theme which, like Ravel's Boléro, rises in a continuous crescendo.... I have never read a report on someone's capacity that has contained so many references to the need for "disinterested advice".'

I enjoyed the discussion on the Mental Capacity Act 2005 in paragraph 2.87—'How should practitioners deal with the MCA in practice?' It is ironic that *Banks v Goodfellow* (1870) has withstood the test of time so far, but the days of the MCA are already numbered. We need to reappraise it in order to comply with the United Nations Convention on the Rights of Persons with Disabilities, which the United Kingdom ratified in 2009. The UNCRPD requires statutory safeguards whereby the exercise of legal capacity is 'free of conflict of interest and undue influence.' Undue influence is currently outside the scope of the MCA, though it has been identified by the court of Appeal as forming part of the residual inherent jurisdiction of the High Court, which survived the coming into force of the Act: *DL v A Local Authority and Others* [2012] EWCA Civ 253. When we get round to reconsidering the MCA, we shall need to include undue influence with capacity in a more holistic piece of legislation on decision-making generally.

I must congratulate the authors and the Oxford University Press on their insight in identifying the need for a work of this kind. As a *vade mecum* for members of the medical and legal professions, its provenance includes *Assessment of Capacity: Guidance for Doctors and Lawyers*, the first edition of which was published jointly by the Law Society and the British Medical Association twenty years ago. I wrote the chapter on capacity to make a will in that guidance, but it was only a brief summary, and I am surprised that no one has produced a detailed study of testamentary capacity until now. I must also commend the authors and the publisher on succeeding in their objective by producing a very practical and readable guide, packed with information that most readers will have no difficulty in understanding, retaining, using, and weighing.

Denzil Lush
Senior Judge of the Court of Protection
1 February 2015

AUTHORS' PREFACE

As we hope we will have succeeded in making clear in this book, the twin imperatives of an ageing population and the rise in numbers of people affected by dementia increase the already challenging nature of this area of the law. It is an everyday area of law for a will draftsman, but the very frequency with which wills for the elderly are prepared tends to mask the complexities of the law, and drafting can all too frequently become a routine task, which it should not be. We fear that this is being made more difficult to manage as knowledge of this area of law is being compromised by the pressures of costs, uncertainty about correct practice, and lack of training. The sheer number of cases cited in the text with modern dates is a clue to how many disputes there must be over issues of capacity (particularly because what is reported is the small tip of a large iceberg).

Draftsmen today are in a difficult position:

- The market price of wills is low and the perception of clients is that they are simple matters.
- A draftsman's knowledge is expensive to acquire and maintain.
- Estates generally have a value worth arguing over.
- The court has available to it ever greater expertise in analysis of medical conditions and the effects on capacity.
- The work of the draftsman is much more complex if matters are to be dealt with correctly.

Trying to tie together law, practice, and medicine has not been an easy task, but it has been illuminating, and we hope that it will assist those who want a better understanding of the subject.

While we have been working on this book, the Law Commission has announced a major project to review the law of wills. One thing that has struck us in our research is how persistent the problems of the disposing mind have been and how much common sense can be found in so many of the old decisions in this area. At least one of us would dissent from the Law Commission's view that the 1837 Act is outdated—while it is not beyond reform, it still has much of merit in it. It is heartening to read, however, that reform in this area of law will provide greater certainty and protection both for those making wills and for those who stand to benefit from them. However, whether or not it will avoid the need for expensive litigation, which can divide families and cause great distress, remains to be seen. Disputed inheritance does seem to have an enduring quality in England, from William of Normandy's rather bloody solution down to the present day's disputes that are resolved in a somewhat less murderous way than his.

In our text we have used the masculine such as 'draftsman', 'testator', etc. No offence is intended to women readers. We have used this approach only to avoid clumsiness of language.

The law is as stated at 1 September 2014.
Martyn Frost
Stephen Lawson
Robin Jacoby

ACKNOWLEDGEMENTS

We should like to thank friends and colleagues who have assisted us by reviewing parts of the text and have offered very helpful suggestions. Any errors or omissions remain ours. In particular, we should like to thank: Alex Ruck Keene of 39 Essex Street for his views on parts of Chapter 2; Matthew Hall of Kings Chambers Manchester; Jennifer McGuinness and John Spittle, both of FDR Law; Denise Kitchener; and Dr Catherine Oppenheimer for her invaluable comments on early drafts of Chapters 12 and 13.

Finally, we must express our love and gratitude to our families for their tolerance of obsessives at work.

CONTENTS

TABLE OF CASES

Where cases are discussed fully, references to them are **bold**

TABLE OF LEGISLATION

STATUTES

STATUTORY INSTRUMENTS

TREATIES AND CONVENTIONS

LIST OF ABBREVIATIONS

ACE-R	Addenbrooke's Cognitive Examination—Revised
ACTAPS	Association of Contentious Trust and Probate Specialists
ADL	activities of daily living
ADR	Alternative Dispute Resolution
BADLS	Bristol Activities of Daily Living Scale
CEDR	Centre for Effective Dispute Resolution
CPA	Conservative Party Association
CPR	Civil Procedure Rules
CT	computed tomography
DLB	Dementia with Lewy bodies
GPCog	General Practitioner assessment of Cognition
HMCTS	Her Majesty's Courts & Tribunals Service
ICD	International Classification of Disease
IHT	Inheritance Tax
IQCODE	Informant Questionnaire on Cognitive Decline in the Elderly
MCI	mild cognitive impairment
MMSE	Mini Mental State Examination
MoCA	Montreal Cognitive Assessment
MRI	magnetic resonance imaging
NOS	not otherwise specified
PACP	Pre-Action Conduct Protocol
PAR	Psychological Assessment Resources
PD	Parkinson's disease
STEP	Society of Trust and Estate Practitioners
SVD	small vessel disease
TIA	transient ischaemic attack

1

INTRODUCTION AND GENERAL PRINCIPLES

Introduction

Last scene of all, that ends this strange eventful history,
Is second childishness and mere oblivion,
Sans teeth, sans eyes, sans taste, sans everything.[1]

Shakespeare's very bleak view of the seventh age of man was written at a time when a member of the aristocracy who survived to 21 (in itself something of a major achievement given the high levels of child mortality and royal whims) had a life expectancy of 71. The general population had a much lower life expectancy. In Elizabethan England, there were five times as many under-16-year-olds in relation to over-60-year-olds as there are today. The median age[2] was 22 compared to almost 40 today. Today, we have a greatly enhanced life expectancy, but we have not escaped the seventh age, indeed for many it can be a far longer period than Shakespeare would have thought possible. **1.01**

The Biblical view of the natural lifespan being three score years and ten[3] was not yet a reality in 1900 when the average life expectancy in England and Wales at birth for both males and females was barely 30[4]. It was in the late 1970s that male life **1.02**

[1] William Shakespeare, *As You Like It* Act 2 Scene 7.

[2] The age that divides the population into two numerically equal blocks, i.e. half the population is above the median age and half the population is below it.

[3] King James Bible, Psalms 90:10 '*the days of our years are three score years and ten*'.

[4] Adrian Gallop, actuary, *Mortality Improvements and Evolution of Life Expectancies* UK Government actuary's department; these figures are depressed, in part, by the shocking levels of infant mortality.

expectancy at birth reached 70 in England and Wales (for females it was the late 1940s).

Aspects of Current Population

1.03 Table 1.1 Recent increase in life expectancy

	1963	1980/2	2010/2	Increase 1963 to date	
Life expectancy at birth					
Male	67.9	71.0	79.1	11.2	16.49%
Female	73.9	77.0	82.9	9.0	12.18%
Life expectancy at 65					
Male	76.7	78	83.5	6.8	8.87%
Female	80.1	82	86.1	6.0	7.49%

1.04 Table 1.1 really speaks for itself in highlighting the size of the increase in life expectancy in recent years. While it may not continue to increase at the same rate, it is expected to increase.

1.05 Current percentage survival to older ages for England and Wales is expressed in the following.[5]

- At birth, survival to 65 is - 86.7% for men and 91.2% for women.
- At birth, survival to 85 is - 39.1% for men and 52.5% for women.
- At 65, survival to 85 is - 45% for men and 57.6% for women.

An Office of National Statistics note to these percentage survival figures adds

> Mortality rates at older ages are thought to be improving because of a combination of factors. One major factor is the improvements in mortality from circulatory diseases, such as heart disease and stroke, partly driven by changing smoking habits and medical and technological advances.

1.06 In 2012 it was estimated that 465,500 of the population of England and Wales was aged over 90.[6] This represented just short of 1% of the total population and it was a 33% increase in numbers between 2002 and 2012.[7] The number of persons over 65 was estimated in 2011 at 10.8 million and this represented 16.4% of the total population (or approximately 21% of the adult population).[8]

---

5 Office of National Statistics: <http://www.ons.gov.uk/ons/dcp171778_329858.pdf>.

6 In December 2013 ONS estimated that one-third of babies born in 2013 will live to 100. Of those aged 65 in 2013 8% of males and 14% of females are projected to reach 100.

7 *ONS Statistical Bulletin: Estimates of the Very Old 2002–12 England and Wales* (27 September 2013).

8 It is estimated that by 2025 the population of the United Kingdom that is 65 and over will have reached 17,812,000, or 24.89% of the estimated population of 71,554,000 (UN Population Division

Testamentary capacity has become a much more common problem in recent years because of the implications of the increased longevity shown above. Modern medicine has provided new treatments for diseases which, in the past, would have been fatal at much younger ages or would have substantially reduced a person's lifespan. These advances in medical science have contributed substantially towards survival to older ages. This is also aided by changes in lifestyle e.g. reduction in use of tobacco. The other side of this ageing coin is that, generally, a greater lifespan has brought with it an increased likelihood of some degree of mental deterioration in old age. **1.07**

The same period has seen significant advances in psychiatric knowledge and in diagnosis and treatment, both of which make the assessment of mental illness, and consequently mental capacity, a far more nuanced issue than it was even 50 years ago. A draftsman is not expected to have the same detailed knowledge of mental illness as a medical practitioner practising in this area. The draftsman's contribution is made through observation and questioning and drawing from that a reasonable conclusion as to capacity. While there is obviously no expectation on the part of the court that the draftsman should have the same detailed knowledge as the medical practitioner, the draftsman can still learn from such practitioners. This is particularly true in areas such as questioning, what to observe, and the difference in importance between short- and long-term memory. **1.08**

It is also quite possible that the existence of greater individual wealth (wealth that is also more widely held in post-1945 generations) has generated more reasons for family members to argue about the validity of a will and the distribution of the elderly person's share of this higher value wealth. Why there is greater mass affluence is relatively easy to see, given the long-term rise in property values, the post-war spread of savings/investment culture, higher wages and salaries, and increased pension provision. All of these may have been affected to some extent by the recent economic crisis, but the long-term change over the last 60 years still remains significant. There is also some evidence to show that wealth is a factor in longevity, which, if correct, would suggest that the elderly sector of the population will contain a disproportionate number of wealthy people when compared to other age sectors. **1.09**

An additional complication for the will draftsman is that during this period of increasing wealth there have been significant changes in society, particularly the shift away from the typical family unit most commonly encountered in the early 1960s. It is much more difficult today to say if there is such a thing as a typical family unit in England and Wales.[9] The much greater variety in the family and legal relationships, **1.10**

World Population Prospects; The 2012 Revision). Globally it is estimated that over the next twenty years the world population aged over 65 will double to 1.1 billion, i.e. 13% of the population (*The Economist* 26 April 2014, citing UN population projections).

[9] Consider the reform of divorce law and the rise in second or third marriages; legal and social recognition of same-sex relationships; much greater levels of cohabitation outside marriage/civil partnership; more children born outside marriage; significant changes in women's wealth and their role in

now encountered within households, gives rise to greater problems of equitable distribution for a testator. In consequence, this can easily sow the seeds of a will dispute. There is also less care of the elderly within family units. This in turn has the potential for will disputes to arise out of provision made by testators for friends and carers—who may have provided greater support in old age to the testator than his family members. There are also very real problems of financial abuse of the elderly and vulnerable. These can affect both the terms of a will or the size of estate that remains at the time of death. All of these issues can, and do, make the task of the draftsman harder when dealing with the elderly or vulnerable, in addition to questions of capacity.

Dementia

1.11 The website for Alzheimer's Research UK[10] contains significant data on diagnosed dementia[11] cases in the UK. Their table of percentage sufferers per age band is set out in Table 1.2.

Table 1.2 Percentage of dementia sufferers per age band

Age band	Male	Female
30–59	0.16%	0.09%
60–64	1.58%	0.47%
65–69	2.17%	1.10%
70–74	4.61%	3.86%
75–79	5.04%	6.67%
80–84	12.12%	13.50%
85–89	18.45%	22.76%
90–94	32.10%	32.25%
95–99	31.56%	36.00%

1.12 The Alzheimer's Research UK website estimates that over 820,000 people are currently living with dementia in the UK and that this number is forecast to rise 'rapidly' as the population ages further. Thus, there is an increasing number of people reaching their 80s, and of those who get to 85 approximately 20% will have a form of dementia.[12]

society of women; reform of gender change issues; increased social and geographic mobility of population; reduction in the age of majority; and more people living alone. These are all significant areas of change that have increased during the past fifty years and have continued to change the structure of society.

10 <http://www.alzheimersresearchuk.org>

11 While the issue of dementia is the most significant issue for the elderly and questions of capacity, it must be remembered that dementia is not the only medical condition that can deprive a person of testamentary capacity; nor, sadly, are younger generations free from it.

12 A US report (5 March 2014, in *Neurology*) suggests that the *under-reporting* of deaths where Alzheimer's disease is *a* cause of death in the over 75s was five deaths in six for 2010. It is not known if

The statistics so far in this chapter must give any will draftsman pause for thought. The statistical likelihood that any given elderly client who seeks assistance with a will, or with changes to an existing will, may have a diagnosed, or undiagnosed, degree of dementia means that much greater care is now required in ascertaining capacity. Notwithstanding this, the elderly client is and will remain a very important component of the private client market. Not only does age tend to focus people's attention on the questions of devolution of their wealth, but the rise in the level of private wealth post-war, referred to above, also makes the current elderly generation one that genuinely needs wills. The elderly client's need for a will now requires an increased level of skill on the part of the will draftsman, given the increased likelihood of some degree of reduced mental capacity. It is not possible to meet the needs of such clients without a sound understanding of both the law and practice relating to capacity. **1.13**

In trying to meet the client's needs, the draftsman needs to be aware that allegations of the invalidity of a will, because of a lack of testamentary capacity, lie at the heart of many family disputes and contentious probate actions. Both of these have the potential to do significant damage to family relationships or cause a complete rupture between parts of a family. **1.14**

> Most unfortunately, the circumstances of the making of the 2006 will, and of the manner in which [the testator's sons], on learning of it, subsequently investigated his testamentary capacity, have transformed the formerly close relationship between his sons and daughters into one of mutual suspicion, recrimination and distrust....[13]

The knowledge of this risk ought to ensure that capacity matters are at the forefront when will instructions are taken from the elderly or vulnerable.

General Issues Relating to Testamentary Capacity

The need for mental capacity

The need for testamentary capacity when executing a will is not a statutory requirement: '...from time immemorial...by the law of England no person is considered capable of making a valid will unless he be—to adopt the language of the pleader—of sound mind, memory and understanding'[14]. The requirements of the Wills Act 1837 are concerned with the formalities necessary for a valid will, not the need for capacity. **1.15**

---

the same research would be valid for the UK, but Alzheimer's Research UK has indicated that a level of under-reporting is suspected here. If this is the case, this estimate may be low.

[13] *Re Key, Key v Key* [2010] WTLR 623; see also *Burgess v Hawes* [2012] WTLR 423 at [9] '...the rift in the family is likely to be beyond repair. It is also likely that any assets in the estate will have been eaten up by this litigation. Both of these matters are the unfortunate consequences of this litigation.'

[14] *Mortimer on Probate* 1st edn., 1911, at page 42 cited in *Re Perrins, Perrins v Holland* [2010] WTLR 1415 at [13].

1.16 The need for mental capacity is not confined to wills; 'It is a general requirement of the law that for a juristic act to be valid the person performing it should have the mental capacity (with the assistance of such explanation as he may be given) to understand the effect of that particular act…'.[15] Otherwise explained as

> The general rule of English law, whatever the context, is that the test of capacity is the ability (whether or not one chooses to exercise it) to understand the nature and quality of the transaction. The classic statement of principle goes back to the advice of the judges to the House of Lords in M'Naghten's case (1843) 10 Cl & F 200. That, of course, was a criminal case where the judges were concerned to define the ambit of the defence of insanity. But on this very general level of abstraction—that capacity is dependent upon the ability to understand the nature and quality of the transaction—the same basic principle applies whether the question is as to capacity to enter into a contract, to execute a deed, to marry, to make a will, to conduct litigation, to consent to a decree of divorce, or to consent to medical treatment.
>
> Munby J (as he then was)[16]

Test of mental capacity generally

1.17 The general principle applied in any test of mental capacity, for any transaction that a person undertakes, is that the level of mental capacity required is tested on

1. the individual involved and
2. the complexity of the task being undertaken.[17]

This is not to be regarded simply as making a will, or entering into a contract at some generalized or abstract level, it means the particular task that is to be undertaken by that person.[18]

> …an idiot cannot make any testament, nor may dispose either of his lands or goods. But if a man be of mean understanding (neither of the wise sort nor the foolish) but indifferent, as it were betwixt a wise man and a fool, yea though he rather incline to the foolish sort, so that for his dull capacity he might worthily be termed grossum caput, a dull pate or a dunce, such a one is not prohibited to make a testament: unless he be yet more foolish, and so very simple and sottish, that he may easily be made to believe things incredible or impossible, as that an ass can fly, or that in old time trees did walk, beasts and birds could speak…
>
> Henry Swinburne *A Treatise of Testaments and last Wills etc* (7th edn., London, 1803) p 127

[15] *Hoff v Atherton* [2005] WTLR 99 at [33] per Peter Gibson LJ citing *Re K (Enduring Power of Attorney)* [1988] Ch 310 at page 313.

[16] *Re E, Sheffield City Council v E & S* [2004] EWHC 2808 (Fam) at [19]; *In re K (Enduring Power of Attorney), In re F* [1988] Ch 310 at 313 F-G Hoffman J (as he then was) said that it was well established that '*capacity to perform a juristic act exists when the person who purported to do the act had at the time the mental capacity, with the assistance of such explanation as he may have been given, to understand the nature and effect of that particular transaction.*'

[17] *Masterman-Lister v Brutton* [2003] WTLR 259 CA; *Gibbons v Wright* (1954) 91 CLR 423 at 438 '*The mental capacity required by the law in respect of any instrument is relative to the particular transaction which is being effected … and may be described as the capacity to understand the nature of that transaction when it is explained.*' (applied in *Re Beaney deceased* [1978] 2 All ER 595 and *In the estate of Park deceased* [1954] P112).

[18] '*One cannot consider soundness of mind in the air, so to speak, but only in relation to the facts and the subject matter of the particular case.*' *Gibbons v Wright* (1954) 91 CLR 423.

This has also been expressed by Chadwick LJ as 'first that the mental capacity required by the law is capacity in relation to the transaction which is to be effected. Second that what is required is the capacity to understand the nature of that transaction when it is explained.'[19] There is in this statement the additional qualification of the explanation being given to the client. In other circumstances, and this point is considered further in Chapter 2 on the test for testamentary capacity, a person's capacity to understand the transaction can be aided by an adviser's explanation of what is entailed in the act and its consequences. This is a realistic approach, as few laymen will understand fully the nature of many of the legal transactions they enter into, such as that of making a will, without an explanation of what the act entails. But, in providing the explanation, the adviser cannot simply rely upon having given advice in order to have enabled the client to understand—understanding must be checked and ascertained by the advisor. Explanation, in other words, is not merely telling. **1.18**

A person under 18 is not capable of making a will.[20] **1.19**

Degree of impairment

For any individual, it is not a mental impairment per se that might prevent the testator from having sufficient capacity, but it is the degree of that impairment[21] and its effect on the person's understanding of the transaction.[22] Thus, a person with dementia is not automatically disqualified from making a will—it is the degree of dementia that disqualifies him.[23] This apparently simple proposition will, however, often involve issues of very fine judgement—see Lord Cranworth's famous remark that 'between [a manifestly incapable person] and that of a man of perfectly sound and vigorous understanding there is every shade of intellect, every degree of mental capacity. There is no possibility of mistaking midnight for noon, but at what precise moment twilight becomes darkness is hard to determine.'[24] **1.20**

---

[19] *Masterman-Lister v Brutton* [2003] WTLR 259 CA at [58] Chadwick LJ citing *Ball v Mallin* (1829) 3 Bligh NS 1 and *Harwood v Baker* (1840) 3 Moore 282.

[20] s. 7 Wills Act 1837 as amended by s. 3(1)(a) Family Law Reform Act 1970 for wills after 1 January 1970; the exception to this is a privileged will s. 11 Wills Act 1837 and Wills (Soldiers and Sailors) Act 1918, see later at 1.38.

[21] There is no distinction for this purpose between the types of illness that may affect capacity; the matter is approached on the basis of its outcome, i.e. whether there is the ability there to make a will. *Banks v Goodfellow* (1870) LR 5 QB 549 at 569–70.

[22] *Viva! Campaigns Ltd & The Vegetarian Society v Scott* [2014] WTLR 525 at [64] 'The sanity or otherwise of [a legacy of £800,000] turns not on [the testator's] partiality for food such as sausages, a full English breakfast or a traditional roast turkey at Christmas; nor does it turn on the fact he was a schizophrenic with severe thought disorder. It really turns on the rationality or otherwise of his instructions.'

[23] *Hoff v Atherton* [2005] WTLR 99; *McClintock v Calderwood* [2005] EWHC 836; *Blackman v Man* [2008] WTLR 389; *Carr v Beaven* [2008] EWHC 2582 (Ch); *Vadakathu v George* [2010] WTLR 135 (Singapore High Court) where it was found that the more serious the illness, the higher was the threshold of proof.

[24] *Boyce v Rossborough* (1857) 6 HL C 2 at 45.

1.21 It is to be noted that a person who is detained on mental health grounds, for example under the powers contained in the Mental Health Act 1983, cannot be assumed to be incapable of making a will, or of undertaking other legal acts, simply because he is subject to an order.[25] Such a person's ability to make a will should be tested in exactly the same way as any other testator. In similar circumstances, in *D'Eye v Avery*[26] a will was made by a stroke patient in respect of whom a receiver had been appointed by the Court of Protection. The testator was found to have had testamentary capacity.[27]

Alcohol and drugs

1.22 Further, capacity may be absent not as a direct consequence of an illness, but indirectly because of the medication that a person receives to treat or alleviate the effects of his illness or injury. This is potentially a most difficult area, as few draftsmen will have sufficient knowledge to judge the effects of prescribed drugs on the mental capacity of a testator or to give any guidance to the court.[28] It does mean that where a testator is known to be receiving prescribed medication, particularly in substantial quantities, care in the draftsman observing the testator's mental state, actions, and understanding is vital (as is his accurate recording of those observations).

1.23 The abuse of alcohol and drugs (prescribed or unprescribed) does not necessarily mean that a person lacks capacity, including testamentary capacity, unless the effect of the alcohol or drug results in the testator not understanding what he is doing.[29] The effect of alcohol or drugs may be temporary but there is also the risk

---

[25] Nor is a person detained in prison barred from making a will; *Re Crippen* [1911] P 108.

[26] [2001] WTLR 227.

[27] '...this is an absolutely marginal case, on the very cusp, as it were, of testamentary capacity... On the balance of probabilities, and with doubts that I have expressed, I find that he could just have made a valid will' at page 244C—nonetheless the will was invalid for want of knowledge and approval. In *D'Apice v Gutkovich—Estate of Abraham (No 2)* [2010] NSWSC 1333, Mrs Abraham was found to have testamentary capacity despite being subject to a guardianship order and probably lacked the capacity to execute a power of attorney.

[28] Consider also the effect of a regime of several everyday drugs taken together as was the case in *Richards v Allen* [2001] WTLR 1031 where it was found that they were capable of altering the testatrix's cognitive processes.

> It must be remembered that Olive was a diabetic and had a recent history of poor control. In addition she was on a number of drugs; Gliclazide for her diabetes, Sinemet, Dothiepin, Clonazepam, Aspirin and Lactulose. Some of those, on the evidence I have heard, were capable of altering the mental state, so far as that is relevant to capacity—Dothiepin and Clonazepam, for example. One of the experts... referred to the possibility of side-effects affecting a patient's cognitive process arising from the interaction of so many drugs... I find that [her confusion] was due to her medical condition and the drug regime.
>
> Anthony Mann QC (sitting as a Deputy Judge); *Clancy v Clancy* [2003] WTLR 1097.

But not all cocktails of drugs will have this effect *Jeffrey v Jeffrey* [2013] WTLR 1509.

[29] *Chana v Chana* [2001] WTLR 201; *Airey v Hill* (1824) Addison 202; *Brunt v Brunt* (1873) 3 P&D 37 (invalid revocation by destruction during a bout of *delirium tremens*); *Billingshurst v Vickers* (1810) ER 956; *Re Heinke's Estate* [1959] CLY 3449 (an invalid codicil executed at the end of a night of heavy drinking).

of permanent mental impairment from illness brought on by the effects of drug or alcohol abuse.

Eccentric wills

Eccentricity, foolishness, and capriciousness are not in themselves necessarily evidence of a lack of capacity.[30]—although it must be said that there might be a fine line between such characteristics and lack of capacity.[31] This is not to overlook that the plain and obvious rationality of a will can argue for the valid capacity of the testator.[32] **1.24**

In *Bird v Luckie*[33] Wigram V-C observed that although the law requires a person to be capable of understanding the nature and effect of an action, it does not insist that the person behaves '... *in such a manner as to deserve approbation from the prudent, the wise, or the good. A testator is permitted to be capricious and improvident, and is moreover at liberty to conceal the circumstances and the motives by which he has been actuated in his dispositions.* **1.25**

---

30 *Sefton v Hopwood* (1855) 1 F & F 578 at 580;

> That does not mean he should make what other people think a sensible will, or a reasonable will, or a kind will, because by the laws of this country, a man has absolute dominion over his own property, and if he being in possession of his faculties thinks fit to make a capricious will, a harsh will, or a cruel will, you have no right to set it aside on that ground...

Pilkington v Gray [1899] AC 401 (Privy Council) 'eccentricity alone does not prevent a man from disposing of his property by will';

Vaughan v Marquis of Headfort (1840) 10 Sim 639 at 641 'By the laws of this country, every testator, in disposing of his own property, is at liberty to adopt his own nonsense'

Hart v Tulk (1852) 2 De GM & G 300 at p313 'Testators are not bound to have good, or any, reasons for what they do'

Buckenham v Dickinson [2000] WTLR 1083 at 1090D; 'Eccentricity, lack of justice, lack even of common sense in the dispositions is not of itself enough'

Cowderoy v Cranfield [2011] WTLR 1699 at paragraph [133] '... it is made clear that it is possible for a testator to make a valid will even where its provisions are unfair vindictive or perverse' (comment on *Boughton v Knight* (1873) LR 3 P&D 64 and *Gill v RSPCA* [2010] WTLR 251 CA)

Schrader v Schrader [2013] WTLR 701 at [82] 'Testators do strange things and are entitled to be whimsical, capricious, vindictive, wrong in belief or their acts beyond explanation without that of itself proving incapacity.'

Boughton v Knight (1873) LR 3 P&D 64 'may disinherit his children, leave his property to strangers to gratify his spite, or to charities to gratify his pride'

> *Testamentary capacity is not reserved for people who are wise, or fair, or reasonable, or whose values conform to generally accepted standards. A person may disinherit a child for reasons that would shock the conscience of most ordinary members of the community, but that does not make a will invalid.*
>
> per Gleeson CJ Re Estate of Griffith deceased, *Easter v Griffith* NSWCA 7 June 1995 unreported.

31 See *Sharp v Adam* [2006] WTLR 1059 CA where the irrationality of decision making was found to be a symptom of the disease the testator suffered from.

32 *Banks v Goodfellow* (1870) LR 5 QB 549; *Cartwright v Cartwright* (1793) 1 Phillim 90.

33 (1850) 8 Hare 301, but an irrational or capricious will may be easier to get set aside or have its provisions modified by the court.

Many a testamentary provision may seem to the world arbitrary, capricious and eccentric.' [34] A modern version of this view is to be found in *Hawes v Burgess*:[35]

> ...the freedom of testation allowed by English law means that people can make a valid will, even if they are old or infirm or in receipt of help from those whom they wish to benefit, and even if the terms of the will are hurtful, ungrateful or unfair to those whose legitimate expectations of testamentary benefit are disappointed. The basic legal requirements for validity are that people are mentally capable of understanding what they are doing when they make their will and that what is in the will truly reflects what they freely wish to be done with their estate on their death.

A similar comment comes from Canada:

> Will making does not require sound judgement... if it did a great many wills might well be ruled invalid, although no question of insanity could arise.... It is the perverse influence of mental disorders affecting judgement that invalidates the will, not the use of judgement under the influence of 'normal' perverseness, whimsy or fantasy.[36]

1.26 Questions of morality of dispositions are also not necessarily issues of capacity—'the inquiry is directed to the testator's soundness of mind, and not to general questions of perceived morality.'[37] Despite the apparent clarity of that remark, in practice the issue may be less clear cut. In *Sharp v Adam*,[38] the testator made a will which made no provision for his two daughters. At the time that the will was made the testator was severely debilitated by progressive multiple sclerosis and the question of his testamentary capacity arose. The court acknowledged the ability of a capable testator to make an irrational, unjust, or unfair will and that such a will must be upheld by the court. If however the irrational, unjust, or unfair act (here excluding children from benefit) possibly arose through a disorder or disease of the mind then the court must look at the reasons why the testator had acted in that way to determine if it was because of a disease of the mind. But, in the light of the quotation at the start of this paragraph, that investigation should not be tinged with moral judgement. The irrational or unjust cause of the will became a question of whether or not it was a manifestation of the lack of capacity (and it was).

Alleged statements of the testator

1.27 A claim that a will that is inconsistent with what the testator may have said about his will in his lifetime is not normally to be taken as evidence of incapacity.[39] It is an

[34] (1850) 8 Hare 301 at 306.

[35] [2013] WTLR 453 CA per Mummery LJ at [14].

[36] *Re Gregory* (1979) 37 NSR (2d) 640 at 657.

[37] *Sharp v Adam* [2006] WTLR 1059 at [79] per May LJ or 'for many years an English testator has been free to confer a princely endowment upon a prostitute or a charity and leave his family penniless' E. H. Burn and J. Cartwright *Cheshire & Burn Modern Law of Real Property* (16th edn., Oxford: OUP, 2000).

[38] [2006] WTLR 1059.

[39] Nor of undue influence; *Wharton v Bancroft* [2012] WTLR 693 at [112].

old problem that members of a family are often firmly convinced that what a relative has said about his will was the truth, even though others in the family claim to have been given a contradictory account. These statements have long been cautioned against as often being partisan and unreliable with passage of time.[40] The quotations below illustrate the point that this is not a new problem—there are nearly 200 years between the first two.

- It is one of the painful consequences of extreme old age that it ceases to excite interest, and is apt to be left solitary and neglected. The control which the law still gives to a man over the disposal of his property is one of the most efficient means which he has in protracted life to command attention due to his infirmities.[41]
- What testators or intending testators are recollected as having said in casual conversation about wills they have made, or are intending to make, is a notoriously unreliable indicator of true testamentary intention, being often tailored to the audience or said for some temporary advantage in family relationships.[42]
- Wills frequently give rise to feelings of disappointment or worse on the part of relatives and other would-be beneficiaries. Human nature being what it is, such people will often be able to find evidence, or to persuade themselves that evidence exists, which shows that the will did not, could not, or was unlikely to, represent the intention of the testatrix, or that the testatrix was in some way mentally affected so as to cast doubt on the will. If judges were too ready to accept such contentions, it would risk undermining what may be regarded as a fundamental principle of English law, namely that people should in general be free to leave their property as they choose, and it would run the danger of encouraging people to contest wills, which could result in many estates being diminished by substantial legal costs.[43]

The statement that the testator makes when, without assistance or influence, he **1.28**
writes out his own will in rational suitable terms can mean that the will itself then argues, by its rationality, for the capacity of its author: '...unquestionably there must be a complete and absolute proof the party who had so formed it did it without assistance. If the fact be so that he has done as rational an act as can be without the assistance from another person, what there is to be proved I don't know...'[44]

---

[40] See *Gill v Woodall* [2011] WTLR CA 251 at [17]; *Hawes v Burgess* [2013] WTLR 453 CA at [14]; *Re Devillebichot, Brennan v Prior* [2013] WTLR 1701; *The Vegetarian Society v Scott* [2014] WTLR 525 at [23].

[41] *Van Alst v Hunter* [1821] 5 Johnson NY Ch Rep 159 per Chancellor Kent.

[42] *Wharton v Bancroft* [2012] WTLR 693 at paragraph [73] (Norris J as he then was).

[43] *Gill v Woodall* 2011] WTLR 251 per Neuberger MR (as he was then) at [16]; see also *Catling v Catling* [2014] EWHC 180 (Ch) at [53]

> She said that [the testatrix] was often in tears, complaining that her other children did not visit her, and that she intended to leave all her money to Kevin. I accept that [the witness] is reporting what she heard, but I attach very little weight to it. Firstly, elderly demented patients will often say things that are not true. Secondly, it is conceivable that [the testatrix] was angry with her family for not visiting, and that she did not realise that this was Kevin and Shirley's fault. Thirdly, given her vulnerability, she might simply have said whatever she thought Kevin and Shirley wanted to hear.

[44] *Cartwright v Cartwright* (1793) 1 Phill Ecc 90 at 101.

Delegation by the testator

1.29 The testator's power to make a will is personal to him and it is not capable of being delegated to another by him.[45] Thus a testator, fearing his declining capacity or illness, cannot delegate, by lasting power of attorney, his power to make a will to enable his attorney later to make a will on his behalf.[46] Nor could a person away from the country authorize another to make his will for him during his absence.

1.30 It would be a risky course of action to attempt to avoid the impossibility of delegating the will making, by executing a will which simply left the entire estate upon a discretionary trust with the trustee having as wider a power as possible[47] to distribute the estate. It is obviously not suggested that such a will is impossible, particularly where there are valid reasons for the discretionary trust being used. But using a discretionary trust does not obviate the need to establish an ability to understand and appreciate, on the part of the testator, those who have claims on his bounty. Without establishing this ability it could be difficult to demonstrate that the testator passed all parts of the test in *Banks v Goodfellow*.[48] This could be particularly so where it is not apparent that there is the ability to weigh the relative bounty for the individual beneficiary (in terms of appreciating their claim on his bounty) or prepare a coherent letter of wishes. Suggesting a discretionary trust is used simply because the testator is unable to make up his mind which individual[49] or individuals he wants to benefit is not acceptable. The testator should have an understanding of who is to benefit and why there needs to be flexibility in the later distribution by using a discretionary trust.

1.31 Preparing a sharia compliant will,[50] where the distribution will be determined after death by the nominated sharia court or expert, does, on the face of it, have a degree of similarity to the delegation issue, given that the testator will not have determined the provision that each individual will receive, nor will he have weighed the relative needs and merits of the individuals and made his choice between them.[51] This can

---

[45] *Re Morris, Lloyds Bank v Peake* [1970] 1 All ER 591; 'he cannot leave it someone else to make a will for him' *Attorney-General v Nation Provincial and Union Bank of England* [1924] AC 262 at 268; *Hastilow v Stobie* (1865) 1 P&D 64. Such 'a will is void in law. For as thy soul is not my soul, so thy will is not my will, nor thy testament my testament' Henry Swinburne *A Treatise of Testaments and last Wills etc* (7th edn., London, 1803) p 23.

[46] Execution of his will by another at his direction in his presence, s.9 Wills Act 1837, is a different issue that relates to the formalities of execution only and not the decision-making regarding the dispositions.

[47] *Chichester Diocesan Fund and Board of Finance v Simpson* [1944] AC 341; *Re Beatty's Will Trusts* [1990] 3 All ER 844 on the nature and validity of wide powers for these purposes.

[48] See Chapter 2.

[49] The position with a discretionary trust for charities should be a little different provided the testator is able to understand the charities or areas of charity work that he wishes to assist.

[50] See the Law Society Practice Note of 13 March 2014.

[51] The recent Law Society Practice Note on Sharia compliant wills (13 March 2014 (now withdrawn)) did not deal with how the draftsman is to ascertain capacity where the testator is not making decisions as to the individual amounts of benefit.

then present the draftsman with the practical difficulty of establishing the testator's capacity to understand those who have claims on his bounty. This does argue for the draftsman establishing the extent to which the testator comprehends, in broad terms, who he is intending to benefit and to what extent. This seems, in practice, to be little different to the discretionary class issue in the preceding paragraph.[52]

The testator cannot delegate his power to revoke a will.[53] **1.32**

A person who has appointed an attorney, under whatever type of power, still has the power to make a will, provided he has sufficient mental capacity to meet the test for testamentary capacity. It may be the case a person lacks the capacity to manage their own affairs but still has testamentary capacity because the two tests are distinct. Where a testator wants to make a new will under these circumstances, the need for clear evidence of testamentary capacity will figure prominently. **1.33**

A will can be directed to be made for a person, who lacks testamentary capacity, by the court.[54] **1.34**

Partial validity

The test of testamentary capacity is usually considered in respect of the whole will and that therefore it is not viewed as possible to find that there was capacity, or incapacity, in respect of only part of it.[55] Undoubtedly that will usually be case. There is a decision, *In the Estate of Bohrman, Caesar v Bohrman*,[56] where it was found that only one provision in a codicil was invalid (because of an insane delusion that the London County Council was persecuting the testator). The correctness of the decision has been doubted.[57] **1.35**

A further decision on partial validity arose from the application of the rule in *Parker v Felgate*,[58] but the report is lacking in detail and sets out little or no judicial reasoning **1.36**

[52] Both the discretionary trust and sharia-determined distribution are additionally vulnerable to claims under the Inheritance (Provision for Family and Dependents) Act 1975 where it is successfully argued that the provision made is unreasonable for a claimant.

[53] *Re Smith's Goods* (1869) LR 1 P&D 717; *Stockwell v Ritherdon* (1848) 1 Rob Eccl 661; revocation of his will by another at his direction in his presence (s. 20 Wills Act 1837) is a different issue and relates merely to the act of revocation, not the intention or decision to revoke.

[54] ss. 16 and 18, Mental Capacity Act 2005; such wills are outside the scope of this book.

[55] Partial validity of a will could be possible where there are issues of knowledge and approval (*Fuller v Strum* [2002] WTLR 199; *Rhodes v Rhodes* (1882) 7 App Cas 192; *Fulton v Andrew* (1875) LR 7 HL 448; *Re Duane's Goods* (1862) 2 Sw & Tr 590 (words inserted without instruction or knowledge)) or undue influence *Wingrove v Wingrove* (1885) 11 PD 81.

[56] [1938] 1 All ER 271.

[57] 'to be of doubtful validity' *Theobald on Wills* (17th edn., Sweet & Maxwell, 2013) at 3–013; 'a singular decision which should perhaps be treated with caution' Barlow et al. *Williams on Wills* (9th edn., LexisNexis Butterworths, 2013) 4.15. Winegarten et al. *Tristram & Coote's Probate Practice* (30th edn., LexisNexis, 2010) at 34–30 notes the case and finding without further comment.

[58] (1883) 8 PD 171—see Chapter 3 for detailed comment on this rule.

on this point. The decision in question is *Thomas v Jones*,[59] where it was found that the will instructions, for all except the residuary clause, were given when the testator had capacity; but when instructions were given for the residuary gift the testator had lost capacity. The testator retained sufficient capacity under the rule in *Parker v Felgate* to execute the will validly for all of the will apart from the residuary gift. The residuary clause could not be admitted to probate on the same basis as the earlier instructions.

1.37 These two decisions seem to raise the possibility that a will could be partially valid/partially invalid. The most likely possibility for this to happen would be on the basis of a delusion where the will is almost entirely rational but for a bequest driven by a delusion. An example might be where the estate is divided equally between the testator's children and another person that the testator believes, on a wholly irrational basis, to be his child as well. However, the dearth of judicial decisions, particularly recently, in this area mean that it is a possibility that is to be approached with caution.

Privileged wills

1.38 A person under 18 is not capable of making a will,[60] but a person entitled to make a privileged will may do so under this age provided they have the necessary testamentary capacity.[61] The circumstances under which such wills can be made may make evidence of testamentary capacity difficult to establish. There is the possibility of privileged wills being made after severe, even potentially mortal, injury on active service or at sea. Under these circumstances, while being sure that a court would be most considerate as to the issue, there are real issues as to a person's ability to pass the test of the three separate limbs of *Banks v Goodfellow*.[62]

Revocation of a will

1.39 Revocation of a will by a person lacking the capacity to do that act will be an ineffective revocation. Where a later will, containing a revocation clause, is found to be invalid, the valid will it attempted to revoke will remain valid.[63] It is not unknown

---

[59] [1928] All ER Rep 704.

[60] s. 7 Wills Act 1837 as amended by s. 3(1)(a) Family Law Reform Act 1970 for wills after 1 January 1970.

[61] s. 11 Wills Act 1837 and Wills (Soldiers and Sailors) Act 1918. Before the 1837 Act there was no requirement for wills of soldiers on active (now actual military) service, or mariners or seamen at sea, to be in writing and s. 11 continued this position. The 1918 Act extended this to The Royal Navy and Royal Marines when on actual military service (if this was not at sea) and also provided that 'soldier' applied to members of the RAF. For a recent application of s. 11 see *Re Servoz-Gavin deceased, Ayling v Summers* [2009] 1657.

[62] For a detailed discussion of such wills see an article by Christopher Parker at <http://www.trustees.org.uk/review-index/Wills-Privileged-wills-A-timely-reminder.php>.

[63] *Brunt v Brunt* (1873) 3 P&D 37 where revocation by destruction was invalid because of insanity due to delirium tremens.

for several successive wills to be found to be invalid and one would then follow the sequence of wills backwards to find the last valid will.[64] Revocation by destruction[65] where the testator lacks the mental capacity to revoke is invalid.[66] The will of a person with capacity is not revoked if he subsequently loses capacity,[67] just as a will made by a person lacking capacity is made valid if he later regains capacity.[68]

The mental capacity required to revoke a will is the same as that required to make one. In *Re Sabatini*[69] it was argued that there should be a lower level of capacity for revocation by destruction, as it should be sufficient to understand that the person receiving benefit under the will no longer merited the testator's bounty. This argument was rejected by the court finding that testamentary capacity was required for revocation. It follows that a testator must be capable of **1.40**

- understanding the nature of the act of revocation for a will, and
- understanding the effect of revoking this particular will.[70]

The exception to the requirement of testamentary capacity being required to revoke a will is revocation by entering into a marriage or civil partnership. For these two events, revocation is by operation of statute.[71] A will is not revoked if it was made in expectation of a particular marriage or civil partnership and the testator intended the will not be revoked by that marriage or civil partnership.[72] Revocation by marriage, or civil partnership, does not require any intention to revoke the will.[73] **1.41**

The level of mental capacity required to enter into a valid marriage is a lower level of capacity than is needed to make, or revoke, a will—'the contract of marriage is a very simple one which does not require a high degree of intelligence to understand. It is **1.42**

[64] A good argument for not destroying wills of an elderly client, it being simpler to prove the original will rather than a copy.

[65] s. 20 Wills Act 1837.

[66] *Brunt v Brunt* (1873) 3 P&D 37, but nonetheless there is the possibility of effective revocation if the contents of the destroyed will cannot be established from other sources; *Sugden v Lord St Leonards* (1876) 1 PD 154.

[67] *Forse and Hambling's Case* (1588) 4 Co Rep 60 b.

[68] *Bunter v Coke* (1707) 1 Salk 237 (unless it is validly re-executed when he regains capacity).

[69] *Re Sabatini* (1970) 114 SJ 35.

[70] There is no authority to suggest that this entails a detailed understanding of what the distribution on intestacy would be for the testator's estate, any more than a testator would need to have such an understanding when making a will.

[71] s. 18 (marriage) and s. 18B (civil partnership) Wills Act 1837; but divorce, or dissolution of a civil partnership, does not have the same effect; s. 18A and s. 18C. But see also the new s. 18(2) and s. 18D (introduced by the Marriage (Same Sex Couples) Act 2013 (Consequential and Contrary Provisions and Scotland) (No. 2) Order 2014) where a civil partnership is later converted to a marriage following s. 9 Marriage (Same Sex Couples) Act 2013.

[72] ss. 18 and 18B Wills Act 1837; see also *Court v Despallieres* [2010] WTLR 437 if no particular marriage or civil partnership is contemplated.

[73] *Israell v Rodon* (1839) 2 Moo PCC 51 (it is assumed that, although this question has not been before the court in the context of a civil partnership, a court would approach a civil partnership on the same basis).

an engagement between a man and a woman to live together and love one another as husband and wife to the exclusion of all others.'[74] In addition, it is necessary for a person to also have the mental capacity to consent to sexual relations as this is usually taken to be implicit in a marriage.[75] Capacity to marry is to be tested as at the time of the ceremony.[76]

1.43 Given the lower level of mental capacity required, marriage and civil partnership are therefore capable of revoking a will in circumstances where the testator lacks both the capacity to revoke the will and the capacity to make a new will.

1.44 Where either party to the marriage or civil partnership is incapable of understanding[77] the nature of the contract they have entered into, the marriage or civil partnership is voidable. A marriage,[78] or civil partnership, that is voidable, whether subsequently annulled or not, revokes a previously made will[79] (unless that will was made in expectation of the marriage or civil partnership). This leaves the curious, and potentially unwelcome, result that a will is capable of being revoked by marriage not only with a lower level of understanding than is required to make a will, but also with a lower standard of understanding than is required to form a valid marriage or civil partnership. This result is arrived at as s. 16 Matrimonial Causes Act 1973 provides that a decree of nullity only annuls a marriage in respect of time after the decree and not before it.[80]

---

[74] *Durham v Durham* (1885) 10 PD 80; see also *In the Estate of Park, Park v Park* [1954] P 112 (where the testator was found to lack capacity in respect of the will he made on the day of his marriage which made some provision for his new wife. The marriage was valid and she inherited more on his intestacy); *Sheffield City Council v E (An Alleged Patient)* [2004] EWHC 2808 (Fam) at [68] also [at 144] 'There are many people...who may be of limited or borderline capacity but whose lives are immensely enriched by marriage. We must be careful not to set the test of capacity to marry too high, lest it operate as an unfair, unnecessary and indeed discriminatory bar against the mentally disabled.' The test for capacity to marry makes no judgement about the wisdom or suitability of the chosen partner; *Sheffield City Council v E* [2004] EWHC 2808 at [84]; *ABC v XZ* [2013] WTLR 187 at [32].

It is assumed here that the court will follow the same test of capacity to marry for the capacity to enter into a civil partnership.

[75] *X City Council v MB, NB and MAB (By his litigation friend the Official Solicitor)* [2006] EWHC 168 (Fam) at [56] and s. 30 Sexual Offences Act 2003.

[76] *Harrod v Harrod* (1854) 1 K & J 4.

[77] 'did not validly consent to its formation (whether as a result of duress mistake unsoundness of mind or otherwise)' s. 12(c) Matrimonial Causes Act 1973 and also s. 50(1)(a) Civil Partnership Act 2004.

[78] *Re Roberts, Roberts v Roberts* [1978] 3 All ER 225 (it is assumed that, although this question has not been before the court in the context of a civil partnership, a court would approach a civil partnership on the same basis).

[79] A marriage that is voidable, but is not annulled by the time of one party's death, leaves the remaining party as a surviving spouse, i.e. a voidable marriage cannot be annulled after the death of one party; see *Morley-Clarke v Brooks* [2011] WTLR 297 (a marriage voidable for lack of capacity and non-consummation where the surviving spouse was entitled on intestacy as the spouse).

[80] For civil partnerships, a nullity order, made under s. 37(1) Civil Partnership Act 2004 similarly does not take effect retrospectively; see s. 37(3).

A void marriage does not revoke a will.[81] **1.45**

Lost wills

Where a will or codicil is last traced to the testator's possession[82] and, despite all reasonable searches and enquiries, it cannot be traced after his death, it is presumed that he has destroyed the will with the intention of revoking it.[83] This is a rebuttable presumption,[84] of which it was said that **1.46**

> It was clear from the old authorities that those presumptions were not intended to be regarded as rigid statutory rules, when they would produce absurd results, but as indications of the inferences which would always be drawn by the court from a given state of evidence. The court would approach the question by considering what was the most probable explanation of the absence of the will on the testator's death.[85]

Where, after taking possession of the will, the testator loses testamentary capacity, this presumption of revocation by destruction will not apply.[86] It must instead be shown that the will was destroyed by the testator while he had capacity, with intention of revoking it, and the burden of proof will lie on the person alleging revocation.[87] It must be assumed, on the same basis, that where a valid will is made in a lucid interval in an existing mental illness, and the will is retained in the testator's possession, the presumption will not apply. **1.47**

Testamentary capacity and other transactions

It is the case that wills are often dealt with in conjunction with other transactions, e.g. **1.48**

- Completion of a power of attorney
- Sales of assets
- Making a gift[88]

---

[81] *Mette v Mette* (1859) 1 Sw & Tr 416; *Re Roberts, Roberts v Roberts* [1978] 3 All ER 225; for the definition of a void marriage see s. 11 Matrimonial Causes Act 1973 (for civil partnerships s. 49 Civil Partnership Act 2004)

[82] If the will has been handed to a third party to hold for the testator, this presumption cannot apply; *Chana v Chana* [2001] WTLR 205; in *d'Eye v Avery* [2001] WTLR 227 it could not be shown that the will was ever in the testator's possession.

[83] *Allan v Morrison* [1900] AC 604; *Animus revocandi*; an essential requirement for valid revocation s. 20 Wills Act 1837.

[84] *Patten v Poulton* (1858) 1 Sw & Tr 55; *Chana v Chana* [2001] WTLR; *Re Zielinski deceased, Korab-Karpinski v Lucas-Gardiner* [2007] 1655.

[85] *In the Estate of Yule deceased* (1965) 109 Sol Jo 317. For recent decisions see *Re Dickson* [2002] WTLR 1395; *Rowe v Clarke* [2006] WTLR 347; *Nicholls v Hudson* [2007] WTLR 341; *Wren v Wren* [2007] WTLR 531.

[86] It would be unreasonable to presume not only that the testator revoked his will by destroying it but also that this action was carried out during whatever part of the period the testator had sufficient capacity to revoke.

[87] *Sprigge v Sprigge* (1868) LR 1 P&D 608.

[88] See Chapter 2 on the capacity to make a lifetime gift.

- A tax planning exercise
- Severance of a beneficial joint tenancy
- Mutual will agreement

The draftsman will be focussed on the question of capacity for the will, but he should not overlook that each, or any, of the other actions taken will need to be considered for questions of capacity in their own right. This is because the applicable test for capacity for each of those actions may contain different elements, or requirements, from those required for wills. A mutual will agreement, while often seen as an integral part of the will that it applies to, is in fact a contract[89] between the (usually) two testators and therefore should be thought of in terms of the capacity to enter into a contract.

Domicile

Introduction

1.49 In England and Wales,

- *A will disposing of movable property*: the applicable test of testamentary capacity for any testator is determined by the domicile of the testator at the time of the execution of the will.[90]
- *A will disposing of immovable property*: the general rule is that the law governing testamentary capacity will be that of the *lex situs*.[91] This underlines the central importance of understanding the realty in an estate, and where it is located, when preparing a will.

This underlines the central importance that domicile has in the will-making process. Whilst a full exploration of domicile is outside the scope of this book, it is of such importance to the question of testamentary capacity that some salient points are worth covering.

1.50 All interviews for will instructions should contain questions on the domicile of the testator. With many testators this will be a relatively simple matter because of their connection being with a single country. However, the difficulty with questions on domicile is that few, if any, clients have any reasonable understanding of domicile and are therefore unlikely to respond in any meaningful way to the question 'What is your domicile?' The client is more likely to give relevant information if the relevance

[89] If it deals with a will containing a specific gift of land it is a contract the disposition of an interest in land (s. 2 Law Property (Miscellaneous Provisions) Act 1989); *Healey v Brown* [2002] WTLR 849.

[90] *Re Fuld's Estate (No 3), Hartley v Fuld* [1965] 3 All ER 776 citing *In the goods of Maraver* (1828) 1 Hag Ecc 498.

[91] The law of the jurisdiction where the property is situate; see *Re Ross* [1930] 1 Ch 377.

and nature of domicile are explained. Then the draftsman's questions can be focussed on the information that will help the draftsman form a judgement of the issue; this will be much more effective than simply asking what the testator considers his domicile to be.

Summary of principles

In *Morris v Davies*[92] the judgment set out ten principles of domicile in *English* law:[93] **1.51**

1. A person is, in general, domiciled in the country in which he is considered to have his permanent home. A person may sometimes be domiciled in a country although he does not have his permanent home in it.
2. No person can be without a domicile.[94]
3. No person can at the same time, for the same purpose, have more than one domicile.[95]
4. An existing domicile is presumed to continue until it is proved that a new domicile has been acquired.
5. Every person receives at birth a domicile of origin.
6. Every independent person can acquire a domicile of choice by a combination of residence and an intention of permanent or indefinite residence, but not otherwise.
7. Any circumstance that is evidence of a person's residence, or of his intention to reside permanently or indefinitely in a country, must be considered in determining if he has acquired a domicile of choice.
8. In determining whether a person intends to reside permanently or indefinitely, the court may have regard to the motive for which residence was taken up, the fact that residence was not freely chosen, and the fact that residence was precarious.
9. A person abandons a domicile of choice in a country by ceasing to reside there and by ceasing to intend to reside there permanently, or indefinitely, and not otherwise.
10. When a domicile of choice is abandoned, a new domicile may be acquired, but if it is not acquired, the domicile of origin revives.

---

[92] [2011] EWHC 1773 (Ch), but the section quoted on domicile derives from a summary in *Barlow Clowes International Ltd v Henwood* (2008) EWCA Civ 577, which in turn was based on *Conflict of Laws* (14th edn., Dicey Morris and Collins).

[93] Domicile is established for the purposes of English law by the application of English rules and concepts, not the rules and concepts of other jurisdictions that the person might have some connection with; *Lawrence v Lawrence* [1985] Fam 106; *Rowan v Rowan* [1988] ILRM 65 (although there may be statutory exceptions to this).

[94] *Mark v Mark* [2005] UKHL 42.

[95] *Mark v Mark* [2005] UKHL 42; *IRC v Bullock* [1976] 1 WLR 1178. This statement refers to English law. It is possible, and not infrequently encountered, that another jurisdiction, with which a person is connected, can at the same time consider that person to be domiciled there. This does not create a dual domicile for either jurisdiction, but merely that each jurisdiction takes a different view of where the person is exclusively domiciled.

Commentary on principles

Domicile of origin

1.52 All persons will start life with a domicile, conferred on them at birth, which is known as their domicile of origin. This is determined as follows.

1. It is the domicile of a child's father, if the child is legitimate and born in the lifetime of his father.
2. It is the domicile of his mother, in all other cases.[96]
3. A foundling is treated as domiciled in the place where he is found.[97] An adopted child takes the domicile of his adoptive parents.

The domicile of origin remains with a person unless, or until, it is replaced with a domicile of choice.[98]

1.53 The domicile of a child is not taken from the place of birth. A child's domicile of origin can change to a domicile of dependence. This can be acquired while the child is below 16 and the father's domicile is changed. This domicile of dependence will remain even if the father dies before the child attains the age of 16. However, for such a child, there can be a change of domicile of dependency if the mother changes her domicile and the child accompanies her.[99]

Domicile of choice

1.54 Notwithstanding this domicile of origin, a person may later change his or her domicile by acquiring a domicile of choice[100] after attaining the age of 16 or marrying under that age.[101] To change a person's domicile requires that person to have sufficient mental capacity to form that intention.[102] In the case of a domicile of choice it is essential to show not only that the person resided in the country[103] in which he claims a domicile of choice, but that he intended to reside there thereafter as his permanent home,[104] or, if not permanently, at least indefinitely.[105] The length of time in that country to acquire a domicile of choice can be very short, provided the

96 *Udny v Udny* (1869) LR 1 Sc & Div 441.

97 *Re McKenzie* (1951) 51 SRNSW 293.

98 *Re Fuld* [1968] P 675 at 682.

99 *Re Beaumont* [1893] 3 CH 490.

100 Since 1974 married women have been able to acquire a domicile of choice like anyone else; Domicile and Matrimonial Proceedings Act 1973.

101 s. 3(1) Domicile and Matrimonial Proceedings Act 1973.

102 *Urquhart v Butterfield* (1887) 37 Ch D 357; this point is not dealt with by the Mental Capacity Act 2005 (nor was it covered by the Mental Health Act 1983). There is little modern authority in this area, particularly on the level of capacity required.

103 In this context, '*residence*' is physical presence '*as an inhabitant*'; *IRC v Duchess of Portland* [1982] Ch 314.

104 i.e. a domicile of choice requires both fact (residence) and intention (to remain)—*animo et facto*.

105 A person who determines to spend the rest of his life in a country has the necessary intention even though he does not regard his determination as irrevocable—*IRC v Bullock* [1976] 1 WLR 1178.

intention and presence are there, and the evidence supports it.[106] Where the length of time spent in the country of choice is of some length, there is no presumption that a domicile of choice has been acquired,[107] but the length of stay can be an important factor in favour of a domicile of choice (when taken into account with all other factors).[108] This not simply a matter of what a person considers his domicile to be, but it involves factual evidence to prove that the new domicile has been acquired before the previous domicile can be lost. A person can form a domicile of choice in this country even though they have no legal right to be present there.[109] Scarman J (as he then was) said in *Re Fuld*:[110]

> (1) The domicile of origin adheres unless displaced by satisfactory evidence of the acquisition and continuance of a domicile of choice; (2) a domicile of choice is acquired only if it is affirmatively shown that the propositus is resident in a territory subject to a distinctive legal system with the intention, formed independently of external pressures,[111] of residing there indefinitely. If a man intends to return to the land of his birth upon a clearly foreseen and reasonably anticipated contingency, e.g., the end of his job, the intention required by law is lacking; but, if he has in mind only a vague possibility, such as making a fortune (a modern example might be winning a football pool), or some sentiment about dying in the land of his fathers, such a state of mind is consistent with the intention required by law. But no clear line can be drawn; the ultimate decision in each case is one of fact—of the weight to be attached to the various factors and future contingencies in the contemplation of the propositus, their importance to him, and the probability, in his assessment, of the contingencies he has in contemplation being transformed into actualities. (3) It follows that, though a man has left the territory of his domicile of origin with the intention of never returning, though he be resident in a new territory, yet if his mind be not made up or evidence be lacking or unsatisfactory as to what is his state of mind, his domicile of origin adheres ...

Should a person who has established a domicile of choice subsequently lose that domicile: **1.55**

(a) English law will not permit him to lack a domicile for even an instant in time;
(b) his domicile of origin will be revived immediately on losing his domicile of choice[112] and the domicile of origin will continue unless, or until, he acquires another domicile of choice;

---

106 *White v Tennant* (1888) 8 SE 596, a US case where a domicile of choice was found to have been acquired with less than one day's presence.

107 *Agulian v Cyganik* [2006] WTLR 565 CA; *Holliday v Musa* [2010] WTLR 839 CA.

108 *Holliday v Musa* [2010] WTLR 839 CA; *Peters v Pinder* [2011] WTLR 1379.

109 *Mark v Mark* [2005] 2 FLR 1193; [2005] UKHL 42.

110 *Re Fuld* [1968] P 675 at 684F–685D, this passage being expressly approved by the Court of Appeal in both *Agulian v Cyganik* [2006] WTLR 565 CA and *Holliday v Musa* [2010] WTLR 839 CA.

111 *Udny v Udny* [1869] LR 1 Sc & Div 441: '*There must be a residence freely chosen, and not prescribed or dictated by any external necessity, such as duties of office, the demands of creditors or the relief from illness.*' For old age and illness see *Re Sylvester, Sylvester v Sylvester* [2014] WTLR 127.

112 *Udny v Udny* (1869) LR 1 Sc & Div 441.

(c) any previous domicile of choice will not be revived on losing his current domicile of choice unless he re-establishes his physical presence in that country coupled with a renewed intention to permanently reside there i.e. establishes it as a new domicile of choice;

(d) on the loss of a domicile of choice and revival of the domicile of origin there is no requirement for any contact with the jurisdiction of domicile of origin such as physical presence or intention to reside there.

1.56 It is possible that a person's domicile of origin may be that of a country which he has never been present in. He was born in country B, by a father resident in B but domiciled in A. The child then grows up and acquires a domicile of choice in B. He later leaves B to live and work in C although not with any intention to permanently reside there. He will have lost his domicile of choice in B and reverted to his domicile of origin in A.[113]

1.57 Acquisition of a domicile of choice involves the assessment of a wide range of factors—indeed any factors that a court considers relevant—in order to establish both intention and residence:

> All that can be said is that every conceivable event and incident in a man's life should be considered, taking account things said and done after as well as before the time when it is alleged that the chosen domicile has been acquired.[114] . . . Nothing must be overlooked that might possibly show the place which he regarded as his permanent home at the relevant time. No fact is too trifling for consideration.[115,116]

Given the wide range of factors that can be relevant the Court of Appeal has warned of the risks of isolating one factor as being determinative as to domicile.[117]

Where can a person be domiciled?

1.58 A testator can only be domiciled in a 'law district' which is legally recognized and distinct. While this is usually a nation state, in federated states (e.g. the US, Canada, and Australia) it is usually an individual state or province. Within the United

---

[113] *Udny v Udny* (1869) 1 LR Sc & Div 441; *Henwood v Barlow Clowes International Ltd (in liquidation)* [2008] EWCA Civ 557.

[114] *Bheekhun v Williams* (1999) 2 FLR 229 CA.

[115] *Drevon v Drevon* [1864] 34 LJ Ch 129—'*There is no act, no circumstance in a man's life, however trivial it may be in itself, which ought to be left out of consideration in trying the question whether there was an intention to change the domicile. A trivial act might possibly be of more weight with regard to determining this question than an act which was of more importance to a man in his lifetime.*'

[116] J. Fawcett and J. M. Carruthers *Cheshire, North, and Fawcett: Private International Law* (14th edn., Oxford: OUP, 2008) p 164.

[117] *Agulian v Cyganik* [2006] WTLR 565 CA at [46] '*Special care must be taken in the analysis of evidence about isolating individual factors from all the other factors . . . and treating a particular factor as decisive . . . the judge's treatment of that one factor as decisive or conclusive of domicile must be examined with care*', approved in *Holliday v Musa* [2010] WTLR 839 CA at [15].

Kingdom,[118] England and Wales,[119] Scotland,[120] and Northern Ireland are separate jurisdictions, as are the Crown Dependencies.[121]

Will instructions

Will instructions cannot be taken safely without ascertaining the facts relating to domicile. Even so, attempting to advise the client conclusively of what his domicile is at the time of the will, and what it will be later at his death, can be dangerous. Domicile, for the purposes of the effect of a will, can only be determined at death and much can change in a person's life between his will and death. Further, factors that the testator may consider significant in his lifetime can be viewed as less important by a court. **1.59**

Whether or not the testator is domiciled in a particular jurisdiction, and at what time, is, within English law, generally decided on the facts as known at the date of death i.e. when a court has to determine the issue of the validity of the will. Further, the arbiter of domicile is the court[122] and it will assess domicile on the facts as established. In the second of the two Court of Appeal quotations below, there is a reminder of the requirement that clear, cogent, and compelling evidence is required to lose the domicile of origin and obtain a domicile of choice. Without that kind of evidence the domicile of origin remains,[123] which makes the domicile of origin a stronger bond and one which will prevail without a clear weight of evidence for change. **1.60**

The Court of Appeal in *Agulian v Cyganik*[124] made the following two points: **1.61**

1. Although it is helpful to trace Andreas's life events chronologically and to halt on the journey from time to time to take stock, this question cannot be decided in stages. Positioned at the date of death in February 2003 the court must look back at the whole of the deceased's life, at what he had done with his life, at what life had done to him and at what were his inferred intentions in order to decide whether

[118] Deemed domicile, a concept for IHT purposes only, is a United Kingdom taxation domicile only.

[119] After the creation of the Welsh Assembly, law-making powers were devolved to Wales, but for succession law purposes England and Wales are in effect still one jurisdiction.

[120] Scotland has always been a separate jurisdiction for the purpose of domicile.

[121] The Isles of Man, Jersey, Guernsey, Alderney, and Sark.

[122] HMRC may take a view as to a person's domicile, but that is no more than an opinion and domicile ultimately is a decision for the court.

[123] J. Collier and P. Rogerson *Collier's Conflict of Laws* (4th edn., Cambridge: CUP, 2013) at p15: the domicile of origin '*is more tenacious than a domicile of choice. A domicile of origin can only be lost by intentional acquisition of another domicile, but a domicile of choice can simply be lost by leaving the relevant country intending not to return as an inhabitant.*'

The character of a domicile of origin '*is more enduring, its hold stronger and less easily shaken off*' *Winans v A-G* [1904] AC 287.

[124] [2006] WTLR 565.

he had acquired a domicile of choice in England by the date of his death.[125] Soren Kierkegaard's aphorism that 'Life must be lived forwards, but can only be understood backwards' resonates in the biographical data of domicile disputes.

Mummery LJ

2. All the cases state that a domicile of origin can only be replaced by clear[,] cogent and compelling evidence that the relevant person intended to settle permanently and indefinitely in the alleged domicile of choice.

Longmore LJ[126]

1.62 The draftsman must also never lose sight of the fact that the English view of domicile is primarily a common law concept. Other common law jurisdictions may apply a similar domicile test (but it is unlikely to be applied in a completely identical way, given the decisions of the courts within their jurisdictions). Outside common law countries, the concept of domicile is generally unknown. Countries will apply their own tests, for example:

- habitual residence (e.g. Argentina, Belgium, or China);
- nationality (e.g. Germany, Greece, Italy, or Spain).

1.63 Crucially this means that a testator with a connection to more than one jurisdiction might be considered to be subject to the law of more than one jurisdiction by applying separately the tests of each jurisdiction. For example, an English-domiciled person resident in Belgium might have both jurisdictions validly (according to their own law) claiming jurisdiction over the estate. Even where the connection is with two common law jurisdictions applying similar principles it is far from uncommon for both states to maintain that domicile is within their state.[127]

1.64 Some have suggested inserting in to the will a statement as to the testator's domicile, but this may prove to be of very limited value.[128] It might very well be preferable, and more effective, to arrange for a separate document, signed by the testator, that recites

[125] See also Lord Atkinson in *Casdagli v Casdagli* [1919] AC 145 at 178 '*... the tastes, habits, conduct, actions, ambitions, health, hopes and projects of* [him] *were all considered as keys to his intention to make a home in England.*' (referring to the decision in *Winans v A-G* [1904] AC 287).

[126] '*The acquisition of a domicile of choice is a serious matter not lightly to be inferred from slight indications or casual words*' Scarman J (as he then was) in *Re Fuld's Estate (No 3)* [1968] P 675. A domicile of origin '*is more enduring, its hold stronger and less easily shaken off*' than a domicile of choice; *Winans v Attorney-General* [1904] AC 287.

[127] This tends to arise because domicile requires the identification and assessment of relevant facts and the judgement involved in that exercise leaves scope for different conclusions in different courts.

[128] The usefulness of such statements can vary and information matters more to the court than a simple claim of what the testator regards his domicile to be:

> *I am not prepared to attach importance to a declaration by a man as to his domicile unless there is evidence to show that the man knew what 'domicile' means. A declaration by a man made orally or in writing that he intends to remain in a certain country will, if not inconsistent with the facts, be of assistance in determining the question whether he has become domiciled there. Domicile is however a legal conception on which the views of the layman are not of much assistance.*

the information relevant to the domicile of the testator and what his intentions are.[129] Bearing in mind that advice is going to be given to the client, preserving the information and documentation upon which the advice has been based is important, in order to:

(a) substantiate the reasons for the advice,
(b) support the claimed domicile in any future negotiations or proceedings, and
(c) support any future reconsideration of the client's position.

Where the client is clearly domiciled in England and Wales but owns foreign movables and immovables, the position is somewhat different. The draftsman is competent to deal with the client's property in this country, and arguably movables abroad, as these will be governed by the law of the client's domicile. Nonetheless, it should be stressed that this applies only in relation to English private international law and another jurisdiction where the movables were situated might take a different view, especially if the gift was in the form of a trust. In relation, however, to foreign immovables, the English practitioner cannot go ahead without taking advice from a practitioner competent in the jurisdiction in which the immovables are situated. **1.65**

If at all possible, a separate will dealing with foreign immovables and movables should be executed. In that case, the practitioner must make sure that it is clear on the face of the will what property is excluded from it. In particular, the practitioner needs to ensure that the new English will does not revoke any extant foreign wills by accident. **1.66**

It is important for the practitioner to take particular care with instructions from testators who, although resident in England and Wales, originate from Eire or Scotland. Both countries have legal rights of succession to part of a deceased's estate. Because of the degree of mobility of population between these countries and England and Wales it is not uncommon for a proper examination of the acquisition of a domicile of choice to be overlooked.[130] Too often it is assumed to have been acquired simply because of length of residence, or even solely the fact of residence, but if there is a long-term intention to return to the country of origin a domicile of choice will not have been obtained. **1.67**

Any discussion of domicile issues with a testator must be approached with care and the language used should be accurate, clear, and capable of being understood by a **1.68**

Romer LJ in *A-G v Yule and Mercantile Bank of India* (1931) 145 LT 9 at 17. Such statements in a will may simply be self-serving *Henwood v Barlow Clowes International Ltd (in liquidation)* [2008] EWCA Civ 557.

[129] As with most statements relevant to a person's intentions or reasons, such statements may well carry more weight with a court if they are in the words of the individual rather than in a document clearly drafted by a legal adviser. This is not to say that the legal adviser should not advise of issues to be covered or clarity of the language.

[130] Both these jurisdictions apply similar domicile tests to that applied in England and Wales.

layperson. The approach of the court to domicile set out in the first quotation from *Agulian v Cyganik*[131] given above shows what a difficult concept it can be for a client to understand.

Taxation

1.69 Regardless of his or her own intentions, a person may be subject in the UK to 'deemed domicile' rules for the purposes of Inheritance Tax. This is a special rule, without parallel in other taxes, by which a person may be treated as domiciled here if:[132]

- he was domiciled in any part of the UK under general legal principles within the last three years; or
- he was merely resident in any part of the UK in not less than 17 of the last 20 years of assessment in which 'the relevant time' falls.

For this purpose 'the relevant time' means the time of a transfer; which could for example be the date of death. This concept can frequently be a source of confusion in that it is an inheritance tax (IHT) concept only and has no application for other tax purposes or for the general law of domicile. It can have the result that IHT is applied to a testator's entire estate, even though he is not domiciled in England and Wales and the devolution of his movable property is governed by the law of the state in which English law regards him as being domiciled.

[131] [2006] WTLR 565.
[132] s. 267 IHTA 1984.

2

THE CURRENT TEST FOR TESTAMENTARY CAPACITY

Early Formulations of a Testamentary Capacity Test

1598: *Marquess of Winchester's Case*:[1] **2.01**

> It is not sufficient that the testator be of memory when he makes a will to answer familiar and usual questions, but he ought to have a disposing memory, so that he is able to make a disposition of his lands with understanding and reason.

1790: *Greenwood v Greenwood*:[2] **2.02**

> I take it a mind and memory competent to dispose of property, when it is a little explained, perhaps may stand thus: having that degree of recollection about him that would enable him to look about the property he had to dispose of, and the persons to whom he wished to dispose of it. If he had a power of summoning up his mind, so as to know what his property was, and who those persons were that then were the objects of his bounty, then he was competent to make his will.

1822: *Stevens v Vancleve*:[3] **2.03**

> [The testator] must, in the language of the law, be possessed of sound and disposing mind and memory. He must have memory. A man in whom the faculty is totally

[1] (1598) 6 Co Rep 23a; of which Henry Swinburne's *A Treatise of Testaments and last Wills etc* (7th edn., London, 1803) observed on p 118 'It seems that a testator answering ordinary and familiar questions is not a sufficient proof of a disposing memory; because to a disposing memory it is necessary there be an understanding judgment fit to direct an estate.'

[2] (1790) 3 Curt App 30.

[3] (1822) 4 Wash CC 262 per Washington CJ.

extinguished cannot be said to possess understanding to any degree whatever, or for any purpose. But his memory may be very imperfect; it may be greatly impaired by age or disease. He may not be able, at all times, to recollect the names, the persons, or the families of those with whom he had been intimately acquainted; may at times ask idle questions, and repeat those which had before been asked and answered, and yet his understanding may be sufficiently sound for many of the ordinary transactions of life. He may not have sufficient strength of memory and vigour of intellect, to make, and to digest all the parts of a contract, and yet be competent to direct the distribution of his property by will. This is a subject which he may possibly have often thought of, and there is probably no person who has not arranged such a disposition in his mind before he committed it to writing. More especially, in such a reduced state of mind and memory, he may be able to recollect and to understand the disposition of his property which he had made by a former will, when the same is distinctly read over to him. The question is not so much what was the degree of memory possessed by the testator as this—Had he a disposing memory? Was he capable of recollecting the property he was about to bequeath; the manner of distributing it; and the object of his bounty? To sum up the whole in the most simple and intelligible form - Were his mind and memory sufficiently sound to enable him to know and to understand the business in which he was engaged at the time he executed his will?

2.04 1840: *Harwood v Baker*:[4]

> [I]n order to constitute a sound disposing mind, a testator must not only be able to understand that he is by his will giving the whole of his property to one object of his regard; but he must also have capacity to comprehend the extent of his property, and the nature of the claims of others, whom by his will he is excluding from all participation in that property; and that the protection of the law is in no case more needed than it is in those where the mind has been too much enfeebled to comprehend more objects than one; and more especially, when that one object may be so forced upon the attention of the invalid as to shut out all others that might require consideration. And therefore the question ... to decide in this case is, not whether Mr Baker knew, when he executed his will, that he was giving all his property to his wife, and excluding all his other relatives from any share in it, but whether he was at that time capable of recollecting who those relations were, of understanding their respective claims upon his regard and bounty, and of deliberately forming an intelligent purpose of excluding them from any share of his property. If he had not the capacity required, the propriety of the disposition made by the will is a matter of no importance. If he had it, the injustice of the exclusion would not affect the validity of the disposition, though the justice or injustice of the disposition might cast down some light upon the question of his capacity.

2.05 All of the above developed similar themes and contain elements which later reached their definitive expression in *Banks v Goodfellow* (where most of the above cited cases were considered). These quotations are not merely historical curiosities as these judgments, particularly *Harwood v Baker*, are still quite commonly cited in modern cases.

[4] (1840) 3 Moo PC 282 at p 290.

The last extract above, from *Harwood v Baker*, contains the idea of caution where the testator's attention is focussed on one person, present with him, and therefore might be less able to recall merits of those not present. While this is not an expressed factor in the *Banks v Goodfellow* test, it is still a factor for the court to consider when assessing the circumstances to which the test is applied and the understanding of the testator. It is, as well, a factor which can be taken into account when considering both undue influence and knowledge and approval.[5] It is therefore an important aspect for the draftsman to consider when taking instructions. **2.06**

Banks v Goodfellow

Facts of the case

This case[6] has for almost 150 years been accepted and applied as the standard test of testamentary capacity in England and Wales,[7] and applied in many other parts of the world that have derived their law from the common law. **2.07**

John Banks, the testator in *Banks v Goodfellow*, whose will was in dispute, had a violent and irrational aversion towards a man called Featherstone Alexander. John Banks was convinced that this man was harassing him (aided by various devils and demons). This delusion, which continued after Featherstone Alexander's death, was a serious delusion producing on occasion epileptic fits that resulted in his confined in the local lunatic asylum. This delusion did not poison his affections towards his niece as he named her as his sole beneficiary[8] in his last will, but did his mental illness prevent him making a valid will? It was found that the will was valid. The original significance of this judgment[9] was that it corrected an earlier error of the Privy Council[10] in the approach to capacity and restored the more traditional approach to capacity **2.08**

5 *Markou v Goodwin* [2013] EWHC 4570 (Ch).

6 (1870) LR 5 QB 549. The longevity of this decision is quite remarkable. It was handed down in the year that Charles Dickens and General Robert E. Lee died and V. I. Ulyanov (Lenin) was born. W. E. Gladstone was Prime Minister (for the first time), Wyatt Earp was alive (but yet to visit the OK Corral), and Germany was still Prussia (and besieging Paris). Richard Wagner's *Die Walküre* was first performed and Jules Verne's *Twenty Thousand Leagues Under the Sea* was published. Alois Alzheimer was only six and had no disease named after him (yet). There was no FA Cup (1871), no Football League or Rugby League (1888 & 1895), no test match cricket (1877), no telephone (1876), no phonograph (1877), no motor car with an internal combustion engine (1879), and no powered flight (1903). The word schizophrenia was not yet coined (1908) and universal suffrage in the UK national elections was years away (1918 men; 1928 women). It was decided in a very different world from today—but that does not detract from its merits.

7 See below in this chapter for consideration of the Mental Capacity Act 2005 at 2.70 et seq.

8 For a fuller narrative of this case and its circumstances see the article by Senior Judge Lush of the Court of Protection at <http://www.step.org/banks-v-goodfellow-1870>.

9 Which was an appeal judgment upholding the original judgment from Cumberland Spring Assizes (Brett J).

10 '[I]n our day the doctrine has sprung up of the unity and indivisibility of the mind, but the ground on which insanity should cause incapacity appears to have been overlooked in the reasoning

(reflected in the extracts at the opening of this chapter). Although the decision in *Banks v Goodfellow* is of considerable age[11] it has survived because of its twin characteristics of simplicity and common sense. Fundamentally, the test set out in the judgment is a statement of the information, relevant to making a will, that a testator must understand, or be capable of understanding.

The original statement of the test of capacity

2.09 In *Banks v Goodfellow* the test of capacity to make a valid will was set out as follows:

> It is essential to the exercise of such a power that the testator
> 1. shall understand the nature of the act and its effects;
> 2. shall understand the extent of the property of which he is disposing;
> 3. shall be able to comprehend and appreciate the claims to which he ought to give effect;
> 4. and with a view to the latter object that no disorder of the mind shall poison his affections, pervert his sense of right, or prevent the exercise of his natural faculties—that no insane delusion shall influence his will in disposing of his property and bring about a disposal of it which, if the mind had been sound, would not have been made.[12]

2.10 It was observed of this test in the Court of Appeal in *Hawes v Burgess* that 'it is reasonable to expect that a testatrix, who is capable of [passing the first two parts of the test] would normally be capable of understanding the claims arising to which she ought to give effect in her family situation.'[13] This judicial *obiter* did not attempt to raise any general legal presumption that it will be so in all cases and it could not be safe practice to make any such assumption. It is safer practice, and more *Banks v Goodfellow* compliant practice, to continue to assess each limb of the test individually. Indeed, there are quite clearly cases decided on the basis of the failure to pass the third limb of the test after the testator has passed the first two limbs.[14] In particular, it is quite

on which it is founded' (1870) LR 5 QB 549 at 563; *Waring v Waring* (1848) 6 Moo PC 341; this case had followed the then fashionable doctrine of the unity and indivisibility of the mind which maintained that any unsoundness of the mind, no matter how slight or unconnected with the will, was sufficient to prevent testamentary capacity being present (see also *Smith v Tebbitt* (1867) LR 1 P&D 437).

[11] *Sharp v Adam* [2006] WTLR 1059 'A decision that has withstood the test of time' at [66] and '...we do not consider that the *Banks v Goodfellow* formulation needs to be reformulated' at [82]; '...it exerts a gravitational pull on other tests of capacity...There cannot be many other authorities this ancient that still command so much respect today' Senior Judge Lush of the Court of Protection; '...is a remarkable one, which repays reading in full. It is, apart from anything else, a masterpiece of English prose.' *Kostic v Chaplin* [2007] EWHC 2298 (Ch) per Henderson J.

[12] (1870) LR 5 QB 549 at 565; in the original text there is no numbering, it has been added here for the sake of clarity and to clearly identify the manner in which 4. is now treated as a separate limb of the test; *Sharp v Adam* [2006] 1059 CA; see 2.22 et seq. For attempts at modern re-statements see below at 2.55 et seq.

[13] [2013] WTLR 153, per Mummery LJ at [55].

[14] *Sharp v Adam* [2006] 1059; *Kostic v Chaplin* [2007] EWHC 2298 (Ch); *Re Ritchie, Ritchie v Joslin* [2009] EWHC 709 (Ch); *Markou v Goodwin* [2013] EWHC 4570 (Ch).

conceivable that where a testator suffers from a delusion he may very well be able to pass the first two limbs but not the third.[15]

Nature of the test

A legal test

The test in *Banks v Goodfellow* is a not a medical test of capacity. It is a formulation by judges, to be applied by judges, of the necessary level of a testator's understanding for his will to be valid. The question of testamentary capacity is a legal question that is to be resolved by the court: '... the issue as to testamentary capacity is from first to last for the decision of the court. It is not to be delegated to experts, however eminent, albeit that their knowledge, skill and experience may be an invaluable tool in the analysis, affording insights into the workings of the mind otherwise beyond the grasp of laymen, including, for that purpose, lawyers and in particular judges.'[16] It is for this reason that the test was set out in layman's terms and not medical terms.[17] **2.11**

A similar view was expressed in Australia: **2.12**

> The criteria in *Banks v Goodfellow* are not matters that are directly medical questions, in the way that a question whether a person is suffering from cancer is a medical question. They are matters for common sense judicial judgment on the basis of the whole of the evidence. Medical evidence as to the medical condition of a deceased may of course be highly relevant and may sometimes directly support or deny a capacity in the deceased to have understanding of the matters in the *Banks v Goodfellow* criteria. However, evidence of such understanding may come from non-expert witnesses. Indeed, perhaps the most compelling evidence of understanding would be reliable evidence (for example, a tape recording) of a detailed conversation with the deceased at this time of the will displaying understanding of the deceased's assets, the deceased's family and the effect of the will. It is extremely unlikely that medical evidence that the deceased did not understand these things would overcome the effect of evidence of such a conversation.[18]

Role of medical opinions

Medical opinions, or formal diagnoses, as the above quotations show, are not conclusive in determining testamentary capacity; they are views for the court to consider, **2.13**

[15] *Kostic v Chaplin* [2007] EWHC 2298 (Ch); *Re Ritchie, Ritchie v Joslin* [2009] EWHC 709 (Ch); or even pass the first limb, but fail the next two *Pearce v Beverley* [2014] WTLR 85.

[16] *Re Key, Key v Key* [2010] WTLR 623 at [98] (Briggs J as he then was); see also *Re Price* [1964] 2 DLR 592 at 595, '... [it] is a practical question which may be answered by a layman of some good sense with as much authority as by a doctor' per Laidlaw J; *Allen v Emery* [2005] EWHC 2389 (Ch) at [24], 'Ultimately capacity is a question of fact like any other which the court must decide on the evidence as a whole'.

[17] Had it been set out in medical terms used in nineteenth-century psychiatry it would long ago have lost its relevance.

[18] *Zorbas v Sidiropoulous (No 2)* [2009] NSWCA 197.

and accept or reject, as the court considers appropriate, after weighing them with, or against, other non-medical evidence.[19] Medical opinions may be based on observation and testing during the testator's lifetime or they maybe a result of analysis of the medical history after death.

2.14 The Court of Appeal in *Hawes v Burgess*[20] expressed concern about post-death analysis of medical records being used in preference to the views of the draftsman:

> My concern is that the courts should not too readily upset, on the grounds of lack of mental capacity, a will that has been drafted by an experienced independent lawyer. If, as here, an experienced lawyer has been instructed and has formed the opinion from a meeting or meetings that the testatrix understands what she is doing, the will so drafted and executed should only be set aside on the clearest evidence of incapacity.[21]

While this is strongly expressed, it seems to be no more than the weighing of the value of both types of evidence. The will draftsman's evidence will depend on the extent to which he has carried out his job properly and recorded fully his observations and conclusions. The post-death medical report will similarly depend upon its own strength, particularly when it deals with previously undiagnosed conditions or conditions where the implications of the symptoms were not appreciated in the lifetime.

The test is focussed on the individual

2.15 *Bank v Goodfellow* is focussed very much on the individual and his circumstances and as such it matches the general approach of English law to the assessment of mental capacity for any task.[22] By addressing the individual and his circumstances, it is implicit in this test that the level of understanding required for a will, where the circumstances and assets of a testator are simple, will be lower than for the testator with complex circumstances and affairs:[23]

- 'Where the will is complex, or where the family circumstances are complex, or calls upon the testator's bounty are subtle, a greater degree of understanding on the testator's part will be required than where the will and the circumstances are very simple.'[24]
- 'A testator with a complex estate and many potential beneficiaries may need a greater degree of cognitive capability than one with a simple estate and few claimants.'[25]

---

[19] See Chapter 6 on the role of the draftsman.

[20] [2013] WTLR 453 CA.

[21] [2013] WTLR 453 at [60]; see also Chapter 6 for this view to be placed in its practical context.

[22] See Chapter 1.

[23] *McClintock v Calderwood* [2005] EWHC 836 where the simplicity of the estate was a factor.

[24] *Tchilingrian v Ouzounian* [2003] WTLR 709 at [72]; this point also arose recently in *Re Simon, Simon v Byford* [2013] WTLR 1615 at [119]; *Vadakathu v George* [2010] WTLR 135 at [56] to [58] expert evidence was undermined by failing to acknowledge this point.

[25] *Re Perrins deceased, Perrins v Holland* [2009] WTLR 1387 Ch D at [40].

This can mean that, at least to a limited extent, simplicity of drafting and simplicity of gifts will aid the understanding of the testator. There is an Australian decision on testamentary capacity where it was suggested that 'No doubt it is unwise to make a will so late when a codicil will do, because a codicil keeps up the continuity of the testamentary capacity existing at the date of the will, so that in executing a codicil much less intelligence is necessary than in executing a will, and consequently professional men dissuade old persons from making wills where a codicil would be sufficient'.[26] While the words could have more clarity, the tenor of the remarks appears to propose that a minor alteration by way of codicil would be easier to understand particularly in the context of not requiring full understanding of the parts of the earlier will that are left undisturbed. If this is correct (and it has some attractions) the remarks must have less chance of being correct the greater the change that is being made. **2.16**

The quotation in the previous paragraph was noted with approval in a recent Australian decision[27] where White J added to it by observing: **2.17**

> As a matter of principle, it does not appear to me that the same capacity would necessarily be required for a testator or testatrix who wished only to revoke a particular gift. A testatrix, when perfectly capable, may have disposed by her will of an elaborate and valuable estate carefully between numerous potential claimants, having weighed their respective claims to a nicety. If one of the beneficiaries should so misbehave towards the testatrix that she resolved that that person should receive nothing, I see no reason in principle why it should be necessary in order for a revocation of such a particular gift to be effective that the testatrix should still have the capacity to appreciate the general nature and extent of her estate and be able to weigh the claims of all persons who might then be potential objects of her testamentary bounty. In principle, it should be enough that the testatrix is capable of making a judgment as to whether the person deserves to be excluded from the will. If the testatrix's mind is so disordered by mental illness or disease that she is not capable of properly comprehending the continued claims of the beneficiary, so that the gift is revoked when it would not have been had her mind not been so affected, then the revocation should not stand. But in carrying out such a testamentary act, prima facie, it should be irrelevant if the testatrix did not know what was the extent of her assets.[28]

Against the above view is the argument that revoking a gift and leaving the subject matter to pass under the residuary gift is enhancing the value received by others when a testator could not weigh the increased benefit they would receive against the claims of others. Whether or not the views of White J would meet with favour in an English court is uncertain, but using a simple codicil just to remove a gift, when that is all **2.18**

---

[26] *Hay v Simpson* (1898) 11 LR (NSW) Eq 109 at 118 per Manning J.

[27] *D'Apice v Gutkovich—Estate of Abraham (No 2)* [2010] NSWSC 1333 at 98.

[28] *D'Apice v Gutkovich—Estate of Abraham (No 2)* [2010] NSWSC 1333 White J at 96. The judge made these remarks in the context of a codicil that removed a specific gift, the subject matter of which then passed under the residuary bequest. White J added 'It is unnecessary to consider what the position would be if the revocation were of an entire will or a residuary gift.'

that is required, would seem to at least have the advantage of offering the possibility of lower capacity being accepted.

General level of comprehension

2.19 In applying this test it is necessary to consider the approach that has been used to define the general level of understanding in a testator that this test looks to establish.

1. It is not necessary that [the testator] should view his will through the eye of a lawyer, and comprehend its provisions in their legal form. It is sufficient if he has such a mind and memory as will enable him to understand the elements of which it is composed, and the disposition of his property in its simple forms.[29]
2. By the terms 'a sound and disposing mind and memory' it has not been understood that a testator must possess these qualities of the mind in the highest degree; otherwise, very few could make testaments at all; neither has it been understood that he must possess them in as great a degree as he may have formerly done; for even this would disable most men in the decline of life; the mind may have been in some degree debilitated, the memory may have become in some degree enfeebled; and yet there may be enough left clearly to discern and discreetly to judge, of all those things, and all those circumstances, which enter into the nature of a rational, fair, and just testament. But if they have so far failed as that these cannot be discerned and judged of, then he cannot be said to be of sound and disposing mind and memory.[30]
3. ... to hold on the facts of this case that [the testatrix] did not have testamentary capacity would require too much, and would be inconsistent with the authorities which support the right of elderly people to make a will disposing of their property as they see fit, even if their mental faculties are far from being at their peak.[31]
4. In judging the question of testamentary capacity the courts do not overlook the fact that many wills are made by people of advanced years. In such people, slowness, illness, feebleness, and eccentricity will sometimes be apparent—more so than in most persons of younger age. But these are not ordinarily sufficient, if proved, to disentitle the testator of the right to dispose of his or her property by will.... Were the rule to be otherwise, so many wills would be liable to be set aside for want of testamentary capacity that the fundamental principle of our law would be undermined and the expectations of testators unreasonably destroyed.[32]

Draftsmen should at the same time also heed the warning in *Hall v Estate of Bruce Bennett*:[33] 'The jurisprudence abounds with statements that it is not sufficient simply to show that a testator had the capacity to communicate his or her testamentary wishes. Those wishes must be shown to be the product of a sound and

[29] *Harrison v Rowan* (1820) 3 Washington 585, quoted with approval in *Banks v Goodfellow*.

[30] *Den v Vancleve* (1819) 2 Southard 660 quoted with approval in *Banks v Goodfellow*; see also *Frizzo v Frizzo* [2011] QCA 308 'The *Banks v Goodfellow* test does not require perfect mental balance and clarity; it is a question of degree.'

[31] *Re Simon, Simon v Byford* [2013] WTLR 1615 Ch paragraph [14].

[32] *Re Griffith, Easter v Griffith* (1995) 217 ALR 284 per Kirby P at 295.

[33] [2003] WTLR 827 AT [15] per Charron JA.

disposing mind.' Making the point that communication and understanding are not the same issue.

From the draftsman's perspective it is important that he understands the above and does not look for a level of understanding, speed of thought, or sharpness of recall that matches his own. He should form a judgement of his client against the level of understanding that *Banks v Goodfellow* requires and that is not necessarily as high as the understanding of a person free from the infirmities of illness or old age. 'In these cases it is admitted on all hands that though the mental power may be reduced below the ordinary standard, yet if there be sufficient intelligence to understand and appreciate the testamentary act in its different bearings, the power to make a will remains.'[34] **2.20**

Any person's level of understanding may change from day to day, colloquially described perhaps as 'good days and bad days'.[35] The draftsman needs to be aware of this in relation to his aged or ill client. Many factors may affect the individual's mental state or physical stamina. **2.21**

- *Time of day*—tiredness/interaction with prescribed drug regime/visit at time of afternoon sleep/drowsiness after meals
- *Medication*—side effects of prescribed drugs (drowsiness, hallucination, inability to concentrate can all affect capacity)
- *Pain levels*—effect on a person's stamina or powers of concentration
- *Physical illness*—may add to confusion[36]
- *Blood sugar levels*—can affect concentration and low levels can lead to lack of focus or a level of distraction (not only a problem for diabetes sufferers)
- *Stress*—domestic problems/changes to carers' regime/new environment/bad news/bereavement/family problems
- *Interruptions to meeting*—person entering the room, television on, etc. can break concentration or chain of thought and generally distract

The interviewer should be able to be aware of the good day/bad day issues and be prepared to re-interview[37] if this is a possible issue giving problems with capacity (or try to avoid them at the outset).

---

[34] *Banks v Goodfellow* (1870) LR 5 QB 549 at 566.

[35] *Feltham v Freer Bouskell* [2013] WTLR 1363 at [63].

[36] *Westendorp v Warwick* [2006] EWHC 915 (Ch) at [24] '. . . it would be usual for patients with Alzheimer's disease to become measurably more confused when they have a chest infection that is serious enough to restrict them to bed, make them appear tired, and cause breathlessness even when they are at rest'.

[37] *Littlewood v Wilkinson Woodward* [2009] WTLR 1189 where visits on two separate days yielded two different views of capacity.

Elements of the *Banks v Goodfellow* Test

Three- or four-limb test?

2.22 This test has been described as being comprised of three separate elements or limbs (with (4) in the test being a qualification of (3)—see 2.09 above). In *Kostic v Chaplin*[38] it was said of this analysis that it was 'helpful for the purposes of exposition to subdivide the test into four elements as the Court of Appeal did in *Sharp v Adam*.... I should add that the four elements are, in my judgement, separate requirements and element (4) is not a mere subset of element (3).'[39] The four limbs of the test are now therefore to be seen as independent of each other, as distinct tests, and the testator is required to pass each of them in order to have capacity.

2.23 Whether there will be any practical difference in viewing this as a three- or four-limb test, as found in *Sharp v Adam*, is difficult tell.[40] If, as the original wording in *Banks v Goodfellow* suggests, (4) did only operate to qualify (3), what is the effect of a delusion then to be on limbs (1) and (2)? It must surely the case that a delusion as to, for example, the value of an estate, must prevent a testator from passing that limb of the test if that delusion is significant and prevents the testator having a rational view of his assets and consequently their rational disposal. In other words a delusion must be capable of defeating any limb of the test if the delusion prevents the proper understanding of any of the preceding limbs.

2.24 What then would be the effect of the qualifying words in (4) 'and bring about a disposal of it which, if the mind had been sound, would not have been made'? Could this qualification have any application to (1) and (2) if (4) was indeed limited in application to (3) only? These words can be looked at as describing only an outcome and in those terms a failure to pass (1) and/or (2) would tend to give the same outcome. It is recognized that there is the possibility that there could be circumstances where the analysis of the application might be an issue.[41] At the present time, however, despite the view in *Sharp v Adam*, other courts have expressed the test in its original form of three limbs.[42] While there might appear to be some scope to argue the point, the view of the Court of Appeal in *Sharp v Adam*, where the elements of the test were relevant, should be regarded as the authoritative statement of the test.

---

[38] [2007] EWHC 2298 (Ch) Henderson J.

[39] At paragraphs 197–198, following the Court of Appeal in *Sharp v Adam* [2006] WTLR 1059 where, in upholding the decision at first instance, it was found that the testator had satisfied the test in limbs (1), (2), and (3), but failed on limb (4)—see para [69] of the CA judgment; *Re Ritchie, Ritchie v Joslin* [2009] EWHC 709 (Ch); also followed in *Markou v Goodwin* [2013] EWHC 4570 (Ch) at [53].

[40] Some decisions are still found where it is treated as a three-part test e.g. *Williams v Wilmot* [2013] WTLR 1291 at [3].

[41] As was argued unsuccessfully in *Kostic v Chaplin* [2007] EWHC 2298 (Ch) at [198].

[42] *Hawes v Burgess* [2013] WTLR 453 CA at [55].

Explanation by the draftsman to assist the testator's understanding

It has been said of a will that 'there must be a complete and absolute proof that the party who had so formed the will did it without assistance'.[43] Although this is sometimes put forward to support the idea of assistance not being provided to the testator, the quotation is taken from a case where the rational and unassisted nature of a holograph will was itself taken as evidence of the testatrix's capacity. In *Hoff v Atherton*[44] it was recognized that there will be testators whose capacity to understand what they are doing is 'limited by defects in memory and comprehension, so that—absent some proper assistance by way of reminder or explanation—it cannot be said that "his mind and memory [were] sufficiently sound to enable him to know and understand the business in which he was engaged at the time he executed his will"'.[45] With such a testator, quite clearly the giving of advice and the draftsman's recording of it (and the testator's understanding of the advice) will enhance the evidence for the will if it were to be challenged. Indeed this process can also serve to strengthen the draftsman's conclusion that his client has capacity. The reverse may also be possible in that the explanation given may result in identifying the client's lack of understanding and the will cannot proceed. Notwithstanding this, advice is not an essential ingredient of the test of capacity. Indeed, very little worthwhile advice will usually be given in the case of a non-professionally prepared will (a factor that argues strongly against wills for the elderly being prepared other than by professionals). **2.25**

The draftsman can, and should, provide what assistance he can to aid the testator's understanding of the process. There is much about the nature and effect of a will that a layperson will not usually understand and there may be legal issues of devolution of assets that require explanation in order for them to understand value or extent of assets. But there is a line between explanation and leading, or suggesting—particularly with regard to the identity of beneficiaries, or the extent of their individual benefit—that should not be crossed. It is not up to the draftsman to prompt or persuade regarding dispositions, other than how the already-stated objective of the testator can be best achieved. **2.26**

There is a practical difficulty with advice where the testator intends to omit a close relative who is clearly within the classes of s.1 of the Inheritance (Provision for Family and Dependants) Act 1975. Is the omission deliberate, or does it arise from a lack of understanding? The draftsman will clearly want to assist his client and advise of the possible consequences of the omission. He may even be asked to advise on the type and amount of a small gift that would deter a claim. This will be acceptable assistance **2.27**

[43] *Cartwright v Cartwright* (1793) 1 Phill Ecc 90.
[44] [2005] WTLR 99 at [58].
[45] Citing *Stevens v Vancleve* (1819) 4 Washington CC at 267 9, in turn cited in *Banks v Goodfellow* (1870) LR 5 QB at 568.

even if the advice as to amount is given, providing the draftsman is satisfied that his client understands the issues and that the change in provision arises solely out of the legal advice that he has given. It must be the testator's decision and not him doing as he is told.

'Shall understand' and 'shall be capable of understanding'

2.28 On the face of the words used in the first three limbs of the test, the requirement is for different understanding for (1) and (2) on one hand and (3) on the other. The requirement 'shall understand' for limbs (1) and (2) appears on a literal reading to require actual understanding, whereas (3) requires the ability to understand only. These words were considered by the Court of Appeal in *Hoff v Atherton*.[46] The suggestion that 'shall understand' requires actual understanding was described as 'an over-literal approach to a judicial statement'.[47]

2.29 In support of this approach the court took into account several old decisions dealing with the capability to understand rather than actual understanding.[48] The approach that is therefore taken is that these words import no more than a capacity to understand for the first two limbs and bring them into line with the third limb.[49] However, there is within this approach a practical issue for the draftsman. In the absence of establishing the extent of actual knowledge of, for example, assets, on the part of the testator, it is difficult for any judgement to be made by the draftsman not only that the testator passes the second limb, but also that the dispositions in the proposed will are reasonable and appropriate in the light of those who have claims on his bounty. Because of this, the practice of the draftsman is usually to test the actual understanding of the testator of his assets and debts in order to judge the testator's capacity (and similarly for his understanding of the nature of his will); establishing actual understanding must show the capacity to understand.

2.30 However, this approach must have a flaw, as it will not identify the testator who does not have actual understanding but nonetheless has the capacity to understand. How then is the draftsman to establish that in terms of practical questions? Has this testator the capacity to remember despite not showing the knowledge of his assets? How, in practice, can the draftsman establish the difference in understanding between the mind of the testator who says that he has forgotten if he has made an earlier will, or

46 [2005] WTLR 99.

47 [2005] WTLR 99 at [34] per Peter Gibson LJ.

48 *Greenwood v Greenwood* (1790) 3 Curt App 30 'the power of summoning up the mind'; *Stevens v Vancleve* (1822) 4 Wash CC 262 'capable of recollecting'; *Harwood v Baker* (1840) 3 Moo PC 282 'be able to understand' and 'capacity to comprehend'.

49 *Re Loxton, Abbott v Richardson* [2006] WTLR 1567 ay [193] '. . . the question is not whether the testator actually knew the extent of the property, but whether he was capable of understanding it . . .' (citing *Minns v Foster* [2002] All ER (D) 225); The Australian courts appear to be less willing to follow this view particularly where assets are concerned (*Kerr v Badran* [2010] NSWSC 1333).

forgotten what is in it, and the mind of the testator that cannot recall the information? This issue with capacity to understand was highlighted in the Court of Appeal in *Simon v Byford*,[50] but without providing any guidance to the practitioner. It was found that the testatrix had the capacity to understand what the terms of a previous will were, but also had forgotten what they were.[51] It is feared that the category of testators who have the capacity to understand, but not actual understanding, will always represent a category where the draftsman's judgement may not be able to determine capacity.

The original wording in *Banks v Goodfellow* indicates that a capacity to understand is required for the third limb—'shall be able to comprehend and appreciate the claims to which he ought to give effect'. This limb is focussed on those nearest and dearest to the testator. As commented above, the draftsman's approach will usually be to establish actual understanding and for this category this is a reasonable approach. It is quite hard to conceive of someone who has the capacity to remember this class of persons, but has forgotten who they are and, in the words used in *Simon v Byford*, chooses not to remember them, being considered to be a person who has testamentary capacity. In reality, this limb is the one which, despite its wording, must require actual understanding. **2.31**

In *Hoff v Atherton*,[52] it was asserted that knowledge and approval required 'affirmative proof' of the 'knowledge of the testator that the dispositions made by the new will represent a significant change in financial terms to the dispositions made by the previous will'. The Court of Appeal would not accept that this assertion was universally correct, adding that 'in some circumstances the court will rightly insist on evidence that the testator had the earlier testamentary dispositions in mind in order to test whether he truly intended to make the new dispositions'. We are therefore left with the position that actual knowledge of the terms of the previous will may, or may not, be required in order to have capacity and/or knowledge and approval, depending upon the terms and circumstances of the wills in question. Although it should be added that having actual knowledge of the terms of previous wills will generally tend to add to evidence of capacity. **2.32**

[50] [2014] WTLR 1097 at [41] per Lewison LJ 'Once I knew all the dates of the Kings and Queens of England, and the formula for Hooke's law; and was "capable" of remembering them. Now I would have to look them up.'

[51] The will in this case was not professionally drawn, but was prepared by members of the family after a family party—circumstances that a professional draftsman would have deemed wholly inappropriate for such a task.

[52] [2005] WTLR 99 CA at [45] to [51] citing *Marsh v Tyrell* (1828) 2 Hagg Ecc 84 and *Kenward v Adams* (*The Times* 29 November 1975) in support of the assertion.

First limb of the test: 'shall understand the nature of the act and its effects'

2.33 The nature of the act and its effects will mean that a testator must be capable of understanding that[53]

- he is making a will;
- the will can be changed or revoked by him while he is alive (if he has the necessary capacity to do either act);
- the will takes effect when he dies and that therefore the will gives no immediate property rights to others (a frequent misunderstanding); and
- the will disposes of what he owns when he dies, but until then he is free to spend, give away, or otherwise dispose of whatever he owns.

2.34 As many clients will not have knowledge of such technical issues, assessing a testator's capacity to understand these points will usually require an explanation of them. If the testator cannot understand these key features of a will after an explanation, it is likely that he does not have sufficient capacity to pass the test. Implicit in this part of the test is that the testator has an understanding of death and that he will die, as without knowing this he will not understand the nature of a will, the gifts in it, and how it takes effect.

2.35 The principal effects of the act that a testator must be capable of understanding are as follows.

- The will makes gifts on death to those named on the terms specified.
- A gift to a beneficiary will fail if the beneficiary dies before the testator and that alternative provisions, if any, in the will will apply (or that the bequeathed property is added to residue).
- The nature of the gifts he is making (absolute, contingent, or limited) but only in such terms as are necessary to give a non-lawyer sufficient understanding of how and when individuals will benefit.[54] For example, it is sufficient if in the case of a simple trust legacy to know that A receives the income during his life and that B receives the capital after A's death. It is not necessary that the testator should have an understanding of the detailed functions and duties of a trustee.
- Where there is a previous will, what gifts are in it, how the provisions in the new will are different, and what the reasons for change are. This effect has been put forward elsewhere.[55] However, a degree of doubt has now been cast on the issue of the knowledge of the terms of a previous will. In *Re Simon deceased*[56] it was found that

[53] See at 2.28 et seq for '*shall understand*'.

[54] *Re Stolikn, Greaves v Stolkin* [2013] WTLR 1793 at [73].

[55] Penny Letts (ed) *Assessment of Mental Capacity* (3rd edn., London: Law Society, 2010) at page 73; see also *Re Simpson* (1977) 127 NLJ 487 and the Golden Rule.

[56] [2013] WTLR 1615 for appeal see [2014] WTLR 1097.

the testatrix, when making a new will, did not understand her reasons for preferring one child in the previous will or what the terms of that will were. On appeal[57] it was found that the testatrix was capable of remembering what her reasons for the previous will were, but had forgotten them. This view creates difficulty for the draftsman in deciding the difference between the testator having forgotten the terms of the previous will (but being capable of remembering them) and having lost the ability to recall the terms. It would appear to be a distinction that many draftsmen may not be capable of establishing.

The validity of a will was considered by the Court of Appeal in *Simon v Byford* where the Court refused to accept that 'effect' of a will extended to 'consequences' of the terms of the will. Drawing a distinction between what was referred to as 'the direct consequences' and the 'collateral consequences', the Court drew a distinction between the effect (i.e. what it disposed, on what terms, and to whom) and its consequences (i.e. the implications for the family and assets of them being disposed in the manner the will set out after death).[58] It was not necessary for the testatrix, in that case, to have an understanding of the consequences. **2.36**

Second limb of the test: 'shall understand the extent of the property of which he is disposing'

The main issue is not that the testator is aware of the exact worth of his free estate (few people ever are), but that he will be capable of having a broad appreciation of what his assets are and a sensible, but not necessarily exact, idea of their value.[59] The test refers to 'extent' and not 'value' of the property. While extent can also mean value,[60] it usually carries more connotation of range, i.e. what it is comprised of. But that is not to wholly ignore issues of value, as without some broadly realistic understanding of value it is difficult to see how rational decisions between beneficiaries and comparative reward can be made. An unrealistic value of the testator's estate can be found to be evidence of confusion such as to show a lack of capacity.[61] **2.37**

[57] *Simon v Byford* [2014] EWCA Civ 280.

[58] *Simon v Byford* [2014] WTLR 1097 at [44] and [45].

[59] *Schrader v Schrader* [2013] WTLR 701 'I agree she may not have known the value of her house, but that is likely to be the case with a large number of testators... It is not, of itself, a requirement of capacity that a testator has to know the value of his home. It is highly likely that she knew it was her most valuable asset by a long way.'

[60] See the *Chambers Dictionary* 1998 edition.

[61] *Wood v Smith* [1993] Ch 90 where the testator thought he had £17,000 of investments—their actual value was over £105,000; *In the Matter of Fish* 522 NYS 2d 970, 972 (3d Dept 1987) 'While a testator need not have precise knowledge of the size of his estate, the authorities clearly hold that a testator's lack of awareness of or ability to keep in mind without prompting the general nature and extent of one's real and personal property requires denial of probate.'

2.38 In *Scammell v Farmer*[62] it was observed that:

> The... suggestion pressed at trial that [the testatrix] did not know the extent of her estate because she could only give a general indication to [the solicitor] is in my judgment unfair. The general indication is not very wide of the mark. And as the estate comprised principally a house, in a thriving property market its value would be difficult to state with any precision.

2.39 In *Blackman v Mann*:[63]

> There is, it is true, no evidence what value she thought that portfolio had, but actual knowledge of value is not necessary for testamentary capacity. I am satisfied by the evidence... that [she] understood that she had, through the companies, a substantial property portfolio to dispose of. In my judgement that is sufficient in the circumstances of this case to satisfy this head of the *Banks v Goodfellow* test.

2.40 In *Re Loxton*:[64]

> As to her property, I find that she was aware of the house, its furnishings and its main contents.... As to her remaining property, I find that she was aware that she had shares of substantial value, but no more—she did not know approximately what the value was, and probably would not have known this in her earlier years.
>
> ...Nor do I think that Miss Loxston's ignorance of the value of her shares affected her testamentary capacity. There is little authority on the extent of the knowledge which a testator must have of his property for the purposes of testamentary capacity, but it seems to me that it must depend upon the nature of the disposition which he is likely to wish to consider making. In some circumstances, it might well be necessary for the testator to know the approximate value of his assets, and indeed liabilities, particularly if what he is contemplating is making a series of pecuniary legacies, the amount of which would depend upon the value of the assets available. I do not think that this is the case here. Even if Miss Loxston had been considering a wider range of beneficiaries, it is probable that she would have left a proportion of her assets to each beneficiary, and for that purpose it was quite sufficient that she knew that there were shares of substantial value.[65]

2.41 *D'Apice v Gutkovich—Estate of Abraham (No 2)*:[66]

> Mrs Abraham was aware that she owned real estate as an investment and was able to identify the principal asset of that category. *Kerr v Badran*[67] establishes that the *Banks v Goodfellow* test may not require that older people know of each particular asset, let alone the value of each asset comprising the estate. Mrs Abraham knew that she had real estate investments and it is a reasonable inference that she knew that she received income from that source. It does not matter that she did not know how much income from real estate investments she received. Nor does it matter that she did not

62 [2008] WTLR 1261 at paragraph [97].
63 [2008] WTLR] 389 at [118] and [119].
64 *Re Loxston, Abbott v Richardson* [2006] WTLR 1567 at [189].
65 At [192].
66 [2010] NSWSC 1333 White J at 105.
67 See immediately below.

> identify the Coogee unit as being one of those investments. In my view the second element of the *Banks v Goodfellow* test (namely that the testatrix understand the extent of property of which she was disposing) is satisfied.

A more lengthy view from Australia was in *Kerr v Badran*:[68] **2.42**

> In dealing with the *Banks v Goodfellow* test it is, I think, necessary to bear in mind the differences between life in 1870 and life in 1995. The average expectation of life for reasonably affluent people in England in 1870 was probably less than 60 years, and for others less well-off under 50 years: the average life expectation of males in Australia in 1995 was 75 years. Younger people can be expected to have a more accurate understanding of the value of money than older people. Younger people are less likely to suffer memory loss. When there were fewer deaths at advanced age, problems which arise with age, such as dementia, were less common. In England in 1870, if you had property it was likely to be land or bonds or shares in railway companies or government-backed enterprises. Investment in ordinary companies was far less common than now. Older people living today may well be aware that they own substantial shareholdings or substantial real estate, but yet may not have an accurate understanding of the value of those assets, nor for that matter, the addresses of the real estate or the particular shareholdings which they have. Many people have handed over management of share portfolios and even real estate investments to advisers. They may be quite comfortable with what they have; they may understand that they have assets which can provide an acceptable income for them, but at the same time they may not have a proper understanding of the value of the assets which provide the income. They may however be well able to distribute those assets by will. I think that this needs to be kept in mind in 2004 when the requirement of knowing 'the extent' of the estate is considered. This does not necessarily mean knowledge of each particular asset or knowledge of the value of that asset, or even a particular class of assets, particularly when shares in private companies are part of the estate. What is required is the bringing of the principle to bear on existing circumstances in modern life.

It is a well-made point that nineteenth-century words need to be understood in their original context, but applied now in the light of twenty-first-century circumstances. The realities of modern investments and investment management must be taken into account.

The Law Society and BMA guide to mental capacity[69] suggests that a testator should **2.43**
also be able to understand

1. the extent of all the property owned solely by them;
2. the fact that certain types of jointly owned property might automatically pass to the other joint owner, regardless of anything that is said in the will;[70]

---

68 *Estate of Badran, Kerr v Badran* [2004] NSWSC 735 Windeyer J at [49] approved in *Zorbas v Sidiropoulous (No 2)* [2007] NSWCA 197.

69 P. Letts (ed) *Assessment of Mental Capacity: A Practical Guide for Doctors and Lawyers* (3rd edn., The British Medical Association and Law Society, 2010) p 73.

70 Understanding the correct devolution of beneficial joint-tenancy property in particular enables a testator to understand who will inherit his interest by survivor and then make decisions informed by this as to the disposition of his remaining property.

3. whether there are benefits payable on their death which might be unaffected by the terms of their will (e.g. insurance policies and pension rights); and
4. that the extent of their property could change during their lifetime.

These are essential elements in a testator's understanding, not merely of what will be available to others as a consequence of his death, but also what can be controlled by his will. There are however, elements of an estate that very few testators will understand without the assistance of the draftsman (such as (2) and (3), above).

2.44 An understanding of the testator's estate must include knowledge of his indebtedness and the effect that this must have on the value of his free estate. Where the indebtedness is significant in proportion to the value of the estate it will be particularly important; minor or usual household debts are of little or no consequence. Rational decisions about the proportional benefit cannot be made without an understanding of how the estate will be diminished by the debts. Debts attaching to particular assets will be an issue for the testator to understand.

Third limb of the test: 'shall be able to comprehend and appreciate the claims to which he ought to give effect'

2.45 This limb requires that the testator is able to comprehend those who have claims on his bounty. This does not refer to contractual claims or claims that might be made under the terms of the I(PFD)A 1975. It refers to those individuals who are

- related by blood, adoption, marriage, or civil partnership to the testator;
- cohabiting with the testator;
- a dependant of the testator;
- raised by the testator;
- close friends of the testator; and
- conceivably philanthropic institutions that the testator is closely connected with;

which the testator would normally be expected to make provision for when disposing of his estate, recognizing the ties of family, love and affection. In identifying which persons fall into this category, there is a moral element—in the sense of identifying those who a testator with normal ties of family and friendship would reward. There is no moral element in the sense of judging the provision in the will (or omission from the will).

2.46 There is no requirement that in order to make a valid will a testator must make provision for all or any of those in these categories. A testator can have perfectly good reasons why he chooses not to benefit any one or all of them.[71] The requirement is

[71] *Tobin v Ezekiel, Estate of Lily Ezekiel* [2011] NSWSC 81; *Viva! Campaigns Ltd & The Vegetarian Society v Scott* [2014] WTLR 525 at [104] 'The plain fact…is that [the testator] did not feel the bond of natural love and affection with his blood family that usually exists. Accordingly, he consciously decided to leave his estate elsewhere. That is a decision which the law respects and upholds.'

that he is able to understand the relationships, and appreciate the relative value of his relationship with each one, and be capable of making a reasoned judgement on the distribution of his estate on that basis. Being able to understand all this does not mean that the testator is bound to make provision for them. Despite the capacity for understanding and weighing choices, he may still choose to act capriciously or eccentrically.[72]

It is not sufficient for a will to leave property to a person that the testator intended in his will. **2.47**

> [F]or a will to be upheld it is established in the authorities that it is not enough to show that the testator or testatrix wished to benefit the person who was in fact benefited. It must also be shown that no mental disorder or, in modern language, as I have said, cognitive impairment, prevented her from having in mind all the other claims and considerations which she should properly have in mind. This does not just mean recording who else might be potential beneficiaries, but the nature of their claims.[73]

In *Re Simon*[74] it was found that when making a will leaving an estate equally between all children the testatrix did not need precise knowledge of the extent of her estate: **2.48**

> [156] ...the law upholds the right of elderly people to leave their property as they choose, even if their mental faculties have declined considerably. This must include many cases in which they can no longer remember all the circumstances relevant to the division of their property between the people they wished to benefit; to make this a qualification for testamentary capacity would be inconsistent with the case law.
>
> [157] ...while I think that there may be cases in which requirement (c) can only be met if the testator is capable of understanding, and possibly only if she does understand, the different provisions of an earlier will, this is not such a case. It must be a matter of degree, and in this case the previous will was 9 years earlier, and the differences were slight;[75] the beneficiaries under both wills were the obvious ones, and all received substantial gifts under both wills. Nobody was omitted. It would be different if the testator was unable to remember the identity of the beneficiaries under a previous will, whom she would still be likely, if reminded, to wish to benefit.[76]

Fourth limb of the test:

> that no disorder of the mind shall poison his affections, pervert his sense of right, or prevent the exercise of his natural faculties—that no insane delusion shall influence

[72] See Chapter 1 at 1.25.

[73] *Markou v Goodwin* [2013] EWHC 4570 (Ch) per Nugee J.

[74] *Re Simon, Simon v Byford* [2013] WTLR 1615 Ch D; later at [158] there is a clear finding that although the testatrix was not aware of the terms of the earlier will she had the capacity of understanding it.

[75] A small private company shareholding, but it had significant issues in terms of control of the company.

[76] Citing *Re Loxston, Abbott v Richardson* [2006] WTLR 1567 at [187] and [190].

> his will in disposing of his property and bring about a disposal of it which, if the mind had been sound, would not have been made.

2.49 This limb is concerned principally, but not exclusively, with the effect of delusions (a significant issue in *Banks v Goodfellow*):

> If the human instincts and affections, or the moral sense, become perverted by mental disease; if insane suspicion, or aversion, take the place of natural affection; if reason and judgment are lost, and the mind, becomes a prey to insane delusions calculated to interfere with and disturb its functions, and to lead to a testamentary disposition, due only to their baneful influence—in such a case it is obvious that the condition of the testamentary power fails, and that a will made under such circumstances ought not to stand. But what if the mind, though possessing sufficient power, undisturbed by frenzy or delusion, to take into account all the considerations necessary to the proper making of a will, should be subject to some delusion, but such delusion neither exercises nor is calculated to exercise any influence on the particular disposition, and a rational and proper will is the result; ought we, in such case, to deny to the testator the capacity to dispose of his property by will?[77]

2.50 In *Boughton v Knight* the jury were told to put to themselves 'this question, and answer it; can I understand how any man in possession of his senses could have believed such a thing? And if the answer you give is, I cannot understand it, then it is of the necessity of the case that you should say the man is not sane.'[78] Today the test might be expressed a little more scientifically, but this quotation gives the flavour of the approach.[79]

2.51

> [A] delusion has been defined as a false belief originating spontaneously in the imagination without foundation either in fact or evidence, of the falsity of which the person affected cannot be convinced by argument or proof. Also there is abundant authority for the statement that an insane delusion is a belief which has no basis in reason and which cannot be dispelled by argument. There is also ample authority for, and it has been laid down that, a mistaken belief as to a matter of fact or illogical conclusions therefrom is not necessarily an insane delusion, neither is any belief or prejudice however mistaken which has some basis for it.
>
> A person may have a delusion which does not imply or show unsoundness of mind, and even mistaken unnatural prejudice may not be an insane delusion, all persons being subject to likes and dislikes. The mere existence, however, of an insane delusion will not invalidate a will unless shown to affect its provisions ....[80]

[77] *Banks v Goodfellow* (1870) LR 5 QB 549 at 565.

[78] *Boughton v Knight* (1873) 3 P&D 64.

[79] *Banton v Banton* (1998) 164 DLR (4th) 176 at [32] per Cullity J 'A delusion is insanity where one persistently believes supposed facts (which have no real existence except in his perverted imagination) against all evidence and probability and conducts himself however logically upon the assumption of their existence'; *Feeney's Canadian Law of Wills* (4th edn., LexisNexis Canada, 2000) '[A] delusion is a belief in a state of facts which no rational person would believe.'

[80] *Forman v Ryan* [1912] 4 DLR 27.

The delusion in the mind of the testator will deprive him of testamentary capacity, if the delusion influences, or is capable of influencing, the provisions of his will.[81] In *Smee v Smee*[82] the testator thought that he was the child of George IV and this materially affected his will in that he made a bequest in his will to set up a library in Brighton.[83] It was said, by the court, of his delusion that: **2.52**

> It is important to bear in mind the nature of the deceased's delusions. He had an idea that he was the son of George IV; that when he was born a large sum of money was placed in his father's hands in trust for him; that he was robbed by his father by the diversion of a large part of that trust fund from him to his brothers; and that all that his father really had to give to his brothers was a sum of £1,000 each, the rest of the property (about £50,000) left by his father and divided by will between his children, being part of the imaginary trust fund, to which the deceased believed he alone was entitled.

In *Kostic v Chaplin*[84] the testator suffered from a delusional disorder causing him to believe that there was an international conspiracy of dark forces.[85] He left his £8m estate to the Conservative Party, and the judge notably found that his attachment to that political party was to an extent fed by his delusional state, believing that this was the only organization that would fight those dark forces. The issue was, had the delusions brought about a disposal of the testator's estate that he would not have made if of sound mind? The point was also raised as to whether it only has to be shown, in order for the will to be valid, that the delusions did not in fact exercise any influence on the dispositions in the will, or if it also had to be shown that the delusions were not likely to influence the dispositions in the will, whether or not they actually did so.[86] It was not necessary for the court to decide this question as it found overwhelming **2.53**

---

[81] *Theobald on Wills* 16th edn., 3-04, citing *Dew v Clark* (1826) 3 Add 79 (an insane aversion to his only daughter); *Re Belliss* (1929) 141 LT 245 (delusion he had already benefited one daughter far more than the other); *Battan Singh v Amirchand* [1948] PC 161 (delusion that he had no relatives); *Re Nightingale* (1974) 119 SJ 189 (a delusion his son had tried to shorten his life); *in re The Estate of Bohrmann* [1938] 1 All ER 271 'the law has recognised that a man may make a perfectly good will so long as the delusions from which he suffers have no relation to any testamentary capacity'; *Banks v Goodfellow* (1870) LR 5 QB 549 at 570 per Cockburn CJ 'But where in the result a jury are satisfied that the delusion has not affected the general faculties of the mind, and can have had no effect upon the will, we see no sufficient reason why the testator should be held to have lost his right to make a will, or why a will made under such circumstances should not be upheld.'

[82] (1879) 5 PD 84.

[83] Where George IV, as Prince Regent, had built and furnished the Brighton Pavilion.

[84] [2007] EWHC 2298 (Ch); other recent decisions on delusions are *Re Ritchie, Ritchie v Joslin* [2009] EWHC 709 (her sons were stealing from her and her daughters never visited her); *Walters v Smee* [2009] WTLR 521 (the claimants had been abusing her (physically and verbally), stealing money and jewellery from her, and displaying inappropriate sexual behaviour—all of which was unfounded); *Hinton v Leigh* [2009] EWHC 2658 (delusions about his blood relatives, but not his adopted children).

[85] The conspiracy involved the legal profession, the accountancy profession, the banking profession, his colleagues in the pharmaceutical industry, and his family.

[86] For example, were the delusions the reason for excluding a member of the family or if, without the delusions, would he have still been excluded through a rational antipathy towards him?

evidence that the delusions did influence the testator in excluding his son from the will and in favouring the Conservative Party. This point remains unsettled.

2.54 If a delusion exists, and does not affect the dispositions in the will, then the will will be valid.[87] The view has been put forward that delusions being described as a false belief which defies logic need to be distinguished from other false beliefs which might arise for reasons which, whilst wrong or mistaken, are not delusional.[88]

Modern re-statements of *Banks v Goodfellow*

2.55 From Australia:

> 'testamentary capacity' encompasses the following concepts:
> 1. that the testator or testatrix is aware, and appreciates the significance, of the act in the law which he is about to embark upon;
> 2. that the testator or testatrix is aware, at least in general terms, of the nature, and extent, and value, of the estate over which he has a disposing power;
> 3. that the testator or testatrix is aware of those [who have] or may reasonably be thought to have a claim upon his or her testamentary bounty, and the basis for, and nature of, the claims of such persons;
> 4. that the testator or testatrix has the ability to evaluate, and to discriminate between, the respective strengths of the claims of such persons.
>
> The necessary corollary of this is that, if, at the relevant time the testator or testatrix is found to suffer from a condition—whether 'mental illness' (or psychosis) in the strict sense or any other form of 'mental disorder' (including, but not limited to, deterioration in higher intellectual function or dementia)—which detrimentally affects his consciousness or sense of orientation, or has brought about disturbances to his intelligence, cognition, thought content and thought processes, judgement and the like, then, even though that condition may be transient, or, if appropriately treated, reversible, the testator/testatrix will, more probably than not, be held to lack testamentary capacity.[89]

2.56 From Canada:

> [The testator must be] capable to comprehend, of its own initiative and volition, the essential elements of will making, property, objects, just claims to consideration,

---

[87] *Banks v Goodfellow* (1870) 5 QB 549 at 570 (delusion of being pursued by evil spirits); *Hope v Campbell* [1899] AC 1 where the testator left a large estate to be held on trust for the promotion of certain charitable or benevolent objects: 'Shortly stated, these objects were total abstinence from the use of alcoholic or fermented liquors, or of tobacco or opium, the dissemination of the true doctrines of the Protestant religion, the inculcation of the danger arising to civil and religious liberty from the doctrines of the Church of Rome, the promotion of Sabbath observance, of Church and State connection, and the union of all Christian Churches on the basis of a united established Church.' It was found that the voice from heaven telling him to do this did not make the will invalid.

[88] *Viva Campaigns Ltd & The Vegetarian Society v Scott* [2014] WTLR 525 at [42].

[89] *Read v Carmody* NSWCA 23rd July 1998 unreported (per Powell JA) applied in *Grynberg v Muller* [2001] NSWC 532 and *Challen v Pitt* [2004] QSC 365; also in *Timbury v Coffee* (1941) 66 CLR 277, 'The factors of competency are that the party must know what he is about, have sense and knowledge of what he is doing and the effect his dispositions will have, knowledge of what his property was, and who those persons were that then were the objects of his bounty.'

> revocation of existing documents and the like.... merely to be able to make rational responses is not enough, nor to repeat a tutored formula of simple terms.[90]

From England: **2.57**

> the testator must:
> 1. be able to understand the nature of the act of making a will;
> 2. know which persons he should consider as possible beneficiaries;[91]
> 3. be able to understand the extent of the property of which he is disposing;
> 4. not be subject to any disorder of the mind as 'poison his affections, pervert his sense of right, or prevent the exercise of his natural faculties'; and
> 5. have the mental capacity to make decisions which take into account the relevant property, persons and circumstances and arrive at a 'rational, fair and just' testament.[92]

Although such restatements may assist a little in illustrating the issues involved by using different words, the Court of Appeal in *Sharp v Adam* was of the opinion that '...we do not consider on reflection that the *Banks v Goodfellow* formulation needs to be reformulated, nor is it perhaps open to this court to do so...'[93] **2.58**

The Draftsman's Duty to Assess the Testator's Capacity

The draftsman has no general duty to obtain a medical report for testamentary capacity purposes for all clients,[94] but where the circumstances of the testator (age, illness, etc.) or the circumstances of the interview, or the terms of the new will, raise **2.59**

---

[90] Rand J paraphrasing the test in *Leger v Poirier* (1944) 3 DLR 1 (SCC); *Re Schwartz* [1970] 2 OR 61 per Laskin JA

> The testator must be sufficiently clear in his understanding and memory to know, on his own, and in a general way, (1) the nature and extent of his property, (2) the persons who are the natural objects of his bounty and (3) the testamentary provisions he is making; and he must, moreover, be capable of (4) appreciating these factors in relation to each other, and (5) forming an orderly desire as to the disposition of his property.

[91] *Banks v Goodfellow* does require actual knowledge of this point; see 2.30.

[92] In *Re Loxston, Abbott v Richardson* [2006] WTLR 1567, Nicholas Strauss QC sitting as a deputy judge.

[93] [2006] 1059 at [82].

[94] In *Thorpe v Fellowes* [2011] EWHC 61 (QB) it was said of a contract issue that 'A solicitor is generally only required to make inquiries into a person's capacity to contract if there are circumstances such as to raise doubt as to this in the mind of the reasonably competent practitioner.' The authors have found that in practice this sentence is misunderstood and cited as authority for there being no need to make any enquiry into testamentary capacity in the absence of patently obviously impaired capacity. This is not what the judgment says. Further, it was not a decision about will instructions and understandably none of the English authorities in this section of this book were considered by the court. There are other issues with this judgment; see <http://www.step.org/thorpe-v-fellowes-solicitors-llp-decision-any-help-us>.

Furthermore, the presumption of capacity in s. 1(2) Mental Capacity Act 2005, is also often wrongly cited in this context. It is not an authority for the draftsman to proceed without enquiry into substantial issues of capacity[95] then the draftsman would be very ill advised to ignore the question of a medical report.

2.60 Obtaining a medical report is a separate issue from the need for the draftsman to otherwise satisfy himself as to his client's capacity. There is generally the point that in order to be able to accept instructions, the draftsman should be satisfied that the client has the capacity to engage him.[96] In *Feltham v Freer Bouskell*[97] it was put that 'Where a solicitor is instructed to prepare and execute a will for a client, if the client does not have capacity, he has no client and cannot accept instructions. If he has concerns as to mental capacity, he must either refuse the instructions and make the position clear to the client, or take steps to satisfy himself as to his client's mental capacity promptly' (note the final word). Simply failing to consider the issue is not sufficient.

2.61 Where the circumstances of the testator, the manner of the instructions, and the terms of the new will raise no concerns, clearly it would be inappropriate to expect a draftsman to expend both time and the client's resources on capacity issues, provided that the draftsman is satisfied that his client has capacity from his dealings with him.[98] The problem with such a general statement is the substantial middle ground between the extremes. However, the draftsman will be acting more prudently and providing better client care if he considers capacity, and where he has any concerns at all asks further questions of his client and seeks to evaluate the client's capacity to understand against the test in *Banks v Goodfellow*.[99] As capacity issues are more often encountered with the elderly and infirm, ignoring the possibility of incapacity

the capacity of the testator. It is also a presumption 'for the purposes of this Act' only and therefore does not apply to testamentary capacity until the court chooses to adopt it (see later in this chapter).

[95] And also undue influence, fraud, or want of knowledge and approval.

[96] 'The relationship of solicitor and client is primarily a contractual one and, as with any contractual relationship, a solicitor's retainer is governed by the terms of the contract agreed with his or her client' Flenley and Leech *Solicitors' Negligence and Liability* (3rd edn., Haywards Heath: Bloomsbury Professional, 2013). There is no single standard for the capacity to enter into a contract; the person must be able to understand the nature and effect of the particular contract (*Boughton v Knight* (1873) LR PD 64 at 72). Where an individual lacks capacity when entering into the contract, unless it can be shown that the other contracting party was aware, or ought to have been aware, of the other party's incapacity, he is bound by it (*Imperial Loan Co v Stone* [1892] 1 QB 599 CA). It is difficult to see that the capacity to contract for a will can require capacity any lower than that to make a will. The Law Society Practice Note on 'Financial Abuse' 13 June 2013 when dealing with precautions to be taken against financial abuse: 'If you are in any doubt as to whether a client has capacity to provide instructions, you must perform a capacity assessment before any instructions are acted upon.'

[97] [2013] WTLR 1363 at [52].

[98] *Jeffrey v Jeffrey* [2013] WTLR 1509.

[99] *Legal Services Commissioner v Ford* [2008] LPT 12 (Queensland) and a finding of unsatisfactory professional conduct where the solicitor's conduct in preparing and arranging for the execution of an EPA and a will 'fell short of a standard of competence and diligence that a member of the public was entitled to expect of a reasonably competent Australian legal practitioner.' Also, see the criticism of the draftsman in *Re Key, Key v Key* [2010] WTLR 623 for failing to address the issue of capacity.

and assuming capacity, rather than observing and establishing relevant information, appears to fall well short of the standards expressed in English judgments.[100]

Templeman J (as he was then) in setting out the Golden Rule[101] clearly accepted that, for the aged or seriously ill testator, there was a duty for the draftsman to take steps to satisfy himself as to capacity. However, the Golden Rule is now acknowledged not to be a rule,[102] although it has been repeatedly accepted by the court as a sound guide to practice. There is still strong support from the court for the application of the rule by draftsmen[103] with often adverse comment where there has been non-compliance. This makes it all the more dangerous for a draftsman to ignore the Rule without good, and documented, reasons. As was said in *Re Key*, 'Contrary to the clearest guidance in well-known cases, academic texts and from the Law Society, [he] accepted instructions for the preparation of the 2006 will . . . without taking any proper steps to satisfy himself of Mr Key's testamentary capacity . . . '[104] **2.62**

In practice, it appears to be acceptable to the court for the Golden Rule be complied with by either **2.63**

- the draftsman following the Golden Rule and involving a medical practitioner; or
- the draftsman otherwise satisfying himself properly as to his client's capacity, at least sufficiently as to reasonably not require any medical view of capacity.

Either of these two courses will arrive at the point of the draftsman being satisfied, at least on balance, as to the client's capacity and this will satisfy the court as to proper conduct, even if ultimately the court concludes that the testator lacked capacity.[105] The importance is not not being mistaken as to capacity, but taking adequate steps to form a reasonable view as to capacity.

There are many English decisions that start from the implied position that the draftsman has a duty to satisfy himself of his client's capacity where the circumstances of the client require it.[106] Much clearer articulation of the duty of the draftsman to be satisfied as to capacity is to be found in the following series of Canadian cases. **2.64**

- *Murphy v Lamphier*[107] . . . the solicitor does not discharge his duty by simply taking down and giving legal expression to the words of the client, without being satisfied

[100] *Re Key, Key v Key* [2010] WTLR 623 at [6].

[101] *Re Simpson* (1977) 127 NLJ 487—See Chapter 6.

[102] *Hoff v Atherton* [2005] WTLR 99 CA at [49] per Peter Gibson LJ 'too briefly reported to be of much assistance, contains prudent guidance for solicitors and does not purport to lay down the law.' See Chapter 6 for more detailed comment on the Golden Rule.

[103] *Re Key, Key v Key* [2010] WTLR 623; *Re Morris deceased, The Special Trustees for the Great Ormond Street Hospital for Children v Rushin* [2001] WTLR 1127.

[104] [2010] WTLR 623 at [6].

[105] *Scammell v Farmer* [2008] WTLR 1261.

[106] *Wintle v Nye* [1959] 1 WLR 284; *Re Parsons, Borman v Lel* [2002] WTLR 237 at 257H; *Re Key, Key v Key* [2010] WTLR 623; *Feltham v Freer Bouskell* [2013] WTLR 1363.

[107] (1914) 31 OLR 287 (affirmed (1914) 32 OLR 19), cited in *Hall v Estate of Bruce Bennett.*

by all available means that the testable capacity exists and is being freely and intelligently exercised… The solicitor is brought in for the very purpose of ascertaining the mind and will of the testator…

- *Maw v Dickey*[108] I find therefore a specific duty on the part of the solicitor to ask questions in order to satisfy himself that his client had testamentary capacity and… a duty to reduce to some permanent form [his] impressions.
- *Friesen v Friesen Estate*[109] The duty of a solicitor taking instructions for a will is always a heavy one. When the client is weak and ill, and particularly when the solicitor knows that he is revoking an existing will, the responsibility will be particularly onerous.
- A solicitor cannot discharge his duty by asking perfunctory questions, getting apparently rational answers, and then simply recording in legal form the words expressed by the client. He must first satisfy himself that true testamentary capacity exists, that the instructions are freely given, and that the effect of the will is understood.
- *Scott v Cousins*[110] The obligations of solicitors when taking instructions for wills have been repeatedly emphasised in cases of this nature. At the very least, the solicitor must make a serious attempt to determine whether the testator… has capacity and if there is any possible doubt—or other reason to suspect that the will may be challenged…
- *Hall v Estate of Bruce Bennett*[111] The law is equally clear that a solicitor who undertakes to prepare a will has duty to inquire into his or her client's testamentary capacity.

This is emphasized by being further considered from the point of view of the client's capacity to engage the draftsman, and understand and accept the terms of the retainer.[112]

2.65 While the authors have not been able to find that any of the above have been considered and expressly approved by the English court, there is a strong likelihood that they would be accepted in support of the implicit recognition of a duty mentioned above. In *Feltham v Freer Bouskell* the court made the clearest statement yet that the

---

108 (1974) 52 DLR (3rd) 178.

109 (1985) 33 Man R (2d) 98 per Kroft J at [88] and [89]; at [70] there is the explanation that

> Other than asking for the nurse's opinion and making his own general assessment [the solicitor] did not ask any questions specifically designed to test Jake's testamentary capacity. [The solicitor] knew the extent of Jake's property, but did not determine the state of Jake's own recollection. He did not ask any questions designed to evaluate the extent of Jake's appreciation of his family obligations, nor did he ask why, after only a few weeks, he was making another will.

Other Canadian cases include *Re Carvell Estate* (1977) 21 NBR (2d) 642 and *Re Worrell* (1970) 8 DLR (3rd) 36.

110 (2001) 37 ETR (2d) 113.

111 [2003] WTLR 827 [22] Ontario CA.

112 See for example The Law Society's Practice Note on Financial Abuse (13 June 2013) and the need to ascertain capacity to instruct (paragraph 4.3.2).

English court regards there as being a requirement that the draftsman must satisfy himself of his client's capacity:

> [The solicitor] accepted instructions to act for [the testatrix] in relation to her desire to change her will. He did so subject to the requirement to satisfy himself that she was of sufficient mental capacity to alter her will.[113]

Should the draftsman then proceed to refuse to prepare a will where he is not satisfied that the client has capacity? The implication of cases such as *Re Simpson*,[114] *Re Morris*,[115] and *Re Key*[116] is that he should. Indeed, it would be an unusual position, both ethically and practically, if a draftsman proceeded with will instructions if he believed the testator lacked capacity. In the New Zealand case of *Knox v Till*[117] the court found that there was no duty to refuse to prepare a will where the client lacked capacity: **2.66**

> There is generally an obligation to carry out the client's instructions. In the situation under discussion no disqualifying factor such as illegality, unlawfulness or breach of ethical responsibilities arises to negate that duty. The giving of advice on the question of testamentary capacity and recording the advice which would appear to be possible appropriate responses to a situation where capacity is apparently in question, are far removed from a possible refusal to act.

The difficulty with these New Zealand views are that they do appear to be out of step with the English and Canadian authorities and do not seem to take into account fully how it can be that a retainer to prepare a will can be offered to, and accepted by, someone who, the draftsman believes, lacks the capacity to understand the subject matter of the retainer.[118]

In Australia the following has been expressed regarding the draftsman's duty.[119] **2.67**

> That does not, however, mean that no ethical considerations arise in such a circumstance. The essence of a solicitor's fiduciary obligations to a client is the unfettered service of that client's interests... The testator should be assisted by his or her legal adviser only in making a valid will.
>
> There is an additional consideration, not dependent of the question of conflict of interest. That is, the duty of the solicitor taking instructions from an obviously enfeebled testator, where capacity is potentially in doubt, to take particular care to gain

113 [2013] WTLR 1363 at [64] per Charles Hollander QC sitting as deputy judge.

114 *Re Simpson* (1977) 127 NLJ 487.

115 *Re Morris deceased, The Special Trustees for the Great Ormond Street Hospital for Children v Rushin* [2001] WTLR 1127.

116 *Re Key, Key v Key* [2010] WTLR 623.

117 [2000] Lloyd's Rep PN 49 there was a further attempt, *Public Trustee v Till* [2002] WTLR 1169, in the same estate where the executors attempted to recoup the probate costs, which also failed.

118 See further in Chapter 6 on the role of the draftsman.

119 *Pates v Craig, the Estate of the late Joyce Jean Cole* [1995] NSWSC 87 at [143] and [147] per Santow J.

> reasonable assurance as to the testamentary capacity of the testator. It is clearly undesirable to attempt to lay down precise and specific rules as to what that necessarily entails for every case. Such rules may lead to a perfunctory, mechanical checklist approach. What should be done in each case will depend on the apparent state of the testator at the time and other relevant surrounding circumstances. Any suggestion that someone, potentially interested, has instigated the will, whether or not a client of the will draftsperson, should particularly place the solicitor concerned on the alert. At the least, a solicitor should ask the kind of questions designed to probe the testator's understanding of the basic matters which connote testamentary capacity.

While one might hesitate to say that an English court would adopt these views, they contain eminently sound practical advice as to good practice that could well be accepted by the English court.

2.68 For the elderly or infirm there is a greater possibility that their instructions are given in imprecise or non-legal terms. Under these circumstances, the draftsman has a duty to clarify what it is that the client requires of him.[120] The extent of the retainer and duty of care will then be determined by the extent and nature of the advice required.

2.69 When considering the duty of care of the draftsman, *White v Jones*[121] established that the duty of care that is owed by the draftsman to his client transfers to the beneficiaries of the will and they can sue upon that duty of care if they have suffered loss through a breach of that duty of care and the testator has not. There is no separate duty of care owed to the beneficiaries.[122] What is less clear is, where a will is prepared negligently, and it is later found to be invalid with costs (in whole or in part) being left in the estate, can the personal representatives recover those costs from the draftsman on the basis that he breached his duty of care? The possibility of this was not ruled out by the Court of Appeal in *Worby v Rosser*.[123] However this is view is not easy to reconcile with the later Court of Appeal judgment in *Corbett v Bond Pearce*.[124] This point remains to be fully explored by the court.[125]

---

[120] *Gray v Buss Murton* [1999] PNLR 882 (noted with approval in *Feltham v Freer Bouskell* [2013] WTLR 1363); *Groom v Crocker* [1939] 1 KB 194 'it is an incident of that duty that the solicitor shall consult with his client on all questions of doubt which do not fall within the express or implied retainer.'

[121] [1995] 2 AC 207.

[122] For a fuller examination of this issue see Chapter 2 Frost, Reed QC, and Baxter *Risk and Negligence in Wills Estates and Trusts* (Oxford: OUP, 2014).

[123] [1999] Lloyd's Rep PN 972.

[124] [2001] WTLR 419. For a fuller examination of this issue see Chapter 3 *Risk and Negligence* Frost, Reed QC, and Baxter (OUP, 2014).

[125] The claimant was successful on this point in *Sifri v Clough Willis* [2007] WTLR 1453, where she recovered in part the costs of the successful want of knowledge and approval claim, but there appears not to have been a full consideration of the two Court of Appeal cases. There is a strong suspicion that given the severe remarks made about the draftsman's conduct in *Re Key, Key v Key* [2010] WTLR 623 that his insurers paid some of the costs, but this suspicion cannot be confirmed.

Mental Capacity Act 2005

Was this Act[126] intended to replace the test in *Banks v Goodfellow*? The answer has to be that there is an unfortunate degree of uncertainty since the commencement of the Act, but for the reasons set out below it is considered that it has not. The MCA 2005 is certainly not retrospective in effect[127] and so it can have no application to any will made before it commenced.[128] **2.70**

The statutory Code of Conduct issued with the MCA 2005 set out the following view: **2.71**

> What other legal tests of capacity are there?
>
> 4.31 The Act makes clear that the definition of 'lack of capacity' and the two-stage test for capacity set out in the Act are 'for the purposes of this Act'. This means that the definition and test are to be used in situations covered by this Act. Schedule 6 of the Act also amends existing laws to ensure that the definition and test are used in other areas of law not covered directly by this Act.
> For example, Schedule 6, paragraph 20 allows a person to be disqualified from jury service if they lack the capacity (using this Act's definition) to carry out a juror's tasks.
>
> 4.32 There are several tests of capacity that have been produced following judgments in court cases (known as common law tests). These cover:
> - capacity to make a will (*Banks v Goodfellow* (1870) LR 5 QB 549)
> - capacity to make a gift (*Re Beaney (deceased)* [1978] 2 All ER 595)
> - capacity to enter into a contract (*Boughton v Knight* (1873) LR 3 PD 64)
> - capacity to litigate (take part in legal cases), (*Masterman-Lister v Brutton & Co and Jewell Home Counties Dairies* [2003] 3 All ER 162 (CA)) and
> - capacity to enter into marriage. (*Sheffield City Council v E & S* [2005] 1 FLR 965).
>
> 4.33 The Act's new definition of capacity is in line with the existing common law tests, *and the Act does not replace them. When cases come before the court on the above issues, judges can adopt the new definition if they think it is appropriate. The Act will apply to all other cases relating to financial, healthcare or welfare decisions.*[129]

The above seems to be fairly clear in the view that the Act's test of capacity does not apply to testamentary capacity (amongst other areas) but that the court could adopt it (or elements of it) if it saw fit.[130] The emphasized passage above concerns the court **2.72**

---

[126] There is an important issue as to the extent to which this Act is compliant with the United Nations Convention on the Rights of Persons with Disabilities. This Convention was ratified by the UK on 8 June 2009. This area is not within the scope of this work, but it will most likely be a major issue for future reform of this area of law.

[127] *Scammell v Farmer* [2008] WTLR 1261; [2008] EWHC 1100 (Ch); *Re Key, Key v Key* [2010] WTLR 623; *Simon v Byford* [2013] WTLR 1615 Ch D.

[128] The MCA 2005 commenced 01/10/07.

[129] Authors' emphasis: this passage seems to make it clear that the authors of the Code did not think that the Act had replaced the listed common law tests.

[130] In *Saulle v Nouvet* [2008] WTLR 729 at [15] the view that appeared to be expressed in the Code of Practice that a court could adopt the MCA test if it thought it appropriate was described as

choosing to adopt the test, or more probably elements of it. It is not an invitation to practitioners to adopt the statutory test without the authority of the court. It is quite possible that the court will adopt any parts of the Act's test so as to align more closely the two tests of capacity. This would be the voluntary adoption to augment the test. There is no reason to suppose that this would extend to adopting the Act's presumption of capacity (see Chapter 5 on the Burden of Proof) even if this was possible.

2.73 In *Re MM*[131] Munby J (as he then was) said of the above emphasized passage:

> The meaning of the observation is clear and the sentiment unexceptional. It is not being said—it could not properly be said—that a judge sitting in the (new) Court of Protection and exercising the statutory jurisdiction under the Mental Capacity Act 2005 is in some mysterious and undefined way entitled to disregard the statutory test in s 3. Certainly not. What is being said is that judges sitting elsewhere than in the Court of Protection and deciding cases where what is in issue is, for example, capacity to make a will, capacity to make a gift, capacity to enter into a contract, capacity to litigate or capacity to enter into marriage, can adopt the new definition if it is appropriate—appropriate, that is, having regard to the existing principles of the common law.

2.74 In *Scammell v Farmer*[132] it was commented that the MCA 2005 would not supplant the common law test. In this case:

> 24. There was a large measure of agreement between counsel that the test of mental capacity under Section 3 of the 2005 Act is a modern restatement of the test propounded in Banks v Goodfellow (1870) LR 5 QB 549, to which I shall turn below. There is, however, an obvious difference between the position at common law and the position under the 2005 Act, in that the onus of proof of incapacity under the 2005 Act (Section 1(2)) is from the outset, and remains, on the complainant. At common law, the position is different.
> 25. I do not consider that the 2005 Act applies in this case, for either (or both) of two reasons. First, this is not a case within the purposes of the 2005 Act, as required by section 1(1). I was referred... to sections 16–18 of the 2005 Act, but those provisions concern the power of the Court to make or authorise the making of Wills on behalf of persons who lack capacity, not the ascertainment of whether a particular testator had capacity when a Will was made.[133]
> 26. I was also referred to the Code of Practice under the Mental Capacity Act issued by the Lord Chancellor on 23 April 2007, and it was suggested that parts of that Code of

'an unorthodox proposition', but see the commentary upon the Code in *Re MM* in the next paragraph. Too recent to be considered in the text are *Walker v Badmin* (Chancery 20/11/14) and *Kicks v Leigh* [2014] EWHC 3926 (Ch) both of which contain detailed reasoning rejecting the MCA as having replaced the common law tests in respect of wills and gifts.

[131] *Re MM, Local Authority X v MM (an adult)* [2007] EWHC 2003 (Fam) at para 80; considered and approved in *Saulle v Nouvet* [2008] WTLR 729.

[132] [2008] WTLR 1261; expressly followed in *Pearce v Beverley* [2014] WTLR 85 (HHJ Behrens) at [87].

[133] In *Bray v Pearce* (unreported Ch D 6 March 2014) it was observed as *obiter* at [88] of this paragraph that 'the meaning and reasoning in the judgment in Scammell on these points is not entirely obvious to me. I cannot and do not say that it was wrong, and these issues are not decisive for this present judgment.' The reasons behind this comment were not set out.

Practice suggest that the Act was intended to apply in a case such as this. Even if that was a correct reading of the Code of Practice, it would not change my interpretation of the 2005 Act. But I do not think that it is a correct reading of the Code of Practice at all, see especially paragraphs 4.31 to 4.33. The latter paragraph actually states that when cases concerning, e.g., a testator's capacity to make a will come before the court, 'judges can adopt the new definition if they think it is appropriate.'[134]

28. [Secondly] to apply MCA 2005 to the disposition of the estate in this case would be to give it retrospective effect.[135]

Further support of these views is to be found in *Saulle v Nouvet*:[136] **2.75**

- [9]...the Act concerns decisions which the Court of Protection has jurisdiction to make, and not decisions of the High Court Queen's Bench Division in civil proceedings.[137]
- [10] The definition of 'capacity' in s. 2(1) is a definition 'for the purposes of this Act'. It is not one of the purposes of the Act to regulate or in any way address the way in which the Court approaches the question of capacity to litigate, and...s. 64 defines 'the court' as 'the Court of Protection established by s. 45'. The Act does not purport to regulate the conduct of any other 'court'.
- [12] The Code of Practice was published in advance of the coming into force of the new CPR Pt 21, and is, in my judgement, inaccurate in asserting that the only capacity decisions which may be taken by a court to which the act does not apply are those identified in the bullet points in para 4.32. That is not what the Act says.

In an article by Senior Judge Lush of the Court of Protection, he expressed a similar view: **2.76**

The Mental Capacity Act doesn't supersede *Banks v Goodfellow*. It merely complements it. The Act requires that someone should be able to understand, retain and use and weigh the information relevant to the particular decision they are making at a particular time.

What *Banks v Goodfellow* does is summarise—in simple and succinct terms—the information that is relevant to the decision of making a will.[138]

Against the above views: **2.77**

1. There was an *obiter* remark in *Perrins v Holland*,[139] without further explanation, that the common law test of testamentary capacity is 'now superseded' by the MCA 2005.

---

134 This view was not followed in *Bray v Pearce* (unreported Ch D 6 March 2014) where the MCA was regarded as the start point when considering testamentary capacity and this conclusion was in line with paragraphs 4.31 to 4.33—a view with which the authors respectfully disagree.

135 Both will and death predated the commencement of the MCA 2005. A point supported in *Gorjat v Gorjat* [2010] EWHC 1537 (Ch) at [132].

136 [2008] WTLR 729.

137 This point is echoed in *A County Council v MS* [2014] WTLR 931, a Court of Protection matter, which concerned a proposed gift by a patient to the Church of the Latter Saints. At [55] 'The Mental Capacity Act 2005—including, therefore, the capacity test set out in it—applies to proceedings in the Court of Protection, and this case is in the Court of Protection.' At [64] 'The statutory capacity test set out in the 2005 Act applies to declarations and decisions made under that Act.'

138 October 2012 published at <http://www.step.org/banks-v-goodfellow-1870>.

139 [2009] WTLR 1387 (Lewison J as he was then).

2. In *Fischer v Diffley*[140] the view was expressed that the common law test 'has been recently supplemented by statute to which, it seems to me, that I am entitled to have regard as a starting point in connection with the question of capacity.' This was applied by starting out with an assumption of capacity.[141] The question of capacity was then approached as a two-part statutory test. 'First the court has to determine whether there is an impairment or disturbance in the functioning of the mind or brain and secondly it has to determine whether, as a consequence of that impairment, etc. the person in question is unable to make a decision for himself in relation to the specific transaction which the court is considering at the time.'[142] Unfortunately the court did not provide us with any reasoning[143] as to why the court considered the MCA 2005 was applicable.
3. In *Bray v Pearce*[144] the court found that the purposes of the 2005 Act should not be narrowly construed and it could be applied, at least by analogy, to testamentary capacity. It is not wholly clear why it was necessary to adopt this approach when the existing common law test was quite appropriate to resolve the issue facing the court without extending the application of the Act by analogy. This judgment also proposed that for the purpose of s. 1(2) MCA 2005 it is 'established' that a person lacks capacity if only a real doubt is raised as to capacity but this then not rebutted.[145]
4. *Theobald on Wills*[146] takes the view that the MCA 2005 will be used once wills, executed after the Act came into force, come to be considered by the court. This view is also taken by the authors of *Williams on Wills*.[147] Neither *Theobald* nor *Williams* cite, or comment on, the views of Munby J set out above.

2.78 It is sometimes said that the MCA 2005 test is simply a modern restatement of the common law test of testamentary capacity and it is true that there are, unsurprisingly, a number of similarities. There are however differences that can be of substance.

(a) The burden of proof at general law for a will shifts testing both the objections to the will and the will, whereas the MCA 2005 starts with a presumption that the testator has testamentary capacity (see Chapter 4 for more detail on this issue).
(b) Section 3 of the Act sets out specific features relating to the inability to take decisions:

140 [2013] EWHC 4567 (Ch) HHJ Dight at [25]—Chapter 4 for burden of proof issues and this decision; *Fisher* was cited with approval in another effectively undefended case *Bray v Pearce* unreported Ch D 6 March 2014.
141 At [27] applying the presumption in s. 1(2) of the act.
142 At [30].
143 At [24] it was simply observed that 'the law is not in dispute'.
144 Unreported Ch D 6 March 2014.
145 Chambers English Dictionary 'doubt *n* uncertainty of opinion: a suspicion'; 'establish *vt* to prove'.
146 17th edn., Sweet & Maxwell 2010 at 3-006.
147 9th edn., LexisNexis Butterworth (2008), 4th Cumulative Supplement (2013) at 4.9.

1. For the purposes of section 2, a person is unable to make a decision for himself if he is unable
   (a) to understand the information relevant to the decision;
   (b) to retain that information;
   (c) to use or weigh that information as part of the process of making the decision; or
   (d) to communicate his decision (whether by talking, using sign language or any other means).
2. A person is not to be regarded as unable to understand the information relevant to a decision if he is able to understand an explanation of it given to him in a way that is appropriate to his circumstances (using simple language, visual aids or any other means).
3. The fact that a person is able to retain the information relevant to a decision for a short period only does not prevent him from being regarded as able to make the decision.
4. The information relevant to a decision includes information about the reasonably foreseeable consequences of
   (a) deciding one way or another; or
   (b) failing to make the decision.

The common law test of capacity is about understanding, or the ability to understand, at the time that the will is executed. There is no requirement that the testator be able to retain that information after the event. A requirement to 'retain that information' in s. 3(1)(b) is far more relevant to continuing functions, such as management of one's affairs, than it is to a will, which is a single transaction not linked in any way to continuing abilities.

c) There is a further requirement in s. 3(4) of requiring that the information, specified in s. 3(1), includes information about the 'reasonably foreseeable consequences' of the decisions or failing to make the decisions. This goes significantly beyond the test in *Banks v Goodfellow*. For example, understanding the reasonably foreseeable consequence of not making a will would entail understanding in broad terms how the estate would devolve on intestacy, in its principal features, and the comparative benefit that would be received by individuals.[148] The Court of Appeal in *Simon v Byford*[149] rejected the suggestion that *Banks v Goodfellow* required a requirement to understand consequences.
d) Section 1(3) provides that 'A person is not to be treated as unable to make a decision unless all practicable steps to help him to do so have been taken without success.' This is about decision making rather than the capacity to understand (which is the essence of *Banks v Goodfellow*).

Has any court applied the MCA 2005 in preference to *Banks v Goodfellow* (other **2.79**
than *Fischer v Diffley* and *Bray v Pearce* referred to above)? In the recent *Re Wilson*[150]

[148] *Re Devillebichot, Brennan v Prior* [2013] WTLR 1701; see also earlier in this chapter at 2.33.
[149] [2014] WTLR 1097 at [44] and [45].
[150] *Re Wilson, Turner v Phythian* [2013] WTLR 899 at [39].

the dispute concerned a will executed on 31 August 2010.[151] The judge noted: 'I did not hear any submissions as to whether the [MCA] test differed from the common law test, though the latter is more expressly tailored to the issue in this case.' He then proceeded to consider the matter on the basis of *Banks v Goodfellow*. To a similar effect, were remarks in *Re Stolkin*[152] where it was said that neither counsel suggested that s. 2 MCA 2005 'adds anything of importance to the common law authorities for the purposes of the present case'. The judge also described s. 2 as merely providing guidance on this question. *Re Devillebichot*[153] concerned, *inter alia*, testamentary capacity regarding a will executed on 19 February 2011—there was no discussion of the MCA 2005 and the matter was judged on the basis of the general law test.[154]

2.80 Therefore, to date, the application of the MCA test, to a will executed after that Act came into effect, has not been fully argued in court and certainly not reviewed by a higher court (but see note 130 to paragraph 2.72).

Banks v Goodfellow is a common law test

2.81 In understanding this issue it is helpful to remember that, as *Banks v Goodfellow* is a common law test, the original test is capable of being developed by the court as modern needs and circumstances require. This ability to develop the definition has enabled the court to adjust the way it is applied rather than leaving matters constrained by the original wording of the judgment (and early applications of it).

2.82 In *Perrins v Holland*,[155] Lewison J (as he then was) observed that:

> First, since the test is a common law test it is capable of being influenced by contemporary attitudes.[156]
>
> Second, our general understanding of impaired mental capacity of adults has increased enormously since 1870.
>
> Third, we now recognise that an adult with impaired mental capacity is capable of making some decisions for himself, given help.
>
> Thus fourth, we recognise that the test of mental capacity is not monolithic but is tailored to the task in hand.[157]
>
> Fifth, contemporary attitudes towards adults with impaired capacity are more respectful of adult autonomy.

---

[151] i.e. after the commencement of the MCA 2005.

[152] *Re Stolkin, Greaves v Stolkin* [2013] WTLR 1793 at [50].

[153] *Re Devillebichot, Brennan v Prior* [2013] WTLR 1701.

[154] It may be relevant to note that the claimant represented herself.

[155] [2009] WTLR 1387 at [40].

[156] See early in this chapter for the extract from *Estate of Badran, Kerr v Badran* [2004] NSWSC 735 Windeyer J at [49] (approved in *Zorbas v Sidiropoulous (No 2)* [2007] NSWCA 197) which is very much in a similar vein with regard to the understanding of assets.

[157] See also *Hoff v Atherton* [2005] WTLR 99.

> Sixth, even the traditional test must be applied in the context of the particular testator and the particular estate. A testator with a complex estate and many potential beneficiaries may need a greater degree of cognitive capability than one with a simple estate and few claimants.[158]

The first of these points shows the way ahead for the court to be able to adapt the test. The second, third, fourth, and fifth points introduce an identification of specific areas where adaptation is foreseeable.

In *Re Key, Key v Key*[159] the judgment reflects particularly the second point (above from the *Perrins* judgment) and extends the traditional test by taking into account the decision-making powers of the testator: **2.83**

> This is not one of those cases in which it is possible to point simply to a conspicuous inability of the deceased to satisfy one of the distinct limbs of the *Banks v Goodfellow* test. Rather it is a case in which I have been persuaded, taking the evidence as a whole, that Mr Key was simply unable during the week following his wife's death to exercise the decision-making powers of a testator... To the extent that such a conclusion involves a slight development of the *Banks v Goodfellow* test, taking into account decision-making powers rather than just comprehension, I consider that it is necessitated by the greater understanding of the mind now available from modern psychiatric medicine, in particular in relation to affective disorder.[160]
>
> Without in any way detracting from the continuing authority of *Banks v Goodfellow*, it must be recognised that psychiatric medicine has come a long way since 1870 in recognising an ever-widening range of circumstances now regarded as sufficient at least to give some risk to a mental disorder, sufficient to deprive a patient of the power of rational decision making, quite distinct from old age and infirmity. The mental shock of witnessing an injury to a loved one is an example recognised by the law, and the affective disorder which may be caused by bereavement is an example recognised by the psychiatrists...[161]

It appears that in taking this developmental approach judges have actually been doing what Munby J envisaged in his comments on the Code of Conduct[162] and the **2.84**

[158] This is consistent with the view in *Masterman-Lister v Brutton* [2003] WTLR 259 CA. Also, see *Tchilingrian v Ouzounian* [2003] WTLR 709 'Where the will is complex, or where the family circumstances are complex, or calls upon the testator's bounty are subtle, a greater degree of understanding on the testator's part will be required than where the will and the circumstances are very simple.' This point also arose in *Re Simon, Simon v Byford* [2013] WTLR 161 Ch D.

[159] [2010] WTLR 623 at [115].

[160] At [108]. The Court heard expert evidence that in some cases of bereavement there could be a severe reaction that could, like depression, impair attention and concentration and the ability to take things in and remember them. There was further evidence that this condition could lead to increased suggestibility so that the testator would simply assent to suggestions of others, not caring to form his own views on the subject. (This is not to suggest that bereavement will cause loss of capacity in all cases.) Although the court regarded this as an extension of the traditional test, it could be argued that the inability to take decision because of mental illness fell within 'that no disorder of the mind shall... prevent the exercise of his natural faculties' (from the fourth limb of *Banks v Goodfellow*).

[161] *Re Key, Key v Key* [2010] 623 at [95].

[162] Which does seem to have been a quite rational reading of the Code on his part see *Re MM, Local Authority X v MM (an adult)* [2007] EWHC 2003 (Fam) at para 80 and 2.65 (above).

application of the *Banks v Goodfellow* test. By not applying the test in a rigid way, but in a way that takes into account changes in society and psychiatric knowledge, the test has already been adapted to twenty-first-century circumstances.[163] There is no reason why factors from ss. 2 and 3 MCA 2005 cannot be applied to develop the application of *Banks v Goodfellow*, within the existing framework of the test, where to do so the development would fit more closely with modern circumstances and knowledge. Indeed, it is arguable that decision making, considered as a factor in *Re Key*, merely echoes s. 2: 'a person lacks capacity in relation to a matter if at the material time he is unable to make a decision for himself... because of impairment...'. Ultimately it is open to the court to add or subtract elements from the common law test, but it is unlikely that major, as opposed incremental, changes would be made without legislative provision.

Statutory wills

2.85 The Court of Protection has the power to order the execution of a will for a patient.[164] The general approach of the court when considering if it should order such a will is that it must act in the best interests of the patient: '... the decision maker must then form a value judgment of his own giving effect to the paramount statutory instruction that any decision must be in P's best interests... this process is quite different to that which is applied under the former Mental Health Acts.'[165] The wishes of P are to be taken into account in this process.[166]

2.86 There is the potential for tension between the common law test of capacity and the statutory test. The Court of Protection has no power to rule on the validity of a will[167] and yet this is a factor if the Court is approached, during the testator's lifetime, to make a statutory will where the previous will might be open to doubt on testamentary grounds.[168] This would serve to highlight not only any differences in the tests, but also what the point is in having different tests. From this point of view, the two tests coalescing into one would solve the issue, but this would not solve the issue of the burden of proof (see Chapter 5).

2.87 How should practitioners deal with the MCA in practice?

- In the absence of an authoritative judgment one way or the other on the application of the MCA test in this area, there seems to be little risk in continuing to

[163] Even in 1941—'We are not bound to go on applying views held over a century ago about mental disturbance and insanity and to disregard modern knowledge and understanding of such conditions.' *Timbury v Coffee* (1941) 66 CLR 277.

[164] ss. 16–18 Mental Capacity Act 2005 and paragraphs 2, 3, and 4 Schedule 2.

[165] *Re P* [2009] WTLR 651 at [39] per Lewison J as he was then.

[166] *Re S and S (Protected Persons)* 2009 WTLR 315, but see also *Re P* [2009] WTLR 651 at [41] et seq.

[167] *Re M* [2009] EWHC 2525 (Fam) at [50].

[168] The position which arose in *ABC v XZ* [2013] WTLR 193.

work with the long-established common law test. Quite clearly the Chancery Division is at ease with this test and the chances of a will preparer being criticized for applying *Banks v Goodfellow* in preference to the MCA test seem very remote indeed.

- We have a substantial body of precedent relating to the application of *Banks v Goodfellow* and this has created a better understanding of the application of the traditional approach to capacity. Departing from these precedents, without good reason, has risks in terms of diversity of approach.
- The application of the MCA test to testamentary capacity is not properly backed by any authoritative judgment in the area of wills and it would appear that there is more chance of being in error, or of misapplication, if the MCA test is applied at this time instead of *Banks v Goodfellow*.
- Augmenting our understanding of *Banks v Goodfellow* by considering the elements in the MCA test is no bad thing, but at the present time it is suggested that those elements do no more than that, unless or until a court provides us with a different answer.

The detailed analysis of *Banks v Goodfellow* (or the MCA 2005) in this chapter is, of course, a matter that will rarely be considered, if ever, when holograph wills are prepared or wills are prepared for the testator by members of the family or friends. This means that little recording of relevant factors will take place. In consequence, it is far safer for testators who are elderly or infirm to have their wills not only professionally prepared, but prepared by professionals who are fully conversant the law's requirements. **2.88**

Gifts and Mental Capacity

Timing of test

The court will require capacity to be shown at the time when the gift is made. As for testamentary capacity, where a professional adviser is involved, to advise on or carry out the transaction on the client's behalf, he will want to ensure that capacity to make the gift exists at the time of the instructions.[169] Without this, it is doubtful that the client would have the capacity to engage him in connection with the gift. The more substantial the gift, or the more unusual the gift (or the circumstances surrounding it), the more important the question of capacity becomes. **2.89**

[169] See Law Society Practice Note 'Financial Abuse' of 13 June 2013 dealing with risk to vulnerable clients at 4.3.2 'if you are in any doubt as to whether a client has capacity to provide instructions, you must perform a capacity assessment before any instructions are acted upon.'

Common law test

2.90 As for testamentary capacity, the capacity to make *inter vivos* gifts is considered to be outside of the provisions of the MCA 2005[170] unless the donor is already subject to the Court of Protection's jurisdiction and the gift requires the approval of the Court of Protection.

2.91 *Re Beaney*[171] is generally accepted as the most authoritative statement of the common law principles involved. Having observed that the mental capacity required to make a gift is the capacity to understand the nature of the transaction once it has been explained to him,[172] the judgment reads:

> In the circumstances, it seems to me that the law is this. The degree or extent of understanding required in respect of any instrument is *relative to the particular transaction which it is to effect*. In the case of a will the degree required is always high. In the case of a contract, a deed made for consideration, or a gift *inter vivos*, whether by deed or otherwise, the degree required *varies with the circumstances of the transaction*. Thus, at one extreme, if the subject matter and value of a gift are trivial in relation to the donor's other assets, a low degree of understanding will suffice. But, at the other extreme, if its effect is to dispose of the donor's only asset of value and thus, for practical purposes, to preempt the devolution of his estate under his will or on his intestacy, then the degree of understanding required is as high as that required for a will, and the donor understands the claims of all potential donees and the extent of the property to be disposed of.[173]

2.92 As explained earlier in this chapter, the common law test of testamentary capacity is capable of being modified by the court to meet the circumstances of modern testators and to reflect the advances in psychiatric medicine. There is no reason to suppose when applying the test of testamentary capacity to large *inter vivos* gifts that the test will not be the modern test of capacity.

2.93 In essence, for a large gift, the level of ability to understand the transaction is not merely akin to that for a will;[174] it will also be partly comprised of the same elements as in *Banks v Goodfellow*.

- The nature of the transaction
- The ability of the donor to understand the nature and extent of his estate
- The donor must also be able to comprehend and appreciate the claims to which he ought to give effect. That is to say to be able to make the evaluation of those who

[170] See above at 2.70.

[171] [1978] 1 WLR 770 at 774 per Nourse QC (as he then was) citing *Ball v Mannin* (1829) 3 Bli NS 1.

[172] *Gibbons v Wright* (1954) 91 CLR 423.

[173] Authors' emphasis; for an example of the application of this decision see *In re Morris, The Special Trustees for Great Ormond Street Hospital for Children v Rushin* [2001] WTLR 1137 where the gift of a house was found to require the same capacity as a will as it was the bulk of the donor's estate (the court also found the transaction was procured by undue influence).

[174] *Pesticcio v Huet* [2003] 1327.

have claims on his bounty and to be able to understand the effect of the gift on the provisions of his will. This is obviously not a significant issue for small gifts.

An example of a large gift can be found in *Sutton v Sutton*[175] where the gift made was unlikely to have been the only asset of value owned by the donor when the gift was made, but the court was prepared to infer that it was his principal asset and apply the view in *Re Beaney* (above). Where a gift is not outright, for example placing bank balances into joint names, do the same considerations apply?

In *Gorjat v Gorjat*[176] substantial balances were placed in joint names and it was observed that capacity should be judged in the light of the balances in question being the donor's greatest asset, but he was not parting with 'entire dominion' over them. He remained equally entitled to the balances while he was alive but on death they would pass to the donee/co-owner. But, the potential consequences of the gift, together with its size, meant that the 'necessary standard of capacity does not fall far short' of testamentary capacity. **2.94**

Issues will arise if the donor makes a series of gifts, each of which is relatively small, but which cumulatively represent a large part of the estate. Under these circumstances, approaching each gift separately for the purpose of evaluating capacity on the basis of this test would be incorrect.[177] The correct basis would be to look at the series as a whole, although this is difficult if the scale of the gifts is not at first apparent. **2.95**

Ability of donor to understand consequences

There were further remarks in *Re Beaney* that the donor must be capable of understanding the nature of an outright gift, e.g. that a gift takes effect at the time of the gift and not later or on death, donor is parting with ownership, the property is non-returnable. This, unlike the test of capacity for wills, adds an extra dimension to the *Banks v Goodfellow* test and that is the understanding of the gift's immediate effect—i.e. the ability of the donor to comprehend the reduction the gift will make to the value of his estate and his consequent ability, or inability, to maintain himself at an adequate standard of living (if at all) from his remaining assets/income. For an extreme example of a gift, see *Hammond v Osborn*[178] where the gift would have been 91.6 per cent of the donor's liquid assets. The sales of investments to raise the cash for the gift gave rise to a CGT liability of almost £50,000 which in turn would have required the sale of the donor's house to pay the tax. **2.96**

---

[175] [2010] WTLR 115.
[176] [2010] EWHC 1537 (Ch) at [138].
[177] *Gorjat v Gorjat* [2010] EWHC 1537 (Ch) at [136].
[178] [2002] WTLR 1125 CA, although capacity was an issue in this case, it was ultimately decided on grounds of undue influence by the donee.

2.97 In *Williams v Williams*[179] this was taken to include

> an understanding of the general nature and effect of a gift of this kind, and thus not just that he was giving away half of his property but also what were the general implications of becoming a joint owner by way of a tenant in common. Since Buckingham Crescent was his only asset of any substantial value, he must also have an understanding of the claims of all potential donees and the extent of the property he was disposing of.

The final two points reflect the second and third limbs of *Banks v Goodfellow*, but the first issue on the implications of the gift requires more understanding of the consequences of the type of transaction.

2.98 The Law Society Practice Note on making gifts of assets[180] advises that the role of a solicitor when acting for a client contemplating a gift is not merely to prepare the paperwork. 'You must[181] ensure that the client fully understands the nature, effect, benefits, risks and foreseeable consequences of making the gift, in order to enable them to form a view as to the wisdom of the proposed transaction.' It sets out three areas of information that must be established:

- what they are seeking to achieve;
- who they wish to receive the gift; and
- what types of asset are to be involved.

The solicitor is then, through contact with the client, enabled to

- evaluate their instructions;
- clarify their domestic and financial circumstances;
- establish that they own the assets they wish to dispose of; and
- assess whether they have the mental capacity to make the gift.

There is further, more detailed commentary on these points. This Practice Note sets out a clear standard required of solicitors and one that should result in greater efforts to establish capacity in particular.[182]

2.99 The role of the solicitor was scrutinized in *Re Morris*[183] in relation to lifetime gifts (as well as a will) and Rimer J was critical of the solicitor's failure to ascertain the capacity of her

---

179 [2003] WTLR 1371 at [43] drawing on remarks in *Re K* [1988] Ch 310 at 316 by Hoffman J (as he then was).

180 6 October 2011, but see also the Practice Note on 'Financial Abuse', 13 June 2013 at 5 2, which, when dealing with gifts, should be read in conjunction with the earlier Practice Note.

181 Defined as 'A specific requirement in legislation or of a principle, rule, outcome or other mandatory provision of the SRA Handbook. You must comply unless there are specific exemptions or defences provided for in the relevant legislation of the SRA Handbook.'

182 It is noted that although this Practice Note was issued after the decision in *Thorpe v Fellowes Solicitors LLP* [2011] EWHC 61 (QB) it makes no reference to it and clearly sets a more desirable standard.

183 *In Re Morris, The Special Trustees for Great Ormond Street Hospital for Children v Rushin* [2001] WTLR 1137 at 1198F.

client to make the gifts and executed her will. *Thorpe v Fellowes Solicitors LLP*[184]—where a gift of the proceeds of sale of a house made by a person later established as suffering from dementia was involved—is sometimes, mistakenly, cited as authority for the solicitor not to ascertain capacity for a client to make a gift. The above passage from *Re Beaney* was neither cited nor considered in *Thorpe*.[185] For reasons that are not wholly clear, the case was about the solicitor's duty in relation to the contract to sell the property, not the solicitor's duty assisting in the gift of the proceeds by the client. This case is not regarded as having effect on the principles in *Re Beaney*, nor the later advice from the Law Society.

A deed of variation to dispose of an inheritance is a gift[186] that is made by the person making the variation. The mental capacity to make such a gift is judged in exactly the same way as any other gift. An inheritance can also be disclaimed. While a disclaimer is not a gift, it is an act which deprives the person disclaiming it of a financial asset which then passes to others under the terms of the will or intestacy.[187] This would appear to require the same test of capacity as for a gift. **2.100**

Consequences of a finding of lack of capacity

The consequence of the donor lacking capacity has been found to be that the gift is void.[188] Despite such an order being made in *Re Beaney*, the correctness of this view has been questioned.[189] *Snell's Equity* also suggests that this may be open to doubt and that the better view is that it is voidable.[190] The authorities in this area were thoroughly reviewed in *Sutton v Sutton*[191] where it was suggested that, in most of the cases where an order was made that the gift was void, the point was either not fully argued or the finding of void or voidable made no difference. **2.101**

184 [2011] EWHC 61 QB see also the footnote to 2.59 on this case.

185 The gift was large in proportion to her assets.

186 It is in essence only a gift that can be given special treatment for the purposes of IHT and CGT; s. 142(1) Inheritance Tax Act 1984 and s. 62(6) Taxation of Chargeable Gains Act 1992.

187 s. 33A Wills Act 1837 and s. 46A Administration of Estates Act 1925 (both as amended by the Estates of Deceased Persons (Forfeiture Rule and Law of Succession) Act 2011) in respect of deaths after 1 February 2012.

188 *In re Morris, The Special Trustees for Great Ormond Street Hospital for Children v Rushin* [2001] WTLR 1137 at 1200A; *Williams v Williams* [2003] WTLR 1371.

189 *Quth v Hussain* [2005] EWHC 157(Ch) per Warren J at [25] 'is not an authority in support of the proposition that a gift made by a person lacking capacity is void rather than voidable.'

190 32nd edn. (Sweet & Maxwell, 2010) at 8–035; a view supported by *Gibbons v Wright* (1954) 91 CLR 423 and *Craigo v McIntyre* [1976] 1 NSWLR 729.

191 [2010] WTLR 115, despite clearly being of the view that the right answer was voidable it was not necessary to make such an order.

3

THE TIME AT WHICH TESTAMENTARY CAPACITY IS REQUIRED

Dual Timing of Test

When the court is asked to consider the question of testamentary capacity, the relevant time at which capacity will be required, for the will to be valid, will be the time of execution of the will.[1] While this is quite logical, there is attached to it an intensely practical issue for the draftsman. He must also be concerned with the capacity of his client at the time that he takes instructions. 'A diagnosis of mild or even moderate dementia is not of itself an obstacle to satisfying the requirements of testamentary capacity . . . a testator may lack capacity on a particular day, but may possess it on a particular day many months later. What is crucial is the condition of the testator on the day he gives his instructions and the day he makes the will.'[2] **3.01**

The draftsman will not be able to proceed with the client's instructions if he is not satisfied that his client had the capacity to give them.[3] If he is not so satisfied, it is highly improbable that the testator could give valid instructions to agree a retainer or a contract to prepare a will from those instructions. **3.02**

To ensure that the testator meets the requirement of testamentary capacity at the time of signing the will, it is incumbent upon the draftsman to satisfy himself that the testator has that capacity, notwithstanding that he will have already done so when **3.03**

---

1 *Arthur v Bokenham* (1708) Mod Rep 148; *Stevens v Vancleve* (1822) 4 Wash CC 262; *Banks v Goodfellow* (1870) LR 5 QB 549.

2 *Carr v Beaven* [2008] EWHC 2582 (Ch): per Floyd J at [81].

3 *Re Barker-Benfield, Hansen v Barker-Benfield* [2006] ETLR 1141 at [42]; see Chapter 5 generally on the Role of the Draftsman.

the instructions were taken. It is much more than merely good practice for the draftsman to determine how well the testator understands the will and the significance of execution at the time of execution—it is a matter where his evidence is highly relevant to the validity of the will.[4] Where the draftsman is aware of possible issues of capacity, even though he has satisfied himself that his client has capacity when giving instructions, it would weaken his evidence as to capacity if has not supervised the execution of the will, and recorded his observation as to capacity at that meeting. Treating the execution solely as a matter of formalities would be dangerous; it should involve consideration of capacity (as well as knowledge and approval).

Change in Capacity Between Tests

3.04 Of particular concern for the draftsman will be any medical events, occurring after the instructions were taken, that might have the effect of reducing capacity at the time of execution. Therefore, recording any apparent deterioration of behaviour, communication, or understanding will be important, if, notwithstanding the deterioration, the draftsman concludes that the testator retains testamentary capacity and can execute his will.

3.05 A further problem is where there is some deterioration in the testator's mental capacity between instructions being given and the execution of the will, such that the testator no longer has testamentary capacity when he is called upon to execute his will. On the face of it, his intentions will be frustrated. The risk of this occurring is of course a factor producing urgency in the preparation of wills for the elderly and infirm.[5] However, there is the possibility that, even with reduced capacity, the will could be validly executed.

The Rule in *Parker v Felgate*

3.06 Where there is a reduction in mental capacity[6] between taking instructions and execution of the will, and the testator no longer has testamentary capacity, the will could still be validly executed, as long as the testator has sufficient capacity to understand that

i. he is executing his will;
ii. it is the will for which he has previously given instructions;[7] and
iii. the will has been drawn in accordance with those instructions.

---

[4] See Chapter 5 generally on the Role of the Draftsman.

[5] See Chapter 7 on the time taken to prepare a will.

[6] This rule could also apply where the loss of capacity is due to the effects of alcohol *Chana v Chana* [2001] WTLR 201.

[7] If the will was prepared from instructions given through an intermediary this rule may not apply (see 3.14 and 3.15, below).

This has become known as the rule in *Parker v Felgate*.[8] In this case, the testatrix suffered severely from Bright's disease.[9] In July 1882 she gave instructions for a new will. Later, in August, her condition deteriorated to the extent of renal failure and, as a result, she fell into a coma. She was considered to have lost testamentary capacity by 26 August. She was roused from her coma sufficiently for her to agree that she wanted her will to be executed. This was done by another at her direction and in her presence[10] on the 29 August. She died on 2 September. **3.07**

The judge, Sir James Hannen, directed that three questions must be addressed by the jury. **3.08**

1. If a person has given instructions to a solicitor to make a will, and the solicitor prepares it in accordance with those instructions, all that is necessary to make it a good will, if executed by the testator, is that he should be able to think thus far: 'I gave my solicitor instructions to prepare a will making a certain disposition of my property. I have no doubt that he has given effect to my intention, and I accept the document which is put before me as carrying it out.'
2. Even if she could not recollect all that had gone between her and the solicitor, was she in a condition that, if each clause of this will had been put to her, and she had been asked, 'Do you wish to leave So-and-So so much?', or 'Do you wish to do this?' (as the case might be) she would have been able to answer intelligently 'Yes' to each question?
3. A person might no longer have capacity to go over the whole transaction, and take up the thread of business from the beginning to the end, and think it all over again, but if he is able to say to himself, 'I have settled that business with my solicitor. I rely upon his having embodied it in proper words, and I accept the paper which is put before me as embodying it.'[11]

These questions should be asked in order of priority and any one question answered 'yes' is sufficient for the will to be valid. The jury found, in respect of the testatrix, that the first two questions were answered 'no', but the third was answered 'yes'—the will was therefore found to be valid.

The words used by Sir James Hannen clearly meant that this is a rule that can only be applied where it can be shown that the instructions given are definite ('I have settled that business with my solicitor') and therefore can have no application to indefinite **3.09**

---

[8] (1883) 8 PD 171 *Parker v Felgate* was not the invention of this rule, the Court of Appeal in *Re Perrins (deceased), Perrins v Holland* [2010] WTLR 1415 CA drew attention to five pre-1837 cases starting with *Seeman v Seeman* (1752) 1 Lee 181.

[9] Which today would be described as acute or chronic nephritis—it was named after Richard Bright who first described the illness in 1827.

[10] s. 9(a) Wills Act 1837 see later at 3.25.

[11] (1883) LR 8 PD 171 at 173.

or unsettled wishes.[12] Having sufficient capacity at the execution of the will, applying this rule, will not lead to a valid will unless capacity at the time of instructions can be shown as well.[13]

3.10 Earlier, in *Harwood v Baker*,[14] the Privy Council had expressed the following view.

> Now if their Lordships had found from other evidence that [the testator] had, while in a state of health, compared and weighed the claims of his relations, and had formed the deliberate purpose of rejecting them all in favour of his wife, but had omitted to carry that purpose into effect before the attack of illness under which he dies; and that during that illness he had acted upon that previous intention, and executed a will in question, less evidence of the capacity to weigh those claims during his illness might have been sufficient to show the will propounded really did contain the expression of the mind of the deceased.

While this shows an earlier inclination towards the position later in *Parker v Felgate*, it is not expressed as precisely, or with the certainty, of Sir James Hannen's three questions.

3.11 In terms of a modern re-statement of the three questions, Moore-Bick LJ put it as:

> Where the testator loses some of his faculties between giving instructions and executing the will, however, the position is different. One must then ask:
> (i) whether at the time he gave the instructions he had the ability to understand and give proper consideration to the various matters which are called for, that is, whether he had testamentary capacity;
> (ii) whether the document gives effect to his instructions;
> (iii) whether those instructions continued to reflect his intentions; and
> (iv) whether at the time he executed the will he knew what he was doing and thus had sufficient mental capacity to carry out the juristic act which that involves.
> If all those questions can be answered in the affirmative, one can be satisfied that the will accurately reflects the deceased's intentions formed at a time when he was capable of making fully informed decisions.[15]

3.12 A further explanation is to be found in *Re Flynn*:

> The authorities appear to show that in a case where a testator, even in a state approaching insensibility, has executed a testamentary instrument drawn up in accordance with previous instructions, he will be held to have known and approved of its contents if, at the time of execution, he was capable of understanding and did understand that he was engaged in executing a will for which he had given instructions, even though at the moment of execution he might not have remembered those previous instructions and would not, at that moment, have understood the provisions of the will, if

[12] For consideration of this point see *Re Perrins (deceased), Perrins v Holland* [2010] WTLR 1415 CA at [33] to [36].

[13] *Re Barker-Benfield, Hansen v Barker-Benfield* [2006] WTLR 1141 at [54]; *Richards v Allan* [2001] WTLR 1031.

[14] (1840) Moo PC 282 at page 313.

[15] *Re Perrins (deceased), Perrins v Holland* [2010] WTLR 1415 CA at [55].

> read to him clause by clause. However, if a litigant is successfully to avail himself of this principle he must, I think, satisfy the court at least that the testator at the time of execution was capable of understanding and did understand that he was executing the will for which he had previously given instructions.[16]

The justification for this rule was set out in *Re Perrins deceased* as: **3.13**

> The reasons lie, I believe, in the freedom of testamentary disposition which the law favours, as explained by the court in *Banks v Goodfellow*, the usual preference of the court, if reasonably possible, to uphold transactions (cf in the context of the interpretation of contracts the maxim *res magis valeat quam pereat*[17]), and the pragmatic recognition in that context that the testator has no further opportunity to give expression to his wishes.[18]

The rule has subsequently been applied, but reported cases have been, until recently, comparatively rare.[19] The recent cases perhaps serve to illustrate its increased relevance with an ageing population. Fairly soon after *Parker v Felgate* was decided, the rule received Privy Council endorsement in *Pereira v Periera*.[20] While the rule is of some age, it quite clearly has modern relevance with the increasing issues of old age and capacity.[21] The rule has received strong modern court approval.[22]

Communication of will instructions

Battan Singh v Armichand[23] is an example where the rule in *Parker v Felgate* was not applied. The circumstances of the deceased were such that his health had declined significantly by the time the will was presented for signature. The Privy Council would not save the will by applying this rule. The court was concerned at the inconsistency in the evidence as to the instructions relayed to the will draftsman. An **3.14**

---

[16] [1982] 1 WLR 310 at 320 per Slade J; cited in *Re Baker, Baker v Baker* [2008] WTLR 565.

[17] 'That the thing may rather have effect than be destroyed.'

[18] *Re Perrins (deceased), Perrins v Holland* [2010] WTLR 1415 CA at [23] per the Chancellor.

[19] See *Kenny v Wilson* (1911) 11 State Reporter (NSW) 460; *In the Estate of Wallace: Solicitor of the Duchy of Cornwall v Batten* [1952] 2 TLR 925; *Re Flynn* [1982] 1 WLR 310; *Clancy v Clancy* [2003] WTLR 1097; *Re Baker, Baker v Baker* [2008] WTLR 565; *Markou v Goodwin* [2014] WTLR 605; the principle was also considered in *Richards v Allan* [2001] WTLR 1031 (by reference to *Re Flynn*) but could not be applied; see also *Catling v Catling* [2014] WTLR 955 where the rule was not applied because of the inherent improbability of the draftsman's evidence regarding his instructions; recent unreported cases include *Barrett v Kasprzyk* 3 July 2000 and *Otuka v Alozie* 19 December 2005.

[20] [1901] AC 354—'Their Lordships think that the ruling of Sir James Hannen is good law and good sense.' This approval was *obiter*, but it was described by the Court of Appeal in *Re Perrins (deceased), Perrins v Holland* [2010] WTLR 1415 CA at [49] and [23] as being of 'high' and 'strong' 'persuasive authority'.

[21] This rule can also apply where a person has written out their own will instructions and their mental capacity declines after preparing it, but before executing the engrossment prepared from it: *In the Estate of Wallace: Solicitor of the Duchy of Cornwall v Batten* [1952] TLR 925.

[22] Most notably from the CA in *Re Perrins (deceased), Perrins v Holland* [2010] WTLR 1415 CA.

[23] [1948] AC 161.

intermediary was used; a young man of slight acquaintance to the testator in the past. The young man's evidence was that he was asked to get a lawyer for the testator as he wanted a new will, but under examination his evidence changed to the effect that his instructions were to get a will prepared to leave the estate to two non-relatives of the testator who were both indebted to him. The Court was reluctant also to accept the evidence as to the terms of the will representing the complete and settled wishes of the testator.

3.15 The court was of view that the principle in *Parker v Felgate* should be applied only with the greatest caution when the testator did not himself give instructions to the solicitor who drew the will, but instead gave them to a lay intermediary who then repeated the instructions to the solicitor.[24] The opportunities for errors in transmission, misunderstanding, and even deception in such a method of delivering instructions are obvious. The court must be 'strictly satisfied'[25] that there are no grounds for suspicion and that the instructions, given to the intermediary, were unambiguous and clearly understood by him. Then, that they are accurately transmitted to, and fully understood by, the draftsman, before the court could make any finding in favour of validity. While these views of the Privy Council do not amount to an absolute bar on the principle applying where an intermediary has been used, they are a clear warning of the difficulties inherent in such a process, and that very clear evidence in favour of the will would be needed.[26]

3.16 Communication of the will instructions directly from client to solicitor is much more helpful, giving, as it does, greater certainty that the instructions are those of the testator and giving better evidence of testamentary capacity when the instructions were given. Written instructions from the testator may help, as occurred in *In the Estate of Wallace* [27] provided that the draftsman still has an opportunity to assess capacity and issues of undue influence.[28]

3.17 It is conceivable that where the execution of the will is by acknowledgement of the testator's signature, in front of two witnesses who validly witness it, and a loss of capacity occurs between signature and acknowledgement, it could be saved by the application of this rule (although no examples can be traced).

---

[24] [1948] AC 161 at [6].

[25] [1948] AC 161 at [6].

[26] *Richards v Allan* [2001] WTLR 1031 is an example of a failed application where instructions were via a third party (or conceivably originated from the third party). The evidence as to the instructions for the will also changed in the course of evidence—at 1043F.

[27] *In the Estate of Wallace: Solicitor of the Duchy of Cornwall v Batten* [1952] 2 TLR 925.

[28] Or even issues of impersonation of the testator; *R v Spillman, Spillman & Russill* [2001] 1 Cr. App. R.(S.) 139 or *Re Willis Estate, Willis v Wilson* 2009 NSSC 231; [2010] WTLR 169.

The testator's understanding of the document

3.18 It is not sufficient for the testator to be aware merely that he is executing a will; he must understand that the will is the will for which he had earlier given instructions.[29] If the testator is unable to remember giving the instructions he will be outside of the application of this rule.

- However, if a litigant is successfully to avail himself of this principle he must, I think, satisfy the court at least that the testator at the time of execution was capable of understanding and did understand that he was executing the will for which he had given instructions.[30]
- It was sufficient that she executed the will knowing what she was doing and acting in the understanding that she was giving effect to her earlier instructions.[31]

Time delay

3.19 In most reported cases the time delay between instructions and execution of the will has been fairly short.[32] The longer the passage of time, the greater the difficulty there could be in showing that

a) the testator was capable of addressing Sir James Hannen's questions (see 3.08 and 3.11);
b) there was no chance of testamentary intention altering during this period, but before the testator lost capacity.

3.20 However, in *Re Perrins (deceased), Perrins v Holland*[33] a lengthy period was involved—5 April 2000 to 26 September 2001. At the time of the will instructions, the testator was unable to read or write, had reduced control of his movements, and was confined to a wheelchair.[34] The draft will was provided on12 April. There were letters, phone calls, and a meeting, and there was also a suggestion that on 27 June the view was expressed that some issues regarding the will were 'not clear or satisfactory' as far as the testator was concerned. Almost a year and a half after the meeting at which the instructions were given, the will was executed[35] in the car park at the solicitors' office after the will was explained to the testator.

---

29 *Perrins v Holland* [2010] WTLR 1415 CA per Moore-Bick LJ at [56] and [70]; *Markou v Goodwin* [2013] EWHC (Ch).

30 *Re Flynn* [1982] 1 WLR 310 per Slade J.

31 *Clancy v Clancy* [2003] WTLR 1097 per Rimer J.

32 *Parker v Felgate* (1883) 8 PD 171 20 days (inclusive); *In the Estate of Wallace: Solicitor of the Duchy of Cornwall v Batten* [1952] 2 TLR 925 3 days (inclusive); *Re Flynn* [1982] 1 WLR 310 5 days (inclusive); *Clancy v Clancy* [2003] WTLR 1097 5 days (inclusive).

33 [2010] WTLR 1415 CA (reported at first instance as *Perrins v Holland* [2009] WTLR 1387 Ch D and for costs see *Perrins v Holland (costs)* [2010] WTLR 95 Ch D.

34 He had been diagnosed with primary progressive multiple sclerosis.

35 The signature was by rubber stamp with the weight of the testator's arm or hand making the impression. See below in this chapter on physical deterioration of the testator. The testator's arm or

3.21 At first instance the judge found that the testator had testamentary capacity when the will instructions were given, but that he lacked such capacity when the will was executed. This finding was endorsed by the Court of Appeal after a thorough review of the origins of the rule and its application.[36]

Partial validity

3.22 Partial validity of a will is also commented on in Chapter 1 at 1.35–1.37. There is one reported decision,[37] where the application of the rule in *Parker v Felgate* has produced a partially valid will. Unfortunately the reported judgment is more about the costs consequence of the probate action than about the previous action on validity (both heard by the same judge). The judgment recites that:

> The result of the evidence as found by the President was that before April 29, 1927, the later will had been determined on as to all its contents except the residuary clause, that the details of the residuary clause remained at large when on April 29 the testator ceased to be of testamentary capacity, and that on the date of execution of the will, although the testator remembered that he had been engaged with Thomas in preparing a will and appreciated the fact that he was being asked to execute it, he remained without present testamentary capacity.

There do not appear to be any subsequent cases reported that consider a similar point. The view that partial validity could result from the application of this rule must remain tentative.

Knowledge and approval of the will

3.23 The requirement of the testator's knowledge and approval of the contents of the will would[38] could cause a problem when *Parker v Felgate* is applied if it was, as usual, required at the time of execution of the will. While it is the case that knowledge and approval must exist at the time of execution, *Parker v Felgate* could not stand if it was an absolute requirement that knowledge and approval must exist at that time. The Court of Appeal considered this point in *Re Perrins (deceased)*.[39] The finding at first instance was that 'in a case in which the principle in *Parker v Felgate* is applied it is not necessary to prove knowledge and approval of the will, provided that (a) the testator believes that it gives effect to instructions and (b) it does in fact do so.' The Court of Appeal added, 'If the testator had full testamentary capacity at the time when he gave instructions, it is possible that at a later date, when he

hand was placed on the stamp, by another; signature by a stamped name is sufficient *In the Goods of Savory* (1851) 15 Jur 1042; for assistance with signature see *Barrett v Bem* [2012] WTLR 567.

[36] An element of the appeal was that the original decision in *Parker v Felgate* was wrong in principle and should not be followed. This did not find favour with the court.

[37] *Thomas v Jones* [1928] P 162.

[38] See later in Chapter 4.

[39] *Re Perrins (deceased), Perrins v Holland* [2010] WTLR 1415 CA at [55].

had ceased to have full capacity, he intended to carry them out. Proof that that was his intention should not depend on his being capable of exercising judgement of the kind that is necessary for full testamentary capacity.'[40] In effect, where the rule is applied, it is moving both capacity and knowledge and approval to the time of instructions[41]—increasing the responsibility of the draftsman when taking instructions to satisfy himself of both the testator's capacity and knowledge and approval. A finding of knowledge and approval of the will's contents may be harder to establish where there is involvement of a third party (particularly a beneficiary) in the instruction meeting.[42]

Physical deterioration of the testator

It was a feature of *Re Perrins (deceased)*[43] that the deterioration in the testator's condition was physical, as well as mental; hence the need for the draftsman, when supervising the will's execution, to be fully conversant with how the testator can be assisted. **3.24**

Firstly, s. 9(a) Wills Act 1837 permits a will to be signed on behalf of a testator 'by some other person in his presence and by his direction'. The two requirements of direction and presence are essential and without either, or both, the execution will fail and the will will be invalid. **3.25**

'Direction' requires some positive communication from the testator, not mere acquiescence to what is being done: **3.26**

> In my judgment the court should not find that a will has been signed by a third party at the direction of the testator unless there is positive and discernible communication (which may be verbal or non-verbal) by the testator that he wishes the will to be signed on his behalf by the third party.[44]

The person signing the will may use his own name or that of the testator for the signature.[45] In either case the attestation of the will should be amended to reflect the facts, i.e. that: **3.27**

1. the will had been read over to the testator and that he appeared to understand it, or that he read it over himself, whichever is the case;
2. the will was signed by another on behalf of the testator;
3. it was signed at the testator's direction; and
4. this was done in his presence.

---

40 *Re Perrins (deceased), Perrins v Holland* [2010] WTLR 1415 CA at [65].

41 *In the Estate of Wallace: Solicitor of the Duchy of Cornwall v Batten* [1952] 2 TLR 925; *Re Flynn* [1982] 1 WLR 310.

42 *Hawes v Burgess* [2013] WTLR 453 at [63] and [65].

43 [2010] WTLR 1415 CA.

44 Lewison LJ in *Barrett v Bem* [2012] WTLR 567 CA.

45 *Re Clarke's Goods* (1839) 2 Curt 239.

3.28 'It is of course good practice that the attestation clause should show that the will was signed by another person signing his own or the testator's name, by the direction and in the presence of the testator, and (as also in the case of a mark) that it had been read over to the testator and that he appeared thoroughly to understand it.'[46]

3.29 The person signing on behalf of the testator may be

1. one of the attesting witnesses;[47]
2. a beneficiary under the will.[48]

The will will be valid if the person signing on behalf of the testator is both of the above, but his bequest will be void.[49]

3.30 'Presence' of the testator is usually considered in the context of witnesses to the will.[50] Presence is not synonymous with sight of the signature. The testator, in this context, does not have to see the signature being made on his behalf (although it is simpler if he can). The test will usually be if he could have seen had he chosen to.[51]

3.31 The physically impaired testator can sign in various ways apart from a signature, e.g.

- by the testator's mark;[52]
- by his thumbprint;[53]
- by his initials;[54]
- by stamped name.[55]

---

[46] *Barrett v Bem* [2012] WTLR 567 CA citing *Tristram and Coote Probate Practice* (LexisNexis 30th edn) at para 3.79.

[47] *Re Bailey's Goods* (1838) 1 Curt 914; although where possible using someone who is not an attesting witness would seem to give greater integrity in the execution and provide potential evidence of due execution from another.

[48] This apparent omission from the Wills Act 1837 whereby a beneficiary witnessing the will could not take benefit, but a beneficiary signing on behalf of the testator could, was deplored by the Court of Appeal and the court urged Parliament to change the law on this point *Barrett v Bem* [2012] WTLR 567 CA.

[49] s. 15 Wills Act 1837.

[50] s. 9(c) Wills Act 1837.

[51] *Casson v Dade* (1781) 1 Bro CC 99; *Doe d Wright v Manifold* (1813) 1 M&S 294; *Jenner v Ffinch* (1879) 5 PD 106; *Re Groffman, Groffman v Groffman* [1969] 2 All ER 108. For a blind testator the test is thought to be the same i.e. by attributing sight to him would he have been able to see (had he chosen to) *Re Piercy's Goods* (1845) 1 Rob Eccl 278. This notional attribution of sight would not appear to extend to a blind witness (*Re Gibson* [1949] 2 All ER 90), but the distinction does appear to be practical.

[52] *In the Estate of Selwood* (1964) 108 SJ 523.

[53] *Borman v Lel* [2002] WTLR 237; *Battan Singh v Armichand* [1948] AC 161 involved an assisted signature by thumbprint.

[54] *In the Goods of Savory* (1851) 15 Jur 1042 provided that the initials are intended to be a signature to the will.

[55] *Jenkins v Gaisford* (1863) 3 Sw & Tr 93.

The act of signing can be assisted by another.[56] However, for this assistance to result in valid execution, the testator must **3.32**

- want to sign his will;
- hold the pen; and
- contribute some physical effort to the signature.

If the testator's hand holds the pen and is guided by another, without any physical input from the testator, the execution will not be valid.[57]

Practicalities for *Parker v Felgate*

Where the draftsman takes instructions from someone of advanced years, or whose health is precarious, there will be a risk of deterioration in capacity before execution of the will. **3.33**

1. Delay must be avoided.[58]
2. Full observations, accurately recorded, are required of the testator's mental capacity when taking instructions.
3. It is worth being more careful than usual to establish that the instructions are
   a. the settled intention of the testator;
   b. understood by him;
   c. agreed by him (countersigning a good handwritten copy of the dispositive wishes at the meeting, with the note reciting that they have be read over and explained would be helpful);
   d. expressly confirmed as being his firm and decided wishes for his will (and that he is not intending further changes before execution).
4. Careful observation and recording of the testator's understanding at the time of execution and why the conclusion was reached that he had sufficient capacity will assist.
5. The manner in which the will was read over, or other way in which the testator was taken through the will, and how understanding was established (and to what degree), if possible with reference to the three questions set by Sir James Hannen in *Parker v Felgate*, should be recorded.[59]

Lifetime Gifts

The rule in *Parker v Felgate* has now been applied to lifetime transactions in *Re Singellos*.[60] Here the donor had agreed to enter into an estate planning transaction **3.34**

---

56 *Fulton v Kee* [1961] NILR 1.

57 *Barrett v Bem* [2012] WTLR 567 CA.

58 Chapter 7 on control of risk.

59 See above at paragraph 3.08.

60 *Re Singellos, Singellos v Singellos* [2011] WTLR 327 Ch D at [166] 'the mere fact that the application of the *Parker v Felgate* approach to *inter vivos* dispositions has not been recognised before cannot

at a time when she was very near to death in hospital. The necessary documents could not be signed together and some needed to be executed later than the initial documents. The documents were therefore executed in batches on 17, 18, 21, and 28 April. The court found that capacity existed when the transaction was set in motion and the initial documents were executed, but the final documents (28 April) were executed when she only understood 'that she was signing documents which gave effect to her earlier instructions ... on the balance of probabilities I do not consider that she had any greater understanding than that.'[61]

3.35 In *Re Singellos*, this rule was extended to a lifetime transaction applying the reasoning in *Perrins*.[62] The reasons given there were found to 'reflect broader considerations of policy which appear equally applicable to *inter vivos* dispositions'[63]:

1. *Perrins* was about testamentary freedom, 'but English law has long recognised a policy of freedom to alienate property *inter vivos* also'.
2. If the rule in *Parker v Felgate* is accepted for wills, but rejected for *inter vivos* gifts, it would make for a more onerous approach to disposal of property by gift than by will.[64]
3. The usual 'preference of the court to uphold transactions' applied to gifts as well as wills.
4. '... the pragmatic recognition that the testator has no further opportunity to give expression to his wishes, applies just as much to a donor's wish to dispose of certain property *inter vivos* when incapacity intervenes before completion.'
5. 'The pragmatic considerations' on the relevant time of the test ensure that the capacity test does not frustrate the legitimate intentions.

be sufficient reason to reject [it]'; the judgment reveals that neither counsel involved had been able to find any earlier authority on this point.

61 [2011] WTLR 327 at [153]; interestingly there was no medical evidence available and the court findings were based on the evidence of a family member and the donor's solicitor and accountant.

62 *Re Perrins (deceased), Perrins v Holland* [2010] WTLR 1415.

63 [2011] WTLR 327 at [162], but see subsequent paragraphs for consideration of counter arguments.

64 This would be counter intuitive and illogical when *Re Beaney (deceased)* [1978] 1 WLR 770 applied the test of testamentary capacity to substantial *inter vivos* gifts; at [167].

4

UNDUE INFLUENCE AND KNOWLEDGE AND APPROVAL

Matters of undue influence and knowledge and approval are frequently alleged at the same time that a claim of lack of testamentary capacity is made. All three are distinct areas, each touching the validity of a will in different ways, but evidence for each may also be relevant to the others. **4.01**

Undue Influence

The doctrine relating to undue influence comes from the need for the court 'to protect people from being forced, tricked or misled in any way by others into parting with their property . . . and the equitable doctrine of undue influence has grown out of and been developed by the necessity of grappling with insidious forms of spiritual tyranny and with infinite varieties of fraud.'[1] This doctrine is not designed to protect a person from the result of their own foolish actions—they remain a person's own responsibility.[2] It was developed instead to prevent abuse of the individual by another.[3] Undue influence should be understood as being distinct from what is commonly referred to as fraud—fraud deceives a testator whereas undue influence coerces him.[4] **4.02**

The doctrine was described Lord Nicholls in *Etridge* as **4.03**

> one of the grounds of relief developed by the courts of equity as a court of conscience. The objective is to ensure that the influence of one person over another is not abused.

[1] *Allcard v Skinner* (1887) 36 Ch D 145 at 183.

[2] *Allcard v Skinner* (1887) 36 Ch D 145.

[3] 'the victimisation of one party by another' *National Westminster Bank plc v Morgan* [1985] AC 686 at 705 per Lord Scarman; *Johnson v Buttress* (1936) 56 CLR 113.

[4] *Theobald on Wills* 17th edn., at 3-031.

> In everyday life people constantly seek to influence the decisions of others. They seek to persuade those with whom they are dealing to enter into transactions, whether great or small. The law has set limits to the means properly employable for this purpose. To this end the common law developed a principle of duress. Originally this was narrow in its scope, restricted to the more blatant forms of physical coercion, such as personal violence.[5]

Note the distinction made between influence and persuasion, which is lawful, and undue influence, which is where influence and persuasion are abused and the pressure becomes unlawful. It is clear that persuasion is lawful, but undue influence is not.

> This passage, which I repeat applies to both forms of undue influence, demonstrates to me that in all cases of undue influence the critical question is whether or not the persuasion or the advice, in other words the influence, has invaded the free volition of the donor to accept or reject the persuasion or advice or withstand the influence. The donor may be led but she must not be driven and her will must be the offspring of her own volition, not a record of someone else's. There is no undue influence unless the donor if she were free and informed could say 'This is not my wish but I must do it'.[6]

The difficulty in practice is that there is no clear bright dividing line between being led and being driven.

4.04 Lord Nicholls in *Etridge* explained that

> ... equity supplemented the common law. Equity extended the reach of the law to other unacceptable forms of persuasion. The law will investigate the manner in which the intention to enter into the transaction was secured: 'how the intention was produced', in the oft repeated words of Lord Eldon LC, from as long ago as 1807 (*Huguenin v Baseley* 14 Ves 273, 300). If the intention was produced by an unacceptable means, the law will not permit the transaction to stand. The means used is regarded as an exercise of improper or 'undue' influence, and hence unacceptable, whenever the consent thus procured ought not fairly to be treated as the expression of a person's free will. It is impossible to be more precise or definitive. The circumstances in which one person acquires influence over another, and the manner in which influence may be exercised, vary too widely to permit of any more specific criterion.[7]

4.05 The remarks in the above paragraph on the impossibility of a defining undue influence are a clear warning to avoid trying to do so. The remarks also heed earlier warnings on this point; 'There is no precisely defined law setting limits to the equitable jurisdiction of a court to relieve against undue influence. This is a world of doctrine,

---

[5] *Royal Bank of Scotland v Etridge (No 2)* [2001] UKHL 44 at [6].

[6] *Daniel v Drew* [2005] WTLR 807 at [36] per Ward LJ; applied in *Thompson v Foy* [2009] EWHC 1076 (Ch) at [101].

[7] *Royal Bank of Scotland v Etridge (No 2)* [2001] UKHL 44 at [7].

not neat, tidy rules.'[8] As a consequence, the court has not done so.[9] The lack of a definition does have the virtue of allowing the court to examine novel circumstances and, where appropriate, bring them within the accepted scope of undue influence.

4.06 The extracts quoted earlier from *Royal Bank of Scotland v Etridge (No. 2)*[10] are part of what is the leading modern examination of undue influence by the House of Lords. The principles that are to be found in this judgment were later summarized by Lewison J (as he then was) in *Thompson v Foy*:[11]

(i) The objective of the doctrine of undue influence is to ensure that the influence of one person ('the donee') over another ('the donor') is not abused.[12]
(ii) If the donee intends to enter into a transaction, but the intention was produced by means which lead to the conclusion that the intention thus procured ought not fairly to be treated as the expression of the donor's free will, the law will not permit the transaction to stand.[13]
(iii) Broadly there are two forms of unacceptable conduct. The first comprises overt acts of improper pressure or coercion such as unlawful threats. The second form arises out of a relationship between two persons where one has acquired a measure of influence, or ascendency, of which the ascendant person then takes unfair advantage.[14]
(iv) The principle is not confined to abuse of trust or confidence. It also extends to the exploitation of the vulnerable.[15]
(v) Disadvantage to the donor is not a necessary ingredient of undue influence.[16] However, it may have evidential value, because it is relevant to the questions whether any allegation of abuse of confidence can properly be made, and whether abuse actually occurred.[17]
(vi) Whether a transaction has been brought about by undue influence is a question of fact.[18]

---

[8] *National Westminster Bank plc v Morgan* [1985] AC 686 at 709 per Lord Scarman who also, at 709, said attempts at a definition were both 'futile' and 'undesirable'; *Royal Bank of Scotland v Etridge (No 2)* [2001] UKHL 44 at [92] where Lord Clyde said it was 'not easy to define'.

[9] '[N]o court has ever attempted to define undue influence' *Allcard v Skinner* (1887) 36 Ch D 145 at 183 per Lindley LJ; 'It is impossible to define...I certainly do not propose to do so', *Governor & Company of the Bank of Scotland v Bennett* [1997] 1 FLR 801 at 822.

[10] [2001] UKHL 44.

[11] [2009] EWHC 1076 (Ch) at [99].

[12] [2001] UKHL 44 at [6]; abuse does necessarily require deliberate exploitation, sharp practice, or criminal behaviour. It can simply be where the donee has exhibited a failure of candour and fairness towards the donor and has preferred his interests to those of the donor *Evans v Lloyd* [2013] 1137 at [38].

[13] [2001] UKHL 44 at [7].

[14] [2001] UKHL 44 at [8].

[15] [2001] UKHL 44 at [11] 'Several expressions have been used in an endeavour to encapsulate the essence: trust and confidence, reliance, dependence or vulnerability on the one hand and ascendancy, domination or control on the other. None of these descriptions is perfect. None is all embracing. Each has its proper place.' Although in Lord Hobhouse's speech he described the relationship as 'typically' fiduciary or similar this has not been followed see *Evans v Lloyd* [2013] 1137 at [40].

[16] [2001] UKHL 44 at [12].

[17] [2001] UKHL 44 at [104].

[18] [2001] UKHL 44 at [13].

(vii) The legal burden of proving undue influence rests on the person alleging it. The evidence required to discharge the burden of proof depends upon the nature of the undue influence alleged, the personality of the parties, their relationship, the extent to which the transaction cannot readily be accounted for by the ordinary motives of ordinary persons in that relationship, and all the circumstances of the case.[19]

(viii) If the claimant proves (a) that the donor placed trust and confidence in the donee or that the donee acquired ascendancy over the donor, and (b) that the transaction calls out for explanation, the claimant has discharged an evidential burden, which will also enable an inference of undue influence to be drawn and thus satisfy the legal burden, unless the donee produces evidence to counter the inference which would otherwise be drawn.[20]

(ix) This is simply a question of evidence and proof. At the end of the day, after trial, there will either be proof of undue influence or that proof will fail and it will be found that there is no undue influence. In the former case, whatever the relationship between the parties and however the influence was exerted, there will have been found to have been an actual case of undue influence. In the latter there will be none.[21]

(x) Proof that the donor received advice from a third party before entering into the impugned transaction is one of the matters a court takes into account when weighing all the evidence. The weight, or importance, to be attached to such advice depends on all the circumstances. In the normal course, advice from a solicitor or other outside adviser can be expected to bring home to a donor a proper understanding of what he or she is about to do. But a person may understand fully the implications of a proposed transaction, for instance, a substantial gift, and yet still be acting under the undue influence of another. Proof of outside advice does not, of itself, necessarily show that the subsequent completion of the transaction was free from the exercise of undue influence. Whether it will be proper to infer that outside advice had an emancipating effect, so that the transaction was not brought about by the exercise of undue influence, is a question of fact to be decided having regard to all the evidence in the case.[22]

(xi) The nature of the advice required is that someone free from the taint of undue influence should put before the donor the nature and consequences of the proposed transaction. It is not necessary for the adviser to recommend the transaction. An adult of competent mind is entitled to enter into a financially unwise transaction if he or she wants to.[23]

4.07 The above makes clear that there are two types of undue influence; actual undue influence and presumed undue influence. For the purpose of this chapter, actual undue influence is dealt with in relation to wills and presumed undue influence is dealt with in relation to gifts.

---

19 [2001] UKHL 44 at [13].
20 [2001] UKHL 44 at [14], [21] and [156].
21 [2001] UKHL 44 at [93].
22 [2001] UKHL 44 at [20].
23 [2001] UKHL 44 at [60] and [61].

Undue influence and duress

There is much overlap between undue influence and the common law doctrine of duress.[24] Relief on the grounds of duress was only available originally where there was a threat of violence or detention to the person, or similar to a third party. Equity expanded the grounds for relief where the pressure is unconscionable to the court, but was less than the common law duress. **4.08**

Undue Influence and Wills

Most modern examinations of undue influence and wills start with Sir J P Wilde's direction to the jury in *Hall v Hall*[25] as he set out the key principles. **4.09**

- To make a good will a man must be a free agent.
- But all influences are not unlawful. Persuasion, appeals to the affection or ties of kindred, to a sentiment of gratitude for past services, or pity for future destitution, or the like—these are all legitimate, and may be fairly pressed on a testator.
- On the other hand, pressure of whatever character, whether acting on the fears or the hopes, if so exerted as to overpower the volition without convincing the judgement, is a species of restraint under which no valid will can be made.
- Importunity or threats, such as the testator has not the courage to resist, moral command asserted and yielded to for the sake of peace and quiet, or of escaping from distress of mind or social discomfort; these, if carried to a degree in which the free play of the testator's judgement, discretion or wishes, is overborne, will constitute undue influence, though no force is either used or threatened.
- In a word, a testator may be led but not driven; and his will must be the offspring of his own volition, and not the record of someone else's.

The fourth bullet (above) highlights the risk in wills for the elderly or infirm because of their probable lower ability to resist pressure.

In *Re Edwards*,[26] Lewison J (as he was then) provided a modern summary of the current law on undue influence as it relates to wills: **4.10**

> There is no serious dispute about the law. The approach that I should adopt may be summarised as follows:
>
> (i) In a case of a testamentary disposition of assets, unlike a lifetime disposition, there is no presumption of undue influence.
>
> (ii) Whether undue influence has procured the execution of a will is therefore a question of fact.
>
> (iii) The burden of proving it lies on the person who asserts it. It is not enough to prove that the facts are consistent with the hypothesis of undue influence. What must be shown is that the facts are inconsistent with any other hypothesis. In the

[24] *Royal Bank of Scotland v Etridge (No 2)* [2001] UKHL 44 at [8].

[25] (1868) 1 P&D 481 at 482.

[26] *Re Edwards, Edwards v Edwards* [2007] WTLR 1387 Ch D at [47].

modern law this is, perhaps, no more than a reminder of the high burden even on the civil standard, that a claimant bears in proving undue influence as vitiating a testamentary disposition.

(iv) In this context undue influence means influence exercised either by coercion, in the sense that the testator's will must be overborne, or by fraud.

(v) Coercion is pressure that overpowers the volition without convincing the testator's judgement. It is to be distinguished from mere persuasion, appeals to ties of affection or pity for future destitution, all of which are legitimate. Pressure which causes a testator to succumb for the sake of a quiet life, if carried to an extent that overbears the testator's free judgement, discretion or wishes, is enough to amount to coercion in this sense.

(vi) The physical and mental strength of the testator are relevant factors in determining how much pressure is necessary in order to overbear the will. The will of a weak and ill person may be more easily overborne than that of a hale and hearty one. As was said in one case, simply to talk to a weak and feeble testator may so fatigue the brain that a sick person may be induced for quietness' sake to do anything. A 'drip... drip' approach may be highly effective in sapping the will.

(vii) There is a separate ground for avoiding a testamentary disposition on the ground of fraud. The shorthand used to refer to this species of fraud is fraudulent calumny. The basic idea is that if A poisons the testator's mind against B, who would otherwise be a natural beneficiary of the testator's bounty, by casting dishonest aspersions on his character, then the will is liable to be set aside.

(viii) The essence of fraudulent calumny is that the person alleged to have been poisoning the testator's mind must either know that the aspersions are false or not care whether they are true or false. In my judgement if a person believes that he is telling the truth about a potential beneficiary then even if what he tells the testator is objectively untrue, the will is not liable to be set aside on that ground alone.

(ix) The question is not whether the court considers that the testator's testamentary disposition is fair because, subject to statutory powers of intervention, a testator may dispose of his estate as he wishes. The question, in the end, is whether in making his dispositions, the testator has acted as a free agent.

The factors set out in this summary provide a useful basis for more detailed comment.

(i) In a case of a testamentary disposition of assets, unlike a lifetime disposition, there is no presumption of undue influence.

4.11 For a will, unlike a gift (see later in this chapter), there is no presumption of undue influence arising out the relationship between a testator and another, no matter what the relationship involved might be.[27] It is a more stringent approach to undue

[27] *Boyse v Rossborough* (1857) 6 HLC 3 'Undue influence cannot be presumed' per Lord Cranworth; *Parfitt v Lawless* (1872) LR 2 P&D 462; *Craig v Lamoureaux* [1920] AC 349; *Tchiligirian v Ouzounian* [2003] 709.

influence that is applied for wills than is the equitable test set out in *Royal Bank of Scotland plc v Etridge (No 2)* for transactions other than wills.[28] Actual undue influence must always be shown in the case of a will.[29]

One reason why this might be so is provided by: 4.12

> I do just pause to say this: it is not abnormal for husbands and wives to discuss what is to go in each other's wills, and indeed to suggest sometimes forcefully what should be done. It is all part of the married state. It is this sort of thing, among others no doubt, that cause courts of equity to decline to hold that the relationship of husband and wife was of itself enough to presume undue influence in *inter vivos* transactions. It is how, after all, real people work in the real world. It is to be remembered that testators may be led, but not driven. Very often a spouse may state quite forcibly that a testator is being unfair. It is undue influence and not influence which is objectionable. It does, however, make it important to inquire whether if the thoughts came from Edith, and as will appear Edith did most of the talking, that they do in fact represent the instructions of the testator himself.[30]

This is not to say that issues of undue influence will not arise between spouses[31] (or other occasions when two people are seen together for mirror-image wills). The problems for the draftsman, when seeing two people together, will usually centre on the extent to which either party is expressing their own intentions. 4.13

- Is one party letting the other speak for both because they are already in agreement and it is easier that way?
- Is one speaking for both, without prior discussion, because that party takes all the decisions and the other habitually acquiesces?
- Is the party that is silent, silent through fear?[32]

Without both participating in the interview, it can certainly be difficult to ascertain testamentary capacity of both. This can be made more complex where either or both have family from a previous relationship and protecting property for issue can be seen as disloyal or untrusting towards the new partner.

(ii) Whether undue influence has procured the execution of a will is therefore a question of fact.

Fact in this area can be difficult to prove as most undue influence will not be openly effected in full view of others. Fact is very often determined from the aggregate of circumstances. *Schrader v Schrader*[33] is a recent example of a successful claim of undue influence. 4.14

[28] [2001] UKHL 44—the justification of a different standard is not wholly clear, but it will require statutory reform or a review by the Supreme Court if it is to be altered.

[29] *Hubbard v Scott* [2012] WTLR 29 at [44]; *Re Edwards, Edwards v Edwards* [2007] WTLR 1387.

[30] *Buckenham v Dickson* [2000] WTLR 1083 at 1089H.

[31] The first instance decision in *Gill v Woodall* [2009] EWHC B34 (Ch) found there was undue influence although this was not found on appeal.

[32] Or not understanding what is going on?

[33] [2013] WTLR 701.

1. The testatrix had a will prepared by solicitors in 1990 which left some specific gifts to grandchildren and divided residue between her two sons.
2. In May 2005, one son moved in with her to act as her carer after she had a fall (his house was sold by his trustee in bankruptcy around the same time).
3. In April 2006 she executed a new will. The son made all the arrangements for this will using a will-writing company. This will differed from the 1990 will in leaving her house to this son. The house was the main asset of the estate and therefore she was substantially excluding the other son from benefit.

4.15 The court found that the testatrix had capacity and that she knew and approved of the contents of the will. Notwithstanding this finding, the court further found that that she had been unduly influenced by the son in making this will. The finding of undue influence was not based on direct proof, but was based on inference from the circumstances:[34]

i. The testatrix was vulnerable. She was in her mid 90s and was less capable than before her fall.
ii. She was very dependent upon the son since her fall. This was not total dependence and she clearly had a mind of her own. She would have been very worried at the prospect of the son moving out and ceasing to care for her.
iii. Not using the previously used solicitors raised issues and the explanation given by the son was unsatisfactory. Turning to a will writer instead ensured that the will would be prepared with no prior knowledge of the testatrix and her circumstances.[35]
iv. The testatrix's reason for leaving the house to the son was factually incorrect and the source of that information was found by the court to be the son himself.
v. There was an absence of any evidence that the testatrix would have wanted to alter the will in respect of the house.
vi. The son was a forceful man with a forceful physical presence, but there was no finding of threat or violence. He had a grievance that he perceived he had not been treated equally with his brother. The judge refers to his 'hatred' of his brother.[36]

---

[34] Drawing inference from the circumstances—*Re Good, Carapeto v Good* [2002] WTLR 801 at [124]-[125]; *Cowderoy v Cranfield* [2011] WTLR 1699 at [141].

[35] A curiosity of the procedure was that the will writer wrote on her instruction form 'I have asked and received confirmation that [the testatrix] was not being put under any undue pressure or influence as to the distribution of the property. I confirmed this with [her] while [the son] was out of the room'

In our experience asking the question 'Are you subject to any undue influence?' is highly unlikely to produce the answer 'yes'. The judge later observed that he did not think this attempt 'to ascertain whether there was pressure on her, the fruits of which are recorded on her instruction form, are a particularly strong counter-indication in this case. If the more subtle form of undue influence is being applied, its victim would hardly be likely to answer "yes" to the question'.

[36] Para [97](viii).

vii. The son's evidence regarding the will was unsatisfactory. He was involved more than he admitted and, despite his denials, was involved directly in amendments to the draft will.

The cumulative effect of these points was, in the court's view, sufficient to support the finding of undue influence.[37]

(iii) The burden of proving it lies on the person who asserts it. It is not enough to prove that the facts are consistent with the hypothesis of undue influence. What must be shown is that the facts are inconsistent with any other hypothesis. In the modern law this is, perhaps, no more than a reminder of the high burden even on the civil standard, that a claimant bears in proving undue influence as vitiating a testamentary disposition.

In order to establish undue influence a five-question test was proposed in *Killick v Poutney*.[38] In order to answer the question 'had the plaintiff established his case?', the following five points were to be satisfied. **4.16**

1. Was the defendant in a position to exercise influence over the testator?
2. Did the defendant exercise influence over the testator?
3. Was the influence exercised undue?
4. Was the undue influence exercised in relation to the disputed will?
5. Was it by means of the undue influence that the will was executed?

In *Re Wilkes* [39]it was observed: **4.17**

> Undue influence means coercion to make a will in particular terms... The proof of motive and opportunity for the exercise of such influence is required but the existence of such, coupled with the fact that the person who has such motive and opportunity has benefitted by the will to the exclusion of others, is not sufficient proof of undue influence. There must be positive proof of coercion overpowering the volition of the testator.[40]

The reference to coercion is significant as the presumption of undue influence cannot apply to a will, coercion becomes an alternative description for undue influence in the context of a will.[41] Coercion may involve violence, imprisonment, threats, emotional blackmail, or simply persistent mental pressure that overcomes the free will.

---

[37] See Chapter 5 on the Burden and Standard of Proof.

[38] [2000] WTLR 41 at 72 B-D per James Munby QC (as he was then).

[39] [2006] WTLR 1097.

[40] In *Vaughan v Vaughan* [2005] WTLR 401 at [87] 'The plea of undue influence will only succeed when it is shown by admissible evidence that the testator was coerced into doing that which he did not wish to do'.

[41] *Hall v Hall* (1868) 1 P&D 481; *Wingrove v Wingrove* (1885) 11 PD 81; *Re Good, Carapeto v Good* [2002] WTLR 801.

4.18 It is not sufficient for a claim of undue influence merely to show that someone has the ability to influence another unduly: '... it is not sufficient to establish that a person has the power unduly to overbear the will of the testator. It must be shown that in the particular case the power was exercised, and that it was by means of the exercise of that power that the will was obtained.'[42]

4.19 Further, it is not enough to prove that the facts are consistent with a claim of undue influence, but the facts must also be shown to be inconsistent with any other rational hypothesis.[43] In finding for the will in *Hubbard v Scott*[44] the judge observed:

> Undue influence is not the only hypothesis with which the making of the 2009 will is consistent. There is another perfectly rational explanation. The testator was elderly and lonely. The visits of the claimants and their mother had become less frequent. He had no-one else to whom he wanted to leave his estate. There was no-one at all for whom he was, or felt, obliged to provide. He described himself to [the solicitor] as an orphan. [The defendant] came into his life and he became fond of her. In all these circumstances I find that undue influence is not made out.

In *Cowderoy v Cranfield*,[45] Morgan J noted the point about being inconsistent with any other hypothesis, but taking note of the considerable evidence surrounding the circumstances of the will, felt it more appropriate simply to ask 'whether the party asserting undue influence has satisfied me to the requisite standard of proof that the will was executed as a result of undue influence'. This view points towards the nature and amount of the evidence itself ruling out the likelihood of any other hypothesis in some cases.

(iv) In this context undue influence means influence exercised either by coercion, in the sense that the testator's will must be overborne, or by fraud.

4.20

> To be undue influence in the eye of the law there must be—to sum it up in one word—coercion. It must not be the case in which a person has been induced... to come to a conclusion that he will make a will in a particular person's favour, because if the testator has only been persuaded or induced by considerations which you may condemn, really and truly to intend to give his property to another, though you may disapprove of the act, yet it is strictly legitimate in the sense of its being legal. It is only when the will of the person who becomes a testator is coerced into doing that which he does not desire to do, that is undue influence.[46]

[42] *Craig v Lamoureux* [1920] AC 349 at 357.

[43] *Boyse v Rossborough* (1857) 6 HLC 2 at 51.

[44] [2012] WTLR 29 at [53] per Proudman J.

[45] [2011] WTLR 1699 at [141]; cited with approval in *Schomberg v Taylor* [2013] WTLR 1413 at [30].

[46] *Wingrove v Wingrove* (1885)11 PD 81 at page 82 per Sir James Hannen; *Parfitt v Lawless* (1872) LR 2 P&D 462 at 471 undue influence for a will 'raises the question of coercion and that only' per Lord Penzance; *Hubbard v Scott* [2012] WTLR 29 at [52] where Proudman J observed that 'persuasion without more is not coercion.'

Coercion for this purpose may arise from a variety of conduct. At the most extreme it could be imprisonment or actual physical violence. But, it will also encompass conduct such as threatened violence, bullying, threatened withdrawal of help and services to the testator, or ostracism of the testator. **4.21**

In *Walker v Walker*[47] it was said that **4.22**

> ... actual undue influence ... may take many forms and may be subtle. It need not just be an instant act of pressure, intimidation or domination, but may take the form of control, domination, or emotional pressure over a period of time, so that a person is so controlled, crushed, or so intimidated or dominated that they will do almost anything to please another, to prevent anger, or to avoid conflict, to have a peaceful existence....

The suggestions here that undue influence may be 'subtle' or use 'pressure over a period of time' highlight that matters of undue influence may well be neither blatant nor immediately apparent. The draftsman cannot expect undue influence to be clear and openly apparent. His questions and recorded observations need in turn to be less direct and aimed at establishing as much detail of the surrounding circumstances as he can in order to gain as full a picture as possible of circumstances that might excite the suspicion of the court. Simple questions about undue influence will rarely be adequate.

(v) Coercion is pressure that overpowers the volition without convincing the testator's judgement. It is to be distinguished from mere persuasion, appeals to ties of affection, or pity for future destitution, all of which are legitimate. Pressure which causes a testator to succumb for the sake of a quiet life, if carried to an extent that overbears the testator's free judgement, discretion or wishes, is enough to amount to coercion in this sense.

The point at which at which pressure overcomes free will is very hard to identify and any draftsman should recognize that it will not always be possible to be sufficiently certain that the will instructions are a result of undue influence. What is important is that the possibility is investigated where circumstances warrant it. A decision to proceed with the will or refuse the instructions needs to be made after a careful weighing of the factors discovered. **4.23**

(vi) The physical and mental strength of the testator are relevant factors in determining how much pressure is necessary in order to overbear the will. The will of a weak and ill person may be more easily overborne than that of a hale and hearty one. As was said in one case, simply to talk to a weak and feeble testator may so fatigue the brain that a sick person may be induced for quietness' sake to do anything. A 'drip ... drip' approach may be highly effective in sapping the will.

[47] [2007] All ER (D) 418 at [221] per Roger Kaye QC (sitting as a deputy judge).

4.24 It is clear that 'not all influence is undue influence. Even very strong persuasion and "heavy family pressures" are not, of themselves, sufficient'.[48] There is a line that must be crossed from mere influence to undue influence, but the point at which it is crossed is hard to determine.[49] Pressure which caused the testator to succumb for the sake of a quiet life, if carried further, to the extent that it overcame his free judgement, discretion, or wishes, is enough to amount to coercion. It is hard to determine this because there is no abstract set of criteria against which all influence could be judged.

4.25 Whether or not actions amount to undue influence will be dependent heavily on the individual circumstances of each case. Significant factors will be

- the mental capacity of the person being influenced;
- the physical strength of the person being influenced, particularly in the context of terminal or debilitating illness;
- the extent to which the person being influenced is isolated from friends, relatives, neighbours, and advisers;
- the strength of character of the person influencing them;
- the nature and manner of the influence exerted;
- the duration and frequency of the influence being exerted; and
- the value, or significance, of the benefit conferred on the person influencing the testator.

4.26 The influence may be much slighter in cases where the testator is of limited mental or physical strength.

> [A] person in the last days or hours of life may have become so weak and feeble, that a very little pressure will be sufficient to bring about the desired result, and it may even be that mere talking to him at that stage of illness and pressing something upon him may so fatigue the brain, that the sick person may be induced, for quietness' sake, to do anything. This would be coercion, though not actual violence.[50]

The will of a vigorous, healthy person of normal capacity would, by contrast, normally require greater pressure. Much will depend upon the strength of character of the individual. For example, in the case of a will, the testator who has impaired capacity but still retains sufficient capacity for his will is less likely to be able to resist undue influence than would the person with a mind that is sharp and vigorous. Similarly, physical frailty, particularly through illness, may mean that the person being

---

[48] *Governor & Company of the Bank of Scotland v Bennett* [1997] 1 FLR 801 at 822; *Re Devillebichot, Brennan v Prior* [2013] WTLR 1701 where there was 'plenty of evidence' of opportunity to influence the testator and that this was opportunity was taken, but the coercion or pressure was not sufficient to amount to undue influence.

[49] 'It is difficult to determine in any case the point at which the influence of one mind upon another amounts to undue influence' *National Bank of Montreal v Stuart* [1911] AC 120 at 137 per Lord Macnaghten.

[50] *Wingrove v Wingrove* (1885) 11 PD 81 at page 82 per Sir James Hannen; *Schomberg v Taylor* [2013] WTLR 1413 at [107].

influenced has less will to resist the process.[51] In *Hampson v Guy*,[52] the testatrix lived for the last years of her life in a convent, but not as member of the order. In her will, made while she lived at the convent, a large part of her estate was left to the order. The finding of the jury was that the will was procured through undue influence. There was evidence of a degree of diminished capacity, but not such as to deprive the testatrix of testamentary capacity. The Court of Appeal, in dismissing the appeal, found that the diminished capacity rendered her very susceptible to influence.

(vii) There is a separate ground for avoiding a testamentary disposition on the ground of fraud. The shorthand used to refer to this species of fraud is fraudulent calumny. The basic idea is that if A poisons the testator's mind against B, who would otherwise be a natural beneficiary of the testator's bounty, by casting dishonest aspersions on his character, then the will is liable to be set aside.

(viii) The essence of fraudulent calumny is that the person alleged to have been poisoning the testator's mind must either know that the aspersions are false or not care whether they are true or false. In my judgement if a person believes that he is telling the truth about a potential beneficiary then even if what he tells the testator is objectively untrue, the will is not liable to be set aside on that ground alone.

Taken together, these two points deal with a more rare type of undue influence. The only recent reported case is *Edwards*,[53] where there were complex family relationships and the claimed undue influence by fraudulent calumny was alleged by one son against another regarding their mother's will. The testatrix was clearly frightened of son *A*, who had removed her from care against medical advice. *A* drank, was very aggressive, and prevented other members of the family from visiting his mother. The testatrix later alleged to the solicitor when justifying a change to her will that **4.27**

1. *A* was the one who looked after her (which was demonstrably untrue);
2. son *B* wanted to put her in a home (which again was demonstrably untrue); and
3. *B* and his wife had stolen from her (found to be untrue).

The judge concluded that son *A* had exerted undue influence by fraudulent calumny against son *B* in order to obtain a will in his favour and ordered that it be set aside and an earlier will be proved.[54] **4.28**

[51] *Hampson v Guy* (1891) 64 LT 778; *Hubbard v Scott* [2012] WTLR 29 at [7] where Proudman J observed that 'persistent pestering of a frail person . . . is more likely to overbear his will than mere pestering of someone who is hale and hearty'; *Pearce v Beverley* [2014] WTLR 85 where the donor was 'infirm and vulnerable'.

[52] (1891) 64 LT 778.

[53] *Re Edwards* [2007] WTLR 1387; also *Re Boyes deceased* [2013] EWHC 4027 (Ch) where the claim failed.

[54] Which divided the estate equally between *A* and *B*.

(ix) **The question is not whether the court considers that the testator's testamentary disposition is fair because, subject to statutory powers of intervention,[55] a testator may dispose of his estate as he wishes. The question, in the end, is whether in making his dispositions, the testator has acted as a free agent.**

Summary

4.29 The above points together make it clear that when considering undue influence in the context of wills:

- It is not influence that is solely bad or immoral.[56]
- It is not judged from a moral standpoint or as an issue of fairness[57] in the terms of the will.
- It is judged from fact.
- It is concerned with a degree of coercion to overcome the free will of the testator.[58]

Undue influence over part of a will

4.30 Where it can be shown that only part of a will resulted from undue influence, that part of the will can be rejected by the court, and probate then granted to the remainder.[59] This should only be done where it is possible to sever the part that is rejected without altering the meaning of what is left.[60]

Undue Influence and Gifts

The nature of the test

4.31 It is a different test to that applied to wills for undue influence in respect of lifetime transactions—thus probate cases are of no direct application when examining lifetime transfers and vice versa.[61]

4.32 The professional adviser must be alert to the possibility of undue influence being brought to bear on a donor in respect of *inter vivos* gifts. While, like wills, a

---

[55] e.g. Inheritance (Provision for Family and Dependants) Act 1965.

[56] *Wingrove v Wingrove* (1885)11 PD 81 where Sir James Hannen referred to 'a young man…caught in tolls of a harlot' being subject to an evil or immoral influence, but that was insufficient without coercion—'…even very immoral considerations either on the part of the testator, or of someone else offering them, do not amount to undue influence unless the testator is in such a condition, that if he could speak his wishes to the last, he would say, "this is not my wish, but I must do it"'; *Baudains v Richardson* [1906] AC 169.

[57] *Re Edwards, Edwards v Edwards* [2007] WTLR 1387.

[58] *Hall v Hall* (1868) 1 P&D 481; *Wingrove v Wingrove* (1885) 11 PD 81.

[59] *Billinghurst v Vickers* (1810) 1 Phill. 187.

[60] *Rhodes v Rhodes* (1882) 7 App Cas 192.

[61] *Theobald on Wills* (1st Supplement to the 17th edn., at 3-030; *Hart v Burbridge* [2013] WTLR 1191 at [49] per Sir William Blackburne '…it is not helpful in this area to have regard to authorities' on undue influence and wills. But he added 'This is not the place to explore whether there is any material difference beyond saying that, in principle, it is difficult to see why there should be.'

gift may be procured through actual undue influence, undue influence relating to gifts will also be presumed[62] (but this presumption is capable of being rebutted) where

1. the gift is so substantial that it cannot be accounted for by ordinary motives; and
2. there is a relationship between the donor and the recipient in which the donor has such trust and confidence in the recipient as to place the recipient in a position to exercise undue influence over the donor in making the gift.[63]

The gifts that attract suspicion have been described '...as if the gift is so large as not to be reasonably accounted for on the ground of friendship, relationship, charity or other ordinary motives on which ordinary men act, the burden is upon the donee to support the gift.'[64] **4.33**

Presumed undue influence does not require wrongful conduct;[65] 'the basis of the court's intervention is not the commission or a wrongful or dishonest act by the defendant, but that, as a matter of public policy, the presumed influence arising from the relationship of trust and confidence should not operate to the disadvantage of the victim...'[66] The court will intervene 'not on the ground that any wrongful act has in fact been committed by the donee, but on the ground of public policy, and to prevent the relations which existed between the parties and the influence arising therefrom being abused.'[67] **4.34**

The distinction between actual and presumed undue influence was described as follows. 'In the broadest possible way, the difference between the two classes is that in the case of actual undue influence something has been done to twist the mind of a donor, whereas in cases of presumed undue influence it is more a case of what has not been done, namely ensuring that independent advice is available to the donor.'[68] **4.35**

---

[62] *Daniel v Drew* [2005] WTLR 807 CA; *Evans v Lloyd* [2013] 1137; *Hart v Burbridge* [2013] WTLR 1191.

[63] *Royal Bank of Scotland v Etridge (No 2)* [2001] UKHL 44; *Macklin v Dowsett* [2005] WTLR 1561

[64] *Allcard v Skinner* (1887) 36 Ch D 145; *Nel v Kean* [2003] WTLR 501; *Pearce v Beverley* [2014] WTLR 85 at [102] '...cannot in my view be reasonably accounted for on the ground of friendship, charity or other ordinary motives on which ordinary men act.'

[65] 'A transaction may be set aside by the court, even though the actions and conduct of the person who benefits from it could not be criticised as wrongful' *Niersmans v Pesticcio* [2004] 699 CA at [20] per Mummery LJ.

[66] *Niersmans v Pesticcio* [2004] 699 CA at [20] per Mummery LJ—in view of the point being made the word 'victim' rather undermines it.

[67] *Allcard v Skinner* (1887) 36 Ch D 145 at 171 per Cotton LJ; *Hammond v Osborn* [2002] WTLR 1126; *Wright v Hodgkinson* [2005] WTLR 435.

[68] *Daniel v Drew* [2005] WTLR 807 CA at [31] per Ward LJ.

Spontaneous action of the donor

4.36 In *Goldsworthy v Brickell*:[69] 'The gift or transaction will be set aside, unless it is proved to have been the spontaneous act of the donor or grantor acting in circumstances which enable him to exercise an independent will and which justify the court holding that the gift or transaction was the result of a free exercise of his will.' 'Spontaneous' here means in the sense of resulting from a person's free will or arising without external pressure, rather than its perhaps more common meaning of impulsive or unpremeditated. In *Hammond v Osborn*[70] rebuttal was defined as requiring proof that the gift was

1. 'the spontaneous act of the donor acting under circumstances which enabled him to exercise an independent will and which justifies the court in holding that the gift was the result of a free exercise of the donor's will';[71] or
2. made by the donor only after full, free, and informed thought about it.[72]

Rebuttal of the presumption

4.37 In *Smith v Cooper*:[73]

> [Where] the test of undue influence applies... the court will presume that the transaction was procured by undue influence exercised by one party over the other; in other words by the abuse by the one of the position of influence that he has over the other. In such a case it is then up to the one party to prove that the transaction was not procured by an abuse of his position of influence but was rather the free exercise of the will of the other party as a result of full, free and informed thought.

Showing that the donor was properly advised as to the nature and effect of transaction is generally taken as the surest form of rebuttal.

4.38 Rebuttal of the presumption of undue influence has been the subject of much judicial comment. *Inche Noriah v Shaik Allie Bin Omar*:[74]

> ... it is necessary for the donee to prove that the gift was the result of the free exercise of independent will. The most obvious way to prove this is by establishing that the gift was made after the nature and effect of the transaction had been fully explained to the donor by some independent and qualified person so completely[75] as to satisfy the court that the donor was acting independently of any influence from the donee and with the full appreciation of what he was doing...

---

[69] [1987] Ch 378 at 401.
[70] *Hammond v Osborn* [2002] WTLR 1125 at [1].
[71] From *Allcard v Skinner* (1887) 36 Ch D 145.
[72] From *Zamet v Hyman* [1961] 1 WLR 1442 at 1446; *Hammond v Osborn* [2002] WTLR 1125.
[73] [2011] WTLR 691 CA at [61].
[74] [1929] AC 127 PC; *Royal Bank of Scotland v Etridge (No 2)* [2001] UKHL 44 at [20].
[75] On the sufficiency of advice required see, for example, *Wright v Hodgkinson* [2005] WTLR 435.

Note that the person who gives the advice is described as 'qualified'. No particular qualification is stated, but it should be taken to be someone who

- has knowledge, by training, formal qualification, or practical experience in the area;
- is sufficiently able to describe in clear terms (intelligible to the donor) what is the nature of the act and what the consequences of it will be for the donor.

That the adviser is both qualified and independent does not guarantee that the advice will be sufficient. It must be shown that the advice met the standard required to fully inform the donor.

The nature of the advice given that is necessary to rebut the presumption of undue influence was explored in *Re Coomber*.[76] The advice **4.39**

- should be provided by an independent person who is free 'from any taint in the relationship' or any self interest;[77]
- should provide a clear explanation of the nature and consequences of the act;[78]
- does not require any approval of the act by the adviser ('independent and competent advice does not mean independent and competent approval').

In addition it has been made clear that the decision to make the gift is not that of the adviser.[79]

It is not sufficient to rebut the presumption by showing merely that the donor understood the transaction; it has to be shown further that the decision to make the gift was an independent one. 'A person may fully understand the implications of the transaction, but still be under the influence of another. The question will be whether the outside advice had an emancipating effect.'[80] It is not sufficient to rebut the **4.40**

[76] *In re Coomber, Coomber v Coomber* [1911] 1 Ch 723 at 730 per Fletcher-Moulton LJ; applied in *Nel v Kean* [2003] WTLR 501.

[77] *Hodson v Hodson* [2006] EWHC 2878 (Ch) at [27] per Patten J 'It is commonly the case that the donor has a full understanding of the nature of what he or she is being asked to do but no real ability to resist the demands being made of them. It is lack of independence which is the key to the intervention of equity.'

[78] The consequences, or effect, of the gift must be explained *Randall v Randall* [2005] WTLR 119 at [37] consequences 'may come in many guises depending on the facts... clearly the effect of the gift on what is left for the donor or the possible fiscal consequences' are essential parts of the advice. Without this a person could not be fully informed about the gift.

[79] *Royal Bank of Scotland v Etridge (No 2)* [2001] UKHL 44 at [61].

[80] *Nel v Kean* [2003] WTLR 501 at [82] (x) and *In re Coomber* [1911] 1 Ch 723; In *Banco Exterior Internacional v Mann* [1995] 1 All ER 936 CA at [947]:

> An understanding of the document may be the first step in the exercise of a free choice whether or not to sign it, but it is not the point at which the law of undue influence is directed. A person may be fully informed as to the content of the document and its legal effect and yet be acting under the influence of another when she signs it. It is the undue influence not the lack of comprehension that gives the wife the defence.

presumption to only show that the donee acted unfairly or wrongly.[81] In the Court of Appeal in *Etridge* [82] the following was said:

> A solicitor who is instructed to advise a person who may be subject to the undue influence of another must bear in mind that it is not sufficient that she understands the nature and effect of the transaction if she is so affected by the influence of the other that she cannot make an independent decision of her own. It is not sufficient to explain the documentation and ensure that she understands the nature of the transaction and wishes to carry it out: see *Powell v Powell* [1900] 1 Ch 243 at 247, approved in *Wright v Carter*.[83] His duty is to satisfy himself that his client is free from improper influence, and the first step must be to ascertain whether it is one into which she could sensibly be advised to enter if free from such influence. If he is not so satisfied it is his duty to advise her not to enter into it, and to refuse to act further for her in the implementation of the transaction is she persists....

In re Morris contains substantial criticism of a solicitor who did not meet this standard when dealing with an elderly client.[84] The Court of Appeal's view of the solicitor's duty was not approved by the House of Lords when it heard the *Etridge* appeal.[85] However, that disapproval was in respect of the type of case before them (a wife charging her share of the matrimonial home in support of a loan for her husband's business). The general tenor of the Court of Appeal's remarks has otherwise been followed in respect of gifts (see the next two paragraphs).

4.41 'When the nature of [the burden of proof to rebut the presumption] is understood it is clear why the cases are dominated by consideration of the role of independent advice to [the donor] before the transaction was entered into.'[86]

4.42 In *Wright v Hodgkinson*,[87] there was no direct judicial criticism of the solicitor who advised an elderly client in the matter of a gift. However, the court found that the legal advice given was insufficient as it could not be shown that the advice 'must have led to a decision based upon full, free and informed thought'. This finding reinforces the need for the adviser to clearly record the nature and extent of the advice given where there might be a presumption of undue influence because of the relationship between the parties.

[81] *Hammond v Osborn* [2002] WTLR 1125; *Wright v Hodgkinson* [2005] WTLR 435.

[82] [1998] 4 All ER 705 per Stuart-Smith LJ at 714; Millett LJ had earlier said much the same in *Credit Lyonnais Bank Nederland NV v Burch* [1997] 1 All ER 144, at 155/156; *Royal Bank of Scotland v Etridge (No 2)* [2001] UKHL 44 at [20].

[83] [1903] 1 Ch 27.

[84] [2001] WTLR 1137 at 1197C.

[85] [2001] UKHL 44 at [59] per Lord Nicholls 'I am unable to accept this as an accurate formulation of a solicitor's duties in cases such as those now under consideration.'

[86] *Evans v Lloyd* [2013] 1137 at [46].

[87] [2005] WTLR 435 at [125] and at [146] it was found that the advice given was insufficient to ensure that the donor could give 'full, free and informed consideration' to the gift; *Meredith v Lackschewitz-Martin* [2002] WTLR 1451 at 35(d) 'received inadequate advice, nothing that could fairly be described as independent.'

It is important that the legal adviser is quite clear which of the parties to the transaction is his client[88] and that he frames his advice accordingly. Trying to advise both parties is out of the question. Recognizing that the potential exists for issues of undue influence to be raised at a later stage (either because of actual or presumed undue influence) should ensure that the adviser can not only show that the advice was independent, and given to the client, but that it was given in absence of the donee. **4.43**

Relationships where undue influence is presumed

In general, undue influence will be presumed where the relationship is one where it can be shown that the donor has placed trust and confidence in the donee; 'the party in whom it is reposed, either because he is or has become an adviser of the other or because he has become entrusted with the management of his affairs or everyday needs or for some other reason, is in a position to influence him into effecting the transaction of which the complaint is made.'[89] This is not so much determined by the nature of the parties as by the fact that the donor places trust and confidence in the other. For the relationships listed below it is the nature of the relationships that gives rise to presumption. **4.44**

Parent upon child: a parent's influence upon a child in matters of gifts to the parent has long aroused the suspicion of the court;[90] 'it is a thing that is assumed between parent and child.'[91] The suspicion does not arise out of fear, or even domination, it arises out the usual nature of such family relationships; 'When we talk of parental influence we do not think of terror in connection with it—that is not the primary idea—it is not terror and coercion, but kindness and affection, which may bias the child's mind, and induce the child to do that which may be highly imprudent, and which, if the child were properly protected, he would never do.'[92] **4.45**

The presumption applies irrespective of sex of the parent or child.[93] It will also apply to a step relationship between parent and child.[94] There is no assumption that that will cease on a child attaining its majority; much will depend upon its independence and emancipation from parental control.[95] **4.46**

There is no presumption of the reverse position for child on parent,[96] even where the parent is old and frail. **4.47**

88 *Meredith v Luckschewitz-Martin* [2002] WTLR 1451 at 23.
89 *Goldsworthy v Brickell* [1987] Ch 378 at 401D.
90 *Wright v Vanderplank* (1855) 2 K & J 1; *Bainbrigge v Browne* (1881) 18 Ch D 1888.
91 *Turner v Collins* (1871) 7 Ch App 329 at 339—per Lord Hatherley LC.
92 *Turner v Collins* (1871) 7 Ch App 329 at 340—per Lord Hatherley LC.
93 *Lancashire Loans Ltd v Black* [1934] 1 KB 380.
94 *Powell v Powell* [1900] 1 Ch 243.
95 *Lancashire Loans Ltd v Black* [1934] 1 KB 380; *Re Pauling's Settlement Trusts (No 1), Younghusband v Coutts & Co* [1963] 3 All ER 1.
96 *Avon Finance v Bridger* [1985] 2 All ER 281; *McCreanney v McCreanney* [2003] All ER (D) 161.

4.48 *Guardians upon wards*: the position with guardians is similar to that of parents (and for the same reasons).[97]

4.49 *Trustees upon beneficiaries*: as for parents the court has long viewed the relationship as being one where the trustee will acquire influence over the beneficiary[98] and the beneficiary will repose trust and confidence in the trustee. It has been suggested that not all trusteeships will give rise to this presumption and that it will only arise where the trusteeship gives rise to influence.[99] Cited in support of this are Lord Cranworth's comments in *Smith v Kay* that it is only a particular sort of trusteeship that gives influence to the trustee.[100] This seems to suggest that the principle may be more limited than is sometimes assumed. It would point to trustees with perhaps more vulnerable beneficiaries (minors, the infirm, beneficiaries that are unworldly or naïve, etc.).

4.50 *Religious and spiritual advisers upon members of congregations or followers*: 'The influence of one mind over another is very subtle, and of all influences religious influence is the most dangerous and the most powerful, and to counteract it Courts of Equity have gone very far.'[101] For this presumption to apply it must be shown that the relationship was more than merely an attendee at a church; there must be a closer relationship.[102]

4.51 *Medical advisers upon patients*: this will cover a range of medical practitioners.[103] There is old authority that this will cover the management of a lunatic asylum[104] and more that it applies to governors of a hospital.[105] It would be easy to see this applying to those who run nursing homes. For this presumption to apply it will require more to the relationship than simple medical treatment; there will need to be a close or longing enduring relationship, therefore much will depend upon the individual facts.

4.52 *Solicitors upon clients*: it is generally accepted that a client will repose trust and confidence in his legal adviser.[106] The relationship of solicitor and client should exist at the time of the transaction, but whether or not the presumption can continue

[97] *Hylton v Hylton* (1754) 2 Ves Sen 547; *Wright v Vanderplank* (1855) 2 K & J 1.

[98] *Hunter v Atkins* (1834) My & K 113.

[99] N. Enonchong *Duress, Undue Influence and Unconscionable Dealing* (2nd edn., London: Sweet & Maxwell, 2012) at 10-016.

[100] (1859) 7 HLC 750.

[101] *Allcard v Skinner* (1887) 36 Ch D 145 at 183 per Lindley LJ.

[102] *Nel v Keen* [2003] WTLR 501 at [100] and [101].

[103] *Claughton v Price* [1997] EG 51.

[104] *Wright v Proud* (1806) 33 ER 246.

[105] *In re CMG* [1970] 1 Ch 574.

[106] 'The great power and influence that an attorney has over his client' *Walmesley v Booth* (1739) 2 Atk 27 at 29 per Lord Hardwicke; 'The crushing influence of the power of an attorney' *Welles v Middleton* (1784) Cox 112 at 125.

to apply after that relationship ceases will depend very much on the individual circumstances.

There is presumption of undue influence between spouses,[107] fiancé and fiancée,[108] or between cohabitants. **4.53**

The above is not an exhaustive list and it has been stressed that the list of relationships in this context is never closed.[109] In *Royal Bank of Scotland v Etridge (No 2)* it was said of these relationships that they **4.54**

> cannot be listed exhaustively. Relationships are infinitely various... the question is whether one party has reposed sufficient trust and confidence in the other, rather than whether the relationship belongs to a particular type... Even this test is not comprehensive. The principle is not confined to cases of abuse of trust and confidence. It also includes, for instance, cases where a vulnerable person has been exploited. Indeed, there is no single touchstone for determining whether the principle is applicable. Several expressions have been used in an endeavour to encapsulate the essence: trust and confidence, reliance, dependence or vulnerability on the one hand and ascendancy, domination or control on the other. None of these descriptions is perfect. None is all embracing. Each has its proper place.

Exploitation

Distinct from undue influence, but nonetheless having some similarity, is what is described in *Snell's Equity* as 'exploitation of a special disadvantage'.[110] This is a separate equitable jurisdiction to set aside a transaction where **4.55**

1. one party to the transaction suffers from a disadvantage or disability;
2. the transaction is oppressive[111] to that party (imprudent is not enough); and
3. the conduct of the other party is unconscionable, i.e. that it is 'morally culpable or reprehensive',[112] and this is more than merely being a bad bargain or that one party secured a better deal than the other.

---

107 *Royal Bank of Scotland v Etridge (No 2)* [2001] UKHL 44; *Barclays Bank plc v O'Brien* [1994] 1 AC 180.

108 *Zamet v Hyman* [1961] 1 WLR 1442.

109 *Pesticcio v Huet* [2003] 1327 where the presumption was considered to exist for brother and sister (where the brother was mentally and physically disadvantaged); *Randall v Randall* [2005] WTLR where the relationship was aunt/nephew where aunt had placed trust and confidence in the nephew to manage her financial affairs (at [55] the nephew was described as having all the hallmarks of a bully); *Wright v Hodgkinson* [2005] WTLR 435 where an elderly man with no family and a man half his age through friendship developed a relationship of trust and confidence; *Pearce v Beverly* [2014] WTLR 85 where an elderly, frail, and vulnerable man placed his trust and confidence, particularly in financial matters, in a female friend 24 years his junior.

110 32nd edn., at 8-036; reviewed and approved in *Evans v Lloyd* [2013] WTLR 1137.

111 'Overreaching and oppressive' and 'shock the conscience of the court' *Snell* (n 110) 8-038.

112 *Snell* op cit 8-039.

4.56 The Privy Council review of this area in *Boustany v Piggott*[113] made the following points on conduct:

1. It is not sufficient to attract the jurisdiction of equity to prove that a bargain is hard, unreasonable, or foolish; it must be proved to be unconscionable, in the sense that 'one of the parties to it has imposed the objectionable terms in a morally reprehensible manner, that is to say, in a way which affects his conscience.'[114]
2. 'Unconscionable' relates not merely to the terms of the bargain but to the behaviour of the stronger party, which must be characterized by some moral culpability or impropriety.[115]
3. Unequal bargaining power, or objectively unreasonable terms, provide no basis for equitable interference in the absence of unconscientious or extortionate abuse of power where exceptionally, and as a matter of common fairness, 'it was not right that the strong should be allowed to push the weak to the wall'.[116]
4. A contract cannot be set aside in equity as an unconscionable bargain against a party innocent of actual or constructive fraud. Even if the terms of the contract are unfair in the sense that they are more favourable to one party than the other ('contractual imbalance'), equity will not provide relief unless the beneficiary is guilty of unconscionable conduct.[117]
5. 'In situations of this kind it is necessary for the plaintiff who seeks relief to establish unconscionable conduct, namely that unconscientious advantage has been taken of his disabling condition or circumstance.'[118]

4.57 Disadvantage or disability is not precisely defined, but decisions have regarded poverty (when compared to the other party) and lack of education as being included. Disadvantage appears generally considered to be in relation to the other party to the transaction.[119]

4.58 Most of the authorities in this area deal with bargains, but in *Evans v Lloyd* [120] it was held that despite an earlier view to the contrary this equitable doctrine did apply to gifts.[121] It was said in this case, where both undue influence and an unconscionable transaction were pleaded, that 'if the claimants succeeded on the ground of undue

113 [1993] UKPC 17; (1995) 69 P & CR 298 at 302–303 per Lord Templeman.
114 *Multiservice Bookbinding v Marden* [1979] Ch 84 at 110.
115 *Lobb (Alec) (Garages) Ltd v Total Oil (GB) Ltd* [1983] 1 WLR 87 at 94.
116 *Lobb (Alec) (Garages) Ltd v Total Oil (GB) Ltd* [1983] 1 WLR 87 at 183.
117 *Hart v O'Connor* [1985] AC 1000; *Nichols v Jessup* [1986] NZLR 226.
118 *Commercial Bank of Australia Ltd v Amadio* (1983) 46 ALR 402 at 413.
119 *Fry v Lane* (1888) 40 Ch D; *Cresswell v Potter* [1978] 1 WLR 255; 'judged in the light of the transaction in question and the documentation it involves' *Chagos Islanders v Attorney General* [2003] EWHC 2222 (QB) at [559].
120 WTLR [2013] 1137.
121 WTLR [2013] 1137 at [51] on *Langton v Langton* [1995] 2 FLR 890 and *Randall v Randall* [2005] WTLR 119.

influence, they would not need to rely on this alternative head of claim, whereas if they fail (as they do) on the ground of undue influence they cannot conceivably succeed on this alternative ground.'[122] While that remark was based on the facts in question, it does illustrate the difficulty of an unconscionable transaction plea succeeding if undue influence fails.

Knowledge and Approval

Frequently challenges to wills are based on a want of capacity as well as want of knowledge and approval. It is useful therefore to summarize the requirement for knowledge and approval. Knowledge and approval has been defined in several recent cases, all to the same effect. **4.59**

- 'Knowing and approving of the contents of one's will is traditional language for saying that the will "represented [one's] testamentary intentions".'[123]
- 'Knowledge and approval of the contents means only that the testator knows that he is making a will, knows what the terms of it are and intends that those terms should be incorporated into and given effect by the will.'[124]
- '. . . that he understood what he was doing, and its effect (that is to say that he was making a will containing certain dispositive provisions) so that the document represents his testamentary intentions.'[125]

See also 5.22 regarding the inclusion of understanding in the definition.

In order for a will to be valid, the testator must know and approve of its contents[126] at the time that he executes it.[127] Knowledge and approval is not a statutory requirement for a will, nor is it part of the test of testamentary capacity. It is a separate requirement for the validity of a will and comes from the necessity of showing that a will is 'the result of the testator's own intelligence and volition'.[128] A person will not have knowledge and approval of a will if it has been signed by mistake. Where such a mistake is made by a husband and wife, for example signing each other's wills in error, the position may different. This occurred in *Marley v Rawlings*.[129] The **4.60**

[122] WTLR [2013] 1137 at [76].

[123] *Gill v Woodall* [2011] WTLR 251 CA at [14], Neuberger MR (as he then was) quoting Chadwick LJ in *Fuller v Strum* [2002] WTLR 199 CA at [59].

[124] *Ark v Kaur* [2010] EWHC 2314 (Ch) WTLR (w) 2010-10 at [19].

[125] *Wharton v Bancroft* [2012] WTLR 693 at [28] per Norris J.

[126] *Hastilow v Stobie* (1865) LR 1 P&D 64; *Guardhouse v Blackburn* (1866) LR 1 P&D 109; *Fuller v Strum* [2002] WTLR 199 CA.

[127] *Hastilow v Stobie* (1865) LR 1 P&D 64; *Guardhouse v Blackburn* (1866) LR 1 P&D 109; but see Chapter 3 regarding knowledge and approval when the rule in *Parker v Felgate* is applied.

[128] *Theobald on Wills* 17th edn., at 3-015.

[129] [2014] WTLR 299 SC.

intention to execute their own wills, and knowledge and approval of the contents, existed and but for the mistake they would have executed the correct documents with knowledge and approval. It was found that the wills could be saved by rectification[130] which entailed swapping the entire typed text between the two documents.

4.61 There is no requirement that a testator understands the legal effect of his will, as he is reliant on his will draftsman as to the legal operation of the words that he has used.[131] The fact that the will might not operate as was explained to him does not negate his knowledge and approval of it.[132]

4.62 Testamentary capacity can exist in the absence of knowledge and approval[133]—but both must be present for a valid will. The question of whether or not knowledge and approval can exist where capacity is lacking is less clear (although the point is perhaps less important). In *Perrins*[134] it was found that capacity was not a prerequisite of knowledge and approval. Earlier, in *Hoff v Atherton*, Chadwick LJ had commented that 'capacity... is a prerequisite to a finding of knowledge and approval. A testator cannot be said to know and approve the contents of his will unless he is able to, and does, understand what he is doing and its effects.'[135] In *Perrins*, the Court of Appeal would not agree with this comment, except insofar as it would be true that if a court found there was no capacity it would not normally be necessary to go on to consider knowledge and approval.[136] It does seem logical that a person may have actual understanding of what they are doing by their will even though they lack the necessary capacity to make one. For example, a testator might clearly know and approve of what he has put in his will even though he cannot make one because he failed the

[130] s. 20(1)(a) Administration of Justice Act 1982.

[131] *Re Morris, Lloyds Bank Ltd v Peake* [1971] P 62.

[132] *Morrell v Morrell* (1882) 7 PD 68; *Re Morris, Lloyds Bank Ltd v Peake* [1971] P 62; *Kell v Jones* [2013] WTLR 507. Where the explanation reflected the testator's intention but was incorrect it will open up the possibility of a negligence claim against the draftsman—applying the general principle of the draftsman's duty of care from *White v Jones* [1995] 1 All ER 691.

[133] *Franks v Sinclair* [2007] WTLR 439.

[134] *Perrins v Holland* [2010] WTLR 1415 CA at [28] and [29] following *Battan Singh v Amirchand* [1948] AC 161 at 170 'A testator may have a clear apprehension of the meaning of the draft will submitted to him and may approve it, and yet if he was at the time through infirmity or disease so deficient in memory that he was oblivious of the claims of his relations, and if that forgetfulness is an inducing cause of his choosing strangers to be his legatees, the will is invalid.'—observing also that this was followed in *Re Wallace* [1952] 2 TLR 925; *Re Flynn* [1982] 1 WLR 310 and *Clancy v Clancy* [2003] WTLR 1097. See also *Re Loxton, Abbott v Richardson* [2006] WTLR 1567 at [196] and *Markou v Goodwin* [2014] WTLR 605.

[135] [2005] WTLR 99 CA at [62]. This was followed in *Re Key, Key v Key* [2010] WTLR 623 at [116] 'A conclusion that a testator lacks capacity necessarily compels a conclusion that he did not know and approve the contents of his will... he could not approve his will, even though he may have manifested an apparent assent to it, after hearing it read over to him.' (the testator lacked testamentary capacity).

[136] [2010] WTLR 1415 CA at [31].

second, third, or fourth limbs of the test of capacity. It might be much harder to say this if he failed the first limb.

The suspicious circumstances that will excite the suspicion of the court, necessary for this issue to arise, are dealt with in Chapter 5. **4.63**

The possibility that knowledge and approval may be lacking for only part of a will is established, but there must be evidence that clearly addresses the probability of a person approving part of the document (and executing it) while not approving another part of the same document. **4.64**

> I do not doubt that it is possible for a court to find that part of a will did have the knowledge and approval of the deceased and that another part did not... Where a will has been duly executed by a deceased of testamentary capacity who knew he was making a will and is shown to have known and approved of a specific part of the will, the court must consider how real is the possibility that the deceased did not know and approve of the remainder of the will and that requires a careful examination of all the circumstances including the directions and dispositions of the will.[137]

[137] *Fuller v Strum* [2002] WTLR 199 CA at 212H and 213A per Peter Gibson LJ.

5

BURDEN AND STANDARD OF PROOF

> In our legal system, if a judge finds it more likely than not that something did take place, then it is treated as having taken place. If he finds it more likely than not that it did not take place, then it is treated as not having taken place. He is not allowed to sit on the fence. He has to find for one side or the other. Sometimes the burden of proof will come to his rescue: the party with the burden of showing that something took place will not have satisfied him that it did. But generally speaking a judge is able to make up his mind where the truth lies without needing to rely upon the burden of proof.[1] **5.01**

As a general statement Baroness Hale's words reflect the reality of decision making in the court. However, the burden of proof can have significance in the areas covered by this book. The validity of a will can be affected by where the burden of proof lies[2] although the court would look to decide the issue without recourse to it: 'Cases are only decided on the burden of proof if, exceptionally, the court is unable to reach an evaluative decision taken as a whole. This is not such a case. The decision may be difficult, but it is neither necessary nor satisfactory to resort to the burden of proof.'[3]

Burden of Proof for Testamentary Capacity

The starting point is that where a will is **5.02**

- rational,
- professionally drawn,

[1] *In re B (Children) (FC)* [2008] UKHL 35 at [32] per Baroness Hale.
[2] See 5.05 below on *Ledger v Wootton*.
[3] *Sharp v Adam* [2006] WTLR 1059 at [74] per May LJ.

- seemingly regular in form, and
- made by a testator whose capacity is not in doubt

there is a presumption in favour of the will being valid.[4] It has been suggested that the force and applicability of this presumption must vary from case to case.[5] This presumption has also been described as 'an arid exercise', not worth dwelling on, where there was substantial doubt about capacity from the outset.[6] For a will that is irrational the initial presumption of validity is much weaker—to what extent will depend upon the terms of the will (i.e. the degree of irrationality).

5.03 The Probate Court has the power, where it sees cause to do so, to initiate its own enquiries into the validity of a will.[7]

5.04 The burden of proof when testamentary incapacity is alleged was summarized in *Re Key* as follows.

> The burden of proof in relation to testamentary capacity is subject to the following rules:
> 1. While the burden starts with the propounder of a will to establish capacity,[8] where the will is duly executed and appears rational on its face, then the court will presume capacity.
> 2. In such a case the evidential burden then shifts to the objector to raise a real doubt about capacity.[9]
> 3. If a real doubt is raised, the evidential burden shifts back to the propounder to establish capacity nonetheless.[10]

5.05 This shifting burden, in a sense, evens out the contest between those propounding the will and those challenging it. Starting with the presumption of capacity (for a will that meets the conditions of paragraph 5.02 (above)), the burden is on those challenging it to show sufficient doubt about the testator's capacity as to remove the presumption of validity. This does not require proof that the testator lacked testamentary capacity, merely that the evidence produced shows sufficient grounds for the court to accept there is a real doubt as to capacity.[11] At this point the burden

[4] *Sutton v Sadler* (1857) 3 CBNS 87. This is distinct from the presumption of due execution of a will based on the principle of *Omnia praesumuntur rite esse acta*—all things are presumed to have been correctly done *Harris v Knight* (1890) LR 15 PD 170; for Canada *Re Laxer* [1963] 1 OR 343; *Hsia v Yen-Zimmerman* [2012] BCSC 1620.

[5] *Re Parsons, Borman v Lel* [2002] WTLR 237 at 243C.

[6] *Symes v Green* (1859) 1 Sw & Tr 401; *Sutton v Sadler* (1857) 3 CB (NS) 87; *Re Parsons, Borman v Lel* [2002] WTLR 237 at 243C.

[7] rr. 12–16 Non-Contentious Probate Rules 1987.

[8] This remains the case even if the propounder has already obtained a grant in common form and revocation of that grant is sought *Ledger v Wootton* [2008] WTLR 235.

[9] 'Real doubt' in this context does not include weak or insubstantial evidence; *Waring v Waring* (1848) 6 Moo PC 341; *Sutton v Sadler* (1857) 3 CB (NS) 87.

[10] Briggs J (as he was then) in *Re Key, Key v Key* [2010] WTLR 623 at [97] citing *Ledger v Wootton* [2008] WTLR 235 at [5] (Norris J).

[11] *Turner v Turner* [2007] All ER (D) 238 (May) where medical records, showing the testator suffered physical effects from a stroke (slurred speech, right sight weakness) and a degree of forgetfulness,

moves away from the challengers to those propounding the will to then show that there was testamentary capacity.[12] Failure to produce evidence on the part of the propounder will, in most circumstances, lead to a finding against the will.[13] In *Ledger v Wootton* the medical evidence for the claimant showed 'real doubt' as to capacity, but did not show conclusively that the testatrix lacked capacity. The defendants 'adduced no evidence' as to capacity: 'On this state of evidence I am compelled to hold that the deceased lacked testamentary capacity at the date of the will.'[14] The invalidity of the will was decided not on sufficient proof of incapacity, but on the defendants' failure to discharge their burden of proof, after real doubt had been raised.

This approach was not followed in *Fischer v Diffley*[15] where the court took the view that it should apply the Mental Capacity Act 2005 to a challenge to a will on capacity grounds: 'As far as capacity is concerned, there are many reported decisions setting out the common law—the principal case being *Banks v Goodfellow*, which has recently been supplemented by statute—to which, it seems to me, that I am entitled to have regard as a starting point in connection with questions of capacity... one starts from an assumption of capacity...'[16] The Court therefore started from the assumption of capacity[17] even where there was a genuine dispute as to validity (and eventually the court found against both wills). 5.06

The Act imposes, for the matters covered by the Act, a statutory presumption of capacity which will, if applied to testamentary capacity, place the burden of proof upon the person alleging incapacity.[18] The difference with the approach summarized in *Key v Key* (above) may appear to be slight, but if the presumption is applied, in an action to test the validity of a will, it would mean a presumption in favour of capacity (and therefore in favour of the will) operating throughout. This would 5.07

were insufficient to show real doubt as to capacity. *Re Key, Key v Key* [2010] WTLR 623 '... this is a case where the element of suspicion arising from the circumstances, although by no means overpowering, is sufficient to call for affirmative proof of knowledge and approval, beyond that constituted by the due execution of a rational will.'

[12] *Vaughan v Vaughan* [2005] WTLR 401 at[105] the propounder 'does not come within a measurable distance... of establishing testamentary capacity'; *Pearce v Beverley* [2014] WTLR 85.

[13] *Ledger v Wootton* [2008] WTLR 235 at [12]; *Fraser v Lee* [2007] All ER (D) 203 (Jun).

[14] *Ledger v Wootton* [2008] WTLR 235 at [12].

[15] [2014] WTLR 757 HHJ Dight; this was the first case, of which the authors are aware, where the MCA 2005 has been applied in determining testamentary capacity. It appears from a subsequent article written by counsel for the claimant in this case (*Trusts and Estates Law & Tax Journal* July/August 2014) that the application of the MCA 2005 was not argued for in court—'Judge Dight approached the law of testamentary capacity in a manner unprecedented as far as the writer is aware.'

[16] [2014] WTLR 757 at [27].

[17] s. 1(2) Mental Capacity Act 2005 'A person must be assumed to have capacity unless it is established that he lacks capacity' n.b. s. 1(1) directs that this principle only applies for the purpose of the Act.

[18] s. 1(2) MCA 2005; the standard of proof will be the same for both—see later in this chapter; see also an excellent analysis of issues regarding the burden of proof by Alex Ruck Keen at <http://www.39essex.com/docs/articles/statutory_wills_and_testamentary_capacity_update.pdf>.

have the effect of always giving an edge in favour of the person propounding the will. It is difficult to see that such advantage is reasonable or justified when the decision for or against capacity will often be a finely judged one which really calls for the arguments for and against the will to be weighed equally. It is suggested that the approach of the court in *Fischer v Diffley* is treated with caution until the application of the MCA to testamentary capacity issues is considered specifically by the court (see Chapter 2). In *Bray v Pearce*[19] the court appeared to approach the 2005 Act on the basis that it supplemented the common law test. In setting out the approach to the burden of proof[20] the court effectively restated the common law position as the court did not consider that the burden of proof would lie throughout on the complainant.[21]

5.08 Where the testator suffered from a mental illness prior to the making of the will, the initial presumption of validity will be replaced by the presumption that the illness continued up to the time of the will.[22] This presumption can be rebutted[23] by showing that the will was made either after recovery from the illness, or during a lucid interval in the illness.[24] The burden of proof for this will will lie with those seeking to prove the will.[25] In the absence of the propounder producing sufficient evidence probate to the will will be refused.[26]

5.09 A lucid interval in this context need not be complete relief from the illness, but sufficient improvement in condition to pass the test of testamentary capacity. If a will is claimed to have been made in a lucid interval, the rational nature of the will, particularly one that is prepared by the testator without assistance can provide substantial evidence towards the will having been made in a lucid interval.[27]

5.10 Where the testator suffers from a delusion, 'a will should be regarded with great distrust, and every presumption should in the first instance be made against it'. The presumption against such a will 'becomes additionally strong where the will is . . . one in which natural affection and the claims of near relationship have been disregarded.'[28]

---

19 Unreported Ch D 6 March 2014 HM Rosen QC sitting as a Deputy Judge; the defendant played no significant role in the matter and offered no evidence.

20 Paragraph [74].

21 *Scammell v Farmer* [2008] WTLR 1261 at [24]; 'The onus of proof of capacity under the 2005 Act . . . is from the outset, and remains, on the complainant. At common law the position is different.'

22 *Smith v Tebbitt* (1867) LR 1 P&D 354.

23 *Bannatyne v Bannatyne* (1852) 2 Rob 472; *Banks v Goodfellow* (1870) LR 5 QB 549; *Brown v Deacy* [2002] WTLR 781.

24 *Hall v Warren* (1804) 9 Ves 605.

25 *Hall v Warren* (1804) 9 Ves 605.

26 See 5.05 above.

27 *Bannatyne v Bannatyne* (1852) 2 Rob 472.

28 *Banks v Goodfellow* LR 5 QB 549 at 570.

Burden of Proof for the Capacity to Make a Gift

The burden of proof initially lies with the person who asserts that the donor did not have the capacity to make the gift. Once it has been shown that the evidence raises a *prima facie* case of a lack of capacity, the burden shifts to the donee to show that the donor had the requisite capacity at that time.[29] In *Williams v Williams* this idea was referred to as being 'normally a sterile point', but in the circumstances of that case it was a point of significance. The evidence against capacity had shown that the donor would only have understood the transaction if it had been carefully explained to him. As that then had to be shown (on the balance of probabilities) this shifted the burden to the donee.[30] In *Re W*[31] the concept of shifting burdens of proof had been disparaged, but in *William v Williams*[32] the application of a shifting burden was described as 'common sense'. If the recipient of the gift cannot establish the capacity of the donor, the gift is set aside.[33] **5.11**

Burden of Proof for a Claim of Want of Knowledge and Approval of a Will

The traditional approach to the burden of proof for knowledge and approval lies initially with the propounder of the will.[34] Where there are no suspicious circumstances surrounding the preparation and execution of the will, and the testator was of capacity, it is presumed that the testator knew and approved of the contents of the document he executed.[35] '... if testamentary capacity ... is established, then it is open to the court to infer that a testator who does know what is written in the document which he signs does, in fact, understand what he is doing. And, where there is nothing to excite suspicion, the court may infer (without more) that a testator who signs a document as his will does know its contents. It would be surprising if he did not.'[36] **5.12**

---

[29] *In re Morris, The Special Trustees for Great Ormond Street Hospital for Children v Rushin* [2001] WTLR 1137 at 1196 D; *Williams v Williams* [3003] WTLR 1371 at [44]; *Smith v Cooper* [2011] WTLR 691.

[30] The evidence of the advice was unsatisfactory and failed to establish the validity of the gift.

[31] [2001] Ch 601.

[32] [2003] WTLR 1371 a5 [45].

[33] Whether a gift that is set aside in this way is void or voidable is not wholly clear; see Chapter 2.

[34] *Barry v Butlin* (1838) 2 Moo PC 480 at 482 'the *onus probandi* lies in every case upon the party propounding the will and he must satisfy the conscience of the court that the instrument so propounded is the last will of a free and capable testator'; *Wharton v Bancroft* [2012] WTLR 693 at [28].

[35] *Barry v Butlin* (1838) 2 Moo PC 480; *Fuller v Strum* [2002] WTLR 199 CA; *Re Sherrington, Sherrington v Sherrington* [2005] 587 CA (at [99] if the testator had ample opportunity to read his will it was 'nothing short of fanciful' to conclude that knowledge and approval was absent); *Channon v Perkins* [2006] WTLR 425 CA; *Wharton v Bancroft* [2012] WTLR 693 at [28].

[36] *Hoff v Atherton* [2005] WTLR 91 at [62] per Chadwick LJ; *Atter v Atkinson* (1869) LR 1 P&D 665 'Once get the facts admitted or proved that a testator is capable, that there is no fraud, that the will

The test was therefore in two stages.[37]

1. Could the challenger to the will show that the circumstances of the will were such as to excite the suspicion of the court?
2. If this was shown to be the case, then the burden of proof was placed on the propounder to dispel the suspicions.[38]

If the circumstances were not sufficient as to excite the suspicion of the court then knowledge and approval would be presumed from the valid execution.

5.13 In *Gill v Woodall* the Court of Appeal took the view that when considering knowledge and approval the court should not treat the burden of proof in the above way (the two-stage approach), but instead should proceed as proposed by Sachs J in *Crerar v Crerar*.[39] On this basis the court would

> ... consider all the relevant evidence available and then, drawing such inferences as it can from the totality of that material, it has to come to a conclusion whether or not those propounding the will have discharged the burden of establishing that the testatrix knew and approved the contents of the document which is put forward as a valid testamentary disposition. The fact that the testatrix read the document, and the fact that she executed it, must be given the full weight apposite in the circumstances, but in law those facts are not conclusive, nor do they raise a presumption.

5.14 This has therefore replaced the traditional approach, although judgments can be found where the traditional approach was applied.[40] Now, in determining an issue of knowledge and approval, the approach of the court should be to pose a single question, albeit one that is in two parts: when executing his will did the testator understand

i. what dispositions were in his will; and
ii. what the effect of those dispositions would be?[41]

was read over to him, and that he put his hand to it and the question whether he knew and approved of its contents is answered' per Sir JP Wilde (while well put this is probably too straightforward for today, lacking as it does anything about understanding the effect of the will).

[37] *Barry v Butlin* (1838) 2 Moo PC 480; *Tyrell v Painton* [1894] P 151.

[38] In *Franks v Sinclair* the view was expressed as: 'It is accepted for Mr Franks that because he was instrumental in taking the instructions for and preparing the 1994 will under which he is a substantial beneficiary and because Mrs Franks did not receive independent advice, the circumstances are such as to put on him the burden to establish affirmatively that Mrs Franks knew and approved the contents of the will.'

[39] (1956) 106 LJ 694; Sachs J observed that 'inquiries touching the validity of a testamentary disposition have always been considered matters touching the conscience of the court', and therefore he rejected 'the idea that there is any rule of law applicable to unusual cases which can so put that conscience into a strait-jacket as to preclude it from drawing inferences in the usual way and thus force the court to a decision which would, on the particular facts, be artificial'; approved by Latey J in *Re Morris, Lloyds Bank v Peake* [1971] P 62; *Gill v Woodall* [2011] WTLR 251 at [22] per Neuberger MR (as he was then); since applied in *Re Stolkin, Greaves v Stolkin* [2013] WTLR 1793 at [69].

[40] *Pearce v Beverley* [2014] WTLR 85.

[41] Or, as Chadwick LJ put it *Hoff v Atherton* [2005] WTLR 99 at [64], 'If the court is to be satisfied that the testator did know and approve the contents of the will—that is to say that he did understand what he was doing and its effect'; followed in *Cowderoy v Cranfield* [2011] WTLR1699.

Matters which formerly would have had to be shown against the will to shift the burden of proof back to the propounder (matters which excite the suspicion of the court) still remain relevant, but form part of the overall case of the challenger against the propounder's case.

How this reformulated test should be applied in practice was analysed by Norris J in *Wharton v Bancroft*[42]: **5.15**

> The Daughters... assert that Mr Wharton did not know or approve the contents of the 2008 Will. My approach to that issue (informed by the familiar authorities as reviewed and commented upon by the Court of Appeal in *Gill v Woodall* [2010] EWCA Civ 1430) is as follows:
>
> a. The assertion that Mr Wharton did not 'know and approve' of the 2008 Will requires the Court, before admitting it to proof, to be satisfied that Mr Wharton understood what he was doing and its effect (that is to say that he was making a will containing certain dispositive provisions) so that the document represents his testamentary intentions.
> b. The burden lies on [the claimant] to show that Mr Wharton knew and approved of the 2008 Will in that sense.
> c. The Court can infer knowledge and approval from proof of capacity and proof of due execution...
> d. It is not in issue that the 2008 Will was read over to Mr Wharton. The Court of Appeal observed in *Gill v Woodall* at paragraph [14], that, as a matter of common sense and authority, the fact that a will has been properly executed, after being prepared by a solicitor and read over to the testator, raises a very strong presumption that it represents the testator's intentions at the relevant time.
> e. But proof of the reading over of a will does not necessarily establish 'knowledge and approval'. Whether more is required in a particular case depends upon the circumstances in which the vigilance of the Court is aroused and the terms (including the complexity) of the Will itself.
> f. So the Daughters must produce evidence of circumstances which arouse the suspicion of the Court as to whether the usual strong inference arising from the manner of signature may properly be drawn.
> g. It is not for them positively to prove that he had some other specific testamentary intention; but only to lead such evidence as leaves the court not satisfied on the balance of probabilities that the testator understood the nature and effect of and sanctioned the dispositions in the will he actually made. But this evidence itself must usually be of weight, because in general the Court is cautious about accepting a contention that a will executed in the circumstances described is open to challenge.
> h. Attention to the legal and evidential burden can be decisive where the evidence is in short supply. But in other circumstances identifying the legal and evidential burden is simply a tool to enable the probate judge to identify and weigh the relevant elements within the evidence, the ultimate task being to consider all the relevant evidence available and, drawing such inferences as the judge can from the totality of that material, to come to a conclusion as to whether or not those

[42] [2012] WTLR 693 at [28].

propounding the will have discharged the burden of establishing that the document represents the testamentary intentions of the testator.

The key to understanding the change to the test appears to lie in the second sentence in (h) above, in the greater freedom allowed to the court in assessing the totality of the evidence produced by either party.

5.16 The fact that a will has been properly executed, after being prepared by a solicitor and read over to the testator raises a very strong presumption that the testator knew and approved of the contents.[43] The reading over of a will, while it raises this presumption of knowledge and approval, does not necessarily conclusively prove it.[44] Much will depend upon the circumstances surrounding the will that excite the suspicion of the court, such as the way in which the will was read over or the complexity of the will, etc.[45] (see later at 5.23 for more on reading over the will).

5.17 Where the circumstances surrounding the preparation or execution of the will, or the contents of the will itself, give rise to suspicion that the testator may not know and approve the contents (in whole or in part), it will not be assumed that there is knowledge and approval. The suspicion must be removed by proof of knowledge and approval. The circumstances giving rise to suspicion were described in *Re R*[46] as 'circumstances attending, or at least relevant to, the preparation and execution of the will itself'. It is thought that this is fairly broadly construed, given that it is frequently the case the allegations of want of capacity, undue influence, and lack of knowledge and approval are all claimed and therefore issues between them will overlap.[47]

5.18 It should be noted that the above contains a significant difference to a claim of undue influence which is quite commonly alleged together with a claim of want of knowledge and approval. A claim of undue influence places the evidential burden on the challenger to the will to prove his claim. By contrast, a claim of want of knowledge and approval will be, in essence, a weighing of the evidence from both sides that will determine the issue. In many circumstances a challenge on the basis of want of knowledge and approval is preferable (and perhaps easier). Where it is thought better to make both claims against a will, it should not be overlooked that making and failing to prove a claim of undue influence will almost certainly leave the claimant with the costs of the action, insofar as they relate to this claim; he has impugned the honesty of his opponent.[48] Where the claimant fails with a claim of want of knowledge

---

43 *Gill v Woodall* [2011] WTLR 251 at [14]; *Wharton v Bancroft* [2012] WTLR 693 at [28].
44 *Wharton v Bancroft* [2012] WTLR 693 at [28]; see *King v King* [2014] EWHC 2827 (Ch) for an example of summary judgment against a claim of want of knowledge and approval (and undue influence) where the solicitor's supervision was an important factor.
45 *Franks v Sinclair* [2007] WTLR 439 at [63] onwards.
46 [1950] 2 All ER 117.
47 *Re Stott, Klouda v Lloyds Bank Ltd* [1980] 1 All ER 259.
48 *Re Flynn* [1982] 1 WLR 310; *Carapeto v Good (costs)* [2002] 1305 at 308H–1309C.

and approval, costs may not be awarded against the losing party (depending upon the circumstances of the claim and particularly the strength of the matters claimed to excite the suspicion of the court).

Excite the suspicion of the court

The circumstances that give rise to the court requiring proof of knowledge and approval have also been referred to as suspicion of 'the righteousness of the transaction'.[49] This alternative expression is not favoured today as it carries with it overtones of morality, which are not part of the subject; 'The question is not whether the court approves of the circumstances in which the document was executed or its contents. The question is whether the court is satisfied that the contents of the document truly represent the testator's testamentary intentions.'[50] This last sentence makes it clear that that suspicion relates to whether or not the testator had knowledge of and approved the terms of the will alone. The behaviour of others connected to the will process may look suspicious but that behaviour, which may turn out to be of no consequence, is not the suspicion that the court is trying to allay. The conduct of those connected with the will or the testator may be disgraceful and yet there may still be knowledge and approval. The test was originally put forward in *Barry v Butlin*, as being where 'a circumstance that ought generally to excite the suspicion of the court, and call upon it to be vigilant and jealous in examining the evidence in support of the instrument, in favour of which it ought not to pronounce unless the suspicion is removed, and it is judicially satisfied that the paper pronounced does express the true will of the deceased.'[51] **5.19**

Circumstances which excite the suspicion of court can be many and varied, but they must relate to the instructions for the will, its preparation, and execution.[52] The proposition is put forward in *Williams Mortimer & Sunnucks*[53] that when setting out the grounds that excite suspicion they should not be used to make allegations of fraud and dishonesty.[54] **5.20**

[49] *Fulton v Andrew* (1875) LR 7 HL 448.

[50] *Fuller v Strum* [2002] WTLR 199 at 211B (see also 228 'merely a more grandiloquent way of expressing exactly the same concept'), this comment was illustrated with reference to *Re Dabbs, Hart v Dabbs* [2001] WTLR 527 where the propounder of the will was alleged to have killed the testator, was the executor of the will, was a specific legatee, and was sole residuary beneficiary. The will was found to be valid.

[51] (1838) 2 Moo PC 480 at 481; 'vigilant and jealous' later repeated in *Wintle v Nye* [1959] 1 WLR 284 at 291.

[52] *Re R (deceased)* [1951] P 10 at 17 'when it is a question of knowledge and approval of the contents of a will the circumstances which are held to excite the suspicions of the court must be circumstances attending, or at least relevant to, the preparation and execution of the will itself'; *Wintle v Nye* [1959] 1 WLR 284; *Re Stott* [1980] 1 WLR 249; *Re Edonya, Knight v Edonya* [2009] EWHC 2181 (Ch) for circumstances surrounding a deathbed will that did not excite the suspicion of the court.

[53] J. R. Martyn and N. Caddick *Williams, Mortimer & Sunnucks—Executors, Administrators and Probate* (20th edn., Sweet & Maxwell, 2013) at 13–32.

[54] This view was approved in *Ark v Kaur* [2010] EWHC 2314 (Ch) at [43] and 'All other points . . . do not bear on the process of preparation and execution of the will and are not . . . matters

5.21 'The degree of suspicion will vary with the circumstances of the case. It may be slight and easily dispelled. It may on the other hand be so grave that it can hardly be resolved.'[55] The evidence involved may well be evidence that is also relevant to testamentary capacity. Examples of suspicious circumstances could include:

- a beneficiary writing out or having the will prepared under which he takes a substantial legacy;[56]
- instructions for the will being given to the draftsman by the sole or main beneficiary;[57]
- the principal beneficiary taking an active part in the will instruction meeting;[58]
- the acting of an intermediary between the testator and the draftsman;[59]
- a radical departure from long-established testamentary wishes, particularly when the new will is in favour of someone in a position of trust such a carer; and[60]
- wills in favour of those who stand in other positions of trust (or members of their close family).[61]

In *Hawes v Burgess*,[62] it was found that a daughter was the 'controlling force' behind the will; she chose the solicitor, made the appointment for her mother, remained in the instruction meeting, and supplied information to the draftsman. She was also present at the execution of the will; a will which the testatrix had not had the opportunity to read and check in advance. These circumstances required affirmative proof of knowledge and approval (which was not forthcoming). The above are only examples of suspicious circumstances and many other factors, or combinations of factors, can excite the suspicion of the court. None of these circumstances are of themselves conclusive and all could be removed with sufficient evidence to the contrary.

that should be treated as exciting suspicion in relation to knowledge and approval' at [45]; an allegation of want of knowledge and approval is not to be used 'as a screen behind which one man is to be at liberty to charge another with fraud or dishonesty without assuming the responsibility for that in plain terms' *Re R* [1950] All ER 117 at 123.

55 *Wintle v Nye* [1959] 1 WLR 284 at 291; *Fuller v Strum* [2002] WTLR 199; *Boudh v Bodh* [2008] WTLR 411; *Re Wilson, Turner v Pythian* [2013] WTLR 899.

56 *Barry v Butlin* (1838) 2 Moo PC 480 at 481; *Wintle v Nye* [1959] 1 WLR 284 (see <http://www.alrc.gov.au/news-media/2011-2012/lament-lost-footnotes-legal-history> for an entertaining pen portrait of the plaintiff); *Re Rowinska, Wyniczenko v Plucinska-Surowka* [2005] WTLR 487; *Franks v Sinclair* [2007] WTLR 439.

57 *Fulton v Andrews* (1875) 7 HL 448; *Re Ticehurst, Midland Bank Executor & Trustee Company Ltd v Hankinson* (1973) *The Times* 6 March; *Reynolds v Reynolds* [2005] EWHC 6; *Pearce v Beverley* [2014] WTLR 85 (where the testator was a vulnerable person); *Richards v Allan* [2001] WTLR 1031.

58 *Hawes v Burgess* [2013] WTLR 453 CA; *Pearce v Beverley* [2014] WTLR 85.

59 *Sifri v Clough & Willis* [2007] WTLR 1453; *Re Key, Key v Key* [2010] WTLR 623.

60 *Re Gallagher* [2008] EWHC 3449 (Ch); *Devas v Mackay* [2009] EWHC 1951 (Ch); *Re Rowinska, Wyniczenko v Plucinska-Surowka* [2005] WTLR 487; *Tociapski v Tociapski* [2013] WTLR 1821.

61 *Re Jones* [1928] P 162; *Franks v Sinclair* [2007] WTLR 439; *Ramacoomarsingh v The Administrator General* [2003] WTLR 291 PC; *Cushway & Elliot v Harris* [2012] EWHC 2273 (Ch) (where the draftsman was a solicitor and the nephew of two aunts, neither of whom could read their wills. The wills were set aside and the judge referred the file to the Director of Public Prosecutions).

62 [2013] WTLR 453 CA at [62]–[64].

In *Hoff v Atherton*,[63] Chadwick LJ set out his observations on the importance of a 'failing mind' when considering knowledge and approval: **5.22**

> Further, it may well be that where there is evidence of a failing mind and—*a fortiori*, where evidence of a failing mind is coupled with the fact that the beneficiary has been concerned in the instructions for the will—the court will require more than proof that the testator knew the contents of the document which he signed. If the court is to be satisfied that the testator did know and approve the contents of his will—that is to say, that he did understand what he was doing and its effect—it may require evidence that the effect of the document was explained, that the testator did know the extent of his property and that he did comprehend and appreciate the claims on his bounty to which he ought to give effect. But that is not because the court has doubts as to the testator's capacity to make a will. It is because the court accepts that the testator was able to understand what he was doing and its effect at the time when he signed the document, but needs to be satisfied that he did, in fact, know and approve the contents—in the wider sense to which I have referred.

This indicates that he considered understanding to be an element of knowledge and approval and certainly merely knowing what is there is insufficient.

Reading over a will to establish knowledge and approval

Where a will has been professionally prepared for a testator and read over to him before signing there will be a strong presumption that the testator knew and approved of its contents.[64] The position will be similar where the will was not read over by the solicitor but instead read through by the testator, provided that he read through it properly and did not merely glance at it.[65] **5.23**

Where affirmative proof of knowledge and approval is required, it can be provided by evidence that the will has been read over to the testator. This is of particular help where a testator is illiterate, blind, or very infirm. Where this is to be done, the will should be read over in a helpful way with explanations and questions to establish knowledge and approval of the terms.[66] Where a will has been read over to the testator by the draftsman there is a strong presumption that it was executed with knowledge and approval. Such a presumption can be rebutted and therefore does not of itself amount to proof of knowledge and approval.[67] However, 'in order to establish knowledge and approval of a will by a testator, more is required than "merely establishing that the testator executed it in the presence of a witness after it had been read to or by him".'[68] **5.24**

---

[63] [2005] WTLR 99 at [64] (also [65]D) applied in *Schrader v Schrader* [2013] WTLR 701.

[64] *Gill v Woodall* [2011] WTLR 251 CA.

[65] *Garnett-Botfield v Garnett-Botfield* [1901] P 335; *Franks v Sinclair* [2007] WTLR 439 at [39] '. . . of little significance as on any basis she did no more than scan the will'.

[66] *Buckenham v Dickenson* [2000] WTLR 1083; *Fulton v Andrew* (1875) LR 7 HL.

[67] *Gill v Woodall* [2011] WTLR 251; *Catling v Catling* [2014] EWHC 180 (Ch).

[68] *Nicholson v Knaggs* [2009] VSC 64 at [387].

5.25 In *Franks v Sinclair*[69] an elderly testatrix, Mrs Franks, had made several wills over a period of time. She had left little or nothing to her son under these wills and she had been on poor terms with him for some time. In 1994 a new will was prepared by the son (who had not prepared the previous wills), a solicitor. The son prepared the new will and took it to his mother. He was accompanied by another solicitor from his firm and a secretary.

5.26 The will was read over carefully and slowly in front of the two witnesses and Mrs Franks signed it without any significant comment. The residuary clause did not name, but merely described, the residuary legatees. The son took the original will back to his office (he did not leave a copy with his mother) and once the new will was prepared he destroyed his notes of the meeting. It was found that the will lacked knowledge and approval.[70]

5.27 The judge made strong points about the manner in which the will was read over.

- Of the verbatim reading over of the will:

  > I think it very unlikely that Mrs Franks understood the effect of clause 8 just as a result of it being read out loud to her. It is expressed in the customary language of wills, which most laypeople will find impenetrable and many may consider to be gobble-degook. There is a long preamble of the administration trusts before one reaches the principle gift, which refers only to 'children' without any names, and is then followed by the dense language of the *per stirpes* substitutional gift.[71]

- Had Mr Franks' intention been that the will would have been understood by Mrs Franks then that would have been more likely to be achieved by a different approach.

  > In my judgement, this reading over of the will was something of a performance, designed to establish the validity of the will in a formal sense, rather than to make sure that Mrs Franks clearly understood what she was signing. If that had been Mr Franks' intention, it would have been more easily and more obviously been accomplished by an explanation of the provisions in terms which Mrs Franks could clearly understand... In my judgement, the reading of the will cannot be relied on as establishing Mrs Franks' knowledge and approval of its terms.[72]

- The judge further observed:

  > One of the duties of a solicitor in these circumstances,[73] even if he is the son of the testator, is to discuss and, if appropriate, question the proposed terms of the will, in order that the testator reaches an informed decision.[74]

---

69 [2007] WTLR 439.

70 In a subsequent costs hearing, costs were awarded against the son on the indemnity basis; *Sinclair v Franks (costs)* [2007] WTLR 785.

71 [2007] WTLR 439 at [64] and [65].

72 [2007] WTLR 439 at [63].

73 i.e. where he was to receive a very significant bequest and the new will would disinherit a member of the family with whom he was not even on speaking terms.

74 [2007] WTLR 439 at [85].

Altogether these points contain valuable pointers as to the effectiveness of reading over a will, particularly to an elderly or frail person, including: **5.28**

- simplicity of drafting;
- simplicity of layout in the sense of administrative provisions being placed together at the end, so that reading over addresses the important matters first while the client is likely to have better concentration;
- verbatim reading of a document straight through from beginning to end is not helpful;
- reading a bequest and then pausing to check the testator's understanding is (a) more helpful to the testator and (b) enables the draftsman to more easily assess the testator's understanding; and
- accurately paraphrasing the wording of clauses is helpful, rather than leaving the testator to struggle to understand unfamiliar wording and expressions—which may distract his attention from the effect of the disposition.

Burden of Proof for a Claim of Undue Influence for a Will

For a claim of undue influence in connection with a will proof of actual undue influence is required. There is no presumption of undue influence in regard to a will and it is necessary to show that the facts of a case are inconsistent with any other hypothesis than that of undue influence (see Chapter 4). The burden then is on the challenger to the will. By the usual nature and circumstances of undue influence, proving undue influence is difficult after the death of the testator.[75] Therefore usually undue influence must be inferred from circumstantial evidence: **5.29**

> It will be a common feature of a large number of undue influence cases that there is no direct evidence of the application of influence. It is of the nature of undue influence that it goes on when no one is looking. That does not stop it being proved. The proof has to come, if at all, from more circumstantial evidence. The allegation is a serious one, so evidence necessary to make out the case has to be commensurately stronger, on normal principle.[76]

Where the person alleged to have unduly influenced the testator declines to take part, or file evidence, in the proceedings no adverse inference should be drawn against him by the court.[77] **5.30**

[75] Successful cases in recent years have not been common (the first instance decision in *Gill v Woodall* [2009] EWHC B34 (Ch) where a finding of undue influence was, on appeal, found to be a matter of knowledge and approval). Other recent cases are to be found in the footnotes to this section.

[76] *Schrader v Schrader* [2013] WTLR 701 para 96; a similar approach was used in *In the estate of Killick, Killick v Pountney* [2000] WTLR 41; *Re Zielinski, Korab-Karpinski v Lucas Gardiner* [2007] WTLR 1655; *Re Edwards, Edwards v Edwards* [2007] WTLR 1387 Ch D; *Ark v Kaur* [2010] EWHC 2314 (Ch) at [47].

[77] *Killick v Pountney* [2000] WTLR 41.

Burden of Proof for a Claim of Undue Influence for a Gift

5.31 A claim of undue influence in respect of a gift is significantly different to one made in respect of a will (see Chapter 4).

1. The claim may be based on actual undue influence, in which case the position is as above for the burden of proof for undue influence and a will.
2. The claim may be based on presumed undue influence arising out of the relationship between donor and donee and the nature of the gift. The burden of proof, that a relationship is one where it could be presumed that undue influence arises, lies with the person claiming it.[78] However, there are established classes of relationship where it is accepted by the court that undue influence will be presumed without requiring anything further from the claimant about the relationship.
3. In both cases, having established that the relationship is one where undue influence is presumed, it should be shown that the transaction is one which calls for an explanation.[79] If the explanation is not forthcoming, the burden then shifts to the donee to prove that the court should not apply the presumption to the transaction at issue. In this context it is insufficient to show that the donor understood what he was doing and intended to do it. It must be shown that his actions were independent.[80]

Standard of Proof

5.32 The standard of proof applied to all of the above is the civil standard, i.e. the balance of probabilities.[81]

---

78 *Nel v Keen* [2003] WTLR 501 at [100] and [101].

79 '...provided the transaction itself is one that calls for an explanation and is not satisfactorily explained' *Thompson v Foy* [2009] EWHC 1076 (Ch) at [100]; *Evans v Lloyd* [2013] 1137 at [41]; *Turkey v Awadh* [2006] WTLR 553 CA at [15].

80

> If on the evidence the transaction cannot so be explained—that is to say, the transaction calls for an explanation and that explanation is not forthcoming—the burden then shifts to the claimant to show that in fact, and despite the terms and nature of the agreement, he did not in truth abuse the position that he held. He would normally discharge that burden—as, for instance, now at least occurs in husband and wife cases—by showing that the defendant entered into the matter with his will fully unconstrained, usually with the benefit of independent legal advice.
>
> *Turkey v Awadh* at [2006] WTLR 553 [15] per Buxton LJ.

Hammond v Osborn [2002] WTLR 1125 CA; *Inche Noriah v Shaik Allie Bin Omar* [192] AC 127 PC; *Evans v Lloyd* [2013] 1137 at [38]; *BCCI v Aboody* [1989] 1 QB 923 at 967E–F.

81 *Fuller v Strum* [2002] WTLR 199 CA at [65] and [70]; *Re Parsons, Borman v Lel* [2002] WTLR 237 as opposed to the criminal standard of beyond reasonable doubt.

[72] Where the matters in issue are facts the standard of proof required in non-criminal proceedings is the preponderance of probability, usually referred to as the balance of probability…

[73] The balance of probability standard means that a court is satisfied an event occurred if the court considers that, on the evidence, the occurrence of the event was more likely than not. When assessing the probabilities the court will have in mind as a factor, to whatever extent is appropriate in the particular case, that the more serious the allegation the less likely it is that the event occurred and, hence, the stronger should be the evidence before the court concludes that the allegation is established on the balance of probability.[82]

Application of this standard to capacity, undue influence, and knowledge and approval issues allows for a degree of flexibility, as may be appropriate in the circumstances, to meet the seriousness of the claim. **5.33**

> [T]his does not mean that where a serious allegation is in issue the standard of proof required is higher. It means only that the inherent probability or improbability of the event is itself a matter to be taken into account when weighing the probabilities and deciding whether, on balance, the event occurred. The more improbable the event, the stronger must be the evidence that it did occur before, on the balance of probability, its occurrence will be established.[83]

and

> This approach also provides a means by which the balance of probability standard can accommodate one's instinctive feeling that even in civil proceedings a court should be more sure before finding serious allegations proved than when deciding less serious or trivial matters.[84]

This is a process that has been described as proceeding 'with caution' and being 'vigilant'.[85] There has been some criticism of Lord Nicholls' views (above), notably by Baroness Hale in *Re B*,[86] 'Lord Nicholls' nuanced explanation left room for the nostrum "the more serious the allegation, the more cogent the evidence needed to prove it"' but her concerns were in an area outside of that of wills. **5.34**

Earlier in *In Re Dellow's Will Trusts*[87] this approach was similarly described as: 'The more serious the allegation the more cogent is the evidence required to overcome the unlikelihood of what is alleged and thus to prove it.' Likewise in *Wintle v Nye*:[88] 'In all cases the court must be vigilant and jealous. The degree of suspicion will vary with **5.35**

---

82 *Re H (Minors) (Sexual Abuse Standard of Proof)* [1995] UKHL 16 at per Lord Nicholls.

83 *Re H (Minors) (Sexual Abuse Standard of Proof)* [1995] UKHL 16 at [74] per Lord Nicholls; *Ali Heyder v Syed* [2014] WTLR 387; *Fuller v Strum* [2002] WTLR 199 CA; *Killick v Poutney* [2000] WTLR 41.

84 *Re H (Minors) (Sexual Abuse Standard of Proof)* [1995] UKHL 16 at [75] per Lord Nicholls.

85 *Re Parsons, Borman v Lel* [2002] WTLR 237.

86 *In re B (Children) (FC)* [2008] UKHL 35.

87 [1964] 1 WLR 451 at 455 per Ungoed Thomas J.

88 [1959] 1 WLR 284.

the circumstances of the case. It may be slight and easily dispelled. It may, on the other hand, be so grave it can hardly be dispelled'. In *Re Edwards*,[89] a claim of undue influence, because of the seriousness of such an allegation, the evidence needed to meet the standard of proof was described as 'compelling'.

5.36 *Re Good*[90] provides an example of this standard when considering a claim of undue influence: 'In my view, the wholesale overbearing of a testator's will by coercion is an inherently more improbable event...and I bear that in mind in assessing whether, on the evidence, the defendants have discharged the burden of proving coercion.'

5.37 In *Franks v Sinclair* there was comment on the assessment of evidence given by the draftsman of a will under which he took benefit. The judge set out two key considerations in evaluating its worth—the probability of the events described and the credibility of the witness. 'Probability here means the likelihood, assessed against the background facts, that Mrs Franks would have given the contested instructions. Mr Franks' credibility as a witness is to be assessed by reference to the totality of the evidence. The importance of his credibility increases to the extent that the contested instructions are found to be unlikely.'[91]

[89] *Re Edwards, Edwards v Edwards* [2007] WTLR 1387 at [2].

[90] *Re Good, Carapeto v Good* [2002] WTLR 801 AT [125] Per Rimer J; *Schomberg v Taylor* [2013] WTLR 1413 at [31].

[91] [2007] WTLR 439 at [71].

6

THE ROLE OF THE DRAFTSMAN

The role that the draftsman has to play in questions of testamentary capacity is complex, and has become more so in recent years. It is also of central importance[1] in any challenges to validity. **6.01**

Evidence of the Draftsman

The court views the evidence of the draftsman as being of great importance in its decision making for questions of capacity: **6.02**

a. The Court of Appeal in *Hawes v Burgess*[2] expressed strong support for the views of the will draftsman as to the testator's capacity:

> My concern is that the courts should not too readily upset, on the grounds of mental capacity, a will that has been drafted by an experienced independent lawyer. If, as here, an experienced lawyer has been instructed and has formed the opinion from a meeting or meetings that the testatrix understands what she is doing, the will so drafted and executed should only be set aside on the clearest evidence of lack of mental capacity.

The authors of *Theobald on Wills* are critical of this view, noting that there have been more than a few cases where solicitor-prepared wills have been held invalid on grounds of want of capacity. 'That is itself a good reason why the Court of Appeal's confidence in the ability of laypeople to detect mental incapacity is, the

[1] See also Chapter 2 on the duty to assess a testator's capacity.

[2] [2013] WTLR 453 per Mummery LJ at paragraph 60. This is not a new approach; see *Birkin v Wing* (1890) 111 LT 273 for the preferring of the solicitor's evidence to a doctor's. '... the courts, particularly where suspicious circumstances exist, are extremely receptive of the evidence of the careful solicitor'; 'Solicitor's Liability for Failure to Substantiate Testamentary Capacity' by Litman and Robertson *The Canadian Bar Review* December 1984 (62 CBR 457).

authors suggest, misplaced.'[3] We believe that there is much merit in this view and that the views in *Burgess* may have been too strongly put,[4] with regard to the last sentence in the view of Mummery LJ (above). The value of the solicitor's evidence remains, but it can, and is, not followed where the medical evidence is stronger. The view in *Re Ashkettle* (below) does much to counterbalance this and in our view put forward a more realistic position.

b. In *Re Ashkettle*[5] it was commented that:

> I accept the wisdom of [Mummery LJ's] comments though I observe that they do not go so far as to suggest that, in every case, the evidence of an experienced and independent solicitor will, without more, be conclusive. Any view the solicitor may have formed as to the testator's capacity *must be shown to be based on a proper assessment and accurate information or it is worthless*; and (as Mummery LJ acknowledges) the terms of the will may themselves suggest that the solicitor's assessment was not soundly based.[6]

This has a most welcome emphasis on how the draftsman's role is to be undertaken. The use of the strong word 'worthless' indicates well the true value of the draftsman's work when no proper judgement has been exercised at the meetings with the client.

c. In *Scammell v Farmer*:[7] '...I have the unchallenged evidence of an experienced solicitor who witnessed the new will and, appreciative of the need to ascertain that [the testatrix] had capacity, satisfied himself that she clearly did have that

---

[3] *Theobald on Wills* First Supplement to the 17th edn.

[4] See also Barbara Rich 'Aspects of Capacity' *ACTAPS newsletter* 174, May 2014, pp 18–19 for criticism of the view in *Burgess*.

[5] [2013] WTLR 1331 (per Christopher Pymont QC sitting as deputy judge)—n.b. authors' added emphasis. *Jeffrey v Jeffrey* [2013] WTLR 1509 at [112] *et seq.* for the support of contemporaneous notes to the solicitor's witness statement.

[6] This point follows remarks earlier in *Brown v Deacy* [2002] WTLR 781 at 790H.

> I am also not prepared to rely on [the draftsman's] assessment of Mrs Mott's testamentary capacity. It is wholly unclear on what basis he reached that assessment. If it is based on a few minutes' conversation...with an elderly lady he had never met before, the assessment is of little value. It is well known that elderly people are often adept at concealing mental impairment from strangers behind a façade of normal social behaviour.

Similarly in *Nicholson v Knaggs* [2009] VSC 64 at [664]:

> A considered and appropriately structured interview with the testatrix was also called for to ensure that Mrs Dyke had testamentary capacity at the time. In particular two enquiries ought to have been pursued. The first was to establish whether there was any rational basis for the significant reductions proposed in the gift structure of the new will. A second line of enquiry should have been directed to ensuring that Betty Dyke comprehended the nature and extent of her estate. This was an essential step in determining whether or not this elderly person had testamentary capacity. However this was neither done nor attempted...

[7] [2008] WTLR 1261; see also *Barrett v Kasprzyk* (unreported 3 July 2000) and the preference given to the evidence of the experienced legal executive; *Eady v Waring* (1974) 43 DLR (3rd) 667 'my conclusions fly in the face of the testimony of the doctor...but in my view...his observations and conclusions are limited.'

capacity.[8] It would require some persuasive evidence to the contrary to undermine that opinion...'

d. In *Williams v Wilmot*[9] after outlining the solicitor's evidence as to his conclusion as to his client's incapacity, the judge observed: 'The significance of this for these purposes is this: [he] is an experienced private client solicitor with particular knowledge and expertise in the area of testamentary capacity in relation to the elderly derived from practical experience over many years in practice as a solicitor.' The judge accepted that this corroborated the medical expert's view and it assisted the court in concluding that capacity was absent.[10]

These views of the court place a heavy burden on the draftsman to carry out his role correctly, as it is apparent that not much weight will attach to his evidence if the draftsman has carried out his work poorly.[11] In addition, where the work of the draftsman falls well below the standard that the court expects from a draftsman, he may be criticized for his performance[12] and have potential liability for losses, particularly costs, arising from his defaults. **6.03**

Recording information

What transpired at the will instruction meeting and at the execution of the will are central to later challenges to the will. In *Ledger v Wootton*[13] the firm who drafted the will had neither will file nor record of the instructions. The draftsman had no recollection of the preparation of the will, nor did the witnesses from that firm recollect the execution of the will. The will was made approximately ten years before death. While that position did not attract criticism from the court it did give rise to a significant hole in the possible evidence for the validity of the will. Much that is involved in will disputes is factual, and the better and fuller matters are recorded the more helpful this is to the court in establishing what the facts of the matter are. Accurate and full attendance notes will help the court.[14] Considering the following, the manner in which these matters is recorded is important. **6.04**

---

[8] The solicitor was so clear that the testatrix had capacity that he did not seek medical evidence, as he said he would have usually done if there was any doubt.

[9] [2013] WTLR 1291.

[10] The will that was found to be invalid was in favour of a carer who did not choose to defend the action.

[11] *Sprackling v Sprackling* [2009] WTLR 897; *Re Key, Key v Key* [2010] WTLR 623; *Martin v Triggs Turner Bartons* [2009] WTLR 1339; *Winefield v Clarke* [2008] NSWSC 882.

[12] *Re Key, Key v Key* [2010] WTLR 623.

[13] [2008] WTLR 235 at [12].

[14] *Minns v Foster* unreported Chancery 13 December 2002 at [26] '[The solicitor] was a meticulous maker of attendance notes, which have proved to be of considerable assistance.'

Scott v Cousins (2001) 37 ETR (2nd) 113 (Ontario Supreme Court of Justice) at [70] per Cullity J 'In my experience, careful solicitors who are in doubt on the question of capacity... will supervise the execution of the will while taking, and retaining, comprehensive notes of their observations on the question.'

- Where there is a serious dispute as to the validity of the will, in all probability there will be a *Larke v Nugus*[15] request for information sent to the draftsman. This is more easily and accurately[16] dealt with if there are adequate attendance notes, etc.
- Attendance notes are inherently more credible if they are as near to contemporaneous as they can be. A long delay in preparation can diminish their value.[17]
- Lack of attendance notes can not only draw the ire of the court[18] but also lead to a court drawing an adverse inference against the solicitor.[19] Partial, or incomplete, attendance notes raise similar issues.[20]

To assist with this

- Appendix 1 contains an observation sheet to help record potentially useful information about the testator. Not all of the observations listed will apply in every case, but completing information where it is applicable could assist a later review by an expert witness. Completing the relevant sections will also help the draftsman to review his impressions of the testator.
- Appendix 2 contains a specimen attendance note with commentary on areas that can be of importance.

Eady v Waring (1974) 43 DLR (3rd) 667 at 675 'The law imposes a heavy burden on a solicitor confronted with [suspicious circumstances] and the conduct of his inquiries and responses thereto must be minutely surveyed to divine from the vantage point of hindsight how free and unfettered was the mind of the testator.'

When a client's capacity is in doubt: A Practical Guide for Solicitors (New South Wales Law Society, 2009) contains the direction 'It is fundamental that solicitors take thorough, comprehensive and contemporaneous file notes of any consultation with clients where capacity is in issue or where the solicitor is exploring this issue through questioning and by observing the client. These notes will be invaluable if the issue of capacity is subsequently raised in legal proceedings where the question of the client's mental capacity is challenged.'

Sharp v Adam [2006] WTLR 1059 at [25] the solicitor 'made meticulous notes'.

[15] *Re Moss, Larke v Nugus* [2000] WTLR 1033 CA; see later in this chapter for more on this issue.

[16] Remembering that *Larke v Nugus* is actually about providing witness statements and therefore there must be consistency between the answers to a *Larke v Nugus* letter and any eventual witness statement.

[17] *Killick v Pountney* [2000] WTLR 41; *Re Parsons, Borman v Lel* [2002] WTLR 237 at 246H; see Chapter 7 for comment on will instruction forms.

[18] *Re Key, Key v Key* [2010] WTLR 623 at [6] '... without even making an attendance note of his meeting ... at which the instructions were taken'; *In the Estate of Thompson deceased, Thompson v Watton* [2003] NIFam 3 at [5] Girvan J was critical of the solicitor's failure to keep an attendance note in relation to execution, failing to check on earlier wills, failing to ask about the value of land, and failing to ask about medical history (which included the testator's admission on several occasions to mental institutions).

[19] *Low Ah Cheow v Ng Hock Guan* (2009) 3 SLR(R) (Singapore CA) 'we draw adverse inference against [the solicitor] for failing to keep proper attendance notes recording fully and accurately the Testator's instructions as to how the will was to be drawn up', per V K Rajah JA.

[20] *Sprackling v Sprackling* [2009] WTLR 897.

Failing to meet with the client will make it difficult for the draftsman to **6.05**

- form a proper view as to capacity;[21]
- judge the level of urgency in the individual case; and[22]
- provide useful and accurate evidence to the court (which may well cause the conduct of the draftsman to be criticized by the court).[23]

Medical advice

It is clearly established that old age is a factor of urgency in the will preparation process.[24] Whilst not exclusively a problem of old age, testamentary capacity issues are more often encountered with the elderly. Therefore the practitioner is faced with **6.06**

a. attempting to deal with the whole process expeditiously; and
b. managing any medical advice necessary.

The first of these is a factor in all wills but, generally speaking, completing the matter in shorter times for the elderly is necessary.[25] The management of time where there are possible capacity issues remains a substantial practical challenge for the draftsman and, in order to ensure control of this, clear policies on time should be created for any firm involved in this work.[26]

There is no legal requirement that medical advice as to capacity must be obtained for all elderly clients.[27] Much will depend upon the view that the draftsman has formed through his proper contact with the client.[28] The views of others, not medically qualified, must be treated with care by the draftsman, particularly where they might have a financial interest in the question of capacity.[29] The draftsman should not attempt to draw any conclusion as to the testator's capacity without meeting him and forming his own view unless documentary evidence fully demonstrates the position.[30] **6.07**

[21] *Feltham v Freer Bouskell* [2013] WTLR 1363: '[The solicitor] accepted instructions to act for [the testatrix] in relation to her desire to change her will. He did so subject to the requirement to satisfy himself that she was of sufficient mental capacity to alter her will.' See also 2.59 et seq.

[22] See 7.09 et seq.

[23] There are occasions where the solicitor's evidence is well recollected and of value to the court despite the lack of attendance notes (see *Pearce v Beverley* [2014] WTLR 85 at [35]). However, even in such cases the value of the evidence would be strengthened by documentary support.

[24] *White v Jones* [1995] 1 All ER 691 and its subsequent applications; see Chapter 7.

[25] See, for example, Neuberger J (as he then was) in *X v Woollcombe Yonge* [2001] WTLR 301 or Chadwick LJ in *Carr-Glynn v Frearsons* [1998] 4 All ER 225.

[26] See Chapter 7 on Risk Management.

[27] The Golden Rule is not a rule, see 6.13 et seq; on the draftsman's duty to check capacity see also Chapter 2.

[28] *Scammell v Farmer* [2008] WTLR 1261; *Wharton v Bancroft* [2012] WTLR 693; *Hawes v Burgess* [2013] WTLR 453.

[29] *Feltham v Freer v Bouskell* [2013] WTLR 1363.

[30] *Feltham v Freer v Bouskell* [2013] WTLR 1363.

6.08 Where it is useful to obtain medical advice, the draftsman should instruct the medical practitioner himself in order to ensure that the medical practitioner

a. is aware of what is required;[31]
b. has explained to him what the test of testamentary capacity is; and
c. is aware of the urgency and importance of his report (and the importance to the testator/patient).

Appendix 3 has an example of a standard letter of instruction for a medical practitioner.

6.09 Before a medical practitioner can be instructed, the testator's consent to the examination and the disclosure of information is needed. The testator may regard such a thing as unnecessary or intrusive, but it is in his interests to obtain medical evidence to support the will. The possibility that the report might deter later challenges has the potential to save the estate much expense. This is a point worth explaining carefully if the testator is reluctant to agree to a medical examination. The requirement of the testator's consent weakens the apparent imperative nature of the Golden Rule ('always').[32]

6.10 A major issue for the practitioner is that although the testator's GP is the normal choice for advice on capacity, GPs generally may lack the expertise to give a view particularly concerning the more complex mental illnesses. At first instance in *Re Perrins*[33] Lewison J (as he then was) observed

> Dr Gross stressed that the assessment of a person's cognitive capability is a task of great difficulty. He suggested that a medical practitioner such as a specialist MS liaison nurse or a GP might not be capable of the task, which could only be adequately undertaken by a specialist neurologist. Even for a specialist neurologist the determination of testamentary capacity was, in his view, a very difficult exercise. I may say that his evidence cast considerable doubt on the medical validity of the so-called golden rule…

There is really nothing surprising about this view. Lord Cranworth's remark,[34] about the difficulty of identifying when twilight becomes darkness, is still very true. The

---

31

> [T]he doctor who undertakes the task of assessing testamentary capacity MUST understand what tests to administer and MUST produce a clear and concise report…It is fatal for a doctor to assess a patient as capable without the 'task specific' questions having been administered and further to produce a report which shows a failure to appreciate the task which he (apparently) undertook.
>
> *Contentious Probate Claims* Francis and Martin (Sweet & Maxwell, 2003)

32 Or Rimer J's suggestion in *In re Morris, The Special Trustees for Great Ormond Street Hospital for Children v Rushin* [2001] WTLR 1137 that the solicitor should 'insist'.

33 *Re Perrins, Perrins v Holland* [2009] WTLR 1387 at [59].

34 See 1.20.

assistance practitioners might enlist to help them has become more specialized as the knowledge of the mind and its diseases becomes more detailed and more generalist knowledge can become less helpful.

The court has expressed the view that it 'could not be an answer to a claim of negli- **6.11**
gence against [the solicitor] for him to say that he could not proceed until he heard from the doctor—it was part of his obligation to chase him up, or if [the doctor] did not respond promptly, to instruct another doctor.'[35] This raises the issue of what is a reasonable time to allow before chasing the doctor or withdrawing the instructions? There is only limited assistance from reported cases, although in *Feltham v Freer Bouskell* the judgment is clear that times will be dependent upon the specific circumstances of each testator.[36] This places the onus on the draftsman to monitor time and judge, in the light of the testator's age and state of health, when is reasonable. Quite clearly this is a point that benefits from being clarified and agreed with the medical practitioner at the outset.

The draftsman, when he seeks a medical report, should give careful consideration as **6.12**
to the choice of medical practitioner.[37]

General practitioner. Most often, the general practitioner, who the testator is registered with, will be the first choice. Where the GP has treated the testator for some time, he should have existing knowledge. His familiarity with the testator's medical history ought to make assessment easier (and quicker).

Where the GP has had little or no previous contact with the testator these advantages will be lost. The GP may be less ready to undertake an assessment, particularly if he is inexperienced, or lacks knowledge, of this area.

Similar issues might arise with group practices where there has been no consistent treatment by the same GP or where a locum is covering for absence or retirement.

The GP who has close personal links with the testator and his family may feel inhibited from preparing a report.[38]

Where the mental capacity of the testator is a particularly complex issue and/or the estate is of high value the GP may be less appropriate to provide a report. In such circumstances it is important that the GP's file is made available to the consultant.

35 *Feltham v Freer Bouskell* [2013] WTLR 1363 at paragraph [55]; while this is probably common sense, it is the first time that a court has expressed this view so explicitly.

36 *Feltham v Freer Bouskell* [2013] WTLR 1363 at paragraph [78] 'What constitutes a reasonable period of time is case specific' and in this case 10 days was thought appropriate for when the solicitor should have chased the doctor for a report (the client was aged 90 and in a nursing home).

37 See also Chapter 15 for points against using a General Practitioner.

38 The draftsman should also be checking in these circumstances that there is no bequest to the GP as his involvement in assessing capacity should then be avoided.

Consultants. Where the testator is in hospital, the consultant in charge of him would appear to be the person best qualified to express a view as to capacity, particularly where the illness being treated is relevant to capacity. The consultant may be less willing to assist if his area of specialization has little or no relevance to capacity, although any medical practitioner should be able to assess mental capacity if properly instructed.

The Golden Rule

6.13 Templeman J (as he was then) in *Re Simpson*[39] observed:

> In the case of an aged testator or a testator who has suffered a serious illness, there is one golden rule which should always be observed, however straightforward matters may appear and however difficult or tactless[40] it may be to suggest that precautions be taken: the making of a will by such a testator ought to be witnessed or approved by a medical practitioner who satisfied himself of the capacity and understanding of the testator, and records and preserves his examination and finding.
>
> There are other precautions which should be taken. If the testator has made an earlier will this should be considered by the legal and medical advisers of the testator, and if appropriate, discussed with the testator. The instructions of the testator should be taken in the absence of anyone who may stand to benefit, or who may have influence over the testator. These are not counsels of perfection. If proper precautions are not taken injustice may result or be imagined and great expense and misery may be unnecessarily caused.

6.14 This statement sets out separate requirements of the medical practitioner and draftsman.[41]

1. The medical practitioner
   - *witness or approve of the 'making' of the will*. There are two separate elements here. The witnessing of the will by the medical practitioner would not take place unless he accepts that the testator has capacity.[42] In practice however, many medical practitioners may be reluctant to act as a witness. Where a medical practitioner does witness the execution of the will, it should provide better evidence as to capacity at the time of execution.[43] Approval of the will is not a moral approval of its dispositions but is the approval, on the grounds

[39] (1977) 121 Sol Jo 224, better recorded at (1977) 127 NLJ 487 Templeman J had earlier made similar comments and had described them as 'the golden if tactless rule' *Kenward v Adams* (1975) *The Times*, 29 November. Advice to similar effect is to be found in *Pates v Craig, the Estate of the late Joyce Jean Cole* [1995] NSWSC 87 [147].

[40] In *Tchiligirian v Ouzounian* [2003] WTLR 709 it was observed of this that 'All too frequently, of course, it is tact which prevails in practice.'

[41] Although this rule was originally expressed in the context of a solicitor taking instructions, there would seem to be little doubt that it is not limited to solicitors.

[42] For an example see *Re Boyes deceased* [2013] EWHC 4027 (Ch).

[43] But is not, of course, a guarantee of capacity; *Sharp v Adam* [2006] WTLR 1059.

of capacity, of the act itself taking place. This may have some potential for a degree of approval of the dispositions themselves on the basis of the third limb of *Banks v Goodfellow*.[44]

- *satisfy himself that the testator has sufficient capacity*. This is a process, a precursor to the point above, involving an assessment of the client, or, where the testator is currently being treated by the practitioner, a report based on current medical assessments.
- *record his examination and conclusion as to capacity in writing and retain it*. In the event of urgent wills the draftsman may have no option, on the grounds of time, but to act on a verbal agreement from the medical practitioner. Where this is necessary the medical practitioner should write up the verbal advice that he has given (as should the solicitor for the advice he received). In all other circumstances, the opinion should be in writing prior to the execution of the will. Given the time element some practitioners prepare the will in advance, if they have instructions, to save time once the report is received.[45]
- *consider the previous will(s) and if 'appropriate' discuss it with the testator*. This is less clear; the only worthwhile consideration of the previous will would appear to be in the context of identifying what the wishes of the testator were. This would then enable consideration of the capacity of the testator from the point of view of the second and third limbs of *Banks v Goodfellow*. It would also enable consideration of the testator's ability to understand why the changes to the dispositions were being made.[46]

2. The draftsman
    - *instruct the medical practitioner*. There is no direction to instruct a medical practitioner, but it is implicit in the statement of the Rule that where this is done it must be the draftsman who does so. Without the draftsman initiating and controlling the process it is doubtful if the medical practitioner will be properly instructed and time will not be managed.[47]
    - *consider the findings*. The Rule as stated does not mention the need for the draftsman to consider the medical report. However, as a matter of common sense it must be seen by the draftsman in order to establish if he can proceed with the will. There is no suggestion in the Rule, as stated, that the draftsman has any discretion to accept or reject the report's conclusions. Given that the aim of the rule is to prevent wills being prepared where capacity is absent, it is unreasonable that the professional judgement of the draftsman should be suspended in this regard, and where the report is deficient the draftsman

[44] See Chapter 2.

[45] There is of course the risk that in the event of an adverse report the cost of the will may be written off.

[46] Although the recent Court of Appeal judgment in *Simon v Byford* [2014] EWCA Civ 280 appears to be in conflict with the Golden Rule in doubting the need to recollect the terms of the previous will.

[47] *Feltham v Freer Bouskell* [2013] WTLR 1363.

could proceed against the medical advice, only where he has strong grounds to do so.

- *consider the previous will(s) and if 'appropriate' discuss it with the testator.* See the remarks above on this point for the medical practitioner.

Observations on the Golden Rule

6.15 This is not a rule of law, despite its name; it is a guide to good practice.

- The later views of the court on this Rule have made this point clear.
  - '[T]oo briefly reported to be of much assistance, contains prudent guidance for solicitors and does not purport to lay down the law.'[48]
  - '[N]ot itself a touchstone of validity and is not a substitute for the established tests of capacity and knowledge and approval.'[49]
  - 'It is undoubtedly a desirable precaution, and one which can save a great deal of trouble in the future, for a solicitor to observe the golden rule where there is the possibility of dispute as to testamentary capacity. Failure to do so, however, is not determinative; the rule is no more than prudent guidance for a solicitor... Ultimately capacity is a question of fact like any other which the court must decide on the evidence as a whole.'[50]
  - 'Compliance with the Golden Rule does not, of course, operate as a touchstone of the validity of a will, nor does non-compliance demonstrate its invalidity. Its purpose... is to assist in the avoidance of disputes, or at least in the minimisation of their scope.'[51]
- Compliance with the Golden Rule is not proof of capacity, just as non-compliance is not proof of incapacity.[52]
- A draftsman need not follow it where
  - he is satisfied as to his elderly or ill client's capacity;[53]
  - time will not permit it.[54]
- It is foolish to ignore it or be unaware of its significance.[55]
- Where it is not followed, a record of why it was considered and rejected will be useful in the event of later challenge.

[48] *Hoff v Atherton* [2005] WTLR 99 CA.

[49] *Catermole v Prisk* [2006] FLR 697.

[50] *Allen v Emery* [2005] All ER D 175 at [24].

[51] *Re Key, Key v Key* [2010] WTLR 623 at [6]; *Cowderoy v Cranfield* [2011] WTLR 1699 at [137] 'non-compliance with the Golden Rule does not demonstrate a lack of capacity'; *Re Edonya, Knight v Edonya* [2009] EWHC 2181 (Ch) at [74] 'a precaution based on good sense.'

[52] *Sharp v Adam* [2006] WTLR 1059 at [27]; *Buckenham v Dickinson* [2000] WTLR 1093.

[53] *Scammell v Farmer* [2008] WTLR 1261.

[54] *Wharton v Bancroft* [2012] WTLR 693—'His job was to take the will of a dying man. A solicitor so placed cannot simply conjure up a medical attendant.'

[55] *Re Key, Key v Key* [2010] WTLR 623 at [6] 'Failure to comply with... the Golden Rule has greatly increased the difficulties to which this dispute has given rise and aggravated the mistrust into which his client's children have subsequently fallen.'

- Rimer J, in *Re Morris, Special Trustees of the Great Ormond Street Hospital v Rushin*,[56] said of the solicitor that her conduct was 'deplorable'.

> She claimed to have experience of probate matters, and her activities at the meeting on 22 February 1996 were also devoted to Mrs Morris's will. It should have been obvious to her that his was a case in which, in accordance with the guidance of Templeman J in *Re Simpson deceased*... and embarrassing though it might have been to press for it, she should have insisted that some medical assistance was invoked as to Mrs Morris's capacity to enter into this unusual transaction and make the proposed will.

- No reported case can be found where the court has applied the Golden Rule where a will has been prepared by a member of the family, carer, neighbour, etc. Given that this rule is to prevent testators making wills when they are lacking capacity, it is more than a little surprising that the court should accept lower standards where the will may be prompted or drafted by those who stand to gain pecuniary advantage.

To find that meticulous compliance with the Golden Rule should be determinative of a will's validity was a view rejected by the Court of Appeal in *Sharp v Adam*.[57] It is, however, worth considering the remaining comments attached to that view in the judgment: **6.16**

> The opinion of a general practitioner, unimpeachable in itself and supported by that of one or more solicitors, may nevertheless very occasionally be shown by other evidence to be wrong. The golden rule is a rule of solicitors' good practice, not a rule of law giving conclusive status to evidence obtained in compliance with the rule. Nevertheless, where a testator's apparent mental state is observed and recorded at the time when he actually executes the will in complete compliance with the rule and with the care with which it was in the present case; and where professional people concerned reached a properly informed and recorded conclusion that the testator does have testamentary capacity, it will require very persuasive evidence to enable the court to dislodge that conclusion.

This makes it clear that the rule, although merely a statement of good practice, has value, and compliance, where the medical practitioner and solicitor have acted properly, will not often be rejected.[58] Justification of the Golden Rule was offered in *Cowderoy v Cranfield*[59] with the observation that a person who is not medically qualified 'may fail to detect defects in mental capacity which become apparent to a

[56] [2001] WTLR 1137.

[57] *Sharp v Adam* [2006] WTLR 1059 at [27] per May LJ.

[58] However, it was rejected in *Sharp v Adam*. In *Re Ritchie, Ritchie v Joslin* [2009] EWHC 709 (Ch), Behrens J found that a delusion prevented the testatrix from having capacity and thereby found against the evidence of the solicitor and GP. He noted at [187] that the doctor based his opinion on a medical examination five weeks earlier on an unrelated medical matter. His assessment was made as to her circumstances and orientation based on his questions. He was not aware that she was intending to cut her children out of her will. He therefore made no formal assessment of testamentary capacity and his assessment was not made in the light of the unusual terms of the will.

[59] [2011] WTLR 1699 at [137].

trained and experienced medical examiner who understood the legal test for testamentary capacity'. A view with which it is difficult to take exception, but the second half of the observation is as important as the first.

6.17 A major difficulty for the practitioner is the inconsistent approach of the court to compliance with the Golden Rule. Non-compliance has been

- used to castigate the draftsman; and[60]
- ignored in litigation.[61]

The Golden Rule is nonetheless an issue that has to be taken seriously and be understood by all draftsmen. It can be followed, or not, depending upon the careful judgement of the draftsman. Reasons for or against following it should be carefully recorded in order that the draftsman's care with the subject can, if necessary, be demonstrated to the court.

6.18 Where the draftsman has met his client to take will instructions he may be faced with one of the following possibilities:[62]

i. *The client is unable to give coherent or satisfactory instructions.*

The draftsman simply cannot proceed with a will.[63] However the meeting should still be written up recording clearly what was observed and the conclusions reached, with reasons as to why he could not proceed. His evidence as to capacity will be relevant in the event that

a. it is later claimed that the client had capacity; or
b. the client obtained a will from another draftsman and that is then challenged on the grounds of capacity.

ii. *The client can give instructions, but the draftsman is sure that the client does not have testamentary capacity.*

The process would be as for (i) above, with the additional of recording the instructions. The draftsman also needs to consider carefully whether or not the meeting falls under description (iii) below and further action is needed. It may be the case that the client is anxious to proceed and is willing to undergo a medical assessment, notwithstanding the draftsman's conclusion. The draftsman would be justified in not proceeding with the will, given his own conclusion, but if the medical report finds that the client has capacity, the draftsman could be acting reasonably in proceeding notwithstanding his doubts. If, despite the medical practitioner's views, the draftsman still believed his own judgement was correct he could be justified in not proceeding. The testator then could try to engage another draftsman.

---

60 *Re Key, Key v Key* [2010] WTLR 623.

61 *Hawes v Burgess* [2013] 453 CA.

62 This section should be read in conjunction with Chapter 7 on risk and control of time.

63 *Feltham v Freer Bouskell* [2013] WTLR 1363 at [53] 'Where a solicitor is instructed to prepare and execute a will for a client if the client does not have mental capacity he has no client and cannot accept instructions.' *Pates v Craig, the Estate of the late Joyce Jean Cole* [1995] NSWSC 87 at [147] 'If after careful consideration of all the circumstances the solicitor is not satisfied that the testator does not have testamentary capacity he should proceed and prepare the will.'

Time is critical during this process. If the client's capacity is borderline it is most unlikely to improve with time and if the client is elderly the court would expect instructions to be dealt with swiftly because of the risk of death or loss of capacity.[64]

iii. *The client can give instructions, but the draftsman is uncertain whether or not the client has capacity.*

The issue for the draftsman is whether or not he can proceed with the instructions. If he cannot form a conclusion as to capacity, the involvement of a qualified medical practitioner is justified in order to assist, as is not proceeding with the will until a positive medical report has been received. The comments in (iii) above apply as to time. The draftsman should have recorded carefully his observations and conclusions in order to be able to provide evidence as to why he reached the conclusion that he did.

iv. *The client can give instructions, and on balance, but recognizing that there may be some factors against capacity, the draftsman is satisfied that the client has capacity.*

Given the draftsman's conclusion, he would be justified in proceeding straightaway without instructing a medical adviser. Introducing delay to comply with the Golden Rule seems unjustified if the draftsman has concluded that the client has capacity. The draftsman should have recorded carefully his observations and conclusions in order to be able to provide evidence as to why he reached the conclusion that he did.

A medical report may assist in the event that the draftsman's judgement might be challenged, but it seems to contradict the draftsman's view of capacity to delay the will for this. Should the client die where there was a delay waiting for a medical report, where the draftsman had concluded for himself there was capacity, this can cause difficulties for the draftsman if there is a *White v Jones* claim.[65] A medical report shortly after the will is prepared and executed could substantially assist in supporting the draftsman's view.

v. *The client can give instructions and the draftsman is satisfied that the client has capacity.*

This will cover most clients, but where the client is old or ill it should not be the case that the draftsman omits to write up his observations relevant to capacity. A later challenge to the will may well require him to give evidence as to his conclusions.

A not uncommon difficulty encountered is the client who wants a new will but, despite advice, refuses a medical examination (or perhaps refuses to pay for one). There is difficulty in this, but it is clarified, at least to some degree, by focussing on the five points immediately above. **6.19**

- If the draftsman considers that his client lacks capacity, then it would seem that he cannot proceed.[66]

---

[64] *White v Jones* [1995] 1 All ER 691.

[65] See Chapter 7 for a commentary on *White v Jones*.

[66] *Re Simpson* (1977) 127 NLJ 487 and *Re Morris* [2001] WTLR 1137 point to the draftsman insisting on a report and declining to act if the client will not agree.

- If the draftsman considers that his client has capacity, to refuse to proceed without the report would suggest that he has decided to terminate his retainer. Whether this would be reasonable or justified is open to doubt. If the draftsman considered that his client had sufficient capacity to engage him to prepare a will, he cannot insist that the client follows his advice. A solicitor has a duty to follow his instructions from his client and not to do so would breach his duty to his client.[67] The solicitor's duty is to advise his client correctly but he cannot force his client to accept the advice.[68] Further, the expenditure required for a medical report cannot be incurred without the authority of the client.

6.20 When considering the instructions the draftsman must exercise judgement as to the full circumstances of the matter. It is not enough that the testator is able to answer

- simple or familiar questions;[69]
- closed questions (i.e. questions that can be answered 'yes' or 'no');[70]
- leading questions (i.e. questions where the words used suggest or lead to the answer).[71]

The draftsman is trying to establish that the instructions come from rational thought.

> But there is no doubt whatever that we may have testamentary incapacity accompanied by a deceptive ability to answer questions of ordinary or usual matters; that is the mind may be incapable of carrying apprehension beyond a limited range of familiar and suggested topics. A 'disposing mind and memory' is one able to comprehend of its own initiative and volition the essential elements of will-making, property, objects, just claims to consideration, revocation of existing dispositions and the like . . . Merely to be able to make rational responses is not enough, nor to repeat a tutored formula of simple terms . . .[72]
>
> By whatever means the solicitor ultimately employs to do it, he must be sure that he is getting something by way of a reasoned answer from his client and not merely, I think, an apparent approval of somebody else's proposition.[73]

---

[67] *Rey v Graham & Oldham* (a firm) [2000] BPIR 354; *Fraser v Gaskell* [2004] PNLR 32.

[68] *Dutfield v Gilbert H Stephens and Sons* [1988] Fam Law 473 'It was not part of his duty to force his advice on his client.'

[69] *Marsh v Tyrell and Harding* (1828) 2 Hagg Ecc R 84 quoting from *Marquess of Winchester's Case* (1598) 6 Co Rep 23a (see 2.01 for quotation).

[70] *Sharp v Adam* [2006] WTLR 1059.

[71] *Buckenham v Dickenson* [2000] WTLR 1083 at 1098F on communication with a frail testator the judge referred to the minimum standards acceptable from the solicitor's conduct (the '*irreducible minima*') and not asking leading questions was part of this minima.

[72] *Leger v Poirier* [1944] SCR 152, at 161/2; citing in support *Marsh v Tyrell and Harding* (1828) 2 Hagg Ecc R 84 at 122:

> It is a great but not uncommon error to suppose that because a person can understand a question put to him, and can give a rational answer to such a question, he is of perfect, sound mind, and is capable of making a will for any purpose whatever; whereas the rule of law, and it is the rule of common sense, is far otherwise; the competency of the mind must be judged of by the nature of the act to be done and from a consideration of all the circumstances of the case.

[73] *Buckenham v Dickenson* [2000] WTLR 1083 at 1098F.

Selection of witnesses

The Golden Rule suggests the involvement of the medical practitioner in the witnessing of the will. While this may often not be possible, the logic in this point is the quality of evidence that the medical practitioner should be able to give about the testator at that time. This logic is worth pursuing a little further when non-medical witnesses are to be used. The use of witnesses who are intelligent and observant should lead to better evidence of the testator's capacity at that time.[74] Safer practice will be to use witnesses who are unconnected with 6.21

- either the principal beneficiaries under the will, or
- those who would take under any previous will (or if known on intestacy)

in order to avoid any suggestion that their evidence may be partial. Witnesses who are prepared to observe carefully and record what they observed about the testator would be particularly useful, especially if their contemporaneous notes could be added to the will file.[75] Their notes should be as far as possible in their own words, with any assistance being restricted to layout, grammar, etc.

Larke v Nugus Enquiries

The relevant time at which capacity will be required by the court to be present for the will to be valid is the time of execution of the will.[76] Usually (but not always) the will will be witnessed by, or executed in the presence of, the will draftsman. Self-evidently the will draftsman will therefore have primary evidence about the capacity of the testator to make a will at the time it was executed. The witnesses to the will may also have relevant evidence about the capacity of a testator to make a will but their role is generally much more passive (absent compliance with the Golden Rule when a medical practitioner is specifically called upon to assess capacity and witness a will). It is the duty of the will draftsman to record questions asked of the testator and the replies of the client together with the will draftsman's assessment of the client's testamentary capacity. Those questions and answers should be preserved as part of the will file. This best practice is clearly set out in Section 2.7.4 of the Law Society's *Wills & Inheritance Protocol*. 6.22

The Solicitors Regulation Authority Code of Conduct 2011 makes it clear that protection of confidential information is a fundamental feature of a solicitor's relationship with a client. It exists as a concept both as a matter of law and as a matter of conduct. This duty continues despite the end of the retainer and even after the death 6.23

[74] *Pates v Craig, the Estate of the late Joyce Jean Cole* [1995] NSWSC 87 at [147] referring to their 'calibre as witnesses if required to testify where the issue of capacity is raised'.
[75] *Pates v Craig, the Estate of the late Joyce Jean Cole* [1995] NSWSC 87 at [147].
[76] See Chapter 3.

of the client.[77] Indicative Behaviour 4.6 of the SRA Code of Conduct shows that the draftsman may not have achieved the required outcomes if he discloses the content of a will on the death of a client unless consent has been provided by the personal representatives for the content to be released. This is the starting principle of professional conduct law and practice. The severity of this position is tempered by the decision in *Larke v Nugus*.[78] Although framed in the original context of a solicitor, this rule will also apply to non-solicitor will preparers.

A word of caution

6.24 The sending of a *Larke v Nugus* letter is often a first step in potential contested probate proceedings, but it should not be sent lightly. The person receiving the letter will usually, quite properly, report the sending of the letter to the executors. Beneficiaries will probably be made aware of a potential claim. The beneficiaries will probably be grieving the loss of a loved one and the thought of potential proceedings can add significantly to distress and grief.

Larke v Nugus: the facts of the case

6.25 This case was finally reported in 2000.[79] The claimants were the executors who sought proof of the will in solemn form. The first claimant[80] was a solicitor and he had prepared the testatrix's last will in 1973, approximately two months before she died. The testatrix was 79 at the time the will was made. Her health was poor and declined during the making of the will. The testatrix died within three months of executing the will.

6.26 The first defendant,[81] a niece of the deceased, made five requests, after the testatrix's death, for a copy of the will and all of her requests were refused. She was concerned about the validity of the will and therefore a caveat was entered. She was a pecuniary legatee (among many) and the residue was left to charity. The controversial part of the will was the bequest of the testatrix's house to her carers. In the initial exchanges of correspondence each of the five requests for a copy of the will were refused—'not for any reason that is at all apparent, other than the unwillingness to allow one beneficiary of the will to know what other beneficiaries there were'.[82]

---

[77] Chapter 4 SRA Code of Conduct 2011.

[78] *Re Moss, Larke v Nugus* [2000] WTLR 1033 CA.

[79] *Re Moss, Larke v Nugus* [2000] WTLR 1033 CA; although judgment was in 1979. In our view the lack of a published law report hampered both awareness of the decision's existence and its correct application.

[80] The second executor died after commencement of the action but before the hearing.

[81] The second defendant died before the trial took place.

[82] [2000] WTLR 1033 p1037A.

The defendant then lodged a caveat. The District Probate Registry raised issues concerning the 'wobbly' signature of the testatrix. In answer to this, a witness to the will (a clerk in the plaintiff's firm[83]) provided an affidavit regarding the execution and stated that the testatrix appeared to have full knowledge and understanding of the contents. In late 1976 the defendant's solicitor requested in the clearest terms a statement of evidence about the execution of the will (and the circumstances surrounding it) together with statements from the two witnesses. The claimant declined to produce these and referred the matter to counsel. **6.27**

The solemn form action for the will to be pronounced valid was initiated by the executors[84] and it eventually came to court in July 1977. The defendant's case was based on both undue influence and a want of knowledge and approval. However, by the time of the hearing, the defendants had not succeeded in getting a statement of evidence from the first defendant concerning the execution of the will, or the instructions and the other surrounding circumstances of the will. **6.28**

Once the court heard evidence from the claimant and his former employee (who had earlier given the statement to the Probate Registrar regarding the execution of the will), the judge expressed grave doubts about the claim of undue influence. The defendant withdrew this claim and shortly afterwards, presumably in the light of the evidence now revealed, dropped all further opposition to the will. Given that the application was for probate in solemn form, the trial had to continue to hear all the evidence as to the validity of the will, as it was not open to the judge to pronounce in such an action without hearing the evidence.[85] In the light of the evidence given, probate was granted and no order was made as to costs. **6.29**

The judge admitted that under normal circumstances the withdrawal of the claim of undue influence would have led to an award of the costs against the defendant. The judge had nothing to substantiate this allegation. However, the want of knowledge and approval claim raised different issues. **6.30**

The judge accepted that the circumstances of the will raised a suspicion that needed to be dispelled. The will left a considerable bequest (the house) to persons on whom the testatrix was dependent.[86] In the light of this it was not unreasonable for the defendant to require satisfactory evidence of the validity of the will. The judge found that the defendant ('somebody having bona fide *locus standi* to dispute a will') should have been provided with a copy. **6.31**

---

83 As was the other witness.

84 By writ in July 1974.

85 A will cannot be pronounced in solemn form merely on the consent of the opposing party; the validity must be proved to the satisfaction of the court.

86 The testatrix was described as 'obsessional' on the point that she would not go into hospital and needed the carers to look after her.

6.32 In addition, *Halsbury's Laws* contained a statement that a solicitor should, where there is a genuine dispute, make available a statement of evidence about the execution of the will and its surrounding circumstances. This was based on the then Law Society advice and it was implicitly endorsed by the judge. Given the claimant's failure to do this, the judge would have awarded the defendant her costs. In the circumstances therefore the judge made no order as to costs, implicitly treating the costs on each issue as roughly comparable. The Court of Appeal found no reason to interfere with the judge's award.

The 'old' Law Society guidance

6.33 However, the real importance of the Court of Appeal's decision lies in its view of the conduct of the claimants. At the time of the dispute the Law Society had issued guidance.

> - If the testator is dead, the solicitor must not disclose any information before probate is granted, except to the executors, without the consent of the executors. But this will not necessarily apply where a solicitor is asked to disclose information about a will which he has prepared and which is in dispute.
> - Privilege cannot be claimed by one person claiming under a deceased testator's will as against another person having a similar claim in respect of matters communicated by the deceased to the solicitor during the lifetime of the deceased. The testator's solicitor could be compelled by the court under subpoena to answer questions directed to eliciting communications made to him by the testator in the course of preparing the will if put to him by either party...
> - Where a serious dispute arises as to the validity of the will, beyond the mere entering of a caveat, and the solicitor's knowledge makes him a material witness, then the solicitor should make available a statement of his evidence regarding the execution of the will and the circumstances surrounding it to anyone concerned in the proving or challenging of that will, whether or not the solicitor acted for those who were propounding the will.[87]

6.34 In *Larke*, the claimant solicitor took the view that this recommendation was restricted to just the events surrounding the execution of the will and did not cover any of the events concerning the instructions and preparation of the will. The claimant did not act in accordance with this (in particular did not regard the circumstances of a will as extending to the instructions) but the court did not find that his attitude was obtuse, wilful, or obstinate.

6.35 Brandon LJ, in giving the leading judgment in the Court of Appeal, explained that it was necessary to look at the principle behind the Law Society advice:

> [I]n my judgment the principle which applied is that, where there is litigation about a will, *every effort should be made by the executors to avoid costly litigation if that can be avoided* and, when there are circumstances of suspicion attending the execution and

[87] This advice was based on advice from counsel.

> making of the will, *one of the measures which can be taken is to give full and frank information to those who might have an interest in attacking the will as to how the will came to be made*. In a case of this kind, where suspicion attaches to the will because certain persons, who have only recently come into the life of the testatrix, take a substantial benefit under the will, then clearly the circumstances in which the instructions for the will were given are of utmost importance, and it is information as to that matter, even more than information as to the formalities of attestation, that is needed. So I do not think that the matter turns solely on the recommendation of the Law Society; I think it also turns on the principle that I have endeavoured to state.[88]

Buckley LJ amplified the principle: **6.36**

> In my view it is also clear that the statement is not intended to be confined to matters concerned with the execution of the will in the narrow sense of the terms 'execution'. In my judgement it *should extend to all matters surrounding the making of a disputed will which are relevant to the question in the action and, in my view, should consequently extend to the circumstances leading up to the preparation and making of the will.*[89]

Quite clearly the Court of Appeal did not merely endorse the Law Society guidance, **6.37** but found that it went beyond mere guidance as the general principle of disclosure was one of law and not merely good practice. This point was reflected in *Catling v Catling*.[90] The will draftsman there represented himself as a barrister—but in fact he was a chartered builder who was unemployed at the time of the trial. It was accepted by Halpern QC (sitting as a judge at the Chancery Division) that the list of principles set out in *Larke v Nugus* 'is a general statement of best practice that is not confined to solicitors'.

The Law Society Current guidance

The current guidance issued by the Law Society is dated 6 October 2011. The guidance can be found on the Law Society website.[91] The current Law Society guidance **6.38** reflects, in many ways, the previous guidance. It is, however, worthwhile noting that it is plain that a will preparer must not disclose information before probate is granted except to the executors without the consent of the executors. This means that a will draftsman can seek instructions from the executors about what information is to be disclosed. If the executors consent to disclosure then the will draftsman is protected.

If the executors do not consent to information being released then a solicitor **6.39** may be under a separate professional obligation to disclose information. The starting point however remains the duty of confidentiality. This duty of confidentiality can only be breached, without the consent of the executors 'Where a serious

[88] Authors' added emphasis.
[89] Authors' added emphasis.
[90] [2014] EWHC 180 (Ch) at [42].
[91] <http://www.lawsociety.org.uk/advice/practice-notes>.

dispute arises as to the validity of the will beyond the mere entering of a caveat'.[92] A common, but misconceived, practice is for lawyers simply to demand information about the making or execution of a will without showing any evidence that a 'serious dispute' has arisen as to the validity of a will. The Law Society guidance makes it clear that a serious dispute must be more than the entering of a caveat. It would not be necessary for a disappointed beneficiary to have caused a formal letter of claim to be sent (some of the information or allegations to be contained within a letter of claim would, in part, be dependent upon the receipt of replies to a *Larke v Nugus* letter). The will draftsman and executors could however at least expect a disappointed beneficiary to set out with particularity allegations that may be made about the validity of a will—without which any enquiries may be regarded as nothing more than unnecessary, inappropriate interference in the administration of an estate and could render the will draftsman liable to professional sanction for a breach of confidentiality.

6.40 The Association of Contentious Trust and Probate Specialists have produced a specimen *Larke v Nugus* letter. This document is available on their website.[93] The letter forms part of the 'ACTAPS code' documentation.

6.41 The questions asked in the ACTAPS letter are entirely appropriate—but relevant case-specific questions should be added where appropriate.

6.42 It is however appropriate to make further observations about the terms of the draft ACTAPS letter. ACTAPS have not updated their draft letter since the Solicitors Regulation Authority took over responsibility for the regulation of solicitors. The Law Society's *Guide to Professional Conduct of Solicitors* has now been replaced by the *SRA Handbook*. Furthermore, although entirely appropriate, the circumstances envisaged by the draft letter are relatively unusual in practice. The specimen letter purports to be sent by solicitors acting on behalf of executors and solicitors for parties interested in the estate. In reality such a joint letter is rarely sent. A letter sent by or on behalf of executors would not need to particularize a 'serious dispute' before information is requested since it is for the executors to decide whether or not information about the making of the will is to be disclosed. If the executors do not consent or are not party to such a letter then the nature of the serious dispute ought to be particularized, since otherwise a solicitor will draftsman remains under a professional duty of confidentiality.

---

[92] Section 3.1 Law Society Practice Note 'Disputed Wills' 6 October 2011.

[93] <http://www.actaps.com>.

Costs

There is often considerable work associated with an answer to a *Larke v Nugus* letter. **6.43**

- The will preparation file will probably have to be retrieved from archive.
- The will draftsman will have to consider and review the contents.
- The will draftsman will need to respond to questions.
- Often a response leads only to further questions being raised.
- Sometimes *Larke v Nugus* letters are received from more than one disappointed beneficiary (or indeed from advisors representing beneficiaries under the will) who want to form their own view about the prospects of successfully upholding the validity of the will.

The Law Society advise in their practice note[94] that you should 'provide a full statement of evidence as to the preparation of the will and the circumstances it was executed to anyone who has an interest in the dispute whether or not you are acting for any of the parties'. The Law Society also say that 'as a potential witness in proceedings you may not charge for time spent compiling the statement or documents, however a reasonable charge may be made for photocopying'.[95] There appears to be no legal basis for the statement that as a potential witness in proceedings you may not charge for time spent compiling the statement or documents. The SRA have confirmed that there is nothing in their Code that prohibits a will draftsman from charging for producing such a letter—although any charges must obviously be reasonable. Plainly great care needs to be exercised here and a balance needs to be struck between the amount of work a will draftsman is being asked to undertake and the effective and cheap administration of justice. A will draftsman who has, perhaps badly, prepared a will and failed to make a proper assessment of capacity would inevitably face considerable criticism if initial errors were compounded by the presentation of a large bill. Care and caution needs to be exercised. **6.44**

Locus standi

Larke v Nugus requests are applicable where there is a genuine dispute and for such the person on whose behalf the request is being made must have the standing to make the claim in court. Broadly speaking these are going to be **6.45**

a. those with an interest in the estate;
b. those who would be entitled in default of the disputed will or wills;
c. those representing children in (a) and (b) above;
d. those entitled to a grant of representation.

[94] Practice Notes 'Disputed Wills'—paragraph 4.1.
[95] Practice Notes 'Disputed Wills'—paragraph 4.1.

Actions regarding validity of wills

6.46 The context of the Court of Appeal's judgment is that of challenges to the validity of a will. The grounds for challenge are:

i. Lack of testamentary capacity
ii. Lack of testamentary intention
iii. Want of knowledge and approval (in whole or in part)
iv. Undue influence
v. Fraud and forgery
vi. Want of proper formality
vii. Validity of revocation

6.47 Other contentious probate matters which, while they might affect the dispositions in the will, do not challenge its formal validity, and lie outside of the *Larke v Nugus* procedure, are:

i. Mutual wills
ii. Proprietary estoppels
iii. Construction actions
iv. Secret/half secret trusts
v. Rectification
vi. Inheritance (Provision for Family and Dependants) Act 1975 claims

6.48 As a consequence, *Larke v Nugus* letters are inappropriate in, for example an Inheritance (Provision for Family and Dependants) Act 1975 claim. However, the PR of an estate that is subject to such a claim has a duty to bring to the attention of the court in the witness statement, amongst other things, any information that might affect the exercise of the court's discretion. This will include any statements by a testator about his reasons for the dispositions he has made.

6.49 Also outside the scope of *Larke v Nugus* are negligence claims regarding the preparation or non-preparation of a will. This area is difficult, as an action regarding validity, such as a challenge to the formalities of a will (e.g. invalid attestation) might reveal negligent behaviour by the draftsman in the way in which he dealt with the execution.[96]

Sanctions for non-compliance

6.50 It may be thought that if a solicitor will draftsman did not respond to a *Larke v Nugus* request a response could be produced by virtue of a complaint either to the

[96] See *Esterhuizen v Allied Dunbar* [1998] 2 FLR, *Gray v Richards Butler* [2000] WTLR 143, *Corbett v Bond Pearce* [2000] WTLR 655, *Humblestone v Martin Tolhurst Partnership* [2004] WTLR 343 and *Ross v Caunters* [1979] 3 All ER 580 on the duty to supervise execution generally.

Legal Ombudsman or the Solicitors Regulation Authority (SRA). Unfortunately these approaches would be likely to be misconceived, a waste of time, and incur unnecessary cost.

The Legal Ombudsman is independent and impartial. His services are free and his office will investigate complaints about lawyers in England and Wales. The Legal Ombudsman is, however, governed by 'Scheme Rules'. The rules limit the types of individual who complain. The Legal Ombudsman would be likely to reject a complaint made by a person who was not a client of the will draftsman, a personal representative, or a beneficiary of the estate of the client. A *Larke v Nugus* letter sent on behalf of an excluded or disappointed beneficiary may therefore be unlikely to have *locus standi* to make a complaint. The SRA does not typically investigate and report on individual complaints, but collects background information about risk. This has resulted in unsatisfactory positions where the Legal Ombudsman has referred such complaints to the SRA and the SRA has referred such complaints to the Legal Ombudsman. This unsatisfactory position appears to remain. **6.51**

Form and content of a response

A will preparer is to be expected to remain neutral in proceedings about the validity of a will—despite the obvious reaction to the effect that 'how dare someone challenge a will that I have prepared?'. If a will draftsman is also an executor then the executor (in the capacity of executor) has a duty to remain neutral—see *Alsop Wilkinson v Neary*,[97] which was a case under the Insolvency Act 1986, where Lightman J said 'in a case where the dispute is between rival claimants to a beneficial interest in the subject matter of the trust, rather the duty of the trustee is to remain neutral and (in the absence of any court direction to the contrary) offer to submit to the court directions leaving it to the rivals to fight their battles.' If this stance is adopted in respect of the costs necessarily and properly incurred (e.g. in serving a defence agreeing to submit to the court's direction and in making discovery (now termed 'disclosure')), the Trustees will be entitled to an indemnity and a lien. **6.52**

The will draftsman should respond to enquiries in an entirely appropriate and professional manner. It may be worthwhile producing a copy of a draft response to a colleague for approval before the letter is sent—or reflecting upon it overnight. A *Larke v Nugus* letter will be a reflection of the professionalism of the will draftsman. If it contains false or misleading responses the will draftsman will be criticized—and may potentially be condemned to pay costs of a contested probate action (via a subsequent action to recover unnecessary costs incurred by a disappointed beneficiary pursuant to the principle in *White v Jones*).[98] **6.53**

[97] 1995 All ER 431.
[98] [1995] 2 AC 465.

6.54 A will draftsman should obviously answer the questions asked—but the important point to note is that the will draftsman should not be confined to answering only the questions asked. It is for the will draftsman to give whatever statement is thought fit, whilst remaining neutral. If the will draftsman believed that the testator had capacity to make a will there is nothing objectionable to stating this in plain (unbiased) terms. The will draftsman should set out

1. relevant experience;
2. expertise and qualifications—professional qualifications obtained, number of years practice, membership of professional bodies, and number of hours relating to continuing professional development undertaken each year;
3. the steps the will draftsman generally takes to ascertain capacity of a testator to make a will; and
4. the steps a will draftsman takes in cases of doubt before responding to the specific questions raised.

This type of information can often set the tone for the future of a case. A disappointed beneficiary may abandon any claim to the estate upon receipt of a carefully crafted response from an obviously experienced and expert will draftsman.

7

RISK MANAGEMENT

Introduction

Risk is the exposure to harm from future events. Any well-managed business needs to have policies to control this exposure in order to avoid or reduce financial loss or reputational damage (which in all likelihood will eventually lead to financial loss as well). Not all risk can be removed and policies must be designed **7.01**

1. to remove that which can be removed;
2. to reduce to an acceptable level that which can be reduced; and
3. to minimize the impact of risk that is outside businesses' control.

A lot of risk management is about determining how much risk can be accepted.[1]

A solicitor's management of risk is required by Principle 8 of the SRA Code of Conduct 2011. In addition, 'a relevant person', for the purposes of the Money Laundering Regulations 2007,[2] is required to have a risk-management policy 'in order to prevent activities related to money laundering and terrorist financing'.[3] Money laundering must not be overlooked in the context of will preparation. The preparation of a will is not a regulated activity, but for a regulated person the giving of tax advice is a regulated activity—the boundary between a will and tax advice is difficult to draw. **7.02**

[1] It was said of the USA's Saturn V rocket that 'you want a valve that doesn't leak and you try everything possible to develop one. But the real world provides you with a leaky valve. You have to determine how much leaking you can tolerate.'

[2] Regulation 3.

[3] Regulation 2.

7.03 Financial abuse of the elderly is a matter of widespread concern.[4] Deliberate acts of fraud and forgery against persons concerning their wills, and *inter vivos* gifts, are crimes and therefore Part 7 Proceeds of Crime Act 2002[5] can be relevant to any assistance given to someone attempting or committing such frauds.

Risk-management Policies

7.04 Any risk-management policy should be

- in writing (demonstrating awareness of the policy and its application is difficult without it being in writing);
- regularly reviewed and updated; and
- readily accessible to all that will need it for guidance and assistance.

Policies should not be written as pious platitudes but should be at a level that will provide real support to a will draftsman and help to meet the firm's risk-management aims.

7.05 Given the frequency with which capacity issues are encountered, and the practical difficulties that they give rise to, testamentary capacity is an area of work that requires effective risk-management policies within a firm.[6] Any firm involved in will drafting should consider carefully how the risks inherent in will preparation for the elderly, or ill, can be managed to protect and enhance

- the desired, and acceptable, level of client care;
- the firm's management of risk; and
- the professional reputation of the firm.

No practice should want the difficulties of challenges to the validity of a will they prepared, if these are at all avoidable. Worse, no firm should court negligence claims

[4] The following discusses this:

> Financial abuse is one of the most prevalent forms of elder abuse. According to 2007 statistics from the Prevalence Survey Report by King's College, London and the National Centre for Social Research on behalf of Comic Relief and the Department of Health, approximately 57,000 people aged 66 and over had experienced financial abuse in the past year, making it the second most prevalent type of mistreatment (after neglect) in the UK. This echoes previous research carried out by Action on Elder Abuse, which revealed that 20 per cent of calls to its helpline were about financial abuse, making it the second most widespread type to be brought to the helpline's attention.
>
> *The Financial Abuse of Older People* by Crosby, Clark, Hayes, Jones and Lievesley © Help The Aged, 2008.

[5] Part 7 sets out the offences of money laundering; s. 327 concealing, etc.; s. 328 arrangements; s. 329 acquisition, use, and possession; s. 340(11) extends this to aiding, abetting, counselling, or procuring any of those offences.

[6] A more detailed examination of risk and negligence in the area of will preparation generally can be found in Frost, Reed QC, and Baxter *Risk and Negligence in Wills, Estates and Trusts* (2nd edn., Oxford: OUP, 2014).

in respect of wills, when steps to manage risk can reduce the potential of such a claim.

In terms of what the risk is, the basic proposition must be that the will draftsman is not at fault, nor is he potentially liable for the costs of a probate action, simply because the court later finds against the will he prepared on grounds of want of capacity. The risks lie where the preparation process, followed by the draftsman, falls below the standards expected of the reasonably proficient draftsman practising in this area.[7] This can expose the draftsman to a negligence action[8] or a claim for the costs incurred in the action.[9] It must not be overlooked that where the draftsman's conduct is criticized by the court, damage to the reputation of that firm can also occur.[10] **7.06**

Compliance with professional regulation and codes of conduct

Evidence of what constitutes the standards set and widely attained in a profession is of prime importance when matters go wrong and negligence is alleged. Non-compliance with professional standards in not in itself proof of negligence,[11] but it is clearly a significant factor for the court to take into account when considering claims of negligence. Interesting issues are raised for the question of professional standards when, as for wills, different professions provide the same service. There is little judicial comment on this issue, apart from *Esterhuizen v Allied Dunbar*[12] (where it was accepted that the duty of care applying to a solicitor will draftsman should apply to a non-solicitor will draftsman[13]). It seems reasonable that a uniform standard is applied to all will preparers, and the only reasonable standard is that which is applied to solicitors. **7.07**

In order to control actual financial risk and reputational risk, a firm's risk-management policy must been drawn with reference to the regulatory requirements and the codes of conduct applicable to these areas. Given the potential for litigation concerning wills, when questions of testamentary capacity arise, awareness of, and compliance with, the draftsman's professional body's requirements is important. Below are examples of how the issue has been dealt with. **7.08**

---

7 See the critical remarks in *Re Key, Key v Key* [2010] WTLR 623 or *Feltham v Freer Bouskell* [2013] WTLR 1363 see also 2.56 et seq.

8 *Feltham v Freer Bouskell* [2013] WTLR 1363.

9 *Re Key, Key v Key* [2010] WTLR 623, there was no award by the court for costs against the draftsman in the judgment, but it has been widely assumed that the solicitor (through his insurers) will have carried a part of the costs.

10 *Bacon v Kennedy* [2000] WTLR 169; *Sprackling v Sprackling* [2009] WTLR 897.

11 *Johnson v Bingley Dyson Furey* [1997] PNLR 392.

12 [1998] 2 FLR 668.

13 The judgment did not clarify that this only applies to non-solicitor will preparers for gain, but this is thought to be the case.

1. Ethics guidance was issued by the Solicitors Regulation Authority (SRA) for the drafting and preparation of wills.[14] This guidance does not form part of the SRA Handbook and is not mandatory, but the SRA may have regard to it when exercising its regulatory functions. The guidance is a reminder of the need to achieve the outcomes in Chapter 1 (Client Care) of the SAR Code of Conduct 2011[15] and to
   a. act in the best interests of each client;
   b. provide a proper standard of service to clients; and
   c. behave in a way that maintains the trust the public places in you in the provision of legal services.

   It is suggested that when dealing with the elderly or ill these points are considered particularly in the context of the elderly or ill.
2. The Society of Trust and Estate Practitioners (STEP) has a Code of Will Preparation.[16] This is a set of principles that operate for the benefit of clients and demonstrate openly the commitment of STEP members to transparency and client service. It recognizes that, in providing will preparation services, STEP members can be expected to operate within an ethical environment. Section 3 of the Code deals expressly with mental capacity:

   i. A will drafter must not prepare a will where they know, or have reasonable grounds for concluding, that the client lacks the necessary mental capacity, unless despite their conclusion, appropriate medical advice indicates to the contrary.
   ii. Where there is doubt as to mental capacity, the will drafter must endeavour to ascertain if, with their assistance, the client would be capable of making a valid will. Where there is doubt as to capacity an opinion from an appropriately qualified medical practitioner is of great value and may well assist the will drafter in their decision as whether or not to proceed with the will instructions. In this regard, the will drafter must be aware of the court's encouragement to involve a medical practitioner and be prepared to comply with it, or have good reasons for concluding that this is not applicable in the circumstances.
   iii. The will drafter is faced with great practical difficulty in that the involvement of a medical practitioner almost invariably takes time to comply with, while the duty of care to the testator requires the prompt and efficient preparation of a will. The will drafter is required to consider carefully which of the two factors must be given precedence in the circumstances of the individual client.

[14] 06/05/14 (Updated 11/07/14).

[15] Drawing attention in particular to O(1.2) providing services to clients 'in a manner which protects their interests in their matter, subject to the proper administration of justice', O(1.4) requiring 'the resources, skills and procedures to carry out your clients' instructions', O(1.5) requiring that the service provided to clients 'is competent, delivered in a timely manner and takes account of your clients' needs', and O(1.12) clients must be placed 'in a position to make informed decisions about the services they need, how their matter will be dealt with and the options available to them.'

[16] See <http://www.step.org/professional-standards> for Codes of Conduct for STEP members.

iv. It is recognised that assessment of mental capacity is an inexact science and that ultimately the court is the arbiter of capacity. The will drafter has an important role to play in the process and should always carefully record their conclusions as to capacity and their reasons for reaching those conclusions.

Compliance with this Code is required from all STEP members who prepare wills[17] in England and Wales.[18]

3. The Society of Will Writers has a mandatory Code of Practice for its members. There is no specific section dealing with capacity, but, like (1) above it is suggested that, when dealing with the elderly or ill, these points (and the outcomes listed in the footnotes below) are considered in the context of the elderly or ill.
4. The Institute of Professional Willwriters has a mandatory Code of Practice for its members. Principle 4 requires members to 'take special care with vulnerable clients'.

Most Codes of Conduct have provisions relating to competence and training. Compliance with these is a fundamental of an effective risk-management policy.

Control of time

Since 1995,[19] the control of time throughout will preparation should have been a basic element of risk management. For the elderly, or ill, client time management is much more critical than it is for the younger or fitter client. As well as covering the time taken to prepare a will, policies should cover other practicalities of time management—such as how matters are to be dealt with when members of staff are absent, ill,[20] or leave the firm.[21] The policy should also encourage the early reporting of matters that have become difficult or where the draftsman needs support. Files that are left, or fall outside of any time monitoring, represent major risks to a firm.[22] **7.09**

[17] Defined in the Code as 'Preparing wills includes taking instructions, drafting and arranging execution, unless the context makes it clear that it applies to only a part of this process.'

[18] The Code includes 'wills prepared in whole or in part outside England & Wales that deal with significant real or personal property in England & Wales.'

[19] See *White v Jones* [1995] 1 All ER 691.

[20] *Hooper v Fynmores* [2001] 1019.

[21] Zurich *@risk* newsletter April 2003 referred to a claim where a will for an 88-year-old in hospital was not prepared within 17 days because of a three-week typing backlog. A second example, where over five weeks elapsed without a will being prepared for a 93-year-old in a home, was attributed to pressure of work and staff absence on holiday. A third example was of a will not being followed up where the member of staff left the firm and telephone messages and a letter were left on his desk. Systems that produce these errors are not robust enough to control risk. Zurich observe that: 'what is clear is that pressure of work, typing backlogs, or the absence from the office of the will drafter or staff to act as witnesses due to illness or holiday will not provide a defence to a professional negligence claim.'

[22] For an extreme example see *Bacon v Howard Kennedy* [2000] WTLR 169 and the scathing remarks made about a near-nine-year delay.

7.10 *White v Jones* is the start point for considering the duty of care in will preparation. It involved a 78-year-old testator and a period of approximately 45 days was found to be too long for the preparation of his will.[23] The importance of age was also highlighted soon after by Chadwick LJ in *Carr-Glynn v Frearsons*[24] where he observed: '. . . it is necessary to bear in mind that the testatrix was 81 years of age when she made her will in 1989. It must have been within the contemplation of a solicitor who was instructed to make a will for a client of that age that the matter ought to be dealt with promptly, lest the client's testamentary intentions be defeated by events beyond his or her control.' This urgency is not driven solely by the possibility of death, but also by the possibility of medical events, such as a stroke, or medical procedures, such as surgery, which might not immediately result in death, but may nonetheless deprive the client of testamentary capacity.

7.11 The most detailed consideration of time, in this context, was by Neuberger J (as he was then) in *X v Woollcombe Yonge*.[25]

> It can always be said that, when a client indicates to a solicitor that he or she wants to make a will, or wants to make a substantial change to a previous will, the solicitor should draw up something very quickly for the client to sign then and there as a holding operation. There can always be a risk of death from heart attack, stroke or accident. The question as to whether a solicitor should be concerned about that possibility must, as I have said, be one of fact and degree. Where the client is old or ill, the delay which may be acceptable will obviously be less than in the absence of age or illness. Where there is a plain and substantial risk of the client's imminent death, anything other than a handwritten rough codicil prepared on the spot for signature may be negligent. It is a question of the solicitor's judgement based on his assessment of the client's age and state of health . . .
>
> So far as preparing the will promptly is concerned, I consider a period of seven days[26] [for a late-middle-aged cancer sufferer with no imminent expectation of death] as she appeared [to the solicitor] was not an unreasonable period . . .
>
> . . . [the] suggestion that a solicitor should only act urgently when he thought that there was a likelihood, by which I take it to mean a more than 50 per cent risk, of his client dying before he could return with the will, appears to me to be a significantly too generous a test to solicitors. I consider that the right test is whether there was a real prospect of such an eventuality.

7.12 Lord Neuberger was setting out a test for the urgency of all wills, in that the draftsman should

a. establish the client's age, health, and any other factors affecting the urgency of the will;

23 The testator died before the will was prepared.

24 [1998] 4 All ER 225; see also *Gartside v Sheffield Young & Ellis* [1983] NZLR 37 where a seven-day delay was too long for an 89-year-old in a nursing home who had had a fall.

25 [2001] WTLR 301.

26 This was seven calendar days.

b. consider the appropriate time for the will to be prepared in the light of (a) above;
c. agree any holding documents if they are needed; and
d. set a reasonable time for the will, given these individual circumstances.

Omitting this assessment will be a prima facie breach of the draftsman's duty for any will.

Awareness of time and working to a timetable appropriate to that individual testator's becomes essential. The danger in this process is losing control of time, allowing it to become unmanaged[27] or left to those unfamiliar with the issues. In *Littlewood v Wilkinson Woodward*[28] there were concerns about the client's capacity from the initial meeting and it was decided to re-interview the testatrix with a more senior member of the firm accompanying the draftsman. In this instance, the re-interview (which established to the satisfaction of both members of the firm that the client did indeed have capacity) looks to have been a practical way forward. Unfortunately, the second meeting took place some 80 days after the first meeting. This passage of time is unlikely to allow for improvement in the capacity of the elderly. As the testatrix did not die between the two meetings no *White v Jones* claim could arise against the firm. However, it is not hard to see the difficulties that could have arisen if she had died before the will was prepared. A better approach would have been to avoid the delay. **7.13**

A risk-management policy on time should give guidance on the acceptable time where the client is **7.14**

a. neither old nor ill;
b. either elderly or ill, but with no imminent expectation of death;
c. either elderly or ill such that there is a foreseeable risk of death in the near future; or
d. in extremis.

Note:

i. 'Time' in this context is the time taken by the will draftsman; the clock stops running against the draftsman where the delays are those imposed by the client. Having said this, the more thoroughly the will instructions are discussed and recorded the less likely the chance of client delay.
ii. Any policy on time will require some consideration of the time consequences of the Golden Rule[29] and how this is to be dealt with.

---

[27] *Feltham v Freer Bouskell* [2013] WTLR 1363: where a will, requested for a 90-year-old woman in a nursing home, made little significant progress before she died a little over two months after the will was first requested.

[28] [2009] WTLR 1189.

[29] See Chapter 6 for further comment on a policy in this area.

7.15 The most time-critical wills are where the testator has only days or hours of life expectancy. Such wills are fraught with practical difficulty, not the least of which is the likelihood of challenge on grounds of capacity or knowledge and approval.[30] In order to minimize the potential problems, firms should consider carefully the following.

- Training for those who will take initial telephone calls
  - to identify the issues of urgency,
  - to ascertain any communication difficulties with the testator,
  - to be aware of how the matter is to be handled (and who by).
- Who is capable of taking will instructions in these circumstances, taking into account
  - legal knowledge, particularly on capacity, undue influence, knowledge and approval, and coercion,
  - communication skills, in terms of
    - clarity,
    - care and patience,
    - knowledge of reading over a will and establishing knowledge and approval,
    - technique (open/closed question issues, use of check questions, etc.),
  - knowledge of how to secure valid execution and knowledge and approval of the will under unusual circumstances,
  - knowledge of how to read over a will.[31]
- A clear policy on time for such wills.[32]
- How, in practical terms, wills can be prepared quickly enough and with accuracy. This will include[33]
  - the issue of a second witness (apart from the draftsman) given that medical or nursing staff are reluctant, or forbidden, to assist;
  - the use of a laptop computer loaded with precedents and other materials, and a portable printer (with paper);
    - most commonly required precedents can be placed on a lap-top, but this should not overlook precedents for suitable testamonium and attestation clauses as the circumstances of execution may require

---

[30] Also, do not overlook the pressure that such circumstances can place on the draftsman. An Australian decision, *Summerville v Walsh* [1998] NSWSC 52 dealt with a failure to procure effective execution of a deathbed will. The testator having received severe burns (which would prove fatal) gave instructions for a will, but was physically unable to sign it. Instead of following the statutory provision for signing by another at the direction of the testator in his presence, the solicitor merely prepared a statement, signed by himself, of the testator's intention. This fell short of the standard expected of a New South Wales solicitor and the court found him liable to the disappointed beneficiary for her lost interest.

[31] See Chapter 5.

[32] *Knight v Edonya* [2009] EWHC 2181 involved a deathbed will, which appears to have taken five days, with the testator dying less than 48 hours after signing the will. The time seems excessive for a dying man.

[33] The days of writing out a will by hand on a hospital table should be long gone. Laptop computers and small portable printers will provide a better and more professional result.

- other support materials on potentially difficult areas, such as physical difficulties with signature
- notice of severance, in case severance of a beneficial joint tenancy is needed.[34]

Supervision of execution

The issues concerning the supervision of the execution of a will need to be understood. There are two main decisions on the draftsman's duty to supervise the execution of a will[35] and they do not sit easily together. The *Esterhuizen* case, referred to below, made it clear that the duty of care regarding the provision of a will extended to all who provided wills, regardless of professional qualification, and that the appropriate duty of care was the same for all and that was the duty of care of a solicitor. **7.16**

In *Esterhuizen v Allied Dunbar*,[36] the failure to supervise the execution of the will by the draftsman, led to the elderly testator attempting to organize it himself, but his attempt failed.[37] It was said that of the will draftsman's duty: **7.17**

> ... a prudent solicitor regards it as his duty to take reasonable steps to assist his client in and about the execution of his will, rather than merely to inform the client how it is to be signed and attested. This means that once the client has approved the draft of a will a prudent solicitor will either invite the client to his office so that the will can be executed there or visit him with a member of his staff to execute the will at the client's house,[38]

and

> Any testator is entitled to expect reasonable assistance without having to ask expressly for it. It is in my judgement not enough just to leave written instructions with the testator. In ordinary circumstances, just to leave written instructions and to do no more will not only be contrary to good practice but also in my opinion negligent.[39]

The approach in *Esterhuizen*, while admitting that it may be different in exceptional circumstances, was to set out a fairly clear standard for ordinary circumstances. The second case in this area, *Gray v Richards Butler*,[40] was decided earlier, but there is no indication in the *Esterhuizen* judgment that *Gray* was considered.[41] **7.18**

---

34 *Carr-Glynn v Frearsons* [1998] 4 All ER 225.

35 First considered in *Ross v Caunters* [1979] 3 All ER 580.

36 [1998] 2 FLR 668 QB; this is the first of the two decisions to be reported, although it was the second in time. *Esterhuizen* is, as a consequence, probably the better-known decision.

37 Although written notes on the correct method of execution were provided, the testator only had one witness to his signature.

38 [1998] 2 FLR 668 at 674, per Longmore J (as he was then).

39 [1998] 2 FLR 668 at 677.

40 [2000] WTLR 143 Ch D; it was accepted in *Humblestone v Martin Tolhurst Partnership* [2004] WTLR 343 that the solicitor was not in breach of his duty of care in not supervising the execution of the will.

41 *Gray* was not published in a set of law reports until February 2000 although it was handed down in June 1997.

7.19 *Gray* sets out a more flexible approach to the question of supervision of execution: 'What steps are appropriate in discharge of these various duties in any given situation may depend upon who the client is and the view that the solicitor has formed, or ought to have formed if acting with reasonable competence, as to the ability of the client to understand and follow advice as to the relevant procedures.'[42] These remarks contrast with other remarks in *Esterhuizen*:

> Allied Dunbar got... [the formalities of execution]... entirely right in their instructions left with the will... Is it enough for a solicitor or a professional will provider to leave it at that? There was some suggestion in argument that this might depend on how competent or intelligent the testator was perceived to be but I cannot believe that this is correct, save only insofar as actual performance of the duty may vary according to a defendant's perception of his client... The fact is that the process of signature and attestation is not completely straightforward and disaster may ensue if it is not correctly done.[43]

7.20 While there is scope to argue about the nature of the duty in general, for the elderly or ill client greater care will be required and compliance with the duty as described in *Esterhuizen* will be safer practice. There is the additional factor that where the will draftsman supervises the execution of the will he will then be in a better position

- to give evidence as to capacity at the time of execution and,
- where called for, to explain the circumstances surrounding execution;
- to give evidence, if the rule in *Parker v Felgate* is being relied on,[44] as to how the level of capacity was determined.

In Australia the court has recommended as good practice (contained in a practitioner's guide) that 'the solicitor who took instructions to draw the will be present on execution'.[45]

For a risk-management policy, the standards required by a firm for the supervision of the execution of wills of the elderly or ill should be clearly defined, together with the information relevant to capacity that should be recorded about the testator and the circumstances of execution.

7.21 Supervision of execution should not merely be focussed on issues of signature and attestation for s. 9 Wills Act 1837 purposes, but also where wills are prepared for two clients (e.g. husband and wife or brother and sister) execution of the correct document is important.[46] Who should prepare wills for the elderly?

---

42 [2000] WTLR 143 at 157E.
43 [1998] 2 FLR 668 at 676H–677A.
44 See Chapter 3.
45 *Pates v Craig, the Estate of the late Joyce Jean Cole* [1995] NSWSC 87 [147].
46 *Marley v Rawlings* [2014] WTLR 299 SC.

For any will instruction the risk of the matter being dealt with by a person practising outside of his area of expertise must be avoided. An example of the risks of acting outside of a solicitor's area of knowledge and expertise is to be found in *Credit Lyonnais v Russell Jones & Walker*[47] where the defendant firm were found to have breached their duty of care. They assigned responsibility for the claimants' property work to a corporate lawyer who the court found to be 'a lawyer who was not, and never claimed to be, a property lawyer'. The court observed that there was no reason to doubt that the solicitor concerned was: 'an able and industrious corporate lawyer. No lawyer can hope to be an expert in all areas of law and he has never claimed to be an expert in property law. The fault which led to [the claimant's] problems can be traced back to the [defendant firm's] decision to assign a corporate lawyer to a property case.' Similarly in *Hurlingham Estates Ltd v Wilde & Partners*,[48] Lightman J held that a solicitor who had 'next to no knowledge of tax law and was quite unqualified to give tax advice' breached his duty of care to the client in failing to appreciate and advise on an exposure to tax in a property transaction. **7.22**

The Zurich *@risk* newsletter of May 2008 contained the following advice on this area: **7.23**

- '*Both taking instructions and drafting wills require knowledge and skill. Some claims notified to us have resulted from solicitors who do not usually have anything to do with the preparation of wills, dabbling in will drafting and getting it wrong. It may sound blindingly obvious but both taking instructions and the actual drafting should be restricted to those within your firm who have the necessary expertise*', and
- '*Where you have will precedents available on your system why not limit access to these to only those authorised to draft wills? This will prevent others, who don't have the necessary experience and expertise, from using the precedents to "have a go" at will drafting.*'

For the more complex area of the elderly, the view was expressed in *Re Parsons* that 'where a would-be testator is of advanced age or has been seriously ill or is under some other incapacity, it should always be correct practice that... the instructions for the will should be taken, and the execution of the will supervised, by a qualified solicitor with experience of wills. Failure to do so can readily lead to problems which could otherwise be prevented.'[49] Quite clearly, in practice, wills of the type considered in this quotation are prepared competently other than by qualified and experienced solicitors. But nonetheless, the general tenor of this comment holds true that these tasks should not be undertaken by those who are unqualified[50] or inexperienced. In **7.24**

[47] [2002] EWHC 1310 (Ch).

[48] [1997] STC 627.

[49] *Re Parsons, Borman v Lel* [2002] WTLR 237 at 257D; *Re Belliss, Poulson v Bellis* (1929) 141 LT 245.

[50] The quotation from *Re Parsons* refers to 'qualified solicitor'. In this context we use the word 'qualified' in the general sense of having sufficient training and/or examinations to be equipped with adequate knowledge to deal with issues of testamentary capacity.

Pearce v Beverley[51] HHJ Behrens took no notice of the note, with the will instructions, recording the testator's decision to deliberately exclude his daughter. Having found that the testator had an irrational belief that his daughter was not his daughter, he observed of the employee of the will-writing company who took the instructions that 'There is no information about [his] qualifications to assess [the testator's] capacity.' Clearly the lack of information on qualification, training, or experience in this area reduces the value of the draftsman's evidence.[52]

7.25 Any training for taking instructions from the elderly or ill[53] should not only cover capacity, but also undue influence and knowledge and approval. It is important to understand what constitutes undue influence and obvious issues, such as the presence of a third party in the will instruction meeting or the excessive involvement of a third party in procuring the will, that might point towards the possibility of undue influence. These same issues might also hamper knowledge and approval.[54] Practical steps to how to establish more clearly knowledge and approval,[55] for example in reading over a will,[56] communication with the testator, or providing copies, will help to minimize risk and improve the credibility of evidence.

7.26 The draftsman who undertakes this work for a reduced or low fee does not have a lower duty of care to his client. Therefore the increased responsibility in dealing with the elderly or ill cannot be avoided by a low level of charging.[57]

---

[51] [2014] WTLR 85 at [94]—it did not help in this case that a third party was present throughout the instructions and she was later found to have unduly influenced the testator into making substantial gifts. Her presence had raised issues of want of knowledge and approval. She could not affirmatively prove knowledge and approval and the will failed.

[52] *Re Barker-Benfield, Hansen v Barker-Benfield* [2006] WTLR 1141 at [47]

> I accept the evidence of the trainee solicitors ... who attended at the hospital and took instructions for the execution of the will. They were in my opinion insufficiently trained for the task imposed on them. To the extent of their expertise they performed with integrity and to the best of their abilities. It was however indeed the case that the job was sufficiently difficult that it would have challenged even a practitioner with many years' experience.

This was for a will executed four days before death, the instructions had been taken by another trainee who 'had no experience of wills. He might have known that there was potentially an issue as to capacity but did not have the test as to capacity at the forefront of his memory.' The interview lasted ten minutes.

[53] See earlier in this chapter on compliance with professional codes of conduct.

[54] *Hawes v Burgess* [2013] WTLR 453 CA and [2012] WTLR 423 Ch; *Pearce v Beverley* [2014] WTLR 85.

[55] *Hawes v Burgess* [2013] WTLR 453 CA and [2012] WTLR 423 Ch; *Pearce v Beverley* [2014] WTLR 85.

[56] *Franks v Sinclair* [2007] WTLR 439.

[57] *Johnson v Bingley, Dyson & Furey* [1997] PNLR 392; *Investors' Friend Ltd v Leathes Prior* [2011] EWHC 711 QB: 'When solicitors undertake work at a specific fee, they are generally speaking obliged to complete it exercising the ordinary standard of care, even if it has become unremunerative.'; *Paratus AMC Ltd v Countrywide Surveyors Ltd* [2011] EWHC 3307 Ch: 'a valuer is not excused from doing what is necessary to provide a competent valuation merely by the low level of his remuneration'; *Hicks v Russell Jones & Walker* [2007] EWHC 940 Ch: 'As [the claimants] were legally aided, RJW were bound to act on their behalf as if they were private client of moderate means.'

Control of risk really requires a firm to consider who is competent to undertake this work[58] on their behalf and how others, not currently judged to be competent, can gain sufficient knowledge and experience to safely undertake the work. Not to create a policy to manage risk in this area creates a level of risk that should be unacceptable to most firms.[59] **7.27**

An important element in who is qualified to take instructions from the elderly or ill will be communication skills. The requirement should be the ability to communicate succinctly and appropriately,[60] thereby giving the client the maximum opportunity to demonstrate understanding and capacity (and substantially lessen the chances of misunderstanding the testator's wishes). In addition, clarity in communication between draftsman and client increases the chances of accurate information relevant to capacity being established and correctly assessed. **7.28**

Will instruction forms

An obvious area to look at for management of risk in all wills is the data on which advice, and will preparation, is based; 'There are in most cases a raft of questions which the draftsman ought to ask before even putting pen to paper or, as is now the case, searching through a database of precedents.'[61] **7.29**

Will instruction forms are potentially useful as a support to the will draftsman. They: **7.30**

- represent a common framework within a firm and thus a common approach to risk management;
- represent a standardized approach and this sets a baseline of information for client standards within a firm;
- are a prop for the draftsman's memory;
- are a vital support if the circumstances of the meeting are difficult or confused;
- allow for easier control and checking of the work of others; and
- can have reminders and sign off control for completion of work.[62]

---

[58] 'She had no training...in relation to communicating with the severely handicapped...her notes of the meeting record that she was told certain things about the testator's relatives which were not only wholly untrue but were unlikely in the extreme to have been said by [the testator]. He simply could not have said them' *D'Eye v Avery* [2001] WTLR 227 at 239B.

[59] In considering this issue solicitors should keep in mind the SRA Code of Conduct Outcomes 1.4 (having resources, skills, and procedures to carry the client's instructions) and 1.5 (provision of competent service in a timely manner taking into account the client's needs) and Indicative Behaviours 1.6 and 1.7.

[60] e.g. the importance of open as opposed to closed questions *Buckenham v Dickinson* [2002] WTLR 1083; *Williams v Williams* [2003] 1371 at [38] and [48].

[61] Michael Waterworth *Parker's Modern Wills Precedents* (7th edn., Haywards Heath: Bloomsbury Professional, 2011) para 1.7.

[62] An example of a will instruction form can be found at <http://www.trenfieldtrustandestateconsulting.co.uk/martyn-frost-articles.php>.

7.31 For the elderly or ill, additional templates can be designed[63] to record information and prompt observations on the client's

- *physical issues*—e.g. immobility, breathing problems,[64] blindness, deafness, visible injuries, smell of alcohol, etc.;
- *behaviour*—appropriate/inappropriate to such a meeting;
- *appearance*—appropriate dress or inappropriate (e.g. dishevelled, wrong clothing, dirty or torn clothing, obvious personal hygiene issues, etc.);
  - if the meeting is at the client's house include comment on conditions both good and bad (e.g. cleanliness, discarded food, empty bottles, etc.);
- *communication*—verbal and non-verbal (while the draftsman may not be able to attribute anything to persistent avoidance of eye-contact or lack of facial expression it can be useful to later medical review of notes). Noting the facility with which there was verbal communication is useful (both fluency and vocabulary);
- *factors for and against the test in Banks v Goodfellow*—where questions directly related to limbs of the test have been asked, verbatim (as far as possible) recording of answers is helpful. Under this heading could also be included
  - details of responses to any check questions asked during the interview (e.g. checking on who the executors are to be five or ten minutes after originally asking the question);
  - details of any questions asked about current events (if there was no awareness of major issues of the day this may raise concerns—Chapter 15).

The better the observations, the more useful the notes will be in any later capacity dispute and the better the performance of the firm in the eyes of the court. As has been commented in different parts of this work, poor quality notes may be the cause of criticism in court and undermine the evidence (and reputation) of the firm. Standardizing the approach can be a major factor in both risk management and client care.

7.32 A practical issue for these forms is that it is not that easy to design a will-instruction form with a logical order of questions—an illogical order merely serves to confuse the client and, at times, the draftsman. Some time and thought is required in order

[63] See Appendix 1 for an example regarding observations of the elderly client.

[64] In *Westendorp v Warwick* [2006] EWHC 915 (Ch) the testatrix suffered from a chest infection at the time she executed her will. She already suffered from a degree of dementia and it was thought that the additional physical infection lowered her capacity.

to arrive at a logical order of questions and a practical form. *Lines v Porter*[65] contained an example of the difficulties produced by an ill-thought-out form.[66]

Other areas that should be part of the risk-management policy in this area are as follows. **7.33**

- Standardization of instruction letter to medical practitioner—see Appendix 3.
- Guidance on selection of appropriate medical practitioner—see 6.12.
- Policy on management of time taken by medical practitioner—see 6.11.
- Guidelines on what a firm expects of a draftsman when questions of capacity arise. An analysis of the possibilities is to be found at 6.18. It is suggested that a consistent approach across the firm represents better risk management than giving no guidance. With no guidance, critical decision making can be left with the inexperienced and that is usually not an appropriate level for adequate risk management.

[65] [2012] WTLR 629 Ch D.

[66] For married couple

- After an opening gambit of 'Are you thinking of getting divorced?'
- Q1 'Do you intend to marry/remarry in the future', A1 'No'.
- Q2 'Would you like your new will to take this into account?', A2 'Yes'.

8

STARTING A CASE—PRE LITIGATION

Acting for a Claimant

To state the obvious, all claimants are different. Some claimants will contact **8.01** a lawyer within a few days or even hours of the death of a testator. Sometimes disappointed beneficiaries contact lawyers many years after the death of a testator—claiming that they have only recently discovered the death (which tends to speak volumes about the nature and extent of their relationship with a deceased). Some potential claimants will know about the contents of a will and may even have a copy. Some claimants will consult lawyers before a grant of probate has been issued whilst some consult after a grant has been issued. Many will often fail to particularize the nature of their concerns to a lawyer—leaving it to the lawyer to obtain relevant information. Disappointed claimants will often say words to the effect of 'I want to challenge a will', without particularizing the basis, e.g. is there to be a challenge based on technical deficiencies in a will (e.g. it was improperly witnessed) or is there to be a challenge on grounds of lack of capacity, lack of knowledge and approval, or undue influence, etc.? It is worthwhile noting that disappointed beneficiaries will often make unparticularized allegations of undue influence, when the true position is that a testator has exercised his right to 'do strange things and . . . be whimsical, capricious, vindictive, wrong in belief or act beyond explanation without that of itself proving lack of capacity (though these factors may contribute to a bigger picture demonstrating it).

They are entitled to change previous provisions in previous wills without explanation or discussion.'[1]

The lawyer should establish from a disappointed beneficiary the legal basis for challenge to a will—and if none exists then plainly this is the end of the matter. Relevant questions need to be asked to establish at least a potential case on grounds of lack of capacity. As a preliminary screen the lawyer will want to know the following.

1. The age of the testator (absent injury or illness a young testator is less likely to lack capacity).
2. What reason the client has to doubt the testator's testamentary capacity—for example was the testator capable of living on his own; was he frail in mind as opposed to frail in body?
3. Is the client aware of any medical problems for the deceased—if so what are they?
4. Did the testator take any medication (which could have led to a lack of capacity)?

8.02 If a prima facie case is demonstrated that merits investigation, then the lawyer may want to take on the case. These comments are made subject to two observations. First, the value of an estate may affect the willingness of a lawyer to take on the case. Some lawyers will not take on a case where the estate has a value of less than £100,000—simply on a cost/benefit basis. The costs in a complex multi-party contested probate action which went all the way to trial could easily exceed the value of the estate. A lawyer could however agree with a client to take a low-value case but work particularly hard in the early stages to settle the claim without the need for expensive proceedings. Second, and probably most importantly, the advisor will need to check that if the will being challenged is invalid then the disappointed beneficiary would have an interest in the estate. (Nothing would be gained for this claimant to prove that the last will of the deceased was invalid due to lack of capacity, only to discover the existence of an earlier will which is not subject to challenge which also excludes this claimant. The same comments apply if the last will is invalid causing an intestacy which does not benefit this claimant.)

Caveat

8.03 One of the first steps for the lawyer to take is to apply to register a caveat. The disappointed beneficiary will have a much stronger negotiating position if a grant of probate has not been obtained, since the executors/beneficiaries will be forced to deal with the claimant because otherwise a grant of probate cannot be obtained, whilst the caveat remains. This prevents the executors from dealing with the administration of the estate. When making an application for a caveat it is essential to ensure that

[1] *Schrader v Schrader* [2013] EWHC 466 (Ch) at [82].

all relevant documentation is correct (e.g. if an incorrect date of death is given to the Probate Registry then the caveat may not be 'picked up' by the Probate Registry when an application for a grant is made and a grant could be issued. Likewise if an incorrect address is given the caveat may be ineffective. It can be quite difficult to pick up the correct address of a deceased if, for example, a deceased owns more than one property or lives at more than one address—in these circumstances both addresses should be given).

Contact with the Executors

If the lawyer knows that the executors or beneficiaries are represented by lawyers then, in the first instance, a gentle letter should be sent to the lawyers alerting them to the possibility of a claim. These lawyers may, or may not, be the same firm who prepared the will. The lawyers may themselves be executors. In a simple will an executor may also be the sole beneficiary. It is courteous (and at a sensitive time) to make the executor aware in the first instance of the fact that a claim may be made, even before full information is obtained. The lawyer may wish to refrain from notifying the executor of a potential claim until a receipt has been received from the Probate Registry to confirm that the caveat has been lodged. The claimant's lawyer will then inevitably want to make further enquiries by writing a *Larke v Nugus* letter to the will draftsman.[2] (Whilst the *Larke v Nugus* letter could plainly not be sent in the case of a home-made will, similar enquiries could be raised to the witnesses to the will—to find out as much as possible about the capacity of the deceased at the time the will was executed. Of course if the claimant lawyer does not know the identity of the will preparer this information should be sought from the executor.) **8.04**

Acting for Executors

If the lawyer acting for the executors is also the will preparer then the lawyer should give consideration as to whether or not it is appropriate to continue to act (see the Solicitors Regulation Authority Code of Conduct Indicative Behaviour 5.6). It is to be recalled that the executor's duty is to remain neutral in proceedings. The executor should refer the details of the potential claim to the beneficiaries. Judgement needs to be adopted here since plainly costs have the ability to become disproportionate to the claim—particularly if there are numerous beneficiaries under the disputed will. As an illustration, if it is the case that a testator has a net estate worth one million pounds but, say, there are numerous small bequests to friends or charities, it is plainly the residuary beneficiary who has the biggest real interest in the outcome of the **8.05**

[2] See Chapter 6.

litigation. A substantial residuary beneficiary might want to make initial enquiries to see if it is possible to settle the claim—on the basis that the last will is valid (in which case the pecuniary beneficiaries, etc. will get paid and will not have been required to incur legal expenses of their own). If the case does not settle then plainly all parties interested in the disputed document will at least be notified about the extent of the dispute and given the opportunity to decide whether or not they wish to become involved. [3]

Acting for Beneficiaries

8.06 If there is one beneficiary in the disputed will then (absent any other conflict) the same lawyer may wish to act for the executors and beneficiary. Likewise, absent any conflict between lawyer and clients and multiple beneficiaries then the same lawyer may wish to act for all parties. It should be recognized, however, that there could be issues with regards to costs at the conclusion of a case since the executor who remains neutral would usually be entitled to recover costs on an indemnity basis. This distinction would become blurred where the same lawyer acted both for a neutral executor and interested beneficiaries—in any event it is the beneficiaries who have a substantive interest in establishing the validity of the will and it will be for them and their advisors to deal with the claim. The response to be adopted will, subject to general rules and protocols, be guided by what they perceive to be the strength of the claimant's claim. If a beneficiary perceives that there is room for doubt about the capacity of the deceased to make a will then the beneficiary may be more willing to adopt a pragmatic approach to early settlement of a case. Even if the beneficiary perceives there to be little doubt, this beneficiary will still be required to comply with the pre-action protocols (referred to below) and will be required to consider mediation—if offered by the disappointed claimant.

Case Plan

8.07 It may be helpful for a lawyer representing any party in proceedings to draw up a case plan. This will be a helpful document for many reasons. First, it will help the lawyer to establish clarity of thought and also a process by which the dispute at issue could be resolved. It will remain a useful document against which progress can be checked as the case progresses. It will force the lawyer to consider the nature and extent of evidence that will be required to prove the case. The second reason to produce such a document is that it will undoubtedly assist the client to understand the procedures, and likely timescales and costs, that will be involved if a contested

[3] CPR 19.8A—power to make judgments binding on non-parties.

probate case should go all the way to trial. Third, it will act as a framework for a cost budget that would inevitably be required if the case gets to the stage of issuing legal proceedings. A case plan would not be a document that would be disclosed to any of the other parties, but would simply be an internal document for consideration by the solicitor, barrister, and client.

The case plan would be likely to include the following issues: **8.08**

1. Case Summary—what the case is about. Date of will, date of death, value of estate, etc.
2. Objectives—what the client is seeking to establish. Is the litigation about the will purely a point of principle or is it about seeking to recover or preserve a sum of money for the client?
3. Identity of the opponent—who (exactly) should correspondence be sent to? Is there more than one potential opponent? Each beneficiary or potential beneficiary should be identified. Would an opponent be likely to be in a position to meet any cost liability ordered at the conclusion of a trial?—if not, then this would be a litigation risk.
4. Causes of action—what are they? Is the case simply pursued or defended on grounds of capacity or are there other issues such as lack of knowledge and approval, allegations of undue influence, lack of compliance with the Wills Act 1837, etc.?
5. Issues in the case—what are they?
6. Evidence required to deal with the issues in the case—lay and expert evidence. What will lay evidence deal with?
7. What other (non-expert) evidence will be required—e.g. what evidence should be sought from professionals such as doctors, nurses, care workers, etc.?
8. The case of the opponent—what is it? What are the favourable or unfavourable facts available to the opponent?
9. Risks—what are the risks and prospects of success?
10. Relevant protocol—should be identified and a plan set out to follow it.
11. Steps/timetable to trial—what would be likely to be undertaken and when—and at what cost?
12. Alternative dispute resolution/mediation—is this going to be offered to the other side? If an offer is made by the other side what is likely to be the response of your client? What are the costs, benefits, or burdens?
13. Funding—what is the likely cost budget for each stage of the case? How is the client going to be able to fund the claim?
14. Case management information—relevant team personnel (including the names of solicitors, counsel, and expert likely to be involved).

9

ALTERNATIVE DISPUTE RESOLUTION

Litigation Risk

There are many risks in a typical contentious probate case. Both sides will, presumably, be represented by competent lawyers and experts. Both sides will, presumably, be confident of success—but for every trial one party wins and one party loses. The inherent difficulty in litigation is knowing, before judgment, which will be the party to win and which will be the party to lose. Any experienced practitioner will have won cases they thought they might lose and will have lost cases they felt confident about winning. **9.01**

A classic and perhaps unfortunate illustration of the principle of risk in litigation is set out in the case of *Sharp v Adam*.[1] The testator, Mr Adam, was 70 when he died in 2002. For a number of years before his death he had suffered from multiple sclerosis. He made a will just over a year before he died. At that time he was unable to speak, but could communicate by nodding, shaking his head, or by moving his eyes. The will was made by a suitably experienced solicitor. The will made no provision for his daughters. The view that the deceased had capacity to make a will was supported by six doctors, two lawyers, and six lay witnesses. A GP was present at meetings when instructions were taken and at the execution of the will. The trial judge found that the GP was a 'highly qualified general practitioner' and was 'an impressive witness'. The solicitor will preparer was a 'competent and experienced solicitor'. The Court of Appeal said that she had taken instructions **9.02**

[1] First Instant Decision [2005] EWHC 1806 (Ch) Court of Appeal Decision [2006] EWCA Civ 449.

for the will 'in quite an exemplary fashion'. Both doctor and solicitor had acted in a way that was 'beyond criticism'. Despite this endorsement, the Court of Appeal found that the will was invalid. Both the trial judge and the Court of Appeal relied on the existence of an MRI scan that was produced by a clinic in Germany which the deceased attended in 1996. That scan noted a diagnosis of longstanding disseminated encephalomyelitis. Counsel for the unsuccessful parties, Gilead Cooper QC wrote:[2]

> Everyone hates losing a case. Usually, after the passage of time and a few wins it becomes possible to look back a bit more philosophically. Sometimes, even, one might recognise that the court probably got the right answer. But re-reading the judgment in this case I am still not quite sure why the appeal was not allowed. Out of a judgment running to 96 paragraphs, it seems to me that the first 92 paragraphs would have amply justified a conclusion going the other way. Only in the final four paragraphs did the Court of Appeal abruptly change direction, basing the whole decision on a frankly incoherent passage from the transcripts.

He concluded that 'there is no way of drafting a bullet-proof will'. Even the exemplary efforts of the solicitor will preparer were insufficient.

9.03 Risks of litigation relate not only to winning or losing but also to the issues of costs. A practitioner may wish to consider the case of *Carapeto v Good*.[3] There a claim was contested on grounds of undue influence, and want of knowledge and approval. These claims were rejected. The judge said 'the making of a charge of undue influence against any person is a serious matter and to have such a charge levelled against one is unpleasant...it seems to me that, in principle, where a charge of undue influence is levelled against a party and that charge fails the costs of that ought ordinarily to follow the event.' He did however, perhaps surprisingly, continue 'in my judgment the defendants were entitled to put that matter in question and were entitled to test the case advanced by Mrs Carapeto.' He concluded that the defendant should pay only one half of the successful claimant's costs—even though no misconduct or allegations about the way the case was pursued by Carapeto were raised. These two cases alone reflect litigation risk in contentious probate proceedings both in respect of outcome but also in respect of costs. Many such other examples exist.

9.04 It is beyond the role of this book to consider all litigation risks that exist—we just accept that these risks do exist. Against that background most sensible clients of modest means are content to try to settle a claim without the risk, worry, and expense of a trial.

[2] *ACTAPS Journal*, Issue 119.
[3] [2002] EWHC 640.

Alternative Dispute Resolution

The Civil Procedure Rules are supported by a Practice Direction on Pre-Action Conduct. This includes a section on Alternative Dispute Resolution (ADR).[4] This reflects that starting legal proceedings should usually be a step of last resort and urges parties at least to consider whether some form of ADR procedure might enable them to settle the matter without starting proceedings. **9.05**

At this point it is worthwhile mentioning that there is no right time at which to conduct ADR. ADR is sometimes conducted at an early stage, before costs have become substantial and themselves become a hurdle to overcome to achieve a settlement. Sometimes ADR is conducted just before trial—our view is that the nature of the dispute having been identified with the letter of claim and response being sent is a perfect opportunity to consider ADR. **9.06**

There are various forms of ADR, including: **9.07**

1. discussion and negotiation;
2. mediation—a form of negotiation with the help of an independent person;
3. early neutral evaluation—where an independent person gives an opinion on the merits of a dispute; or
4. arbitration—where an independent person makes a binding decision.

Jackson LJ has said 'the aim is that, in general, no case should come to trial without the parties at least having seriously considered some form of ADR to settle their dispute.'[5] This intention has been supported by the Civil Procedure Rules Committee who have approved a draft Case Management Direction in the following terms: '[A]ll parties must consider settling this litigation by any means of Alternative Dispute Resolution (including mediation), any party not engaging in any such means proposed by another must serve a witness statement giving reasons within 21 days of that proposal—such witness statements must not be shown to the Trial Judge until questions of costs arise.'[6] **9.08**

Jackson LJ is undoubtedly a firm believer in the process of mediation. He has, with assistance from others, produced a book known as *The Jackson ADR Handbook*.[7] This book was published in 2013 and has a foreword from Lord Dyson MR. It is said that a copy of the book has been given to all members of the judiciary. Although not all judges share the enthusiasm of Jackson LJ for the ADR process, it may be difficult for **9.09**

---

4 Section 8.1.

5 Preface to *White Book*, Vol. 1 (2014).

6 <http://www.justice.gov.uk/courts/procedure-rules/civil/standard-directions/list-of-cases-of-common-occurrence>.

7 S. Blake, J. Browne, and S. Sime (Oxford: OUP, 2013) ISBN 978-0-19-967646-0.

any judge to refuse to take into account offers or refusals of ADR when considering questions of costs.

9.10 The usual cost rule in litigation is that the loser would be required to pay the costs of the winner.[8] The court does however retain discretion to make a different order. When deciding what order, if any, to make about costs the court must have regard to all of the circumstances of the case including the conduct of the parties—both before as well as during proceedings—and the manner in which a party has pursued or defended the case or a particular allegation or issue. The court has established principles in relation to an offer to embark on mediation—see *Halsey v Milton Keynes General NHS Trust*[9] in *PGF II SA v OMFS Company Limited*;[10] the principles derived from the *Halsey* case were set out as follows:

i. The court should not compel parties to mediate even if it were within its power to do so. This would risk contravening Article 6 of the European Convention on Human Rights and would conflict with a perception that the voluntary nature of most ADR procedures is a key to their effectiveness.
ii. Nevertheless, the court may need to encourage the parties to embark upon ADR in appropriate cases and that encouragement may be robust.
iii. The court's power to have regard to the parties' conduct, when deciding whether to depart from the general rule that the unsuccessful party should pay the successful party's costs, includes power to deprive the successful party of some or all of its costs on the grounds of its unreasonable refusal to agree to ADR.
iv. For that purpose the burden is on the unsuccessful party to show that the successful party's refusal is unreasonable. There is no presumption in favour of ADR.

9.11 Supplementing those statements of principle, the Court of Appeal adopted and explained a non-exclusive list of factors which were likely to be relevant to the question of whether a party had unreasonably refused ADR. These include:

a. the nature of the dispute;
b. the merits of the case;
c. the extent to which other settlement methods had been attempted;
d. whether the costs of the ADR would be disproportionately high;
e. whether any delay in setting up and attending the ADR would have been prejudicial; and
f. whether the ADR had any reasonable prospect of success.

[8] CPR 44.3 (2)(a).
[9] 2004 1 WLR 2002.
[10] 2013 EWCA Civ 1288.

The *PGF* judgment highlighted statistical research conducted by the Centre for Effective Dispute Resolution ('CEDR'). CEDR dealt with approximately 8,000 mediated cases per annum. The cases mediated in 2012 reported success rates of 70 per cent on the day and 20 per cent more settling shortly thereafter. The *Halsey* case also made reference to the Court of Appeal's own pilot scheme which achieved a 50 per cent success rate (it will be appreciated that these figures do not relate only to contentious probate cases—but include statistics in relation to all aspects of civil litigation). **9.12**

The *PGF* case decided by the Court of Appeal in 2013 was significant because the appeal raised, for the first time as a matter of principle, the following question: 'What should be the response of the court to a party which, when invited by its opponent to take part in a process of Alternative Dispute Resolution simply declines to respond to the invitation in any way?'. The Court of Appeal unanimously endorsed the proposition that, as a general rule, silence in the face of an invitation to participate in ADR was itself unreasonable, regardless of whether or not there was a good reason for a refusal to engage in ADR. **9.13**

The *PGF* judgment (above) summarized advice contained within the *Jackson Handbook*. The advice includes: **9.14**

a. Not ignoring an offer to engage in ADR.
b. Responding promptly in writing, giving clear and full reasons why ADR is not appropriate at the stage, based if possible on the *Halsey* decision.[11]
c. Raising with the opposing party any shortage of information or evidence believed to be an obstacle to successful ADR, together with consideration of how that shortage might be overcome.
d. Not closing off ADR of any kind and for all time, in case some other method than that proposed, or ADR at some later date, might prove to be worth pursuing.

It was said 'that advice may be fairly summarised as calling for constructive engagement in ADR rather than flat rejection, or silence'.[12]

[11] [2004] 1 WLR 2002.

[12] Paragraph 30 of *PGF supra*. There can be risks in not approaching the ADR constructively, see *Re Rawlinson (costs)* [2010] WTLR 1443 where refusing an offer because of defendant's conduct did not result in a costs penalty or *Re McKeen, Viva! Campaigns Ltd v Scott* [2014] WTLR 461 where there was no costs penalty for setting conditions to mediation that were reasonable but as a consequence of which the defendant would not continue with his offer of mediation.

Mediation

9.15 In a dispute about capacity to make a will, discussions and negotiations often take place. Early neutral evaluation and arbitration are less common forms of ADR. Mediation appears to be growing in popularity for understandably positive reasons, coupled also with negative reasons for using court determination.

9.16 Once a mediation has been arranged then the parties themselves and not the court are in control of the process and outcome. As has already been reflected, mediation works to achieve settlement. Mediation Service users generally report feedback stating that they like the service. As has been seen, if mediation is unreasonably refused then there is a risk of a finding at trial that the refusing party has failed to comply with the court's objectives regarding proportionality and cost management.

9.17 In accordance with his duties a litigator will undoubtedly discuss the issue of mediation with his client. An ideal time would be after an exchange of correspondence between the parties has identified that there is in fact a serious and genuine dispute (in *PGF*[13] it was argued that a mediation would have been premature because expert evidence was still awaited. This prematurity was not said to be a good reason to decline to mediate). Obviously both sides should have some good evidence to support their case but this need not go to the extent of formal witness statements having been taken. In a dispute about capacity perhaps the GP records should have been made available to both sides which would at least reveal whether there was anything significant brought to the attention of the medical professionals during the lifetime of the deceased to enable the parties to form a provisional view about the strength of their respective positions. As has been indicated above if mediation is conducted at a later stage then the amount of costs can become a hindrance to settlement.

9.18 If a client is amenable to mediation then this should undoubtedly be offered to the other side. If the client is not amenable to an offer of mediation then the client should be warned in writing about the risks (and obvious potential cost consequences) if the client is found to have unreasonably refused. A belief in the strength of one's own case or a desire not to meet the other side at a mediation would not be regarded as a reasonable justification for refusing mediation since this may make acceptance of the offer more likely.

Correspondence with the other side

9.19 If mediation is to be put forward then a formal written offer should be made to the other side, offering to embark on mediation. It is important to deliver an open

[13] 2013 EWCA Civ 1288.

assurance that the claimant would adopt a reasonable, flexible, and pragmatic approach at mediation.

The identity of the appointed mediator can be a critical aspect of the case. The majority of mediators are highly trained, skilled, and experienced—but some are not. The problem is that sometimes parties will engage in a battle to establish their own choice of mediator—with the receiving party simply rejecting the proposing party's nominations, whereupon the proposing party will inevitably reject the receiving party's nominations. It is important to be pragmatic and flexible here—too many mediations flounder at this stage. It is suggested that the proposing party should put forward the names of at least three mediators—perhaps with an invitation to the receiving party to feel free to speak to the mediator (or their clerk) about their experience and expertise, etc. In default, a global suggestion can be put forward by inviting a mediation organization to put forward a mediator of their own choosing—this does somewhat detract from the process since the outcome can be unpredictable, but at least has the advantage of seeming to be a transparent process. **9.20**

The mediation process

If a mediation is agreed by each side (sometimes there are competing interests and sometimes there can be three or more parties to a mediation)—the parties and their advisors should be well prepared. **9.21**

Most advocates will prepare a case summary/position statement for disclosure to the mediator and the other side. It is to be remembered that the position statement has a triple purpose. First, a copy will inevitably be given to your own client, who wants to see that you have properly taken on board all of the strengths of the case. Second, the position statement will, however, be sent to the other side and if there is to be a prospect of a successful outcome it is equally important that the position statement should not provoke the other side into making settlement more difficult. The third purpose is to give the mediator an overview as to the issues in the case. **9.22**

Contents of a position statement

A position statement would usually comprise the following elements: **9.23**

1. The general practice is to head the papers in the same way that a statement of case would be headed. The document should then be marked 'without prejudice and for use in the mediation only'. The statement should also indicate the identity of the party for whom it is served.
2. Introduction—a general introduction as to what the dispute is about.
3. Attendance—who will be attending the mediation on behalf of your side—counsel, solicitor, and the identities of any clients to attend.
4. Brief background to the case.

5. The position of your client—what your client seeks. Remember that objectives can be achieved at a mediation that could not be achieved via the court process. All a judge can decide is whether or not a particular will is valid. In a mediation the parties would be free to achieve any settlement they thought fit.
6. A procedural chronology—dates of letter of claim and response, etc., together with relevant pleadings and orders for directions, etc.
7. Issues—what the legal and factual issues between the parties are.
8. Your client's position on the issues—briefly why your client's version is right. Remember that the position statement will be disclosed to the other side and it should not be written in a confrontational style. Reference may be made to documents or statements, etc. already disclosed, or to be disclosed.
9. Offers—the extent of any offers made by either side, so that the mediator can understand the difference between the parties.
10. Costs to date—careful consideration should be given to this aspect. It is not necessary to include this information in a position statement. Costs are usually dealt with at a mediation so if information is not to be given in the position statement the details of costs should be taken to the mediation in case a settlement is achieved. If costs are shown to be very high then it may worry the other side and make them realize the likely extent of costs if they lose. Alternatively a high figure for costs may simply make the other side more determined to fight the case.

Contents of a mediation bundle

9.24 A mediator should not be overburdened with documents. A mediation is NOT a mini trial. The contents of the bundle will obviously be dependent upon the stage that has been reached. If legal proceedings have not yet been commenced then the bundle would be likely to include:

1. The letter of claim;
2. The letter of response;
3. The relevant will or wills;
4. A family tree;
5. A *Larke v Nugus* letter;[14]
6. A *Larke v Nugus* reply;
7. Any expert reports that have been disclosed by the parties;
8. Any relevant documents—e.g. estate accounts.

9.25 It is not likely that the mediator will need to see all of the medical records, although key documents may be relevant—for example any GP entries at or around the time the will was executed.

[14] See Chapter 6.

If legal proceedings have been commenced then the mediation bundle would normally include: **9.26**

1. All the documents referred to above.
2. Any statements of case the claim form, statement of case, defence, counter-claim, etc., and any key relevant letters passing between each side (NOT the entire correspondence file).
3. Any relevant orders—particularly case-management orders that have been made. This will be relevant so that the mediator can understand and appreciate the procedural timetable.

Preparation for mediation

Brian Dawson, solicitor mediator at Walker Smith Way Cheshire has produced notes for 'preparing for mediation'. These notes are produced below—and they reflect the procedure used by most, if not all, mediators. **9.27**

> ***Preparing for Mediation***
>
> **Introduction**
>
> It is very important the parties and their advisers are well prepared.
>
> Please assist the mediator by supplying him/her with a brief summary of the issues between the parties as soon as possible. The mediator is there to help the parties achieve settlement; the mediator is not a judge and will not impose any decision. The summary should therefore set out the issues, as far as possible, and should not seek to persuade the mediator about the strength of the parties' arguments.
>
> In a time-limited mediation of up to four hours, the summary should not exceed five to ten pages, together with copies of any essential documents.
>
> **Confidential briefings**
>
> You may wish to provide the mediator with a confidential note; it should be clearly marked as 'confidential to the mediator only' and the mediator will respect the confidence.
>
> Such document may provide the mediator with a better understanding of the issues and negotiating position and may speed up the process.
>
> Please be as candid as you are able with the mediator when speaking to him in confidence. Your trust will not be abused, and it will help speed up the process.
>
> **Who should attend the mediation?**
>
> The mediation requires a well-prepared small team, which can:
>
> - identify the issues;
> - present your argument persuasively to the other parties;
> - work well together and with others at the mediation, and be candid with the mediator.
>
> The team should include a decision maker, with the authority to settle, including insurers with authority where relevant.
>
> **What will happen on the day?**
>
> Normally the mediation follows a pattern whereby the mediator is in charge of the process and the parties are in charge of the content.

- The mediator will normally start by chairing an open session, when he/she will provide a full explanation and set the agenda for the day.
- The mediator will normally have private and confidential meetings with each team and may have further joint meetings.
- If a negotiated outcome is reached, the parties will draft the terms of settlement.
- If there is no negotiated outcome, the parties will meet with the mediator to decide on the future progress of the dispute.

Confidentiality

The mediation is without prejudice, which means that what is said at the mediation cannot be quoted by either party subsequently in the dispute and it is non-binding, unless and until agreement is reached and terms of settlement are drawn up.

Note: Although the process is confidential, the mediation will be terminated if anything is said at the mediation, which leads the mediator to believe that some criminal activity may have taken place.

Preparing the parties

It is very helpful if advisers can prepare the parties to the mediation, particularly with regard to the status of the mediator, who is there to assist the parties in trying to achieve settlement. He is not a judge. Please stress that the mediator is completely impartial and can be trusted with the most confidential information. The mediator is not permitted to use or pass on information provided to him/her in confidential session, without the express authority of the person providing that information to him/her.

Costs of mediation

9.28 The usual procedure is that each side will pay half the mediator's fees at or before the mediation and that each side will bear their own costs for attending the mediation—but that all costs incurred would be regarded as costs in the litigation. The mediation agreement should be checked to make sure that there is no contrary provision so that one side effectively writes off the costs of attending mediation. Of course a contrary agreement may be reached. If one side wants there to be a mediation but the other side is relatively impecunious then the person offering mediation may offer to pay all of the mediator's fees or even the costs of the other side—on the basis that those costs would be regarded as litigation costs within the discretion of the court at the conclusion of proceedings if an agreement was reached. Of course if an agreement is reached then the issue of costs would usually be resolved at the mediation. In *Lobster Group Limited v Heidelberg Graphic Equipment Limited* [15] the costs of mediation were not recoverable because each side agreed to bear their own costs. The point is raised here because it does need to be carefully considered so that the intentions of the parties are appropriately reflected.

[15] [2008] EWHC 413.

Reaching a settlement

If a settlement is reached at a mediation meeting, a written agreement will be drawn up to reflect the terms agreed. It would be of assistance if one party starts to prepare a framework settlement document in advance of a mediation in the hope, but not necessarily expectation, that in accordance with statistical probability a settlement will be achieved. The settlement would deal not only with the issue of any payment to be made by one side to the other and resolving issues of costs but would also deal with court formalities if legal proceedings have been commenced—i.e. there will need to be a grant of representation issued to one side or the other (see Chapter 10 on Settlement). Often it takes a considerable period of time to reduce the basis of an agreement to writing in a format that is acceptable to each side. Although a manuscript agreement can, of course, be agreed and signed by the parties (to be typed up later) it is usually of assistance if one side at least has access to a laptop computer and printer so that a typed agreement can be finalized and signed by all sides before they leave the mediation. **9.29**

Finally, the authors recommend a splendid article, freely available on the Internet, called 'The Subversive Lawyer's Guide to Mediation' by David Richbell.[16] The article gives unique insight into the difficulties facing a mediator. **9.30**

16 <http://mataw.essentialsystems.co.uk/wp-content/uploads/2010/06/the-subversive.pdf>.

10

METHOD AND MECHANICS OF SETTLEMENT

Statistically, the vast majority of claims intimated or commenced settle pre-trial. The method of settlement depends on whether or not legal proceedings have been commenced. **10.01**

Settlement Pre Issue

There are many permutations. A disappointed beneficiary may simply abandon the claim, leaving the executors free to make an application for a grant of probate. A caveat could be warned off or simply allowed to lapse. If relevant beneficiaries agree to make a payment to a disappointed beneficiary then an agreement can be reached in correspondence or evidenced by a formal agreement to be signed by the parties. Plainly if an agreement is reached whereby the last purported will is recognized to be invalid then all relevant beneficiaries will have to consent to the terms of settlement. If some of the relevant beneficiaries do not have capacity to consent (e.g. because they are children or lacked capacity themselves) then any settlement would need to be approved by the court using the procedure set out in Part 21 of the Civil Procedure Rules (CPR). **10.02**

Settlement After Issue of Proceedings

The mechanics of settlement in respect of proceedings issued are set out in the Practice Direction to Part 57 CPR—paragraph 6.1: **10.03**

> [I]f at any time the parties agree to settle a probate claim, the court may–
> (1) order the trial of the claim on written evidence which will lead to a Grant in solemn form;

(2) order that the claim be discontinued or dismissed under Rule 57.11 which will lead to a grant in common form; or
(3) pronounce for or against the validity of one or more wills under Section 49 of the Administration of Justice Act 1985.

10.04 Chancery Practice Form 38 sets out the form of order. Section 49 Administration of Justice Act 1985 permits a probate claim to be compromised without a trial if every 'relevant beneficiary' has consented to the proposed order. It is only available in the High Court. A relevant beneficiary means a person who under any such will is beneficially interested in the deceased's estate and where the effect of the pronouncement would be to cause the estate to devolve on an intestacy, or partial intestacy, or to prevent it from so devolving a person who under the law relating to intestacy is beneficially interested in the estate.

10.05 The advantage of a grant in solemn form is that it is regarded as binding; not only on the parties to the action and the persons who claim under them, but also on all those who had knowledge of the action and had the opportunity of intervening, but failed to do so.[1]

10.06 If legal proceedings had been commenced then mechanics of settlement can be quite cumbersome. In the first instance the parties would be best advised to lodge a consent order with the court asking for a 'trial' of the claim on written evidence which will lead to a grant in solemn form. The rules require a 'trial'. Unless district judges are familiar with rules and practice then, although the court should be invited to make the initial order of the claim, it may not do so and the preliminary hearing may be required to persuade the court to adopt this course of action. Thereafter the court should list the case for a 'trial'. This is, of course, not a trial with witnesses since the claim will be tried, as directed, only on 'written evidence'. A judge may need 30 minutes' reading time and 30 minutes' hearing time, depending upon the complexity of the case and issues. A district judge or Master will not have jurisdiction to conduct a 'trial' so the cases thereafter are generally listed before a High Court, or Section 9 circuit judge[2].

10.07 An order from district judge/Master for trial may look like the following.

Usual court heading

District Judge/Master

Upon hearing counsel for the claimant and counsel for the defendant

Upon it being recorded that the claimant and the defendant have agreed terms of settlement and have agreed to implement their settlement by seeking pronunciation in solemn form of the will of the deceased dated the [ ] following the trial of the claim on written evidence.

[1] *Tristram & Coote's Probate Practice* 26.06.
[2] Section 9 of the Senior Courts Act 1981.

It is ordered

By consent

1. The claim shall be listed before a judge in open court for trial upon written evidence only with an estimated length of hearing with 45 minutes prior reading time.
2. For the purpose of the above hearing the parties will agree dates for availability themselves through the clerk for counsel for the claimant as a single point of contact who will by 4:00 pm on the [ ] telephone the listing office and fix the date for trial convenient to the parties and the court. Failure to do so will result in the trial being fixed in any event.
3. There shall be an agreed single hearing bundle to contain all relevant pleadings, orders, affidavits/witness statements, and the draft order with its schedule, such bundle to be lodged at court not less than three clear days before the date set for the hearing. The relevant provisions of the Chancery Guide shall apply to the preparation of the bundle.
4. The hearing bundle shall also contain a skeleton argument prepared by counsel for the claimant, and to be agreed if possible by counsel for the defendant, which will set out the reasons for making the order sought.
5. Costs in the case, etc.

Procedure Prior to 'Trial'

It is likely that counsel would be instructed at least by the party who is seeking a grant. It is in the interests of the other parties to be represented to avoid any difficulty or issues that inevitably arise on the day. **10.08**

It is important to ensure that the file is in procedural good order—a paginated mini trial bundle would be helpful, including relevant pleadings, witness statements, and the order of a district judge leading to 'trial'. The requirements of CPR 57.5 are sometimes neglected—*any* testamentary documents of the deceased in the possession or control of any party MUST be lodged with the Court—by a claimant when the claim form is issued and by a defendant when he acknowledges service. The claimant and every defendant who acknowledges service must serve a witness statement describing knowledge of any relevant testamentary documents. The specimen form for the written evidence about testamentary documents is annexed to Practice Direction 57. Without these statements (and documents) an adjournment to the application may be ordered (if this is omitted a court may be persuaded to make the order subject to the lodgement of the statements and documents rather than take up further court time with a further court hearing). **10.09**

It is desirable to lodge a skeleton argument in advance of the hearing. The skeleton argument would typically deal with the background to the dispute, identify the deceased, the date of death, identify the relevant beneficiaries under relevant wills or **10.10** an intestacy, and deal briefly with the procedural chronology. The skeleton argument should deal with the procedure in relation to settlement (CPR 57.6.1, etc.) and make BRIEF submissions as to why probate should be granted in respect of the will to be propounded. If a caveat has been lodged which remains effective (because it either remains valid or has been made permanent by a notice of appearance) then the order should deal with the dismissal of the caveat. The court order should be sent to the Probate Registry with the application for a grant of probate.

10.11 An order in terms agreed may look like the following:

Usual Court Heading/Parties

HH Judge ....

Sitting at on the........ day of........... 2014

Between

Upon the trial of the claim

And upon the court having read the evidence filed.

And upon the court hearing from counsel for the claimant.

The court pronounces for the force and validity of the last will and testament of Albert Smith being the script bearing the date 3 February 2012 and marked 'A'.

And it is ordered that:

1. A grant of probate in the estate of the above Albert Smith deceased of...........be issued in respect of the last will and testament dated 3 February 2012 to the claimant being the sole executrix named in the said last will.
2. On application for such grant the caveat number.....................originally entered at the Leeds District Probate Registry on 3 March 2014 do cease to have effect.
3. There be no order as to costs between the parties.
4. The terms of the schedule be carried into effect (a schedule will be provided which sets out the terms of any agreement reached).

11

LEGAL PROCEEDINGS

Commencement of Proceedings

If no agreement can be reached as to the validity of a will then, inevitably, one side will issue proceedings against the other. It is open to either side to commence proceedings—i.e. a disappointed beneficiary could issue proceedings seeking a declaration as to intestacy or seeking a grant of probate in respect of a prior will. Equally those seeking to propound the validity of the disputed will could issue proceedings for a grant in solemn form upon that will. **11.01**

Before either side commences proceedings against the other it is important to establish, even at a late stage, that there is no prospect of settling a case. The proposed claimant should, by this stage, have considered Alternative Dispute Resolution (ADR) or mediation and considered whether or not it was appropriate to make a formal offer to settle the claim pre proceedings. The general Pre-Action Conduct Protocol (PACP) recommends that before issuing proceedings both parties should have the opportunity to take stock—to see if it is possible to resolve the matter without needing to start proceedings or alternatively to narrow the scope of the proceedings by seeking to establish what issues can be agreed. The modern philosophy of justice is that litigation is to be viewed as a last resort and all parties should genuinely seek to establish if a settlement can be achieved. **11.02**

Checklist for claimant

11.03 It is useful to have a checklist as an aide memoire before legal proceedings are issued. The checklist may include the following questions and considerations.

1. Has a 'stocktake' type letter been sent to the other side as recommended by the Pre Action Conduct Protocol?
2. Has mediation been offered? If not, are there good reasons for not making that offer?
3. Has a Part 36 offer been made to maximize the client's prospects of recovering costs?
4. If a Part 36 offer has been made is it still appropriate? Has the case been strengthened or weakened since the Part 36 offer was made?
5. Consider who should be the defendant from the outset. Do all relevant beneficiaries or potential beneficiaries know about the claim?
6. Conduct a stocktake with the client. Warn the client about timescales, strengths and weaknesses of the case, and potential cost liability. Once legal proceedings are actually issued the client will potentially become liable for the costs of the other side if the case is not successful.
7. Who is to draft the claim form and particulars of claim? Give consideration to the selection of counsel if not involved before.
8. Consider venue for the claim—is it High Court or county court jurisdiction?
9. On receipt of any defence go through it carefully. Check what allegations in the particulars of claim are accepted and what are denied. Are new allegations raised that need to be investigated or evaluated? Give fresh advice to the client and consider reviewing with counsel.

Issuing Legal Proceedings

11.04 Proceedings are started when the court issues a claim form at the request of a claimant.[1] In respect of a disputed will the proceedings are regarded as 'probate claims'. A probate claim is defined in Part 57(2)(a) CPR as a claim for 'the grant of probate of the will, or letters of administration of the estate, of a deceased person or the revocation of such a grant or a decree pronouncing for or against the validity of an alleged will, not being a claim which is non contentious (or common form) business.'

11.05 By virtue of Schedule 1 Senior Courts Act 1981, probate business, other than non-contentious or common form business, is assigned to the Chancery Division.

11.06 CPR PD 7A(2.5) states that a claim relating to chancery business (and a claim relating to a disputed will qualifies as 'chancery business') may, subject to any

[1] CPR 7.2 (1).

enactment rule or Practice Direction, be dealt with in the High Court or in the county court. County courts with chancery jurisdiction include the Central London County Court together with the county courts at Birmingham, Bristol, Caernarfon, Cardiff, Leeds, Liverpool, Manchester, Mold, Newcastle upon Tyne, and Preston.[2] Contested probate proceedings are, however, rarely issued in the county court. Section 32 of the County Courts Act 1984 gave jurisdiction to the county court in limited circumstances, in particular where it was shown to the satisfaction of the county court that the value of the deceased's net estate at the date of death did not exceed £30,000. This section was, however, repealed by the Crime & Courts Act 2013. The equity jurisdiction for the county court has been substantially increased by virtue of the High Court and county court jurisdiction (Amendment) order 2014.[3] The value of the deceased's net estate, however, remains only at £30,000 and the county court only has jurisdiction when a grant or application is made through the principal registry of the family division or a district probate registry under section 105 of the Senior Courts Act 1981 (Regulation 2(5)(C) of the said 2014 regulations). In reality therefore contentious probate proceedings are rarely commenced in the county court. Proceedings commenced in the 'wrong' court may be transferred to the High Court under section 42 of the County Courts Act 1984.

For the avoidance of doubt contentious probate proceedings are not proceedings which are started in the county court money claims centre at Salford—but are proceedings started in the High Court or district registry. **11.07**

Court form

The general claim form N1 should not be used—there is a specific claim form (Probate Claim)—N2. The claim form should, whether issued in the High Court or in the county court, be marked in the top-right-hand corner 'Chancery Business'.[4] It is usual to issue the claim form with supporting particulars of claim so that the claim form and the particulars of claim are served together upon a defendant. There is however no requirement to issue the claim form with a particulars of claim. Where the claimant does not include the particulars of claim in the claim form then they may be served separately either at the same time as the claim form or within 14 days after service of the claim form (provided that the service of the particulars of claim is within four months after the date of the issue of the claim form). If the particulars of claim are not included in, or have not been **11.08**

[2] CPR PD 57.2.2.

[3] SI 2014/821.

[4] CPR PD 7A (2.5).

served with, the claim form then the claim form must contain a statement that the particulars of claim will follow.[5]

11.09 Although the general rules relating to the issue of proceedings are set out in CPR 7 there is a particular part of the Civil Procedure Rules (CPR) which deals with probate and inheritance claims.[6] In general, contentious probate proceedings follow the same procedure as an ordinary Part 7 claim—subject to the differences contained within CPR 57 (e.g. all probate claims are allocated to the multi-track and judgment cannot be obtained in default of a defence).

Lodging of testamentary documents and filing of evidence about testamentary documents

11.10 The rules impose a specific requirement that any testamentary document of the deceased in the possession or control of any party must be lodged with the court.[7] Unless the court directs otherwise the testamentary documents must be lodged in the court office, by the claimant when the claim form is issued, and by a defendant when he acknowledges service. The claimant and every defendant who acknowledges service of the claim form must lodge a supporting statement describing any testamentary documents of which he has knowledge, or if he does not know of any such testamentary document, stating that fact and giving the name and address of the person in whose possession or under whose control the testamentary document is, or, if he does not know the name and address of that person stating that fact. The words 'testamentary document' are defined in CPR 57.1(2)(c). This definition includes 'a will' or 'a codicil' but also includes a draft of a will, written instructions for a will made by or at the request of or under the instructions of the testator, and any document purporting to be evidence of the contents or to be a copy of a will which is alleged to have been lost or destroyed. The wide scope of this definition should be appreciated by practitioners who often omit draft wills or written instructions for a will that are within their possession or control. A specimen form for the written evidence about testamentary documents is annexed to Practice Direction 57. This rule is sometimes ignored by claimants and defendants in contested probate proceedings. The failure to produce the required statement often displays a lack of knowledge of procedure and lawyers who fail to comply with the rule will often incur the wrath of a judge at case-management hearings. Plainly steps should be taken prior to the issue of proceedings to establish the whereabouts of all or any relevant testamentary documents. It is any original will that should be produced, if available—not simply photocopies.

[5] CPR PD 7A 6.1/6.2.
[6] CPR 57.
[7] CPR 57.5.

Contents of statements of case

A 'statement of case' is defined in CPR 2.3.1 as a claim form, a particulars of claim where these are not included in a claim form, a Defence, a Part 20 claim, a reply to a defence, and any further information given in relation to them voluntarily by court order under CPR 18.1. **11.11**

CPR 57.7 states that the claim form must contain a statement of the nature of the interest of the claimant and each of the defendants in the case. Ensuring compliance with the formal requirements CPR 57.7 is important so the text is quoted below. **11.12**

1. The claim form must contain a statement of the nature of the interest of the claimant and of each defendant in the estate.
2. If a party disputes another party's interest in the estate he must state this in his statement of case and set out his reasons.
3. Any party who contends that at the time when a will was executed the testator did not know of and approve its contents must give particulars of the facts and matters relied on.
4. Any party who wishes to contend that
   a. a will was not duly executed;
   b. at the time of the execution of a will the testator lacked testamentary capacity; or
   c. The execution of a will was obtained by undue influence or fraud must set out the contention specifically and give particulars of the facts and matters relied on.
5.
   a. A defendant may give notice in his defence that he does not raise any positive case, but insists on the will being proved in solemn form and, for that purpose, will cross-examine the witnesses who attested the will.
   b. If a defendant gives such a notice, the court will not make an order for costs against him unless it considers that there was no reasonable ground for opposing the will.

CPR 57.7 must also be read in conjunction with the general requirements relating to a particulars of claim contained within CPR 16.4. There is also a reminder that the Practice Direction Pre-Action Conduct, paragraph 9.7 states that where proceedings are commenced the claimant should state in the claim form or particulars of claim whether they have complied with Sections III and IV of that Practice Direction (exchanging information before starting proceedings etc.). **11.13**

Contents of a particulars of claim

Particulars of claim vary in length considerably depending upon the complexity of the issues required to be identified by the effect of the will being either valid or invalid. The particulars should include the following. **11.14**

1. Statement of the nature of the interest of the claimant and each defendant in the case—i.e. whether they are entitled under the will in dispute, any previous will or an intestacy.

2. Details of any caveat, warning, and notice of appearance.
3. Statement of the extent of the interest under a will.
4. Details of what is being sought, i.e. a decree of probate of the relevant will in solemn form and the seeking of payment costs of the action.
5. The claim form should include a statement of truth which must be signed by the claimant or his lawyer.[8]

Service of Proceedings

11.15 The general rules relating to service of proceedings contained within CPR 6 apply to contentious probate proceedings. The claimant (or his lawyer) can serve the claim form on the defendant (or their solicitors)—or ask the court to serve it.[9] The usual method is for proceedings to be served by post or document exchange. Where both sides are represented by solicitors it is usual for the claimant solicitor to invite the defendant solicitor to accept service of proceedings. Where the solicitor is within the jurisdiction and if the defendant has given notice in writing (or the solicitor acting on his behalf has given notice in writing to the claimant) then service on the solicitor (and no one else) will then be 'good service'.[10] If a defendant resides outside the jurisdiction CPR 6.30 applies.

Responding to the particulars of claim

11.16 If the claimant serves the claim form with a particulars of claim then the defendant (within the jurisdiction) must file an acknowledgement of service within 28 days after service of the claim form. Where the defendant is served with a claim form which states that the particulars of claim are to follow then the defendant has 28 days after service of the particulars of claim.[11] This is longer than the usual period of time allowed to acknowledge service in other proceedings which is usually 14 days. Although CPR 57.4 makes reference to 'acknowledgement of service and defence' the word 'defence' is not further referred to in CPR 57.4. It is usual to serve any defence with the acknowledgement. If, however, a defendant contends that he has any claim or is entitled to any remedy relating to the grant of probate of the will or letters of administration of the estate on his own account then the defendant must serve a counterclaim making that contention.[12] CPR 10.5 contains the formal requirements relating to the contents of the Acknowledgment of Service. In general legal proceedings (e.g. for a debt), if a defendant does not acknowledge receipt of

[8] CPR 22.3.2.
[9] CPR 6.4.
[10] CPR 6.7(i).
[11] CPR 57.4(2).
[12] CPR 57.8(1).

proceedings then it is possible to apply for a 'default judgment' once the time for filing an acknowledgement of service has elapsed. The default judgment procedure is NOT available in respect of a contentious probate claim. Where a defendant does not acknowledge service or does not file a defence then the claimant may apply for an order that the claim proceed to trial and seek a direction that the claim be tried only on written evidence.[13]

Who should be a defendant?

A balance should be struck between the extent and significance of the issues involved and the legal costs that are likely to be incurred joining in all parties who have an interest in the estate if either the will is valid or found to be invalid. If there are numerous individuals who would be beneficiaries under a disputed will then notice should be given to each and every one of them about the fact of the dispute. Likewise if the disputed will would result in an intestacy then those individuals who would benefit under the intestacy also have a right to be informed about the dispute. If, for example, there is one substantial subsidiary beneficiary in a disputed will but numerous other individuals are to receive nominal pecuniary legacies of, say, £250 each, then the claimant may wish to make a pragmatic offer simply to pay those claimants whatever the outcome of the dispute—rather than face the prospect of them becoming involved in proceedings, the claimant losing the claim and then facing an application for costs. These points should be considered prior to the issue of proceedings. As a minimum the executors under a disputed will together with substantial beneficiaries should be added as defendants at the outset. It is likely that the executors, in their capacity as executors, would wish to remain neutral in the dispute and await the decision of the court. **11.17**

For the avoidance of doubt it is, of course, possible that a defendant could admit the claimant's claim—after the issue of legal proceedings. In the event of an agreement it is still necessary to have an order stating to whom the grant is to be made under CPR 57.11. A claimant may consider suggesting that minor beneficiaries may all wish to instruct the same firm of lawyers to represent them all, to reduce costs under CPR 19.6 and CPR 19.8A. **11.18**

Contents of a defence

The general rule relating to the contents of a defence contained within CPR 16.5 applies as follows: **11.19**

1. In his defence, the defendant must state
   a. which of the allegations in the particulars of claim he denies;

[13] CPR 57.10.

   b. which allegations he is unable to admit or deny, but which he requires the claimant to prove; and
   c. which allegations he admits.
2. Where the defendant denies an allegation,
   a. he must state his reasons for doing so; and
   b. if he intends to put forward a different version of events from that given by the claimant, he must state his own version.
3. A defendant who
   a. fails to deal with an allegation; but
   b. has set out in his defence the nature of his case in relation to the issue to which that allegation is relevant,

shall be taken to require that allegation to be proved.

11.20 The general rule set out in CPR 16.5 is supplemented by the rules relating to the contents of a statement of case contained within CPR 57.7. If a party disputes another party's interest in the estate he must state this in the statement of case and set out reasons. Any party who contends that at the time the will was executed the testator did not know of and approve its contents must give particulars of the facts and matters relied upon. Likewise any party who wishes to contend that a will was not duly executed—that at the time of execution the testator lacked testamentary capacity or the execution of the will was obtained by undue influence or fraud—the statement of case must set out the contention specifically and give particulars of the facts and matters relied upon; failure to do so may result in an application for summary judgment and/or an application to strike out the statement of case pursuant to CPR 3.4(2)(c).

Contents of a defence specific to a probate claim—no positive case

11.21 Although there are general rules relating to the contents of a defence, there is a specific defence that is available in contentious probate proceedings. This rule is contained within CPR 57.7(5)(a). A defendant may give notice in his defence that he does not raise any positive case, but insists on the will being proved in solemn form and for that purpose will cross examine the witnesses who attested the will. The rule provides that if a defendant gives such a notice the court will not make an order for costs against him unless it considers that there was no reasonable ground for opposing the will. There are several points to make about this special defence. If a defendant seeks to rely on that defence (in the hope of gaining costs protection if he loses) then the defendant cannot stray into seeking to put a positive case at trial. Unless a positive case is placed before the court it can make it very difficult for the case to be successfully defended. If, with a view to maintaining cost protection, the advocate limits himself to asking each witness if he is sure of his evidence—this may prove to be a fruitless exercise. Furthermore although the rule gives a prima facie defence to a claim for costs, costs always remain within the discretion of the trial judge and some trial judges have been known to make orders for costs against unsuccessful defendants in these circumstances—even though no positive case has been raised. This is a risk that must be drawn to the attention of a defendant seeking to rely on this defence. An unsuccessful defendant has no guaranteed right to avoid a costs order being made against him—but in any event even if the claim was unsuccessful he would still be likely to have to pay his own legal costs.

Revocation

There is no doubt that a claimant is in a relatively strong position if the validity of a will is challenged before a grant of probate has been issued. The caveat procedure can stop a grant being issued—and hence the administration, and distribution, of the estate being concluded. The making permanent of a caveat by a notice of appearance will force a defendant to negotiate or deal with the claim. There is no limitation period in respect of an application to challenge a will. A will can be challenged even if a grant of probate has been issued—but the claimant will be on the back foot since the defendant will already have a grant. There is a specific part of CPR 57 which deals with application for a revocation of an existing grant—CPR 57.6. Every person who is entitled or claims to be entitled to administer the estate under the grant must be made a party to a claim. If a defendant has the probate or letters of administration under his control he must lodge it in the relevant office when he acknowledges service.[14] **11.22**

Summary Judgment

Although it is not possible to obtain a judgment in default of a defence, if the defence served is plainly hopeless it may be possible to obtain summary judgment pursuant to CPR 24. The court may give summary judgment in any case against the claimant or a defendant on the whole of the claim or a particular issue if it considers that party has no real prospect of successfully bringing or defending the case or that there is no other compelling reason why the case or issue should not be disposed of at trial.[15] In the vast majority of cases a claim that is properly pursued or defended will not be appropriate for summary judgment—but there can be cases where, for example, an impecunious, obstructive defendant is using the proceedings as a means of disrupting the administration of the estate and putting a claimant to the potentially considerable expense of a trial. It is important to remember the requirement that it is still not possible to obtain a judgment administratively—so that if the court does decide that the defendant has no real prospects of successfully defending the claim, etc. then **11.23**

[14] CPR 57.6(3).

[15] CPR 24.2.

the case will still need to be listed for trial on written evidence only. The requirements for a summary judgment application are contained within CPR 23 and CPR 24. In addition to the procedural requirement set out in CPR 24, if an order pronouncing for a will in solemn form is sought on an application for summary judgment the evidence in support of the application must include written evidence proving due execution of the will.[16]

11.24 A good illustration of the procedure for summary judgment in a contentious probate case is demonstrated in *King v King*.[17] This was a High Court appeal against the decision of Master Teverson who granted summary judgment dismissing Mrs King's claim disputing the validity of a will made by her late husband in September 2005. The claim was, in substance, a claim for revocation of the grant of probate in relation to the 2005 will. Her claim was on the grounds that her husband made the will without the knowledge or approval of its contents and that the execution of the will was obtained by undue influence. The executor applied for, and obtained, summary judgment. Master Teverson dismissed the claim but gave permission to appeal. The appeal was heard by Edward Murray sitting as a deputy judge of the Chancery Division. He observed that Master Teverson had correctly reminded himself 'that it is not appropriate in many probate claims to dispose of them on a summary basis on written evidence alone'. On the appeal it was submitted on behalf of the claimant appellant that Master Teverson had decided the application for summary judgment in relation to the issue of knowledge and approval on the basis of the balance of probability, rather than the proper basis for summary judgment set out in CPR 24.2, namely whether Mrs King had a real prospect of success in respect of her claim or whether there was some other compelling reason why the case should be disposed of at trial. The appeal judge rejected that submission and held that Master Teverson had indeed correctly applied the appropriate test. Paragraph 35 of the appeal judgment is, however, relevant in the context of disputed capacity cases since the judge noted:

> ... in this case, the testamentary capacity of Mr King was not in dispute and in any event appears to be confirmed by the attendance notes of 21 June 2005 and 27 September 2005. Accordingly, assuming for the moment that there were no circumstances that would or should arouse the suspicion of the court, Master Teverson had sufficient evidence to enable him to conclude that the ordinary test was satisfied in this case, namely that so long as there is no problem of lack of testamentary capacity, the testator's knowledge and approval of the contents of his will will be assumed from the fact that he has signed the document and had it attested in proper form.[18]

There is plainly an argument that the procedure for summary judgment only applies 'so long as there is no problem of lack of testamentary capacity'—but for the reasons

[16] CPR 57 PD 5(1).

[17] [2014] EWHC 2827 (Ch).

[18] *Fuller v Strum* [2001] EWCA Civ 1879 at [77].

we have stated above, in the rare but appropriate case, an application for summary judgment can, and should, be made, even if lack of capacity is alleged—but without appropriate evidence.

An application for summary judgment is often considered with an application pursuant to CPR 3.4 (2). The court has power to strike out a statement of case if it discloses no reasonable ground for bringing a claim. The practitioner would be looking for an argument to the effect that even if everything the other side says is factually true it would still give no claim or defence. An application for summary judgment or an application for a strike out should not be used where the outcome may hinge on the resolution of disputed evidential issues—save, possibly, in the exceptional case where the evidential basis of the case advanced by the other side is so manifestly wrong that it could be characterized as fanciful. **11.25**

Directions Questionnaire

If a defendant files a defence then, upon receipt, a court officer will provisionally decide the track which appears to be most suitable for the claim and serve on each party a notice of the proposed allocation.[19] The notice of proposed allocation will require the parties to file a completed directions questionnaire and serve copies on all of the other parties. It should be noted that there are three 'tracks' for dealing with claims generally, namely the small claims track, the fast track and the multi track. The small claims track is applicable to those claims with a value less than £10,000. The fast track is for those claims which have a value of not more than £25,000—and the multi track is the normal track for any claim for which the small claims track or the fast track is not the normal track. By virtue of CPR 57.2(4) all probate claims are allocated to the multi track so it is to be hoped and expected that the court officer undertaking the provisional allocation of track pursuant to CPR 26.3(a) will provisionally allocate the claim to the multi track. If an error is made and the wrong track is allocated then the court may be persuaded in correspondence (particularly if sent by both sides) to rectify this error either prior to or at a case-management conference. If the case is provisionally allocated to the multi track then other, newer, consequences follow. Unless the court orders otherwise then, in respect of multi track cases commenced on or after 1 April 2013, all parties (except litigants in person) must file and exchange cost budgets as required by the rules.[20] Each party must do so by the date specified in the notice served by the court under Rule 26.3 or, if no such date is specified, 7 days before the first case-management conference. The consequences of failing to file and exchange budgets are severe—by virtue of CPR 3.14 unless the **11.26**

[19] CPR 26.3.
[20] CPR 3.13.

court otherwise orders, any party which fails to file a budget despite being required to do so will be treated as having filed a budget comprising only the applicable court fees. In CPR 3.12 the purpose of cost management is said to be that the court should manage both the steps to be taken and the costs to be incurred by the parties to any proceedings so as to further the overriding objective. The overriding objective is defined in CPR 1 and seeks to enable the court to deal with cases justly *and at proportionate costs* (our emphasis), CPR 1.1(2). Dealing with a case in ways which are proportionate includes taking into account:

i. the amount of money involved; and
ii. the importance of the case; and
iii. the complexity of the issues; and
iv. the financial position of each party.[21]

11.27 The courts are adopting much more proactive steps to manage the costs of litigation. As an illustration, a court may be reluctant to permit the cost of oral witness evidence from numerous witnesses who are going to give evidence on the same issue i.e. about the capacity, or lack of capacity, of the deceased.[22] Equally the court may wish to control the cost of expert evidence. It is yet too soon to comment upon the effectiveness of these reforms which are relatively new but we have seen, for example, a district judge seeking to control the cost of obtaining a jointly instructed psychiatric report to a level lower than is readily obtainable from many of the experts who tend to deal with these cases.

11.28 If a party does not file and serve a directions questionnaire then the claim (or defence) is at risk of being struck out.

11.29 The directions questionnaire for fast track and multi track is Form N181. The form deals with the following issues:

1. Whether the parties wish a one-month stay to try to settle the proceedings.
2. If the claim has been issued in the High Court whether it should remain there (the court may transfer the claim to a county court irrespective of the views of the parties).[23]
3. Which is the appropriate court to deal with the case? (The location of the majority of the witnesses is a relevant feature here.)
4. Whether the parties have complied with the PACPs. The reason for this question is not particularly clear—it only asks whether 'you' have complied with any relevant PACP and does not invite comment on the conduct of the other side.
5. Case-management information—whether any applications have been made.

---

[21] CPR 1.1 (2)(c).
[22] See the new powers contained in CPR 32.3(3).
[23] s. 40 (2) County Courts Act 1984.

6. Which is the relevant track (Small Claims, Fast, or Multi track)?
7. Disclosure of electronic documents (in Multi-track cases) by virtue of CPR 31.5(3).
8. Experts—parties need to explain whether they wish to use expert evidence at the trial or final hearing. The form makes it clear that there is no presumption that expert evidence is necessary in a dispute or that each party will be entitled to their own experts. If expert evidence is required then the Court will at least want to be satisfied why the joint instruction or joint selection of an expert is not appropriate (with a view to saving cost). The court will require the parties to identify an expert by name and their field of expertise—together with a justification for the appointment of that expert and an estimate of costs.
9. Witnesses—the parties must identify which witnesses as to fact they intend to call at the trial and a brief summary as to the facts upon which each witness intends to give evidence.
10. Estimated length of trial.
11. Costs—a cost budget in form Precedent H[24] must be filed in accordance with CPR 3.13 (in Multi-track cases).

Part 18 Request for information

The court may at any time order any party to clarify any matter which is in dispute in the proceedings or give additional information in relation to any such matter—whether or not the matter is contained or referred to in a statement of case.[25] In practice the party seeking clarification or information should first serve on the party from whom it is sought a written request stating a date by which the response to the request should be served. The date must allow the second party a reasonable time to respond.[26] The response may be contained within a letter but a standard format is used which contains the requirements of CPR 18 PD 1.6. It is all too easy to miss essential requirements if the request is contained in a letter. It is good practice for litigators to retain their own standard precedent form which complies with the formalities. If the receiving party refuses to respond then the matter may fall to be decided by a directions judge at a case-management conference. **11.30**

Notice to admit facts

CPR 32.18 gives a party the power to serve notice on another party requiring him to admit the facts, or the part of the case of the serving party, specified in the notice. The notice to admit facts process is used far too infrequently. The standard form **11.31**

[24] Precedent H form can be found at CPR 3E PD 3.
[25] CPR 18.1.
[26] CPR 18 PD.1.

(N266) is one of the easiest to complete. The tactical effect of a notice to admit facts should not be underestimated. To give an illustration, a testator may have suffered an illness, between the date of giving instructions for a will and the date when the will was executed, which impaired his capacity. A claimant may be seeking to rely on the rule in *Parker v Felgate*.[27] Under this rule a will can be valid where a testator had given instructions with capacity but did not execute it until a time when he lacked capacity—in limited circumstances the will may still be found to be valid.[28] A party seeking to propound a will may claim that the deceased had capacity both at the time of instructions for and execution of the will. The case may proceed to trial and the validity of the will upheld on the ground that, for example, the rule in *Parker v Felgate* applies because the deceased had capacity at the time of giving instructions for the will. In the usual scenario the unsuccessful defendant would be likely to have to pay all of the claimant's costs. The unsuccessful defendant could however seek to protect his position by serving a notice to admit facts—i.e. inviting the claimant to concede that the deceased did not have capacity at the date of execution. If this point was not accepted then the court may exercise the discretion under CPR 44.2 and CPR 44.3 to require the successful claimant to pay the costs of the defendant proving that the deceased did not have capacity at the time the will was executed—this could have considerable cost consequences. More than one notice to admit facts may be served in the same case and considerable pressure can be put on the opposing side in a case to narrow down the areas of dispute by reference to the skilful and appropriately timed notice to admit. A similar process can be used in respect of a notice to admit or produce documents.[29]

Disclosure of electronic documents/agreeing directions

11.32 Not less than 14 days before the case-management conference each party must file and serve a report verified by a statement of truth which describes what documents exist or may exist that are, or may be, relevant to the matters in issue in the case, describes where those documents may be found, describes in the case of electronic documents how those documents are stored, and estimates the broad range of costs that could be involved in giving standard disclosure in the case. The parties are directed to attempt to reach agreement about the scope and extent of disclosure of electronic documents.

11.33 Both the parties and the court will be assisted if the parties can at least attempt to agree the majority (if not all) of the directions—together with the respective cost budgets. The Practice Direction[30] requires the parties to consult one another and to

27 [1883] 8 PD 171.
28 See Chapter 3 for a detailed commentary on this rule.
29 CPR 32.19.
30 CPR 26 PD 2.3.

cooperate in the completing of the directions questionnaires and giving information to the court. The parties must try to agree the case-managed directions that they will invite the court to make. Specimen directions for Multi track are available on the Justice website.[31] The website includes a section for 'standard directions'. Wherever possible the court prefers the court standard wording to be used rather than the individual wording adopted by individual solicitors. There are standard directions for standard types of cases including personal injury, clinical negligence, employers' liability, etc. cases—but there are no specific standard directions in respect of contentious probate claims. The 'general' standard directions order (as adapted for a contentious probate case) would comprise:

1. Introduction—warning about the importance of complying with the terms of the order.
2. Allocation to the Multi track.
3. Consideration of ADR (including mediation).
4. Disclosure of documents.
5. Disclosure of evidence of fact statements.
6. Provisions regarding expert evidence—jointly instructed, instructed by each side together with a timetable for disclosure of any questions to the expert, and discussions between experts.
7. Listing of trial.
8. Pre-Trial Directions—and Pre-Trial Review to be listed 4 weeks before the trial window—and a direction as to whether or not the review may be conducted by telephone.
9. Requirements for trial including filing of case summary, chronology, trial timetable, exchange of skeleton arguments, etc.

It is in the interests of the parties to try to reach an agreement as to the directions to be sought.

It is also in the interests of the parties to try to reach an agreement on the cost budgets for each side—it is unlikely that the court would interfere with budgets which had been agreed between the parties, since the court may make an order which 'records the extent to which the budgets are agreed between the parties'.[32] There is little relevant authority upon the extent to which a court will decline to approve the parties' agreed cost budgets and clarification is awaited. **11.34**

It is likely that after filing of directions questionnaires the court will list the matter for a case-management conference to deal with directions and budgets. **11.35**

[31] <http//www.justice.gov.uk/courts/procedure-rules/civil>.
[32] CPR 3.15 (2)(a).

Joining non parties

11.36 CPR PD 57.4 requires the court, in giving case-management directions in a probate claim, to give consideration as to whether any person who may be affected by the claim and who is not joined as a party should be joined as a party or given notice of the claim (under Rule CPR 19.8A) or otherwise, and whether to make a representation order under Rule 19.6 or 19.7.

11.37 If proceedings have been commenced and not all of the parties who would be affected by the outcome of the case have been joined as parties (either as a claimant or as a defendant) then the court will usually make an order that notice of the proceedings should be given to them—together with a copy of the pleadings and orders made to date. This rule gives the court power to make any final judgment binding on them even though they are not parties to the case. The court does have the power to direct that any other witness statements, etc. already served in the proceedings should be served together with the formal documents. Notice of the proceedings is to be given in form 52 (notice of claim). Experience has shown that this form is remarkably difficult to find—it can be found under the Government 'HMCTS' Form Finder Website. The substance of Form 52 is as follows.

No.52

Notice of Claim to non-parties (CPR 19.8A)

IN THE HIGH COURT OF JUSTICE

Claim No.

CHANCERY DIVISION

[ ] DISTRICT REGISTRY

MASTER

.....20...

BETWEEN

Claimant

Defendant

To...................................... [Persons[s] affected by the claim]

TAKE NOTICE THAT:

1. Proceedings have been begun in the Chancery Division of the High Court of Justice in accordance with the attached claim form.
2. You are or may be one of the persons who are interested in the [estate] [trust property] to which the proceedings relate.
3. You may within 14 days after service of this notice acknowledge service of the claim form by completing the attached acknowledgement of service and handing

it in at, or sending it by post to, Chancery Chambers, Room 5.04, Thomas More Building, Royal Courts of Justice, Strand, London WC2A 2LL and you will then become a party to the claim.

4. If you do not acknowledge service of the claim form within 14 days after service of this notice you will be bound by any judgment given in the proceedings as if you were a party to them.

Dated...... [enter date of sealing]

If a party served with a notice files the accompanying acknowledgement of service he will become a party to the claim (and potentially liable to a costs order). If the person served with the notice of the claim does not acknowledge service of the notice he will be bound by any judgment given in the claim as if he were a party.[33] A potential beneficiary who does not have a substantial financial interest in the case may prefer not to become a party to the proceedings but instead (if in possession of relevant evidence which may help his position) wish to contact the claimant or defendant or their lawyers to offer a witness statement—so that they could become involved in the case without exposing themselves to a cost risk. CPR 19.6 deals with the power of the court to make an order where more than one person has the same interest in a claim. CPR 19.7 deals with representation of interested persons who cannot be ascertained e.g. because they are unborn, cannot be found, or are a class of persons who have the same interest in the claim (e.g. if there was a bequest to be shared between all the members of a cricket club at the date of death of a deceased). **11.38**

Cost Budgeting

In respect of cases commenced after 1 April 2013 new powers were given to courts to manage the cost of cases. These powers were introduced by the Civil Procedure (Amendment) Rules 2013[34] and are now contained within CPR 3.12 to CPR 3.18. These powers followed the recommendations made in the 'Access to Justice' final report from Jackson LJ. Unless the court orders otherwise, all parties except litigants in person must file and exchange cost budgets as required by the Rules. The format of the cost budget is set out in CPR Practice Direction 3E—Costs Management. A detailed Precedent H must be completed setting out the cost to be incurred in respect of various elements of work, for example pre-action costs (costs incurred before the issue of proceedings), costs in connection with the issue of proceedings and preparations of statements of case, costs associated with attending a case-management conference, dealing with disclosure of documents, preparing witness statements, obtaining experts reports, attending a pre-trial review, preparing for trial, and attending trial. The cost budget must be filed by a date specified in the notice served **11.39**

33 CPR 19.8 A.

34 SI 2103/262.

by the court under CPR 26.3(1)—or, if no such date is specified, seven days before the first case-management conference. Any party which fails to file a cost budget when required to do so will be treated as having filed a cost budget comprising only of the applicable court fees.[35] If the total costs of the case to trial are not likely to exceed £25,000 then only the first page of Precedent H needs to be completed—otherwise the substantial detail needs to be provided to the court. In the vast majority of probate disputes the costs of a case which goes to trial would be likely to exceed £25,000, so cost budgets will inevitably need to be prepared. There are a few tactical issues that arise in relation to cost budgets.

11.40 The court has no direct power to interfere in those costs which have arisen before proceedings are issued. This leads to some practitioners front-loading cases in an attempt to reduce the powers of the court to control costs. This may involve, for example, preparation of witness statements, obtaining of expert evidence, etc. before proceedings are issued. CPR 3.12 provides that the purpose of case management is that the court should manage both the steps to be taken and the costs *to be incurred* (our emphasis) by the parties to any proceedings. The court may take into account costs already incurred for the purpose both of cost-management and case-management directions. Just because, for example, a party has taken 15 witness statements from lay witnesses to give evidence about the capacity of the deceased to make a will there is no guarantee that a court will allow all witnesses to be called. The Practice Direction does state that 'The court may, however, record its comments on those costs and should take those comments into account when considering the reasonableness and proportionality of all subsequent costs.'[36] Courts are ever-more concerned about their own resources and the unnecessary length of trials. Witnesses who are seen to be giving evidence that duplicates evidence of other witnesses may not be permitted to be called. From the claimants' point of view and the defendants' point of view, if legal proceedings seem inevitable it is tactically important for both sides to work out a case plan—seeking to identify the steps that reasonably need to be taken to prove their case—together with the associated costs. If cost budgets are agreed between the parties then the court will record the extent to which those cost budgets are agreed.[37] It appears on the face of the rules that the court cannot interfere with cost budgets which have been agreed. It is sensible for each party to start dealing with cost budgets with the other side early—to exchange budgets and to attempt to agree them or to narrow down areas of dispute by way of arranged telephone call. Whilst a judge is unlikely to accept an excessive or disproportionate budget, an agreed, reasonable budget may remain undisturbed.

[35] CPR 3.14.
[36] CPR PD 3E 2.4.
[37] CPR 3.15(2)(a).

Disclosure

The court will almost always make an order for each side to disclose relevant documents to the other. The process is set out in CPR 31 together with the supporting Practice Direction. Many or all relevant documents may have already been disclosed on a mutual basis by consent before legal proceedings have been commenced. Documents that must be disclosed include those that are both favourable and unfavourable to a party's case (documents include written, electronic, photographic, video, and audio evidence). It is impossible to be prescriptive about the documents that will be disclosed since the documents that are available will vary from case to case. In a disclosure list the following documents will generally appear. **11.41**

1. Correspondence passing between the parties' lawyers.
2. The statements of case and orders in the action.
3. Medical records—GP, hospital, etc.
4. Social services records.
5. Nursing home records.
6. The relevant will or wills.
7. The relevant will draftsman's file of papers.
8. Estate accounts/HMRC form 400.
9. Relevant documents available to the parties. The list is hugely variable but the following documents are examples of what may be relevant:
   a. Photographs or a DVD of the deceased—a family video taken at a birthday party was regarded as a significant piece of evidence in *Simon v Byford (deceased)*.[38]
   b. The deceased may have generated documents that could be relevant—e.g. an old copy of *The Times* crossword duly completed (this example is mentioned as it became an issue in a case two of the authors dealt with. An ability to complete *The Times* crossword at or around the time a will was made was evidence of a degree of mental acuity—but was not determinative of the issue of capacity to make a will. Damage to the frontal lobe will affect judgement and can deny capacity to make a will—even though the testator was capable of completing *The Times* crossword).
   c. Notes, diaries, or letters written by the deceased at or around the time of the will. The authors have seen documents which would both tend to deny or support the ability to make a will.
   d. Christmas cards, birthday cards or greetings cards—or indeed the absence thereof—can be very relevant to the third limb of the *Banks v Goodfellow* test—the testator should be capable of understanding who may have expectancy to receive a bounty.
   e. Telephone bills—showing the length of calls to advisors, banks, or friends may corroborate lay witness evidence as to the capacity or the testator.

[38] *Simon v Byford* [2014] EWCA Civ 280; [2014] WTLR 1097 CA.

Witness Statements

11.42 Witness statements should be produced from sufficient witnesses to be able to prove the case—and no more. Increased importance is attached to the overriding objective by the court—with particular emphasis on the need to deal with cases at proportionate cost. This seeks to ensure that cases are dealt with expeditiously and fairly and that an appropriate share of the court's resources and time is allocated to a case while taking into account the need to allot resources to other cases.[39]

11.43 Lay witnesses will often have essential evidence to help the court determine a case. Lay witnesses will often have unique knowledge of the conduct, state of health, and capacity of a deceased—but a lay witness should never be asked to give evidence to the effect that 'I believe that the deceased had capacity to make a will'. This is outside the knowledge of a lay witness and would represent impermissible opinion evidence. The lay witness will however be able to give essential evidence one way or the other which would lead an expert or the court to believe that the deceased did, or did not, have capacity to make a will. Factors indicating capacity would include the ability of the deceased to:

- live on his own;
- drive a car;
- handle his own money and financial transactions;
- travel by public transport without getting lost;
- plan—e.g. planning shopping expeditions, the acquisition of items for a household, or holidays, etc.

11.44 Factors which may tend to indicate a lack of capacity could include:

- the inability to conduct the activities referred to above—e.g. by statements from a witness who could give examples of the confusion of the deceased when handling money;
- the increasingly eccentric or bizarre behaviour of the deceased. It is to be stressed that bizarre or eccentric behaviour is not of itself evidence of a lack of capacity but could be indicative of it;
- a lack of orientation as to time and place—e.g. by knocking on a neighbour's door at 3:00 am expecting the neighbours to be up and awake;
- the forgetfulness of the deceased—both short term and long term—e.g. by the deceased forgetting that a close relative had died many years ago or by repeating the same story many times;

[39] CPR 1.1(2).

- delusions suffered by the deceased—e.g. believing that a television programme is reality.

This evidence can be extremely helpful for experts and the court—but often the evidence that a witness has will only represent a partial picture and it requires evidence from a variety of sources to produce a full picture. Those witnesses who are independent and have nothing to gain by virtue of the litigation are often those witnesses who have the most credible evidence to give. Equally these most useful witnesses are often the most reluctant to become involved. **11.45**

It is common for both sides to wish to call a high number of witnesses—where each such witness has something to say about his or her dealings with the deceased. It is often worthwhile taking evidence from persons who met the deceased at different times and in different situations. Such evidence can be crucial to allow a judge to receive a complete, rather than partial, picture of the capacity of the deceased. The practitioner should be ready to counter the reluctance to allow large numbers of witnesses by drafting witness statements to keep them as short and as relevant as possible so that evidence can be dealt with quickly, and by pointing out to the procedural judge giving administrative directions that the trial judge will need to gain an overall picture of the deceased's capacity prior to death. **11.46**

Content and format of witness statements

The requirements as to the format and content of witness statements are contained within CPR 32 and the supporting Practice Direction—the witness statement must, if practicable, be in the intended witness's own words. Considerable credibility for a witness can be lost at trial if the words of the statement are effectively the words of the lawyer of one of the parties. **11.47**

The drafting of poor witness statements may have a disastrous effect on a case, particularly as the witness statement will often stand as the evidence in chief of the witness. Judges are increasingly refusing to allow elaboration of the statement by a witness in chief when he or she takes the stand. The more important the content of the witness statement, the more detail should be provided. Obviously evidence about the capacity of the deceased at the time the will was executed is crucial. Direct words used in conversation should be quoted if possible. Phrases such as 'he confirmed that' or 'I indicated that' or 'he agreed that' should be replaced by a description of what was actually said. If a witness cannot resort to direct speech because of fading memory then the witness should say so. A background narrative from a witness setting the scene for any given incident or conversation could be very relevant. For example, if a witness went to see a testator in hospital, the witness could be asked what the testator had been doing that day, such as reading a book or newspaper, watching television, or making phone calls, etc. **11.48**

Experts

11.49 There is no automatic assumption that expert evidence will be accepted by a court in a will capacity case—indeed the Civil Procedure Rules start from the premise that expert evidence is to be restricted to that which is reasonably required to resolve the proceedings.[40] Furthermore, in *Hawes v Burgess*,[41] Mummery LJ said

> ...my concern is that the court should not too readily upset, on the grounds of lack of mental capacity, a will that has been drafted by an experienced independent lawyer. If, as here, an experienced lawyer has been instructed and has formed the opinion from a meeting or meetings that the testatrix understands what she is doing, the will so drafted and executed should only be set aside on the clearest evidence of lack of mental capacity. The court should be cautious about acting on the basis of evidence of lack of capacity given by a medical expert after the event, particularly when that expert has neither met nor medically examined a testatrix, and particularly in circumstances when the expert accepts that the testatrix understood that she was making a will and also understood the extent of her property.

This quote should, however be contrasted with the comments made by Morgan J in *Cowderoy v Cranfield*:[42]

> [A]s neither psychiatrist had ever had the opportunity of seeing Mrs Blofield, neither was in a position to give me a direct psychiatric appraisal at any point in time, let alone on the day Mrs Blofield executed the disputed will. In principle, psychiatric evidence could assist a court dealing with an issue as to testamentary capacity. For example, the evidence could refer to such medical evidence as is available as to an individual's physical condition from time to time and could explain the likely impact on the mind of that physical condition. Similarly, the evidence could refer to medication being taken by an individual and comment on the likely effect on the mind of such medication being taken.

11.50 Despite these comments, expert evidence is obtained and given in evidence in the vast majority of cases which proceed to trial—particularly where medical issues arise (as they inevitably will) in respect of disputes as to whether or not an individual had capacity to make a will.

In a disputed capacity case expert evidence will usually be obtained from a psychiatrist. If the testator was elderly at the time instructions for the will were given then it is usual to obtain expert evidence from a psychiatrist who specializes in later-life patients. Perusal of recently reported judgments will often identify the experts who practise in this area as medico-legal experts.

40 CPR 35.1.
41 [2013] EWCA Civ 94; [2013] WTLR 453 CA.
42 [2011] EWHC 1616 (Ch).

Unless the expert is instructed by the individual or firm on a regular basis then a full and formal letter of instruction should be sent which includes: 11.51

1. The nature of the instructions—what is being sought from the expert—expertise to help determine whether the deceased had capacity to make a will.
2. Details of the party/parties providing the instruction, in the form of a list of documents that are attached.
3. Introduction—the family circumstances—perhaps a family tree showing the rival claimants to the dispute. Basic information such as date of birth, date of death, illnesses, etc. Reference should also be made to the will and the relevant date, and the complexity of the estate or assets at time of death or time of instruction for the will (if significantly different).
4. The Legal Issue—the test of testamentary capacity as defined by *Banks v Goodfellow* and the Mental Capacity Act 2005.[43]
5. Reference to the form and content of the expert's report and the role of the expert—as set out in CPR 35 in the supporting Practice Direction.
6. Timescale and requirements (e.g. an email address for the provision of a report).

Documents to be sent to the expert may include: 11.52

1. The disputed will.
2. Any relevant earlier wills.
3. A *Larke v Nugus* letter.[44]
4. A *Larke v Nugus* response.
5. The will preparer's file of papers—if relevant or significant.
6. Relevant witness statements, from either side, to the extent that they have been disclosed.
7. GP records—these will be inevitable in virtually every case.
8. Hospital records—particularly if the deceased had been investigated or treated for memory problems.
9. If the deceased was in a nursing home or care home at the time the will was made then nursing home or care home records/diary entries could be relevant.
10. A family tree showing the relevant potential claimants of the deceased's bounty.

The GP's records will usually include letters and correspondence sent by hospitals to the GP advising the nature and outcome of any investigations. If there have been specific investigations as to capacity, the hospital records will become essential—e.g. a letter from a hospital psychiatrist to a GP is likely to record the fact that the patient scored a particular score on a mini mental state examination. It is unlikely that the copy of the actual test will be enclosed. The first point to note here is that it is not unknown for the scores to have been added up incorrectly. The 11.53

[43] See Chapters 2 and 5.
[44] See Chapter 6.

second point to make is that the medical expert will want to consider not just the totality of a score, but will want to give consideration to the nature of the questions that were correctly answered and, perhaps more importantly, the nature of the questions that were answered incorrectly. Nursing-home or care-home records can be particularly relevant and are often ignored. These homes often prepare a care plan which will identify items of risk for a patient. Lack of capacity may have been identified as an area of risk. Daily diary entries may include reference to unusual behaviour or delusions which would not otherwise be picked up from GP or hospital records. Hospital nursing notes often give a much better idea of possible delirium than medical notes. These records are often neglected and can provide an invaluable source of evidence for parties. A care home nurse could also become a highly relevant witness as to the day-to-day behaviour of the deceased—but it must be appreciated that care home staff often do not wish to become involved in what may be seen as a partisan dispute between rival claimants to the estate of one of their patients.

Instructing experts

11.54 An informal general approach should be made to a potential expert to check:

- the availability of the expert and likely cost of the report;
- how long it would be likely to take for the expert to prepare a report—can the expert comply with any court timetable already given, if an expert report has not been obtained before proceedings are starting;
- whether there is a conflict? The selected expert may already have been instructed by the other side or may not want to take a case for professional reasons (e.g. the expert may have an interest in a charity which could stand to benefit if the will was either successfully challenged or maintained).

For these reasons only brief details should be given to the expert in the initial approach. If the expert is willing to act then formal instructions should be given. These will include a detailed letter of instruction together with supporting documents. For a specimen letter of instruction for an expert see Appendix 4.

Experts' reports

11.55 The quality of experts' reports can vary substantially. It is not the case that a longer report is more persuasive than a shorter report—what is significant is the content, substance, and logic of the report. If a report does not comply with the form and content required by the rules, less weight may be applied. If the report contains basic errors—e.g. incorrect date of birth or date of death, etc. it may not inspire confidence. Some reports are written in a remarkably bold and forthright style. This may be evidence of confidence and certainty on the part of the author. Alternatively, the same report may be viewed as an intransigent report without consideration of both sides. It is essential that the lawyer and lay client read and carefully check the report for basic errors—but ultimately the judgement of solicitor and counsel about the persuasiveness and relevance of the report reflects the art of litigation and the judgement of those involved. Follow the rules and procedures. It is obviously not part of an expert's function to adopt a biased or partisan approach. Whilst the approaches of both experts and judges vary, a court will often prefer the expert evidence of a witness who is cautious and willing to consider the position of both sides in a case.

The expert's role is not to go through all of the witness statements and documents and then perform the role of the judge by reaching a conclusion on all of the evidence. The expert will need to have regard to the witness statements and documents but his role should be to pick out the relevant points and discuss and consider how they might fit in with a given medical diagnosis—in other words the expert should be concentrating on bringing medical insight to bear on matters which would not be apparent to the lay person. Further examples of this would be commenting on the effect of any medication known to have been taken by the deceased at the time of the making of the will, commenting on the relevance of notes in hospital records, and translating any relevant medical terminology. This principle was expressed appropriately by Morgan J in *Cowderoy v Cranfield*.[45] **11.56**

It may be necessary for a psychiatrist to defer to a physician on certain points, and sometimes it is necessary for there to be evidence from two doctors on each side.

Contents of an expert's report

By virtue of CPR 35.10, at the end of an experts' report there must be a statement that the expert understands and has complied with their duty to the court. Furthermore the experts report must state the substance of all material instructions, whether written or oral, on the basis of which the report was written. It is generally established that the terms of the instructions to the expert are privileged from disclosure.[46] It is however the practice of most experts to list the documents that have been considered to enable the report to be prepared. It will be appreciated that sometimes an expert may be instructed early in proceedings before certain documents have been discovered or generated. Equally a report prepared later in **11.57**

[45] [2011] WTLR 1699 at [121].

[46] *Lucas v Barking, Havering, and Redbridge Hospitals NHS Trust* [2003] EWCA Civ 1102.

proceedings may take account of documents that have not subsequently been disclosed pursuant to the obligations of disclosure contained within CPR 31. It is a useful tactic for a lawyer to check the list of documents considered by the expert to see if all relevant documents have in fact been disclosed. There may be inadvertent reasons for non disclosure. An expert may place reliance on a witness statement but subsequently find that witness may be unwilling or unable to attend court to give evidence—thus potentially affecting the conclusions of the expert. The *Lucas v Barking* case referred to above together with CPR 35.10(4) make it plain that documents considered by an expert but not disclosed will not automatically attract a right of inspection—but the court may order disclosure if it is satisfied that there are reasonable grounds to consider that the statement of instructions is inaccurate or incomplete. In *Lucas v Barking* the order for disclosure of a witness statement and an earlier expert's report was refused. Such cases tend to be fact-specific but in appropriate cases a request for disclosure should be made. In August 2014 the Civil Justice Council published new and updated guidance for the instruction of experts in civil claims. The guidance is intended to replace the protocol on experts which formed part of the Practice Direction 35 of the Civil Procedure Rules. The new guidance (paragraph 61) states that 'before filing and serving an expert's report solicitors must check that any witness statements and other experts' reports relied upon by the expert are the final served versions'. If this guidance is complied with the problem identified in this section may be ameliorated—but if this guidance is not followed it will provide a fruitful line of cross examination of the expert at trial. The new guidance (paragraph 87) imposes an obligation upon the solicitors to inform the experts they have instructed when a case has been concluded either by settlement or trial—to rectify a long-standing complaint from experts generally that they are left holding papers without knowledge as to how and when a case has been concluded.

Questions to experts

11.58 CPR 35.6 provides that a party may put written questions to an expert who has provided a report. The questions must be proportionate. Questions must be put only once, be put within 28 days of service of the expert's report, and must be for a purpose only for clarification of the report—unless the court gives permission or any other party agrees. The expert's answers to the question are to be treated as part of the expert's report. Paragraph 6.2 of the Practice Direction supporting CPR 35 provides that the party or parties instructing the expert must pay any fees charged by that expert for answering questions put.

It can be useful to put questions to an expert in contentious probate cases. The nature of the questions put can often be fact-specific but the following general generic question may be considered. CPR PD 3.3(6) requires an expert to state in his/her report where there is a range of opinion on the matters dealt with in the report; the expert must summarize the range of opinions and give reasons for their own opinion. Sometimes an expert may not deal with that requirement in a report. A useful question may be to ask the expert if there is a range of opinion in relation to specific conclusions reached—particularly if the expert has not complied with the requirements of the Practice Direction. This can be a useful tactic to 'set up' the expert. If the expert states that there is no such range of opinion but is subsequently met by a different opinion from the expert on the opposing side, this may show the expert's view to be too narrow—or that the expert has not been willing to consider the merits of other opinions. If the expert concedes that there is indeed a range of opinion with regard to the conclusions reached then this may be seen to dilute the certainty of the expert's own opinion.

Some lawyers seek to cross-examine an expert by the presentation of numerous detailed questions. Such questions should be considered carefully. On one hand these questions may be entirely inappropriate and disproportionate, seeking to raise issues that go beyond clarification of the report. On the other hand the questioner may have identified and highlighted elements that have not been properly considered or explained in the expert's report. Judgement should be exercised, perhaps by the expert and instructing solicitor, as to whether or not it is appropriate for all or any such questions to be answered. Ultimately, if no agreement is reached, the issue would be decided by a judge upon application of the questioner as to whether or not it is appropriate for all or any of the questions asked to be answered. **11.59**

If particular documents are missing from the expert's list of all material sent to that expert then it may be appropriate to ask the expert if these documents have indeed been considered—and if not if their consideration affects any opinion. **11.60**

Where each side has their own expert report it is inevitable that the court will **11.61**

- order those reports to be disclosed to the court; and
- use the powers contained in CPR 35.12 to require discussions between experts, requiring the experts to prepare a statement for the court setting out those issues on which they agree and those issues on which they disagree, with a summary of their reasons for disagreement.

In seriously disputed cases where there are arguments on both sides either for or against establishing capacity, the experts may themselves conclude that the issues between them are relatively narrow and it will be a matter for a court hearing to form a view about the credibility of relevant witnesses and determine whether the will is valid or invalid. Often the experts will recognize that the decision about capacity could be a fine one requiring a court to take account of sometimes conflicting lay witness evidence.

Single joint experts

11.62 By virtue of CPR 35.7 the court has power to direct that the expert evidence is to be given by a single joint expert. Although the desire to save costs is understandable and a laudable aim there can be considerable risks for both sides in agreeing the appointment of a single joint expert. Firstly there is a risk that the single joint expert will effectively decide all or many of the issues in a case without challenge from an opposing expert. The second serious difficulty is that where a joint expert has been appointed neither side should interview that expert without the other side being present. This means, for example, that it can be difficult to evaluate the strength of the expert's position in a way that is usually achieved in a pre-trial conference with counsel, solicitor, client, and expert for the parties being present.

Concurrent expert evidence

11.63 The procedure at trial with regard to expert evidence has evolved. The traditional trial would start with lay evidence from the claimant and then deal with expert evidence from the claimant before the defendant called his lay and expert witnesses. More recently judges tended to hear from all lay witnesses and then hear evidence from the expert from the claimant followed by the expert from the defendant (where medical issues remained between them). The court now has power to hear concurrent expert evidence, colloquially known as 'hot tubbing'. This procedure is set out in CPR PD 35 11.1 to 11.4. The court has power to direct that some, or all, of the experts from like disciplines should give their evidence concurrently. The court may direct that the parties agree an agenda for the taking of concurrent evidence based upon the areas of disagreement identified in the experts' joint statements made pursuant to CPR 35.12. At the appropriate time (generally after all lay evidence has been heard) the relevant experts will each take the oath or affirm and the experts then address the items on the agenda. The judge may initiate the discussion by asking the experts in turn for their views. The judge may ask questions about these views or invite either expert to comment upon, or ask the other expert questions. Thereafter the parties' representatives may ask questions of either expert. Jackson LJ says that 'experience has shown that judges have gained much more assistance from experts by hearing evidence concurrently. The extent of disagreement has been reduced and the real issues have been identified.'[47]

Pre-Trial Preparation

11.64 The court will, following a case-management conference, give administrative directions regarding the future conduct of the case. A timetable for directions will be

[47] Refers to the *White Book* 2nd supplement, (Sweet & Maxwell, 2013).

given for administrative steps such as disclosure of documents, disclosure of witness statements, disclosure of expert evidence, etc. This timetable must be followed. Sanctions may be imposed by the court if steps are not taken within the appropriate time. Whilst the parties to litigation are now encouraged to agree reasonably short extensions of time, serious and significant delay will not be tolerated. In *Mitchell v Newsgroup Newspapers Limited*[48] the claimant's solicitors were debarred from claiming any costs in the proceedings because they were late serving a cost budget. This strict approach was considered by the Court of Appeal in July 2014 in three cases which were known as *Denton v TH White Limited & Others*.[49] The court reflected that 'the parties should in any event be ready to agree limited but reasonable extensions of time up to 28 days as envisaged by the new rule CPR 3.8 (4)'. It was reflected by the Master of the Rolls that 'it is as unacceptable for a party to try to take advantage of a minor inadvertent error as it is for rules, orders and Practice Directions to be breached in the first place. Heavy costs sanctions should be imposed on parties who behave unreasonably in refusing to agree extensions of times or unreasonably oppose an application for relief from sanctions pursuant to CPR 3.9.' Litigation, it was said, cannot be conducted efficiently and at proportionate cost without fostering a culture of compliance with rules, Practice Directions and court orders and cooperation between the parties and their lawyers.

If a party finds that they are unlikely to be able to comply with a timetable imposed **11.65** by the court then the first step should be to approach the other side in litigation to ask for an extension of time of up to 28 days pursuant to CPR 3.8(4). If an agreement cannot be reached to extend time then a prospective application should be made to court before the deadline has expired. The court has power to extend the timetable pursuant to CPR 3.1(2)A. The prospect of successfully making an application to extend time is enhanced if the application is made before the deadline has expired and there is a good reason for delay. Of course it is essential to try to obtain a realistic and proportionate timetable at the outset when the court gives directions. The parties will undoubtedly be assisted if all relevant individuals are aware of the timetable from the early stage. This means that the client, counsel, and any relevant experts should be sent a copy of the directions made by the court as soon as the order is received.

At an appropriate stage or stages it may be appropriate for the lawyer for each side to **11.66** consult with counsel—e.g. if significant, perhaps unexpected, developments arise on disclosure of documents, disclosure of witness statements, or disclosure of medical evidence then it may be appropriate to take stock as to merit and to consult with counsel

[48] [2013] EWCA Civ 153.

[49] *Denton v TH White Limited, Decadent Vapours Limited v Bevan & Salter, Utilise TDS Limited v Davies Bolton Community College Corporation & Watertrain Limited* [2014] EWCA Civ 906.

about the issues arising. Each side will probably want to have a pre-trial conference with counsel once the administrative steps pre trial have been concluded. This will be particularly important if counsel has not met the client before. It is often useful in a heavy case where serious issues between expert witnesses arise to have a conference involving the medical expert. Medical experts generally find it helpful to meet counsel and solicitor before a trial. Sometimes clients do not understand that the role of the expert is to help the court—some clients wrongly believe that the expert is 'batting for them'. The solicitor can help to protect the expert by making sure that the client understands the professional obligations upon an expert witness. To state the obvious, it is wise to take heed of the views of the expert expressed in the report, in discussions, and in conference.

Witness summonses

11.67 Once a trial date has been fixed the lawyers for both sides should consider whether a witness summons should be issued and served pursuant to CPR 34.2. It would be wise to consult with any expert witnesses as to whether or not they would like to be served with a witness summons. This may be seen as a means of guaranteeing their attendance at trial—but on the other hand an expert witness may be offended by the service of a witness summons, particularly if that expert has already agreed to attend trial on a given date. An expert witness should be consulted about their preference. Lay witnesses are in a different position. The case of a party to proceedings could be severely damaged by the non attendance of a witness at trial. The lawyer should discuss this issue with the client. A close friend of a claimant or defendant would, in reality, be most likely to attend a trial voluntarily, but a witness of fact who does not have a close personal relationship with the claimant or defendant may have little interest in attending—particularly if that witness is a professional called to give evidence of fact rather than opinion (e.g. a doctor, care-home worker, etc.). In those circumstances it may be appropriate to serve a witness statement. As a matter of courtesy the witness should be consulted. Conduct money should be served with the witness summons.[50]

Trial bundles

11.68 The responsibility is usually upon the claimant to prepare an agreed trial bundle.[51] The rules provide that the claimant must file a trial bundle not more than seven days and not less than three days before a trial. This is sometimes taken as a signal that the preparation of a trial bundle can be left until just before the trial. This is a serious misunderstanding. It often takes some time to agree and prepare a trial bundle. Preparation of a trial bundle index should be commenced as soon as all of

[50] CPR 34.7.
[51] CPR 39.5.

the administrative steps have been concluded. Preparation of a trial bundle should not be delayed in the hope or expectation that the case will settle. The preparation of a good trial bundle can be seen as a mark of the professionalism of the lawyers involved. The bundle of documents should follow CPR 39APD.3. This Practice Direction should be read in conjunction with Appendix 6 of the Chancery Guide—which gives further guidance in relation to the preparation of bundles for use in the Chancery Division. Even an experienced practitioner would do well to re-read the Practice Direction and relevant section of the Chancery Guide prior to preparation of a trial bundle. The bundle should be indexed and paginated.

It is usual for the bundle to include: **11.69**

1. The claim form and all statements of case.
2. A case summary/chronology where appropriate. A judge will often be greatly assisted by a chronology which is agreed by counsel in neutral terms. A dramatis personae may also be included here if numerous individuals are relevant.
3. Requests for further information and responses to requests.
4. All witness statements to be relied on as evidence.
5. Any witness summaries.
6. Any notices of intention to rely on hearsay evidence.
7. Any notice of intention to rely on evidence such as photographs, etc. under CPR 33.6.
8. Any medical reports and responses to them.
9. Any other experts' reports and responses to them.
10. Any order giving directions as to the conduct of the trial.
11. Any other necessary documents (if testamentary documents as defined in CPR 57.2(c) have not been included elsewhere then they must be included here).

The content and format of a trial bundle will vary significantly from case to case depending upon the number of relevant documents, but a few general points should be made: **11.70**

1. It is essential that relevant documents should be properly copied—it is sometimes easy to miss essential text if the relevant page is placed at an angle on a photocopier.
2. Page numbers should be inserted in bold figures at the bottom of the page.
3. Not more than one copy of any document should be included unless there is good reason for doing otherwise.[52]
4. It is rarely, if ever, appropriate to include copies of all correspondence passing between lawyers—it is, of course, permissible to prepare a separate second bundle dealing with cost issues if required. Such a bundle could include correspondence offering mediation, Part 36, offers, etc. This second bundle would obviously be produced only after the judgment on the issues has been delivered.

[52] Chancery Guide 1A-203.

5. Where possible documents should be in A4 format.
6. When any marking or writing in colour on a document is important the document must be copied in colour or marked up correctly in colour.
7. Documents in manuscript that are not easily legible should be transcribed.
8. Bundles should not be overloaded as they tend to break. The Chancery Guide provides that no bundle should contain more than 300 pages.[53]
9. All staples, heavy metal clips, etc. should be removed.
10. Redundant documents—e.g. particulars of claim overtaken by amendments or request for further information recited in answers given should generally be excluded.[54] The Chancery Guide gives clear guidance; however, an advocate may want to question the party about the amendment—for example asking why the new claim or allegation was not included originally—and will need to do so by reference to the original pleading. Practitioners may want to liaise with the advocate about this before removing documents that might usually be expected to be included. More common redundant documents appearing in many trial bundles comprise the full response pack to the defence and allocation questionnaires—where nothing turns on these documents.
11. Documents referred to in, or exhibited to, witness statements, affidavits, and experts reports should be put in a separate bundle and not placed behind the statement concerned so that the reader can see both the text of the statement and the document referred to at the same time.[55]
12. Where the volume of documents needed to be included in the bundles and the nature of the case make it sensible, a separate core bundle should be prepared for the trial containing those documents likely to be referred to most frequently.[56]
13. If authorities, extracts from text books, etc. are photocopied for convenience for use in court, the photocopy should be placed in a separate bundle with an index and dividers.[57]

11.71 Sometimes there is considerable misunderstanding about the nature of the contents of a trial bundle. Attention is drawn to CPR 32 PD 27.2 which states that 'all documents contained in bundles which have been agreed for use at a hearing shall be admissible at that hearing as evidence of their contents unless the court orders otherwise or a party gives written notice of objection to the admissibility of particular documents'. Great care therefore needs to be exercised by lawyers preparing and agreeing a trial bundle. There is sometimes a misconception that all that is being achieved by the production of a trial bundle is the production of relevant documents for the court—without appreciating that those documents will thereby become

[53] Chancery Guide 1A-206.
[54] Chancery Guide 1A-209.
[55] Chancery Guide 1A-210.
[56] Chancery Guide 1A-213.
[57] Chancery Guide 1A-215.

admissible 'as evidence of their contents'—without objection. This principle has particularly been considered in two recent cases (neither of which were contentious probate cases). In *Charnock v Rowan*[58] it was said by the Court of Appeal that

> …the obligation will lie on each party's lawyers to go through the agreed documents with the client or witness and take instruction on any discrepant evidence, albeit hearsay, relevant to the pleaded issues. But a party which has failed to plead its case with sufficient clarity may well find itself barred from adducing any evidence, hearsay or not, in support of an unpleaded contention.

Despite being a Court of Appeal authority Mr Justice Norris (a Chancery Judge) was required to consider this principle in *First Subsea Limited v Balltec Ltd.*[59] His finding (as recited at paragraph 28 of his judgment) is significant since he said

> The consequences of this view, (namely, that the inclusion of a statement in a disclosed document which is not the subject of specific challenge means that there is admissible evidence before the court of a fact stated in that statement) is that in the instant case, although BSW (a) has pleaded in general terms that Mr Lang was in breach of fiduciary duty and in breach of contract but given no particulars, (b) has not pleaded reliance on the so-called admissions made in the Manchester proceedings, (c) has not given any notice of intention to rely on those admissions, and (d) has not drawn attention to the evidence in their skeleton argument in opening, they could nonetheless in closing and after the defendants have closed their case, say, 'Well, there is evidence on which we wish to rely to prove that Mr Lang was in breach of his obligations, because you can find these statements on these pages in one of the many volumes of documents running to thousands of pages in this case'.

He then went on to decide the principles derived which he set out in paragraph 29 of his judgment, which read

> …it seems to me that PD 32 Para 27.2 has to be read in the context of the Civil Procedure Rules as a whole. Whatever the Practice Direction may literally say, there is no doubt that the Civil Procedure Rules contain, in CPR 33.2 and following, express reference to the requirements of the Civil Evidence Act as to the adduction of hearsay evidence. Those provisions are there for a purpose. I would be reluctant to read paragraph 27.2 as completely overriding those other provisions of the CPR, and indeed the statute itself. I accept that there are two expressions of view in the Court of Appeal that it might have that effect in the circumstances of the cases before the court. But for present purposes it seems to me that the guidance which is provided by CPR PD 32 paragraph 27.2 falls to be applied in each individual case by reference to the CPR as a whole, to the existence of the evidential requirements of the Civil Evidence Act, and in particular to the overriding objective. It seems to me that it would not be 'just' in many cases, to rely upon paragraph 27.2 as relieving a party seeking to use it of the obligation of giving fair and proper notice of the matter that is in issue and the evidence that will be used to prove it.

[58] [2012] EWCA Civ 2.
[59] [2013] EWHC 1033 (Pat).

11.72 The point we wish to make here is that great care needs to be taken when seeking to 'agree' a trial bundle. Care and attention needs to be given to establish what the consequence of the inclusion of any given document in a trial bundle will be—in particular whether either side will be able to rely on it as being evidence of a proposition in the case as pleaded.

11.73 These notes represent a summary of the key guidelines contained in the CPR and Chancery Guide. As is indicated above, the lawyers would do well to re-read the relevant sections of both in full.

Skeleton arguments

11.74 A skeleton argument is usually produced in contested will proceedings. Whilst it is likely that the judge hearing the case will be entirely familiar with the legal issues to be adopted, there is no guarantee that this will be the case—particularly in the County Court or if a Chancery Judge is a land law, commercial, or insolvency specialist. Skeleton arguments are essential in appeals and are expressly referred to in CPR 52.4.5, but are not referred to for first instance trials in the Civil Procedure Rules. Guidance for the form and content of skeleton arguments is included in Appendix 7 of the Chancery Guide. The advocate would usually be expected to produce a skeleton argument just prior to trial. These are usually exchanged on a reciprocal basis. There is a specific court form of skeleton argument—Form N163. This form is rarely used in practice, with the advocate producing their own format and style. The Chancery Guide indicates that every skeleton argument should:

1. identify concisely
   a. the nature of the case and the background facts;
   b. the propositions of law relied upon with references to the relevant authorities; and
   c. the submissions of fact to be made with reference to the evidence;
2. be as brief as the nature of the issues allows;
3. be in numbered paragraphs and state the name and contact details of the advocate who prepared it;
4. avoid arguing the case at length; and
5. avoid formality and make use of abbreviations e.g. C for claimant and A/345 for bundle A page 345.

11.75 Self-evidently, it will be likely to take the advocate some time to prepare the skeleton argument. By virtue of the fact that the skeleton argument should refer to the relevant page numbers in the agreed bundle, it is essential to seek to agree the bundle in good time before the trial so that counsel can be given an agreed bundle with the brief. Counsel will not want to go through and mark up a brief in preparation for a trial only to have to go through it again when a paginated bundle is prepared.

There is a misconception that skeleton arguments always have to be simultaneously exchanged. The Chancery Guide, at paragraph 7.19, provides that 'in an appropriate case the court may direct sequential, rather than simultaneous, delivery of skeleton arguments'. This may be particularly appropriate where one party is raising a positive case for the opposing party to respond to—however, quite often in probate claims, there is an argument about who has the burden of proof and so the identity of the person raising the positive case can sometimes be a matter of controversy. This tactical issue should be considered when final directions are given regarding trial. **11.76**

Trial Preparation Checklist **11.77**

A lawyer may use a checklist pre-trial to ensure all relevant steps have been taken or considered. Such a list may include the following:

1. Lawyer to read the complete files of papers to identify relevant documents to be included in the trial bundle.
2. Prepare a draft trial bundle index.
3. Seek to agree the trial bundle index with the defendant.
4. Reconsider with the client the advantages and disadvantages of proceeding to trial in the light of:
   a. the issues between the parties;
   b. the evidence of both sides;
   c. the risks of litigation;
   d. the value of the dispute (it is generally unwise to litigate on a 'principle' despite the expressed wishes of a party to proceedings); and
   e. any offers made by the opposing party.
5. Prepare a chronology of main events and a dramatis personae.
6. Prepare brief to counsel in good time. Ask counsel to prepare a skeleton argument.
7. Arrange pre-trial conference with client, counsel, and medical expert.
8. Inform all experts, witnesses, and counsel's clerk of time, date, place, and trial as soon as date is known. Consider sending a map and timetable.
9. Consider serving witness summons on experts or lay witnesses.
10. Give claimant an opportunity to read the trial bundle—this is important.
11. Give witnesses an opportunity to re-read their own statements prior to trial—send any witnesses a copy of these a few days before. Tell witnesses what the likely issues are going to be.
12. Prepare the client to give evidence and warn about what to expect for cross-examination. Witnesses must not be coached about how to give evidence but preparation is essential. A client might be advised to go to the same court a week or two before trial to find the venue, to become more relaxed, and, perhaps, watch how another trial proceeds to gain experience. This may be the first time a client has gone to court and this client's nervousness will be understandable.
13. Agree a trial timetable with the other side—particularly in a complex case lasting more than a day.

Trial

11.78 In a substantial case the parties should agree a trial timetable so that relevant witnesses and experts know when to attend. Of course all witnesses and experts may choose to listen to all of the evidence—but in a busy world this is rarely the case. The court will generally choose to hear the evidence of the claimant and those lay witnesses supporting the claimant and then hear the defendant and the defendant's witnesses. Generally expert evidence will follow together after lay evidence has been received. Expert witnesses would not generally expect to have been required to listen to all or any lay evidence—particularly if that evidence is likely to last several days or more. The expert witness would, however, expect to be briefed upon the issues that have developed prior to giving evidence of their own.

11.79 Counsel for the claimant, or both sides, would be expected to give opening statements followed by the evidence of the claimant. The judge would be expected to have read the relevant witness statements and so evidence in chief may be limited to the oath/affirmation and any clarification of aspects referred to in a witness statement before being made available for cross-examination and then re-examination. This process would generally be followed for all of the claimant's witnesses before the defendant and the defendant's witnesses give evidence. As indicated above, often expert evidence will follow the hearing of all lay evidence. On completion of evidence, closing submissions will be made followed by a judgment. Generally a judgment is given extempore straight after the trial has concluded. Sometimes judgment will be reserved—particularly in a more complex case.

Opening at trial

11.80 There is relatively little guidance within the Civil Procedure Rules as to which party should open the case at a trial. It is generally presumed that a claimant can open the trial. This assumption is referred to in the Chancery Guide—Conduct of a Trial—Chapter 8 which says 'in general, and subject to any direction to the contrary by the trial judge, there should be a short opening statement on behalf of the claimant, at the conclusion of which the judge may invite short opening statements on behalf of the other parties.[60]' In the vast majority of cases this proposition is correct. The claimant does usually open the trial because it is a claimant who has the burden of proof. It is not always a claimant who has the burden of proof in a probate claim—it is to be remembered that either a person seeking to propound the last purported will may have been the party to have started proceedings, but it may equally be the party who is seeking to propound an earlier purported will who has

[60] Chancery Guide 8.5.

started proceedings and whom, as such, may have the relevant burden. Of course in contentious probate cases the burden of proof can shift.[61] Who has the burden of proof may be an issue at the trial. Is there, for example, 'real doubt' as to whether or not the testator had capacity to make a will and to what extent is the presumption of capacity contained within s. 1(2) Mental Capacity Act 2005 to be applied? Suffice to say that these issues should be considered when the court gives a timetable for trial.[62] It is accepted that in general a claimant will open a case at trial but, for the reasons set out in this paragraph, this is not inevitably the case.

Costs

CPR 44 provides general rules about costs. The preliminary observation to make is that the court has a discretion as to whether costs are payable by one party to another, the amount of those costs, and when those costs are to be paid.[63] That discretion is generally unfettered and is difficult to challenge on an appeal unless the judge steps outside the broad range of discretion available.[64] Having said that, if the court decides to make an order about costs the general rule is that the unsuccessful party will be ordered to pay the costs of the successful party, but the court may make a different order.[65] **11.81**

When deciding what order to make about costs the court will have regard to all the circumstances of a case including the conduct of the parties, whether a party has succeeded on part of its case (even if that party has not been wholly successful), and any admissible offer to settle made by a party which is drawn to the court's attention which is not an offer to which the cost consequences under Part 36 apply. The conduct of the parties includes conduct before as well as during the proceedings and in particular the extent to which the parties followed the Practice Direction—pre-action conduct, whether it was reasonable for a party to raise, pursue, or contest a particular allegation or issue, the manner in which a party has pursued or defended the case or a particular allegation or issue, and whether a claimant who has succeeded in the claim in whole or in part exaggerated its claim. **11.82**

61 *Sherrington v Sherrington* [2005] EWCA Civ 326; [2005] WTLR 587 CA; *Re Ashkettle, Ashkettle v Gwinnett* [2013] EWHC 2125 (Ch); [2013] WTLR 1331; Para 97 *Re Key, Key v Key* [2010] EWHC 408 (Ch). See Chapter 5 on Burden and Standard of Proof.

62 CPR 39.4 and CPR 29.8.

63 CPR 44.2(1).

64 'As is well known, orders for costs are very rarely disturbed' Judge LJ *Voice and Script International Limited v Alghafar* [2003] EWCA Civ 736, and 'costs are in the discretion of the trial judge. This court will only interfere with the exercise of that discretion on well-defined principles' *Adamson v Halifax* [2002] EWCA Civ 1134 'the judge has either erred in principle in his approach or has left out of account or taken into account some feature that he should or should not have considered or that his decision is wholly wrong because the court is forced to the conclusion that he has not balanced the various factors in the scale'.

65 CPR 44.2(2).

11.83 For these reasons it is essential for both sides to act reasonably throughout the conduct of the case. This obligation applies to all aspects of the case. Correspondence should be seen to be written in a reasonable manner. The Pre-Action Protocol should be followed. ADR should be considered. Documents should be disclosed before the issue of legal proceedings. In will capacity cases it is not unusual for a claimant to run a series of causes of action, including lack of capacity, lack of knowledge and approval, and/or allegations of undue influence. If, for example, a claimant succeeds on one of these and a will is declared invalid, but fails on the other two causes of action, perhaps unreasonably having pursued them, a court would be likely to consider the requirement that the unsuccessful party should only pay a proportion of the other party's costs. The application of cost principles can be demonstrated by consideration of the significant case of *Kostic v Chaplin*.[66] In this case it was established that a testator lacked testamentary capacity when he made wills leaving his estate to the Conservative Party Association. The claimant successfully sought a pronouncement against two wills that were made by his deceased father. The deceased's decision to disinherit his son was, unfortunately, influenced by insane delusions. In contentious probate claims there were two long-established exceptions to the general rule that the unsuccessful party should pay the costs of the successful party. First, if a person who made a will had really been the cause of the action or responsible for the litigation it is possible to make out a case for costs to come out of the estate rather than being paid by the unsuccessful party. Second, if circumstances led reasonably to an investigation of the matter then costs might be left to those who had incurred them.[67] Henderson J found the *Kostic* case to be an unusual one. Even though the Conservative Party lost the case he found that its initial costs of investigating the claim should be paid by the estate—at least to the stage where a realistic assessment of the merits of the claim could first properly be made. Even though they lost the case the Conservative Party recovered their costs to a fairly early stage in the litigation when the nature of the claimant's case and the evidence in support of it had been explained to the Conservative Party Association and that the CPA had an opportunity to consider its position, to gather information, and to decide whether or not to contest the proceedings.

11.84 A second case which demonstrates how principles are applied in practice appears in *Wharton v Bancroft*.[68] In that case Norris J found that a challenge to a testator's deathbed will on the ground that it had been procured by undue influence failed. In a separate judgment the judge dealt with the costs issues following the beneficiary's success in proving the will and considered the general circumstances in which it will be appropriate to depart from the general rule as to cost in such cases. He found that the cause of

66 *Kostic v Chaplin Saunders and the Attorney General* [2007] EWHC 2909.
67 *Spiers v English* [1907] P.122.
68 [2012] EWHC 91 (Ch); [2012] WTLR 727 and for original trial see [2012] WTLR 693.

the litigation did not warrant a departure from the general rule as to cost. There was no ground to say that the action had been caused by the conduct of the deceased or the beneficiary under his last, disputed, will. Norris J found that the unsuccessful claimant had taken a commercial decision about the strength of the case which had turned out to be wrong—and this was not a ground to displace the general rule as to cost. A significant element of this case, however, related to the executor's cost of attending to hear and respond to personal criticisms about the way he had prepared the deathbed will. It is usual for an executor will preparer to remain neutral in proceedings. A substantial part of the case advanced at trial was that the will draftsman, Mr Bancroft, had behaved improperly by failing to recognize a conflict of interest in receiving instructions from Mr Wharton and in his failure to arrange for the attendance of a doctor in compliance with the Golden Rule. Norris J concluded that the will draftsman acted reasonably in preparing for and attending trial and was moderate in not seeking his own representation by counsel. The judge found that there was no reason in justice why his costs of attending to hear and respond to personal criticisms of him and to address the court as to the circumstances in which the relevant will was produced should be borne by the unsuccessful claimant. He recovered his costs on an indemnity basis.

The wide discretion for a court to make limited cost orders (as opposed to awarding costs in totality) is contained in CPR 44.2(6). **11.85**

Bases of assessment of costs

Where a court is required to assess the amount of costs it will assess those costs on a standard basis or on the indemnity basis. These distinctions can have important consequences for all parties and their representatives. **11.86**

Where the amount of costs is to be assessed on the standard basis the court will only allow those costs which are proportionate to the matters in issue. Costs which are disproportionate in amount may be disallowed or reduced, even if they were reasonably or necessarily incurred. The court will resolve any doubt as to whether costs were reasonably and proportionately incurred or were reasonable and proportionate in amount in favour of the paying party.[69] Further, if there is any doubt about the reasonableness of such costs that doubt is resolved in favour of the paying party.

Where the amount of any costs is to be assessed on the indemnity basis the court will resolve any doubt which it may have as to whether costs were reasonably incurred or were reasonable in amount in favour of the receiving party.[70] The limiting factors of proportionality are not included within the determination of cost factors when an indemnity order for costs is obtained. A successful advocate therefore has a particular interest in recovering an award of indemnity costs rather than standard costs. The **11.87**

[69] CPR 44.3(2).
[70] CPR 44.3(3).

court has a discretion as to whether to award costs on the standard or indemnity basis. Costs can be awarded on an indemnity basis if the conduct of one unsuccessful party is seen to be extreme. This aspect is rarely invoked.[71] It is more likely however that an order for indemnity costs will be made following a successful party beating their own offer that has been made pursuant to—CPR 36.14(3)(b). Subject to limited exceptions the court will, unless it considers it unjust to do so, order that a claimant is entitled to 'costs on the indemnity basis from the date on which the relevant period (to accept the offer) expired'.

Detailed or summary assessment

11.88 Where a court orders a party to pay costs to another party it has a discretion whether to make a summary assessment of costs or order a detailed assessment of costs.[72] The Practice Direction supporting CPR 44 indicates that the court will make a summary assessment of costs unless it is not practicable to do so at the conclusion of a trial on a case which has been dealt with on the Fast track, or at the conclusion of any other hearing which has lasted not more than one day.[73] If it is likely that there will be a summary assessment of costs then the parties are required to prepare and serve on each other a statement of costs not less than 24 hours before the hearing.[74] The format of the bill should follow court form N260 and the formal requirements are set out in CPR 44 PD 9.5. If a contentious probate case has been heard within one day it will be likely that, following evidence, judgement, and arguments about costs, etc. that court time will be rapidly running out. It is more likely even in those circumstances that a cost assessment would be put off to another day at a detailed assessment. The lawyers for each side cannot take this risk, however, and should still exchange cost schedules if the case is listed for one day or less. Issues in relation to detailed assessment of costs are beyond the scope of this book—but see the provisions set out in CPR 47 and the supporting Practice Direction.

Appeals

11.89 The procedures relating appeals are governed by CPR 52. An appellant or respondent requires permission to appeal in contentious probate proceedings.[75] An application for permission to appeal may be made to the lower court at the hearing at which the decision to be appealed was made or to the Appeal Court in an appeal notice.[76] The

71 For such an example see *Franks v Sinclair* (costs) [2006] EWHC 3656 (Ch).
72 CPR 44.6.
73 CPR PD 44 9.2.
74 CPR PD 44 9.5(4).
75 CPR 52.3.
76 CPR 52.3(2).

procedures are different depending upon the nature of the decision against which an appeal is sought. The procedures differ for a final decision as opposed to an interlocutory decision.

If an appeal is to be considered then the judge making the decision should be asked for permission to appeal, since if this is granted it saves the cost and delay associated with an application for permission to appeal to the Appeal Court. To state the obvious, it is extremely 'bad form' to ask a judge for permission to appeal simply because the advocate or party does not appreciate the decision that has been handed down. Permission to appeal should only be made where there are realistic prospects of success and the client intends to proceed with an appeal. Tom Bingham, the former Senior Law Lord, in his book *The Business of Judging*[77] said 'the judge's usual practice being to grant leave (to appeal) if he has decided a question of law and to refuse it if he concedes himself to have exercised a discretion'. **11.90**

A refusal of permission to appeal by the judge hearing the claim does not necessarily mean that there is no merit in the appeal—but only that the judge is following what he perceives to be traditional practice. **11.91**

Practice and procedure relating to appeals is complex. Careful and detailed consideration needs to be given to CPR 52 and the supporting Practice Direction. **11.92**

The general principle is that an appeal is to the next level of judge in the court hierarchy, but there is an exception to this principle contained within Article 4 Access to Justice Act 1999 (Destination of Appeals) Order 2000.[78] The normal rule (appeal lies to the next level of judge in the court hierarchy) does not apply where a district judge or circuit judge in a county court or Master or district judge in the High Court gives a final decision in a Multi-track Part 7 claim. A final decision includes a decision on the merits or costs but excludes a case-management decision, a summary judgment decision, or a striking out decision. Appeals against final decisions are made directly to the Court of Appeal (table 1, Practice Direction 52a). **11.93**

If a party applies for permission to appeal against a judgment or order at a hearing at which the judgment or order was made CPR 40.2(4) requires the judgment or order to state whether or not the judgment or order is final, whether an appeal lies from the judgment or order and if so to which appeal court, and whether the court gives permission to appeal and if not the appropriate appeal court to which any further application for permission may be made. Although this is a mandatory requirement upon the court, in reality it is, regrettably, frequently neglected. It is, of course, the responsibility of the advocates to draw the attention of the court to this requirement where a request for permission has been sought. **11.94**

[77] T. Bingham (Oxford: OUP, 2011) ISBN 978-0-19-969335-1.
[78] SI 2000/1071.

11.95 Where an appellant seeks permission from the Appeal Court it must be requested in the appellant's notice—there is a standard court form—Form N161. This form should be completed and lodged with the Appeal Court within such period as may be directed by the lower court or, where the court makes no such direction, 21 days after the date of the decision of the lower court[79]—the practitioner should be aware that an application for permission to appeal to the first instance judge must be made 'at the hearing at which the decision to appeal is made'[80]—in other words straight after the judgment has been delivered. It can happen that judgment is delivered in the absence of the advocates, with costs and consequential matters being deferred to another date. In order to preserve the 'first bite of the cherry' the losing party must make sure that the judge, when delivering his or her judgment, adjourns the hearing part heard to the time when costs and any consequential issues are determined.[81] The appellant's notice must be served on each respondent as soon as practicable and in any event not later than seven days after it is filed[82]. There are steps that the practitioner can take to enhance prospects of making a successful appeal. In due course a full transcript of the judgment would be required. Whilst this is easier when a written judgment is handed down, if the judgment is extempore the lawyers should use their best endeavours to make an accurate note of the judgment since this will undoubtedly form the basis for the grounds of appeal. Time is often tight. If there is a genuine expectation of an appeal the first instance judge could be asked to allow a slightly longer period in respect of which an appellant's notice should be lodged with the Appeal Court—this is particularly relevant if the time for appeal falls within a Christmas or other holiday period. Prospects of a successful appeal will be enhanced if the appeal is lodged within time—otherwise there is an additional hurdle to be overcome—namely the requirement to obtain permission to appeal out of time. It is not necessary for a respondent to serve a respondent's notice unless the respondent also seeks permission to appeal from the Appeal Court or wishes to ask the Appeal Court to uphold the order of the lower court for reasons different, or additional to, those given by the lower court.[83] Unless the Appeal Court or lower court orders otherwise, an appeal does not operate as a stay of any appeal against the order of any lower court.[84] In sensitive cases the lower court should be asked to stay the operation of the judgment pending the outcome of an appeal. The grounds for so doing are fact and case specific.

11.96 The parties (particularly the litigants) must appreciate the limitations upon an appeal process. An appeal will not succeed simply because one party is unhappy with the

[79] CPR 52.4(2).
[80] CPR 52.3(2).
[81] *Jackson v Marina Homes Limited* [2007] EWCA Civ 1404.
[82] CPR 52.4(3).
[83] CPR 52.5.
[84] CPR 52.7.

outcome. Every contentious probate appeal will only be limited to a review of the decision of the lower court.[85] The Appeal Court will not receive oral evidence or evidence which was not before the lower court unless it decides to order otherwise. *Ladd v Marshall*[86] was a case decided on the principles of the old Rules of the Supreme Court. This case determined that fresh evidence would not be allowed if it could have been obtained with reasonable diligence for use at the trial and that the evidence must be such that, if given, it will probably have an important influence on the result of the case, and also that the evidence must be of such credibility as to be likely to be believed. Practice Direction 52a includes general provisions relating to appeals and includes the destinations of appeal, the procedure for obtaining permission to appeal, the need for skeleton arguments, and the disposal of applications to appeal by consent. Practice Direction 52b deals specifically with appeals in the county court and High Court and Practice Direction 52c deals with appeals to the Court of Appeal.

Offers to Settle

It is exceptionally rare for there to be a litigated case which involves no risk at all to both sides. Apart from the usual perceived litigation and evidential risk there is always an inherent risk that proceedings may not continue as one party expects. It is generally sensible to seek to settle a claim to reflect the risk involved. This conduct is encouraged by the general thrust of the Civil Procedure Rules and Protocols (ADR is encouraged by the Pre-Action Protocol). It is rare to agree to attend a mediation (with the consequent incurring of costs for both sides) where one party refuses to make any offer at all to the other. CPR Part 36 and CPR 44.2(4)(c) allow a court to consider offers made to settle a claim pre trial. **11.97**

The first point to make is that either party is free to make any offers, including any terms, to the other. Where there is a dispute about the validity of a will this is, on its face, an 'all-or-nothing' claim—i.e. the will is either valid or it is not. A disappointed claimant may, however, have varied or complex reasons for making a claim—and those reasons may not be properly understood by the defendants. A claimant may feel hurt or distressed about being excluded from the will of someone with whom the claimant thought they had a close relationship. A disappointed claimant may simply be seeking a chattel or possession which has personal or sentimental value. A disappointed beneficiary may have particular pressing or urgent debts to pay and feel the need to embark on litigation simply as a last-ditch attempt to escape from financial **11.98**

[85] CPR 52.11(3). The Appeal Court will not allow an appeal unless it can be shown that the decision of the lower court was 'wrong' or 'unjust because of a serious procedural or other irregularity in the proceedings in the lower court'.

[86] [1954] 1 WLR 1489.

difficulty—but within the context of an estate the amount of the debt could be relatively small. Claimants pursue litigation for all sorts of complex and varied reasons.

11.99 Either side is free to make an offer to settle in any terms—and this opportunity should not be neglected. Mediation can sometimes be a splendid opportunity to create a settlement which would not be possible at a court trial where the all-or-nothing outcome is certain.

If an offer (which does not comply with the Part 36 formalities) is not accepted then the case will continue to trial. The court is permitted to take into account the fact that a non-Part 36 offer has been made but may not conclude that the making of the offer has any relevance to the usual cost consequences that may apply since 'the general rule' is that the unsuccessful party will be ordered to pay the costs of the successful party.[87] An offer to settle is therefore a very powerful weapon in the hands of both claimant and defendant.

11.100 If the initial defendant to proceedings is an executor it is important to realize the limitations of the executor's powers—the executors cannot simply give away part of the estate without the consent of the beneficiaries. Any offer made on behalf of a person who lacked capacity (a child or patient) must be approved by the court.[88]

Part 36 offers

11.101 Part 36 of the Civil Procedure Rules allows parties to make formal offers to settle the claim. Those offers will be likely to carry cost consequences for the offering and receiving party if the offer is not accepted and it is beaten at trial. Either side is free to make a formal Part 36 offer.

Part 36 offers can be technical and complex. There are many reported cases with regard to the provisions of CPR 36. Care and caution need to be exercised before making or accepting such an offer. There is an HMCTS form that can be used to make a Part 36 offer—Notice of Offer to Settle Form N242a. This form is frequently not used when offers are made in contentious probate proceedings—but it may, of course, be used suitably amended (e.g. deletion of reference to aspects of the form that are relevant only to personal injury claims).

Form and content of a Part 36 offer

11.102 The formal requirements of a Part 36 offer are set out in CPR 36.2. Specifically it must:

- be in writing;
- state on its face that it is intended to have the consequences of Section 1 of Part 36;

87 CPR 44.2(2)(a).
88 CPR 21.10.

- specify a period of not less than 21 days within which the defendant will be liable for the claimant's costs in accordance with Rule 36.10 if the offer is accepted;
- state whether it relates to the whole of the claim or to part of it, or to an issue that arises in it and if so to which part or issue; and
- state whether it takes into account any counterclaim.

In relation to these last two provisions it is to be appreciated that Part 36 offers can be made in respect of issues that arise in respect of proceedings—not just simply the totality of the claim. A second point to make is that in contested probate proceedings if the claimant makes an application to establish the validity of a will this is often met by a counterclaim to establish the validity of a previous will or to seek an intestacy. A Part 36 offer must deal with this counterclaim. One of the main disadvantages for making a Part 36 offer is the requirement to offer to pay the costs of the claimant.[89] If this offer to pay those costs is not made, or if an attempt is made to limit costs (e.g. by making a contribution to the costs of the other side), then that offer will not be a formal Part 36 offer and will not automatically attract the cost consequences that would usually be expected to apply. The offer would be an offer which excludes or limits costs pursuant to CPR 44.2(4)(c), which a court will take into account along with other factors in the case. From the perspective of either side the timing of the making of a Part 36 order is significant. Plainly an offer made earlier in proceedings will carry responsibility for lower costs than if it was made later in proceedings. Another point to consider is that, of course, more than one Part 36 offer can be made. In contentious probate proceedings often more than one offer is made. For practical reasons the offer should be made not less than 21 days before trial. **11.103**

The person receiving the offer may, within seven days, request that the person making the offer clarify the offer. If the offeror does not give the clarification requested within seven days of receiving the request the offeree may, unless the trial has started, apply for an order that he does so. Subject to the outcome the court may specify the date when the Part 36 offer is to be treated as having been made.[90] **11.104**

A Part 36 offer is accepted by serving written notice of the acceptance on the offeror.[91] In general terms the Part 36 offer may be accepted at any time unless the offeror serves notice of withdrawal on the offeree.[92] If an offer is accepted out of time—i.e. after 21 days have expired—then the offeree would usually be required to pay the offeror's costs incurred after the 21 days for acceptance. A small, but potentially important, point is that unless the parties agree, a Part 36 offer may not be accepted after the end **11.105**

89 CPR 36.10(1).
90 CPR 36.8.
91 CPR 36.9(1).
92 CPR 36.9(2).

of a trial but before judgment is handed down. If the strength of a case varies after time then the offeror should continue to keep the terms of the Part 36 offer under review—since it may be relevant to withdraw, but then make a fresh, reduced, offer.

11.106 The cost consequences of acceptance of a Part 36 offer are set out in detail in CPR 36.10. If the offer is accepted then costs are payable on the standard basis (not the indemnity basis).[93]

11.107 CPR 36.11 states that if a Part 36 offer is accepted then the claim will be stayed. This provision is entirely sensible in respect of proceedings which are not related to an application for a grant of probate—e.g. in a claim for a debt. It is not sufficient for the parties to a contentious probate claim to allow proceedings to remain 'stayed' since this will leave neither side with a grant of representation. The matter will need to be brought back to court in some form so that grant of representation can be issued. These terms should be specifically referred to in any Part 36 offer—if an offer of payment is to be made then how is the estate to devolve?

11.108 A Part 36 offer is treated as 'without prejudice save as to costs'.[94] This means that the fact that offer has been made must not be communicated to the trial judge until the case has been decided. If the offer is not accepted and proceeds to trial the costs consequences will be determined following the substantive judgment.[95] If a claimant fails to obtain a judgment more advantageous than a defendant's Part 36 offer or if a claimant obtains a judgment against the defendant at least as advantageous then specific costs consequences follow.

11.109 Unless he/she considers it unjust to do so then if the claimant fails to obtain a judgment more advantageous than the defendant's offer, the defendant will be entitled to costs from the date on which the relevant period to accept the offer expired and interest on those costs from that same date. Where, however, a claimant obtains a judgment which is at least as advantageous to the claimant as the proposal contained in the claimant's Part 36 offer then the claimant is entitled to:

a. interest of the whole or any part of any sum of money awarded at a rate not exceeding 10 per cent above base rate for some or all of the periods starting with the date on which the relevant period to accept the offer expired; and
b. costs on the indemnity basis from the date on which the relevant period expired; and
c. interest on those costs at a rate not exceeding 10 per cent above base rate; and
d. an additional amount which shall not exceed £75,000 by applying a prescribed percentage. The prescribed percentage is set out in CPR 36.14(3)(d).

---

93 CPR 36.10(3).
94 CPR 36.13.
95 CPR 36.14.

The 'additional amount' is calculated in different ways depending upon whether the claim is a 'money claim' or a 'non-monetary claim'. A dispute about the validity of a will is a non-monetary claim, and the additional amount is calculated by reference to the costs awarded, i.e. 10 per cent of the costs awarded up to £500,000 and 5 per cent of the balance over that sum, up to a maximum of £1 million. This can be potentially a very significant sum, particularly when coupled with the indemnity basis of assessment and interest on those costs. Obviously a clear agreement needs to be reached between the solicitor and the client to whom these windfall sums will be payable in the event of success. Unless an agreement is reached to the contrary then these benefits will be received by the client. CPR 36.14(4) sets out the circumstances that the court will take into account when deciding whether it would be unjust to apply the additional benefits referred to above. These circumstances include the terms of the offer, the stage in proceedings when the offer was made, the information available to the parties at the time when the offer was made, and the conduct of the parties with regard to giving or refusing to give information for the purposes of enabling the offer to be made or evaluated. **11.110**

Although the court has discretion to make an award of up to 10 per cent above bank base rate in times of low interest rates the usual award is considerably less than 10 per cent. **11.111**

There is an argument that, on strict reading of CPR 36, the cost consequences may be of limited applicability in validity claims where the will is either valid or it is not—it could, for example, be argued that if the will sought to be proved by the defendant is found to be valid as claimed then how could a claimant obtain a judgment 'more advantageous' then a defendant's Part 36 offer if the defendant maintains the validity of the will? In reality, however, courts seem to be willing to look beyond the issue of the validity of a will and consider offers. An example of this occurred in *Wharton v Bancroft*.[96] This was a dispute in relation to a deathbed will with an estate worth in the region of £4 million. The will was challenged by daughters of the deceased. The claimant (who was seeking to establish the validity of the last will) made a Part 36 offer to execute a deed of variation under which each of the daughters would receive a legacy of £5,000 and would be entitled to payment of their costs assessed on the standard basis. It was said when the Part 36 offer was made that the claimant was confident that the daughters' case had no merit whatever and that the offer was made to avoid lengthy and expensive litigation. The offer was rejected and the defendant's daughters, who claimed that the will was invalid, allowed the case to proceed to trial. The court upheld the validity of the will. The daughters' counsel submitted that it would be unjust to make an order carrying the usual cost consequences. The defendant's counsel argued that the Part 36 offer must present a genuine and **11.112**

[96] *Wharton v Bancroft* [2012] EWHC.

realistic attempt to resolve the dispute by agreement—as opposed to making an offer which created no real opportunity for settlement but was merely a tactical step designed to secure the benefit of the incentives provided by Part 36. Norris J held that this concept was 'not an easy one to apply'. He concluded that all Part 36 offers are tactical in the sense that they are designed to take advantage of the incentives provided by Part 36. He recognized that, although the sum to be received by each of the daughters was small, the offer was not derisory. When taking into account the cost consequences at the time it was made the offer would have been in the order of £200,000. He concluded that it was not unjust to allow the general rule in CPR 36.14 to have effect. He also had regard to 'aggressive conduct of the action by the defendant solicitors' which reinforced the essential justice of such an order. This case was relatively unusual because Norris J also made a separate order for the costs of the solicitor executor to be paid by the unsuccessful claimants.

Mechanics of settlement

11.113 The vast majority of claims raised settle before trial. Settlement can be achieved pre proceedings, or after proceedings. The mechanics of settlement will vary depending upon the stage at which the claim is reached.

Early settlement

11.114 If a potential claimant lodges a caveat and then enters into negotiations, a settlement may be reached—perhaps by way of an offer to the disappointed claimant (a general warning is again issued to the effect that the executors should take a neutral role in proceedings and should not settle the claim without the consent of the beneficiaries). If one of the beneficiaries is a child or a patient (without capacity to settle a claim) then the consent of the court needs to be obtained.[97] In these circumstances the claimants can write to the Probate Registry to withdraw the caveat or allow it to lapse automatically after six months.

Notice of appearance/warning

11.115 If a caveat has been registered which the propounder has sought to warn off and a notice of appearance has been entered then the caveat becomes permanent. A caveat can only be removed by summons lodged at the Probate Registry dealing with the application for a grant. This summons can be by consent and need not require a personal hearing.[98]

11.116 If legal proceedings have been commenced then the compromise of proceedings can be more complex and administratively cumbersome. The usual rules which

---

[97] CPR 21

[98] Non-Contentious Probate rules 44

apply generally to discontinuance of proceedings contained in CPR 38 do not apply to probate claims.[99] A claimant in a contentious probate case who has started proceedings does not have an automatic right generally available to other claimants to discontinue proceedings. At any stage of a probate claim the court may, on the application of the claimant or of any defendant who has acknowledged service, order the claim to be discontinued or dismissed on such terms as to costs as it thinks just, and order that a grant of probate of the will or letters of administration of the estate may be made to the person entitled to the grant. This procedure can be adopted where the application for the grant is in common form. If it is agreed that the last will is not to be admitted to probate—but an earlier one is—the last will has to be pronounced against, then the earlier will pronounced for, in solemn form.[100]

The Practice Direction supporting CPR 57 sets out the different ways in which settlement of a probate claim can be established.[101] **11.117**

If the parties agree to settle a probate claim then the court may order the trial of the claim on written evidence which will lead to a grant in solemn form. The important point to note here is that it is necessary for all parties to agree. If all parties don't agree then this process cannot be followed. It is assumed that by this stage the court will have received written evidence about the validity of the will from the individual or individuals seeking to propound it. It is also essential to ensure that the witness statement or affidavit about testamentary documents referred to in CPR 57.5 has been produced and filed with the court. A settlement in these terms strictly leads to a trial. It is not necessary for witnesses to appeal or give evidence, because of the order that the claim proceed on written evidence. It is however usual for there to be a—relatively short—hearing to outline the facts to the judge and to provide authority for the mechanics of settlement. **11.118**

It is, of course, possible that the claimant can agree to discontinue or have the proceedings dismissed leading to a grant in common form. The final option, which is less cumbersome, is to seek an order from the court pronouncing for or against the validity of one or more wills under s. 49 of the Administration of Justice Act 1985. It is possible to lodge a consent order in these terms with the court which avoids the expense of a trial. This procedure can be used only if every 'relevant beneficiary' has consented to the proposed order. A relevant beneficiary is an individual who would stand to benefit if either the claim was successful or unsuccessful. Potentially there could be very many relevant beneficiaries and it may be difficult in practice to **11.119**

[99] CPR 57.11
[100] *White Book* 57.11.1
[101] CPR 57 PD.6

persuade each and every one to sign and return a consent order—particularly where such a relevant beneficiary has no financial interest in the outcome. If this section of the Act can be used, then there is no doubt that it is procedurally simpler to conclude an agreement in these terms. In reality, however, it is often administratively complex to employ this method.

12

THE MAIN MEDICAL CAUSES OF IMPAIRED TESTAMENTARY CAPACITY

Introduction

'Hitler and Stalin must have been mad.' This is a common but incorrect remark, the relevance of which to testamentary capacity is the need to understand the difference between mental illness on one hand, and learning disability and personality disorder on the other. In the language of psychiatry all three are mental disorders, but mental illness is what Cockburn LCJ must have meant by a 'disorder of mind' in the *Banks v Goodfellow* judgment. 12.01

What then differentiates mental illness from learning disability and personality disorders? In brief, the latter two are present from birth or by the time adult life is reached, whereas mental illness describes *a change from a person's normal state of mental health*. Mental illnesses may begin abruptly or gradually and may remit, recover,[1] or recur. Or the illness may persist and develop into long-term chronic illness. 12.02

[1] The difference between remission and recovery is a technical one. Remission describes reaching a stage where the mental illness no longer impairs normal function. After an arbitrary period of remission, usually six or twelve months, recovery is said to have been achieved.

Psychiatric Diagnosis

12.03 Psychiatric diagnosis differs from the diagnosis of most physical disorders, because it is *descriptive* and not usually underpinned by laboratory or radiological tests that identify a clear pathological process. At the present time, however, as neuroscience is improving our ability to detect abnormalities in the brain, some areas of psychiatry are moving closer to physical medicine: dementia being a prime example. Psychiatric diagnosis is a description of patterns of history and mental state phenomena that can be observed and documented. These clinical manifestations, or syndromes, tend to follow certain patterns, and respond in predictable ways to treatment. Thus, psychiatric syndromes are described in order to guide treatment, to help in giving a prognosis, and as a means of furthering our knowledge of mental disorders. Even with dementia, which has known underlying physical causes, the diagnosis is a psychiatric one as we have defined it.

12.04 The language of psychiatric description and diagnosis does not map directly onto that of the law. In the present context, the term *capacity* is a legal and not a psychiatric one. It has a legal and not a medical purpose. The same can be said of *undue influence*, which we discuss elsewhere in this book. Psychiatry requires a concept that is similar but not identical to legal capacity. For example, a severely depressed patient may be unable to distinguish between his pathological ideas of worthlessness and his true abilities, as a result of which he cannot temporarily achieve or carry out some particular purpose. This is not a legal problem and psychiatrists in the UK[2] would tend to say that he lacks *competence* not capacity in this context. Similarly, many patients are subject to the influence of others during episodes of illness. If the influence is malign doctors might regard it as undue, but it is not necessarily undue in the narrow legal sense of overcoming a person's will.

12.05 As the subject is now language we shall define some of the terms used in psychiatry which are essential to the diagnostic process.

Disorders of Perception

12.06 *Hallucinations* are false sensory perceptions for which there is no external stimulus. The patient may, for example, hear voices of people talking to him when no one is there (auditory hallucinations); or see things that are not actually present (visual hallucinations). Hallucinations can occur in any type of sensory experience, e.g. smell (olfactory hallucinations) and touch (tactile hallucinations). *Illusions* are false

[2] In the USA it is the other way round. Competence is the legal term and capacity is used by psychiatrists.

sensory perceptions, but for which there is an external stimulus. In delirium tremens which is due to alcohol withdrawal, for example, patients may perceive patterns on curtains or wallpaper as insects crawling up them.

Disorders of Thinking

Disorders of thinking are differentiated into disorders of the *logical form* of thinking and disorders of the *content of thought*. In acute schizophrenia in young adults logical thought disorder is characteristic. Connections between thoughts cannot easily be understood, and at their worst the patient with logical thought disorder is completely incomprehensible. He may invent words (neologisms) or use odd grammatical constructions. For example, a young man with auditory hallucinations commanding him to do things wrote that he was '*roared to smoke*'. In manic states a different form of thought disorder occurs in which the patient is so distracted by individual thoughts that they take off into a flight of ideas. Here it is usually possible to see what the connections between thoughts are. For instance the connection might be a pun. A patient said 'I am off alcohol, but holograms are fine. Just like the weather, and whether to go down to the sea in ships...' and so on in an exhausting fashion. **12.07**

Disorders of the content of thinking are delusions or over-valued ideas. Delusions are false beliefs, and over-valued ideas are beliefs that most people would consider false. As delusions hold a special place within the *Banks v Goodfellow* judgment we shall discuss them separately, later in this chapter. **12.08**

Disorders of Mood

Disorders of mood encompass depression and mania. These can be seen as exaggerations of normal mood states that persist for too long, or are of such intensity that they cannot be considered normal. We discuss them in more detail later in this chapter. **12.09**

Confusion

It is sometimes said that there is no more confusing word in medicine than *confusion*. Strictly speaking it should refer to an inability to think and act with one's customary clarity. Unfortunately, many doctors who are not psychiatrists have tended to use it as a synonym for delirium. Defined in the correct way, confusion can clearly describe the mental states of many people with very acute mental illnesses such as depression and schizophrenia who are in no way delirious. Delirium is a state of altered conscious awareness which is described in detail later in this chapter. **12.10**

Psychosis and Psychotic

12.11 Psychosis is another term, like confusion, that is used too loosely, but it occurs frequently in the documents in contentious probate cases and needs to be explained. The commonest meaning of psychosis is a mental state characterized by hallucinations and/or delusions. However, it is also often applied to any very severe mental illness, in which delusions or hallucinations are not necessarily found. For example, psychiatrists sometimes refer to a *psychotic depression* just meaning a very severe episode, usually with suicidal risk.

Learning Disability

12.12 The terminology to describe what is now called learning disability has been subject to changes in social attitudes, together with a certain amount of political correctness. Terms such as *mental defective*, *idiot*, and *moron* have rightly been abandoned because they have been adopted as insults in general parlance. Mental sub-normality has also been dropped, partly for the same reason, and partly because normality is difficult to define. Mental retardation was the term used in the fourth edition of the *Diagnostic and Statistical Manual (DSM-IV)* of the American Psychiatric Association, and in the International Classification of Disease, tenth version (ICD-10). DSM-5 now calls it intellectual disability. Mental handicap is still permissible, but learning disability is now considered the most acceptable term in the UK. The ICD-10 definition of learning disability states that it 'is a condition of arrested or incomplete development of the mind, which is especially characterized by impairment of skills manifested during the developmental period, which contribute to the overall level of intelligence, i.e. cognitive, language, motor, and social abilities.' DSM-IV classifies severity according to IQ: mild referring to the IQ range of 50–55 up to 70; moderate with IQ 35–40 up to 50–55; severe with IQ 20–25 up to 35–40; and profound with IQ below 20 or 25. The range of, rather than fixed, border-scores is deliberate because factors other than IQ are taken into account and precision is not possible. In DSM-5, intellectual disability is considered to be present in persons whose IQ is approximately two standard deviations or more below the population, i.e. a score of about 70 or below. We should, however, stress that the diagnosis and level of ability should never rely simply on an IQ score. An assessment is always of an individual who has a range of abilities and disabilities that cannot be reduced to a number.

12.13 As a general statement only, those people with mild learning disability are able to make wills. In the spirit of the Mental Capacity Act 2005 every effort should be made to optimize the capacity of people to make their own decisions. Ways of doing this may include presenting the relevant information in different formats (in speech, or writing, or pictures); explaining things step by step, possibly on successive occasions;

and ascertaining from carers what circumstances—such as time of day, physical comfort, absence of anxiety—will make it easier for the person to concentrate on the decision.

Solicitors are advised not to be put off by, or make instant judgements from, appearances when dealing with learning disabled clients. Some may have an abnormal appearance or a speech impediment. This applies especially to people with Down's syndrome and cerebral palsy. In the past they were often institutionalized in establishments for people with severe learning disability when, in fact, they were of normal intelligence. A well-known example was Joey Deacon <http://en.wikipedia.org/wiki/Joey_Deacon>, who had severe cerebral palsy and spent many years in Caterham Hospital but was 'liberated' when with the help of friends he wrote his autobiography, *Tongue Tied: Fifty years of friendship in a subnormality hospital.* **12.14**

In many cases it may well be unreasonable to ask a solicitor to assess whether someone with learning disability has the capacity to make a will. In such cases the assistance of a psychiatrist or psychologist specialized and experienced in the field will be required but, as always, they should be carefully briefed on the legal test for testamentary capacity. **12.15**

Personality Disorder

The fifth version of the *Diagnostic and Statistical Manual* ('DSM-5') of the American Psychiatric Association [2013] defines personality disorder as 'an enduring pattern of inner experience and behaviour that deviates markedly from the expectations of the individual's culture, is pervasive and inflexible, has an onset in adolescence or early childhood, is stable over time, and leads to distress and impairment.' Put another way, someone with a personality disorder has traits that are distributed normally within the population, but in such quantity or of such quality that they cause distress to the individual and to others. Yet another way of looking at it is to see these individuals as immature to a greater or lesser extent in their personality structure, and who have not learned to form normal relationships with others or to deal with childish patterns of behaviour, such as the desire for immediate gratification or lack of impulse control. **12.16**

Personality disorder best illustrates the problems of identifying disorders by their clinical features. Just as each person with a 'normal' personality cannot be adequately captured by a brief description, so neither can people with 'disordered' personalities. One way to approach the problem is to regard everyone's feelings, thoughts, and behaviour as governed by a number of personality traits which, in combination, go to make up their uniqueness. Such traits might include anxiety, meticulousness, generosity, suspiciousness, open-mindedness, impulsiveness, indifference to others, emotional instability, and so on. In so-called *normal* people these traits combine in **12.17**

Table 12.1 ICD-10 Subtypes of personality disorder

Paranoid personality disorder
Schizoid personality disorder
Dissocial personality disorder
Emotionally unstable personality disorder
Impulsive type
Borderline type
Histrionic personality disorder
Anankastic personality disorder
Anxious [avoidant] personality disorder
Dependent personality disorder
Other specific personality disorders
Personality disorder, unspecified

proportions that allow them to lead normal lives. In those with personality disorders their traits bring them into conflict with themselves or others. We should stress here that the use of 'normal' and 'abnormal' clearly illustrates that there is no clear boundary between those with and without disordered personalities, for how can one possibly define normality when it comes to human beings?

12.18 Personality disorders may largely be the result of an individual's genetic predisposition, but they can often be traced back to deprivation in childhood when personality structure is still developing.

12.19 Personality disorder has traditionally been sub-divided into various types, but classifications and names change according to the fashions of the day. Table 12.1 lists the subtypes in the ICD-10 issued by the World Health Organization.

12.20 The sub-type of most relevance to testamentary capacity is paranoid personality disorder, which will be discussed in more detail in the next chapter.

Mental Illnesses

Dementia

12.21 Dementia is a clinical syndrome, i.e. not a pathological diagnosis. The term describes a collection of clinical signs and mental state phenomena seen *in vivo*, but *not* an underlying disease process. There are very many underlying disease processes (between 50 and about 100) that cause dementia. A much smaller number make up the most common causes and these are shown in Table 12.2.

12.22 The most recent revision of the International Classification of Diseases (ICD-10) published by the World Health Organization in 1993 defines it as follows:

> Dementia is a syndrome due to disease of the brain, usually of a chronic or progressive nature, in which there is impairment of multiple higher cortical functions, including

Table 12.2 The more common causes of dementia

Most common	Less common, but not rare
Alzheimer's disease[3]	Chronic alcohol abuse
Cerebrovascular disease	Frontotemporal dementia and Pick's disease[6]
Dementia with Lewy[4] bodies	Huntington's disease[7]
Parkinson's disease[5]	Motor neurone disease
	Primary and secondary brain tumours

> memory, thinking, orientation, comprehension, calculation, learning capacity, language and judgement. Consciousness is not clouded. Cognitive impairments are commonly accompanied, and occasionally preceded, by deterioration in emotional control, social behaviour or motivation. This syndrome occurs in Alzheimer's disease, in cerebrovascular disease and in other conditions primarily or secondarily affecting the brain.

The important thing to note in this definition is that to sustain a diagnosis of dementia there must be *impairment of multiple higher cortical functions*: memory loss alone is not dementia.

Mild cognitive impairment (MCI)

People with MCI show a slight but measurable impairment in one or more cognitive **12.23**
functions, most commonly memory, but this is insufficiently severe to interfere with normal functional activity. The importance of MCI is that a significant proportion of those affected convert to dementia. The conversion rate is between 5–15% per year. It follows, of course, that not all people with MCI do develop dementia.

Alzheimer's disease

Alzheimer's disease is the commonest underlying cause of dementia in the Western **12.24**
world. Alzheimer's disease that comes on in middle age (*early onset* dementia, formerly known as *pre-senile* dementia) is clearly genetically determined, and many cases are due to identified single-gene defects; whereas in Alzheimer's disease developing after middle age (*late-onset* dementia, formerly called *senile* dementia) genetic

[3] First described in 1907 by Alois Alzheimer, a German neurologist and psychiatrist, who studied a woman with dementia and observed abnormal protein deposits in her brain at autopsy.

[4] Named after Friedrich Lewy, a German neurologist, who in 1912 described abnormal deposits in the brains of patients with Parkinson's disease.

[5] Named after James Parkinson, an English apothecary who in 1817, published *An Essay on the Shaking Palsy*.

[6] Pick's disease is a sub-type of frontotemporal dementia, so called because specific abnormalities (Pick bodies) are seen in the brain, first described in 1892 by Arnold Pick, a Czech neurologist and psychiatrist.

[7] Named after George Huntington, an American physician who described a case in 1872, although descriptions of the disease date back to the Middle Ages.

predisposition probably plays a less important role. The pathology of Alzheimer's disease is now quite well understood and, in summary, involves the abnormal deposition of proteins in the brain which cause the death of nerve cells and thus the interruption of neural pathways.

12.25 The most frequent presenting (first) clinical manifestation of Alzheimer's disease is *episodic memory impairment.* Memory is a complex process, which can be roughly separated into a number of different functions. Episodic memory refers to newly acquired information for specific events and the details of the event, with the time and place where it occurred being part of the information. Semantic memory refers to the general knowledge (including knowledge of our own language and of how to act according to social norms) that we build up over our lives, without necessarily being able to say how and where we acquired the information. Semantic memory is that which confers meaning to us. So for example, the statement 'I went with my sons yesterday to visit Stonehenge' draws on episodic memory, while it is semantic memory that allows the speaker to recall where Stonehenge is, what it looks like, and its place in history. Old memories may be episodic ('I remember the Queen's coronation') or semantic ('I remember the poems I learned at school'). In the early stages of Alzheimer's disease it is usually the old memories which are best preserved and can most readily be retrieved, because the typical problem with the disease is an inability to commit new information to memory store.

12.26 Other forms of memory include sensory memory (a sight, a smell, or a sound), remembering to carry out an intention for future action, and working memory. Working memory is the notional store of information that we need for current mental activity. The information is necessarily very complex and includes visual as well as verbal material. As the situation changes, information in working memory has to be manipulated and augmented or reduced. Working memory is also related to executive function, which is defined and discussed in the next chapter. As Alzheimer's disease progresses all the various aspects of memory, including the ability to retrieve from long-term store (those poems learnt at school) gradually become impaired.

12.27 Dementia due to Alzheimer's disease is characterized by a wide variety of cognitive impairments in addition to memory. These include dysphasia, dyspraxia, agnosia and impaired executive function. *Dysphasia* is a disorder of language, both the understanding and production of it, which are located respectively in different parts of the brain. Broca's area, which is for expressive language, is in the lower posterior part of the left frontal lobe; whereas Wernicke's area, which is for the understanding of language, is in the upper posterior part of the left temporal lobe. Figure 12.1 is a cartoon showing the language areas and the lobes of the brain. Receptive dysphasia, impaired understanding of language, is very common in Alzheimer's dementia. Dysphasia, a disorder of *language*, must be distinguished from dysarthria, which is a disorder of

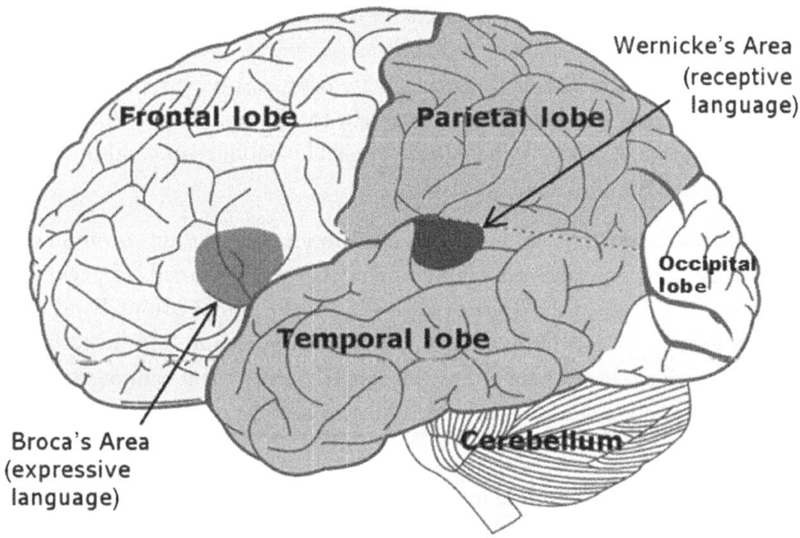

Figure 12.1 Lobes of the brain and language areas.

speech articulation due to weakness or paralysis of the muscles of the speech apparatus, such as may occur after a stroke.

Dyspraxia and agnosia

Dyspraxia and agnosia are almost invariable in the later stages of dementia due to Alzheimer's disease. Dyspraxia is the inability to carry out motor tasks due to a lesion in the brain and not due to paralysis or weakness of the muscles needed for the task. In a computing analogy it is a software disruption; whereas muscular weakness or paralysis are hardware impairments. Dyspraxia often manifests itself first by difficulties in getting dressed or attending to personal hygiene, although the latter is frequently due to loss of social awareness. *Dysgraphia*, impairment in writing ability, is a form of dyspraxia, although located in a different part of the brain. It may be manifest in an inability to sign a will. *Dyscalculia*, impaired ability to calculate, is located in the same brain area as dysgraphia. **12.28**

Agnosia is also a software problem, and is the failure to recognize sensory stimuli due to a brain lesion, and not to any fault of the sensory organs, such as the eye or ear. Agnosia can occur with any type of sensory stimulus. For example, one patient did not recognize the smell of gas when he left the stove turned on but unlit; another patient could hear the doorbell but did not recognize what the noise was. More dangerous examples, sometimes with a fatal outcome, are failure to recognize traffic or rivers and ponds. For relatives the most distressing sort of visual agnosia is a failure to recognize familiar faces, e.g. of offspring or a spouse. This is termed prosopagnosia. **12.29**

12.30 Delusions and hallucinations also occur in dementia due to Alzheimer's disease. Delusions are discussed separately below, because they are specifically mentioned in the *Banks v Goodfellow* test. Hallucinations are false sensory perceptions for which there is no external stimulus. The patient may, for example, hear voices of people talking to him when no one is there (auditory hallucinations); or see things that are not actually present (visual hallucinations).

12.31 Delusions, hallucinations, and delusional misinterpretations are common causes of disturbed and aggressive behaviour. Such behaviour also tends to occur in the more advanced stages of the disease, when the patient cannot comprehend what is going on around him. A frequent example is when nurses are administering intimate care, such as cleaning up after incontinence. The patient cannot understand why he is having his clothes removed, and tries to fight off those he perceives as assaulting him.

12.32 Mood changes are also common in dementia due to Alzheimer's disease. Depressive illness is significantly more frequent in the decade preceding the clinical appearance of Alzheimer's dementia. It is also common in the early stages of the disease when the patient begins to realize what is happening to him. Conversely, it is said to remit when he loses insight. It is important that doctors do not write off depression as part of the dementia, and do nothing about it. All patients with depression have a right to treatment. Euphoria or elevated mood may also occur in dementia due to Alzheimer's disease, notably when the frontal lobes of the brain are involved.

12.33 A definitive diagnosis of Alzheimer's disease cannot be made until after death, and examination of the brain under a microscope. But if sufficient clinical information is obtained, diagnostic accuracy in life has in fact been shown to be high. CT and MRI[8] brain scans may show generalized cerebral atrophy and particular atrophy of the hippocampus, a small part of the temporal lobe that is preferentially affected by the Alzheimer's pathological process.

12.34 The pathological lesions in the brains of people with Alzheimer's disease appear several years before the first mental state changes become evident. Once the latter begin, cognitive decline usually continues steadily over a period of years. The mean survival from diagnosis has increased over time because of both earlier diagnosis and continual improvement in treatment and management. It is currently about seven years, although there is wide variation. Some patients die sooner with a more rapidly progressive disease, or because they fall prey to conditions that all older people may have, such as cancer and heart attacks. But some patients have been known to survive much longer, even up to twenty years. In the late stages of the disease patients become immobile and bed-bound. They lose weight and are prone to infections. The

[8] CT: computed tomography; MRI: magnetic resonance imaging.

commonest immediate cause of death is either pneumonia or a pulmonary embolus (a 'clot on the lungs').

Cerebrovascular disease

Cerebrovascular disease is the second-commonest cause of dementia. The pathological basis of it is death of brain tissue for circulatory reasons. Once dead, brain tissue does not regenerate. Therefore, those mental functions sub-served by the dead tissue are either impaired or absent. It used to be held that the commonest pattern of cerebrovascular dementia is a *stepwise deterioration* in mental function, the mechanism of which goes as follows. A cerebrovascular event occurs, such as a stroke or a transient ischaemic attack (TIA), and mental deterioration follows. There is usually some oedema (fluid in the extra-cellular space) surrounding the brain lesion which does resolve and may result in some improvement in function, but the patient is left overall with some permanent impairment. He stabilizes at a (lower than his normal) mental ability until the next cerebrovascular event occurs. This pattern of cerebrovascular disease is thought to arise from a series of infarcts, and so became known as multi-infarct dementia. It accounts for about twenty per cent of cases of cerebrovascular dementia. **12.35**

More commonly, however, cerebrovascular dementia is due to what is now termed *small vessel disease* (SVD). Here patients have arteriosclerosis of the small vessels of the brain—sometimes in the cerebral cortex, sometimes in subcortical parts of the brain—which in essence starves the tissues they supply of oxygen, resulting in death of nerve cells. This may produce small infarcts (so-called lacunar infarcts) or very small infarcts (micro-infarcts) which do not usually result in obvious strokes or even recognizable transient ischaemic attacks (TIAs), but gradually cause decline in cognitive function over time. Sometimes these infarcts can be seen on CT or MRI scans, but they are often too small for the resolution of even the most modern scanners. Another example of SVD is *subcortical arteriosclerotic encephalopathy* (Binswanger's disease), which is due to widespread damage to deep white matter in the brain. The areas affected can be seen on CT and MRI scanning. Executive dysfunction is characteristic (see Chapter 13). Subcortical dementia is differentiated from cortical dementia (e.g. Alzheimer's disease) by psychomotor retardation—a slowness in translating intention into action. For example, the doctor asks the patient to pick up a piece of paper on the desk, which he can do but only very slowly. Similarly, the doctor might ask a question to which the patient can give a correct or incorrect answer, but only after a considerable pause. **12.36**

Mood and personality changes are prominent in cerebrovascular dementia. Patients may be labile: depressed and tearful one moment and cheerful the next. Lability of mood is particularly common after major strokes. However, significant bouts of depression are also common and, as with Alzheimer's disease, need to be treated. **12.37**

Other features of cerebrovascular dementia include motor deficits due to strokes, especially dysarthria, gait disturbance, and incontinence. Memory is also affected, although often not as severely as in Alzheimer's dementia.

12.38 Some patients with cerebrovascular dementia may die of a major stroke, but others become debilitated and immobile like those with Alzheimer's disease, and have the same terminal event of pneumonia or pulmonary embolus. Many die of one of those diseases that non-demented people die of. It should also be remembered that Alzheimer's disease and cerebrovascular disease are common in the elderly population. It is not surprising, therefore, that they not infrequently coexist in the same patient.

Other causes of dementia

12.39 Most, if not all of the impairments that occur in dementia due to Alzheimer's disease are seen in dementia due to other causes. Thus, there is no need to go into these syndromes in detail.

12.40 Dementia with Lewy bodies (DLB) and dementia in Parkinson's disease (PD) are probably related conditions. They are both caused by deposits of a protein, alpha synuclein, in the brain. In PD these bodies are confined to a sub-cortical structure called the *substantia Nigra*, whereas in DLB they are found in the cerebral cortex. Patients with PD who develop dementia (not all of them do) also show cortical Lewy bodies. Characteristically, DLB patients and those with dementia in PD experience visual hallucinations. They also exhibit fluctuations in their level of awareness, with states equivalent to delirium (see below).

12.41 Dementia in PD is the commonest example of a *sub-cortical dementia*; Huntington's disease is another. The term refers to particular clinical features that are due to abnormalities in structures below the cerebral cortex. The characteristic feature of a sub-cortical dementia is psycho-motor slowing. There is slowing of cognition, and patients also have memory impairment, and difficulty with complex intellectual tasks and problem solving. These features are found on clinical testing, but dementia in Parkinsonian patients often passes unnoticed to the untutored eye.

12.42 Frontotemporal dementia and Pick's disease manifest themselves with behavioural changes. Characteristically, these are disinhibition, apathy, inertia, loss of empathy for others, changes in dietary choice and increased appetite, sometimes stereotyped and ritualistic behaviour, and perseveration. Perseveration is the persistence of a response after the stimulus has ceased to be appropriate. For example, a patient may correctly say it is Tuesday, but when asked what month it is, replies Tuesday, and gives the same response to more questions. Impairment of executive function (see Chapter 13) is a prominent feature of frontotemporal dementia. Judgement is usually severely impaired.

The clinical picture in dementia due to brain tumours depends largely on the location of the tumour in the brain. Frontal tumours in the dominant cerebral hemisphere, for instance, may produce a frontal dementia as described in the preceding paragraph. **12.43**

Chronic alcohol abuse can cause a global dementia, but also a disorder in which new episodic memory is very severely impaired, called Korsakov's syndrome. A characteristic feature of Korsakov's syndrome is *confabulation* which is defined as a falsification of memory due to organic brain disease. It is neither mendacity nor delusion, since the patient really recalls what he describes as a memory. Sometimes, the memories are genuine but placed at the wrong time. A patient, who had been in hospital for several weeks, said that he had been playing cricket in Norfolk the previous day. His wife said that he had indeed played cricket in Norfolk, but only several years ago. Other confabulations are more bizarre and fantastic and can be provoked. The late William Sargent, a well-known psychiatrist at St Thomas's Hospital in London, was interviewing a man with Korsakov's syndrome in front of an audience of medical students. Wishing to provoke a confabulation, Sargent said to the patient 'we've met before haven't we?'. The patient replied 'yes guvnor, the last time I saw you, you was pissing on the lions in Trafalgar Square.' **12.44**

Delirium

Delirium is also a global impairment of multiple higher cortical functions but differs from dementia in certain crucial ways. Its hallmark is *a disturbance of conscious awareness and the sleep–wake cycle*; hence the sentence in the definition of *dementia* in ICD-10 quoted above, 'consciousness is not clouded', which specifically differentiates it from delirium. Consciousness is a term that philosophers have discussed for centuries without reaching a definitive conclusion! The medical meaning is pragmatic and defined as a normal awareness of oneself and one's surroundings. **12.45**

Delirium also differs from dementia in other ways: it is of more rapid onset, i.e. hours or days, compared with years for dementia; and resolution, either by remission or death, occurs within hours, days, or weeks, although it may recur frequently in vulnerable individuals. Delirium fluctuates, which clearly has implications for testamentary capacity, as we shall see in the following chapter. **12.46**

Delirium can be noisy or quiet (alert or hypo-alert). Noisy delirium is familiar to anyone who has visited a general medical ward at their local hospital. Typically there is an older patient who is shouting, or trying to pull out a drip or urinary catheter, perhaps attempting to get out of bed, and obviously confused and disorientated. One of the reasons for such a disturbance is that the patient is experiencing frightening visual hallucinations. If such patients recover, they often describe the experience as a living nightmare. Quiet delirium is what the term says. These **12.47** patients lie in bed and do not cause any trouble to the nursing staff, but if they are engaged in conversation, it is clear that they, too, are thoroughly confused and disorientated in time, place, and person. The differentiation of a quietly delirious person from a demented one might be difficult on a single assessment. However, if a reliable informant says that he was mentally perfectly well before this episode, it is more likely to be delirium. Similarly, if the patient recovers normal or significantly better mental function after treatment for the physical illness that has brought him into hospital, then delirium is the likely cause of the mental disorder. The importance of quiet delirium for testamentary capacity cannot be overemphasized, and is discussed in the next chapter.

12.48 Because delirium involves a disturbance of the sleep–wake cycle, many patients sleep for only short periods during the day and night, and when awake they are both noisy and drowsy. This situation is often made paradoxically worse by giving them sedative drugs.

12.49 The causes of delirium are legion and can be summarized as any underlying physical illness or toxicity, especially toxicity to prescribed drugs. If the underlying cause remits, delirium, too, resolves itself. Treatment is, therefore, primarily that of the underlying cause, which might simply involve stopping medication or giving antibiotics. Older people are at particular risk of delirium because they lack cerebral reserve. Dementia sufferers are at high risk of delirium, often as the result of an unrecognized underlying infection, such as of the urinary tract. Delirium is sometimes termed *an acute confusional state* by physicians and surgeons.

Affective Disorder

12.50 Affective disorders are those mental illnesses characterized by a disorder of mood. Broadly speaking these are depressive and manic states, which are classified under the rubric of *bipolar disorder*. To this we need to add grief reaction which figured prominently in the case of *Key v Key*.[9]

12.51 The primary disturbance in depressive illness is obviously depressed mood. The classic clinical manifestations also include: intense anxiety; feelings of guilt and worthlessness; loss of the capacity to feel pleasure (anhedonia); pessimism about the future; anorexia and weight loss; insomnia, especially early morning waking; and suicidal thoughts. However, some elderly people, including those making wills, may not display obvious low mood. This is referred to as masked depression. In severe cases there may be delusions (see below). Another particular feature of depression in old age is a change in behaviour that can be misinterpreted as simple bad conduct.

[9] *Key v Key* [2010] EWHC 408 (Ch).

Examples of this are patients throwing themselves on the floor, unexplained incontinence, and shoplifting (Lady Barnett syndrome)[10].

Manic states tend to be characterized by elevated mood, although irritability and anger are as frequent as euphoria. Thinking tends to be grandiose. The patient believes that he is capable of more than he realistically can achieve. Grandiose delusions also occur. The patient is hyperactive and may sleep very little but remain awake in a hyperactive state. He is expansive and spends sums of money that bring himself and his family to the brink of ruin. The manic patient can be aggressive, and even dangerously violent, especially if he feels that people are frustrating his ambitions and intentions. He is highly distractible and in conversation may switch topics at an extraordinary rate, a phenomenon known as *flight of ideas*. Disinhibited behaviour is characteristic. An obituary in the *Daily Telegraph* in 2005 relates how a talented barrister with severe bipolar disorder addressed the jury in a fraud case as follows **12.52**

> [M]embers of the jury it is my duty as defence counsel to explain the facts of this case on my client's behalf; the judge will guide you and advise you on the correct interpretation of the law and you will then consider your verdict. Unfortunately, for reasons which I won't go into now, my grasp of the facts is not as it might be. The judge is nearing senility; his knowledge of the law is pathetically out of date, and will be of no use in assisting you to reach a verdict. While by the look of you, the possibility of you reaching a coherent verdict can be excluded.

At which point the barrister was led from the court.

Old age may modify manic illnesses because of reduced mobility. Elderly people are less overtly aggressive and threatening, but quietly irritable, hostile, and grandiose. The extraordinarily rapid flight of ideas seen in younger patients can be slow, but still obviously abnormal and betraying extreme distractibility. **12.53**

Grieving is usually an entirely normal life experience, but symptoms can be identical to a depressive illness. Mostly, grief tends to resolve after about a year, and is not considered pathological until at least a year has elapsed. In pathological grief reactions the symptoms are also essentially the same as in a depressive illness. A person suffering from normal grief or pathological grief reaction is vulnerable when making a will, either from undue influence or because judgement is distorted. **12.54**

Affective disorders are for the most part treatable with the aim of restoring the patient to their normal state. Thus, if there is no urgency to make a will, it is advisable to wait until remission of the illness before making it. **12.55**

---

[10] Isobel Lady Barnett was a television personality in the 1950s. Towards the end of her life she became rather a recluse. In 1980 she was found guilty of stealing a can of tuna and a carton of cream from a local shop. Four days later she committed suicide.

Other Psychoses

12.56 Psychosis, as we have seen, is commonly a shorthand term for mental illnesses characterized by delusions and hallucinations. So far in this chapter we have discussed first the organic psychoses (dementia and delirium), so called because they have identifiable or presumed lesions in the brain, and second the affective psychoses (disorders of mood). There remain the other psychoses that include schizophrenia and related disorders. Schizophrenia does *not* mean split personality, as the media and people who ought to know better sometimes refer to it. The 'schizo-' prefix means disintegration, and specifically disintegration of mental functions that include thinking, perception, and affect. There are also subtle changes in cognition. Schizophrenic illnesses that begin in adolescence or early adulthood—the mean age of onset in males is 20 and in females 25—are characterized by personality deterioration often expressing itself in poor self-care skills and self-neglect. There may be a disorder in the *form* of thinking which manifests itself in unusual or unfathomable logical connections in speech and writing. This is called *logical thought disorder*, and refers only to the logical process of thinking and not the content. Thought content is also affected with delusional, self-referential, and most commonly persecutory beliefs. Frequent perceptual abnormalities are auditory hallucinations: hearing voices that are often abusive. Passivity is the feeling of interference with personal integrity by an external force or agent, whereby the patient experiences, for example, control of his thoughts and actions.

Delusions

12.57 Cockburn LCJ adjudicated *delusions* into a special place in testamentary capacity with the *Banks v Goodfellow* judgment: '... that no insane delusion shall influence his will in disposing of the property and bring about a disposal of it which, if the mind had been sound, would not have been made.'

12.58 Psychiatrists define a delusion as *a fixed, false belief of morbid origin that is inconsistent with the believer's cultural or religious background*. A delusion is *fixed* because no amount of persuasion and even evidence will shake it. *Of morbid origin* means that it arises because of some known or presumed mental illness. The caveat on religious and cultural factors is important because some cultures propose religious and social beliefs that might otherwise be considered delusional. For example, it is normal and not delusional in some rural African cultures to believe that a physical illness is due to an enemy casting an evil spell.

12.59 Psychiatrists also distinguish delusions from *over-valued ideas*. The latter are beliefs that most people would consider false, but instead of arising from a mental illness, i.e. of morbid origin, they are understandable within the context of the believer's personality. A trivial example might be a belief in flying saucers, but there are situations when over-valued ideas can be put forward by claimants as delusions in testamentary capacity cases. This will be discussed in Chapter 13. It is sometimes almost impossible to distinguish over-valued ideas from delusions, especially if they are of a persecutory[11] nature. This situation can arise in individuals with so-called sensitive or paranoid personality disorders, who tend to over-interpret events and remarks as referring to themselves.

The difficulty in differentiating delusions from over-valued ideas is exemplified in the nineteenth-century cases of *Dew v Clark*[12] and *Boughton v Knight*,[13] where fathers disinherited their respective daughters whom they disliked intensely. In both cases the judges felt that the antipathy to the children amounted to unsoundness of mind, i.e. effectively insane delusion in *Banks v Goodfellow* terminology. Here is Sir James Hannen in *Boughton v Knight*: **12.60**

> [I]f a woman believes that she is one of the Trinity, and that the gentleman to whom she leaves the bulk of her property is another person of the Trinity, what more need be said? But, a very different question, no doubt, arises where the nature of the delusion which is said to exist is this, when it is alleged that a totally false, unfounded, unreasonable—because unreasoning—estimate of another person's character is formed. That is necessarily a more difficult question.
>
> [he goes on to talk about parents who are averse to and repulsed by their children:]
>
> I say there is a point at which, taken by itself, such repulsion and aversion becomes evidence of unsoundness of mind.

Another quotation from the judgment in *Boughton v Knight* has come to be considered a good legal test of a delusion. 'You must of necessity put to yourself this question and answer it. "Can I understand how any man in possession of his senses could have believed such and such a thing?" And if the answer you give is "I cannot understand it" then it is of the necessity of the case that you should say that the man is not sane.' However, the present author, having read both cases, is of the view that both fathers were profoundly unpleasant personalities whose ideas about their daughters were not delusional but over-valued. These are, of course, cases well over one-hundred years old, when neither doctors nor judges could have been expected to know what is now standard psychopathology. The specific question of the difference between delusions and over-valued ideas has not been directly tested in court, **12.61**

[11] In lay parlance 'paranoid'. However, we prefer not to use paranoid, because the word defines ideas and beliefs that are *self-referential*. Most self-referential beliefs are indeed persecutory, but not all of them. For example, the delusion that someone (usually of superior status) is in love with you is self-referential, i.e. paranoid, but not persecutory.

[12] *Dew v Clark* (1826) 3 Add. 79.

[13] *Boughton v Knight* (1873) L.R. 3P.D. 64 at 68.

and we cannot know what the modern judicial view would be. But there have been recent cases where courts have effectively had to decide the issue in the context of paranoid personality disorders. These cases are discussed in the next chapter. In summary, it remains a possibility that psychiatrists and judges interpret delusions and over-valued ideas in different ways.

13

HOW MENTAL ILLNESSES IMPACT UPON TESTAMENTARY CAPACITY

It is not the fact of the presence of a mental disorder, or even necessarily its severity, that determines testamentary capacity. It is the particular way in which the illness affects a specific testator that decides the issue. These might appear to be statements of the obvious, but sometimes they seem to be ignored. **13.01**

Learning Disability

People with mild learning disability may well have the necessary capacity to make a will. The importance of Gibson LJ's statement 'with the assistance of such explanation as he may be given'[1] cannot be overemphasized here. Unfortunately, some medical practitioners assume that learning disability equates to lack of capacity. In a case from our experience,[2] the general practitioner of a testatrix with mild learning disability wrote that she had 'a very low IQ throughout her whole life.' It turned out that the testatrix was able to live independently with assistance and could even read and write a little. Her IQ was probably around 70 and could not have been 'very low'. Nevertheless, the GP wrote 'She would have been totally unable to understand the nature of the act of making the will, the extent of her property or the claims of others.' This was at complete variance with the will-drafting solicitor's attendance note which made it clear that she not only understood the nature and consequences **13.02**

[1] *Hoff v Atherton* [2005] WTLR 99.

[2] In this chapter the cases quoted as 'from our experience' are all from contentious probate practice, but were settled before trial, and not, therefore, reported.

of the act of making her will, but had a correct appreciation of her estate, including that she had investments made on her behalf. Her residual beneficiaries were the two people who had long helped her to manage her affairs and to live as independently as possible. They were not present or even in the house when she gave instructions for the will, and there were no other persons who had a greater moral claim to her estate. The challenge to her will was withdrawn.

Dementia

Memory

13.03 Memory failure is usually the first manifestation of mild cognitive impairment (MCI) and dementia. MCI is effectively by definition insufficient to impair testamentary capacity. Its use in the area of capacity is to identify a manifest starting point for dementia, if the person with MCI does go on to develop it. In dementia itself, especially due to Alzheimer's disease, memory impairment calls into question the ability to appreciate the extent of the estate and to know those who might expect to benefit from the will. In cases where the estate is relatively simple, and memory impairment is not too severe, it is reasonable and possible to remind the testator of the components of his estate and even to have a list for him, which he might retain for a sufficient length of time to make the requisite decisions, in accordance with Section 3(1) of the Mental Capacity Act 2005.[3]

13.04 On the other hand, if memory impairment is severe and the estate complex, it may not be possible for the testator to hold the information in working memory (see Chapter 12) for long enough to allow decisions to be made. In Korsakov's syndrome, where episodic memory failure is the defining manifestation, it is doubtful that any new information can be retained, but possible that the testator can be reminded of information that is still embedded in memory store from times past. Difficulty arises when a relative and possible beneficiary has died since the onset of the Korsakov's syndrome, and the testator cannot retain the news. It may then be necessary repeatedly to remind him of this when he gives instructions for the will. Facilitating capacity accords strongly with the spirit of the Mental Capacity Act 2005.

13.05 As noted in Chapter 12 confabulation (false memory) is characteristic of Korsakov's syndrome, but it is found more frequently in Alzheimer's dementia, simply because the latter is more common. In the case of *Hawes v Burgess*[4] the testatrix told the

[3] 'For the purposes of Section 2, a person is unable to make a decision for himself if he is unable:

to understand the information relevant to the decision;
to retain the information;
to use or weigh that information as part of the process of making the decision; or
to communicate his decision (whether by talking, using sign language or any other means).'

[4] *Hawes v Burgess* WTLR [2012] 423.

solicitor who took instructions for the disputed will that her son was 'to be excluded because of the lifetime provision that is to be made for him'. There never was any lifetime provision for him, nor any intention to make it, and what she told her solicitor was a confabulation.

Other cognitive deficits

The other more subtle cognitive deficits certainly may contribute to lack of capacity to make a will. The most important of these is *receptive dysphasia*—failure to understand language. When it is gross, receptive dysphasia is fairly easy to spot, but it is much more difficult as it is developing. It is a common experience of doctors dealing with demented patients to be told by a spouse that 'he is awkward and won't do what I tell him to'. This frequently means that the patient simply has not understood what is said to him. The problem is that neither party recognizes that one of them does not understand. The situation is exacerbated by the fact that many people with dementia maintain *a good social façade*. Whilst not understanding the details of what is said to them they can often grasp that something said, such as a question, requires the answer yes or no. A way to test for receptive dysphasia is to ask the patient to undertake some simple tasks of increasing complexity, such as 'Give me the sheet of paper on the desk. Point to the window then to the door', and so on. It should also be remembered that virtually all tests of cognitive function, which are the subject of the next chapter, require an understanding of language. **13.06**

Expressive dysphasia is common after strokes causing paralysis of the right side of the body, due, usually, to a thrombosis in one of the branches of the left middle cerebral artery. The association between paralysis and expressive dysphasia is because the area involved in expressive language (Broca's area) is close to the motor cortex which controls movement. Some cases of dementia, termed *primary progressive aphasia*, begin with a severe expressive language difficulty before developing into a more widespread cognitive impairment that is identical to Alzheimer's disease. Unlike receptive dysphasia, where the testator might appear normal to the untutored eye of the will draftsman, the testator with expressive dysphasia clearly appears abnormal because he cannot speak. Contrary to appearances, the one with receptive dysphasia as part of his dementia may lack testamentary capacity, whereas the one with expressive dysphasia may not. There are ways of communicating that circumvent the latter. In accordance with the Mental Capacity Act 2005 (see footnote 3) a testator must be able to communicate his decision. If other cognitive functions are intact, the testator might be able to communicate with writing, albeit with the 'wrong' hand; or by means of written or spoken multiple-choice questions; or any other ingenious means that a will draftsman can devise well within the spirit of the Mental Capacity Act 2005. **13.07**

Agnosia—the failure to recognize sensory stimuli—may impair a potential testator's capacity to know who might have a moral claim on his bounty. In a case from **13.08** our experience, a millionaire disinherited his sons because he believed that they had defrauded him in a property deal. In fact, he had misidentified his nephews as his sons. Whether the nephews actually had defrauded him in the property deal was a moot point, but it was they who had been involved in it, and not the sons.

13.09 Dyspraxia—the inability to carry out motor tasks—may not by itself directly affect testamentary capacity, but, as it often leads to deterioration in personal hygiene and in the ability to carry out normal activities of daily living, it is an index of the severity of dementia.

13.10 Dyscalculia—impaired calculating ability—may cause difficulty for a testator in assessing the extent of his estate or judging proportionate parts of the estate to be divided among beneficiaries. However, the assessment of dyscalculia depends on knowing what the patient's premorbid ability was, as discussed in the next chapter.

13.11 Impairment of executive function is one of the most important deficits in dementia that may clearly affect testamentary capacity. A brief definition of executive function is the ability to integrate a variety of different psychological functions for the purpose of goal-directed activity. A review by Perry and Hodges[5] described it as

> ... those higher-order cognitive capabilities that are called upon in order to formulate new plans of action and to select, schedule and monitor appropriate sequences of action. It thus includes many stages by which goal-directed behaviour is manifested. First, the subject must appreciate the meaning of that goal and form an intention to fulfil it. The problems inherent in the task must be assessed and plans made to overcome these. The plan must then be initiated, with continual monitoring of the progress made towards this goal, and if necessary the subject must show sufficient flexibility to change strategy and correct mistakes if the goal is not being achieved. The subject must finally be able to distinguish when the goal has been reached and to judge the effect of his actions relative to the original goal before finally terminating the activity.

Perry and Hodges also point out that impaired executive function has often been attributed to frontal lobe impairment, because the concept emerged from descriptions of the famous case of Phineas Gage[6] who, in a rock-blasting accident in Vermont, USA in 1848, survived an iron bar going through his left (dominant) frontal lobe. The term *frontal executive function* is still frequently used, but is strictly speaking inaccurate because other brain areas are also involved.

13.12 The so-called dysexecutive syndrome is characterized by loss of the ability to plan and initiate goal-directed behaviour. The patient shows inability to control or arrest inappropriate responses, and loses or does not respond to feedback on his psychological

[5] R. J. Perry and J. R. Hodges (1999) 'Attention and executive deficits in Alzheimer's disease: a critical review'. *Brain* 122, 383–404.

[6] <http://en.wikipedia.org/wiki/Phineas_Gage#Gage.27s_accident>.

performance. Loss of such feedback may lead him to show disinhibition, and an uncritical attitude to his behaviour or its impact on others. Impaired internal control renders him more readily influenced by external sources. Diminished initiative leads to reduced ability to switch attention at will, which manifests itself by inflexibility in thinking. Thus, problem-solving is affected because he does not entertain alternative solutions.

It can be seen from this description that, in a word, *judgement* is affected, and it **13.13**
hardly needs to be said that judgement is at the heart of will-making. Nevertheless, we are not aware of any probate case where the validity of a will was rejected primarily on the grounds of executive dysfunction. In *Gorjat v Gorjat*[7] the matter was extensively reviewed in cross-examination of the two experts respectively instructed by the claimants and the defendant, but the will was upheld. In *Sharp v Adam*,[8] where the will was rejected, one of the experts emphasized that the testator had impaired executive function as a part of his overall cognitive impairment caused by multiple sclerosis. As is well known, the grounds for rejection of the will were his failure to appreciate the moral claims of his daughters.

Frontal dementia

Frontal dementia is particularly characterized by impairment of executive function, **13.14**
and of relationships and consideration for others. The first thing that tends to be noticed by close family members is a change in personality. Personal standards of hygiene fall, and initiative and drive are reduced. Disinhibited behaviour with either cheekiness or petulance is seen. As Lishman[9] put it, 'judgement may be markedly impaired in the conduct of affairs. The patient shows little concern about his personal future, and fails to plan ahead or carry through ideas. Inability to forejudge the consequences of actions can lead to foolish or irresponsible behaviour. Social and ethical controls may be weakened and have issue in anti-social conduct.'

Subcortical dementia

Parkinson's disease (PD), being the most common cause of a subcortical dementia, **13.15**
has been at issue in some testamentary capacity cases. In *Wilkes v Wilkes*[10] the testatrix suffered from PD but also diffuse cerebrovascular disease. It is questionable, therefore, whether she actually had true PD, but more probably had a Parkinsonian syndrome due to cerebrovascular disease, which is not uncommon. Her disorder of mind was most likely to have been vascular dementia, but her will was upheld

[7] *Gorjat v Gorjat* [2010] EWHC 1537 (Ch).
[8] *Sharp & Anor v Adam & Ors* [2006] EWCA Civ 449.
[9] W. A. Lishman *Organic Psychiatry* (3rd edn., Oxford: Blackwell Science, 1998) p 77.
[10] *Wilkes v Wilkes* [2000] EWCOP 1562.

anyway. In the case of *Pearce v Beverley* heard in the Leeds County Court,[11] in which a claim was brought of failure duly to execute a will and incapacity to make several *inter vivos* transactions, undue influence was not pleaded and thus not adjudicated, but can be detected reading between the lines. The will was held not to have been duly executed and the transactions were judged invalid. The descriptions in the judgement of the testator are typical of PD. For example a cancer specialist who saw him a year before he died wrote 'I was struck by his blank expressionless face and paucity of movement during the interview. His ex-partner was with him in clinic and felt that the symptoms had progressed over recent months. I understand he had a normal brain scan a few months ago. It struck me that he had many of the features of Parkinson's disease.' A psychiatrist saw him a few months later and wrote: 'His speech was slow in volume, rate and rhythm. The content was appropriate but there was difficulty in understanding things and expressing himself. In terms of cognition he was not orientated to place but he was orientated to time and person. There was some evidence of memory loss both long term and short term. It was very difficult to complete MMSE [mini mental state examination] as he was unable to concentrate or think on any question.' This is a good description of psychomotor slowing, comprehension difficulty, and memory impairment, typical of PD.

13.16 Dementia with Lewy bodies ('DLB') can be considered here as an example of a subcortical dementia because it clearly bears a similar pathological relationship to PD. However, it also has some features of a cortical dementia, not least because the pathological changes often coexist with those of Alzheimer's disease, and the clinical picture depends on which changes are the more prominent. We have not found any UK-recorded cases in which DLB was considered a factor. There are some Australian cases, but the evidence for the diagnosis is not very clear from the judgments. The only one which has a little evidence of this kind is *Tonkiss v Graham*,[12] in which the one expert (a neuropsychologist) stated that the testatrix was subject to delirium-like episodes from which she made a complete recovery, which is certainly consistent with DLB.

13.17 In the description of executive dysfunction above we mentioned that patients are more readily influenced by external sources. Clearly, this has relevance to the question of undue influence (see Chapter 5), but unless coercion can be proved such that the will represents the wishes of the influencer rather than the testator, which happens in only a minority of cases, executive dysfunction is not used as evidence to overturn wills. Experts instructed to write reports, potentially for trial, often find themselves in a difficult position when asked to comment on the possibility of undue influence. In clinical practice as well as contentious probate, doctors tend to take a

---

[11] *Pearce v Beverley* [2013] EW Misc 10 (CC).

[12] *Tonkiss and Anor v Graham and Ors* [2002] NSWSC 891 (4 October 2002).

Table 13.1 'Red flags' for undue influence

Peisah et al 2009
Relationship risk factors
- Anyone in a position of trust or upon whom the testator is dependent for emotional or physical needs

Social or environmental risk factors
- Isolation and sequestration of the person
- Change in family relationships/dynamics
- Recent bereavement
- Family conflict

Psychological and physical risk factors
- Physical disability
- Non-specific psychological factors such as deathbed wills, sexual bargaining, serious medical illness with dependency and regression
- Personality disorders
- Substance abuse
- Mental disorders including dementia, delirium, and mood and paranoid disorders

Legal risk factors
- Beneficiary instigates or procures the will
- Contents of the will include unnatural provisions
- Contents favour the person instigating the will
- Contents not in keeping with previous wishes
- Other documents have changed at the same time

less restricted view of undue influence than current law. For example, the so-called *gold-digger*, usually a female carer of a widower with dementia, is commonly encountered. She may be offering him sexual favours, or threatening directly or by implication to withdraw care, but when he makes a will in her favour disinheriting his own children, there is rarely, if ever, any evidence of coercion. In our experience, the practising clinician and his multi-disciplinary team will consider the situation to be one of undue influence, but if that clinician is instructed to write a report for contentious probate litigation, he knows that undue influence is unlikely to be pleaded, or to succeed if pleaded.

A group of old age psychiatrists were commissioned by the International Psycho- **13.18**
geriatric Association to review undue influence from a medical standpoint. Whilst acknowledging the difficulty in pleading undue influence in anglophone jurisdictions, they came up with a number of indices (called *red flags*) that should at least arouse suspicion.[13] These are shown in Table 13.1. Clearly these red flags derive from clinical experience, and have no legal validity, but they may serve at least to alert the will draftsman. Isolation and sequestration of the testator are particularly common in our experience, even in cases never being pleaded as undue influence. For example,

[13] C. Peisah et al. *International Psychogeriatrics* (2009), 21:1, 7–15.

in *Catling v Catling*[14] in which the pleas were lack of testamentary capacity and want of knowledge and approval, the judge noted as a separate point in his judgment of the latter plea, which overturned the disputed will, 'Mrs Catling was living with Kevin and Shirley and was more or less cut off by them from contact with her other children, even though the others tried to see her.'

13.19 It is not only clinicians who find the current legal situation in England & Wales unsatisfactory. Kerridge,[15] an academic lawyer, wrote that 'it is too easy in England to coerce, or deceive, a vulnerable testator into making a will and it is not easy enough to challenge a suspicious will when one comes to light.' As other authorities have averred, lawyers try to circumvent a plea of undue influence by pleading want of knowledge and approval. But Kerridge calls this use of a 'fiction'. These issues are discussed in full in Chapter 4.

Delirium

13.20 The importance of delirium in relation to testamentary capacity cannot be overestimated. As a rule of thumb, delirious people lack the capacity to make a will. They may not appreciate the extent of their estate but, more importantly, are unable to weigh up the competing claims of those who might expect to benefit from their will. The situation arises most commonly with wills made in hospital. The latter are potentially, but not necessarily, *deathbed wills*. Many older people with dementia are admitted to hospital several times with intercurrent[16] infections, especially of the chest or urinary tract, which make them delirious for a while until antibiotic treatment returns them to their pre-delirious state.

13.21 Noisy delirium is usually not difficult to spot, but quiet delirium can sometimes be so. Usually it will be clear from talking to a quietly delirious patient that he is not orientated to time and place, but if closed questions are asked expecting simple answers such as yes and no, a will draftsman can be deceived into thinking that the patient's mental state is normal. For example, a solicitor might say that he has brought in the will to hospital for which instructions were given before his client was admitted to hospital. The latter says yes. The solicitor asks if he should read the will over clause by clause. The patient answers yes. The solicitor reads the will clause by clause, and for each one asks if this remains his client's wish. The patient answers yes. Does he wish to execute the will? The answer is yes, and the will is signed. This procedure is not a guarantee of testamentary capacity.

[14] *Catling v Catling* [2014] EWHC 180 (Ch).

[15] R. Kerridge (2000) 'Wills made under suspicious circumstances: the problem of the vulnerable testator'. *The Cambridge Law Journal* 59, 310–34.

[16] A common medical term for a new acute illness, usually an infection, arising during the course of a chronic one.

13.22 Delirium, by its very nature, tends to fluctuate, and the course of the mental disturbance may well be punctuated by *lucid intervals*. In the case of *Dench v Dench*[17] the testator had a large frontal brain tumour. He had given instructions for a will in August before the diagnosis was made and before he had significant symptoms. In October he was admitted to hospital in Grantham with fluctuating delirium. At some of the times when he was delirious, he thought that he was respectively in Sheffield and London. His solicitor visited him in Grantham Hospital to have the will executed. She spent two hours with him before he signed the will. She made copious, exemplary notes which were accepted as accurate by the judge, and the will was upheld. The judge ruled that he had full capacity when he executed the will, but stated that he would have ruled that the testator had what he referred to as '*Parker v Felgate*[18] capacity', had he been unable to confirm full capacity.

13.23 One of the most frequent causes of delirium in older people is prescribed medication: for example, opiates (morphine, heroin, and their derivatives) given for terminal cancer care. If this might be the last chance to make a will, and medication is thought to be causing delirium, the drugs can be withdrawn temporarily to see if a sufficiently lucid interval can be achieved in order for a will to be made.

13.24 In cases where wills are signed in hospital and where delirium might be anticipated as grounds for a later challenge, we recommend that will draftsmen consider the following options. The first would be to delay the execution of the will until the patient recovers. Alternatively, if it is feared that the testator will die, but does in fact recover, the will should be confirmed when he is evidently no longer delirious.

Affective Disorder

Depressive illness

13.25 Depressive illness distorts patterns of thought. Most commonly, the patient is dominated by ideas of guilt and worthlessness, which can reach delusional intensity. For example, a patient developed the delusion that the police were going to arrest him for not declaring a single British Gas share certificate to the Inland Revenue (as it then was). On being questioned further he believed that he would be deservedly sentenced to death. In older patients delusional beliefs are not always inwardly directed. For example, some may say that their marriage is stuck so fast on the rocks that it cannot be salvaged. On recovery from the depressive illness, they are amazed that they

[17] *Dench v Dench* [2013] Case No: 1LS30722 Chancery Division (probate) Leeds District Registry. Not elsewhere reported.
[18] *Parker v Felgate* [1883] L.R.8P.D.1712.

had said this. Clearly, a testator who disinherits a spouse in the throes of such a belief is liable to evoke the *insane delusion* limb of the *Banks v Goodfellow* test.

13.26 As the most serious consequence of a depressive illness, suicide calls into question testamentary capacity, but as the judge stated in a 2009 Australian case:[19]

> The fact that the deceased committed suicide does not of itself lead inexorably to the conclusion that the deceased lacked testamentary capacity at the time of the execution of either of the instruments [two home-made wills] although this is recognised as a factor of significance.

The *Banks v Goodfellow* test has to be applied, and in this particular case the two wills were upheld, notwithstanding clear evidence of a depressive illness and a variety of false beliefs.

13.27 *Key v Key*[20] was the recent case that changed the position of affective disorder on the contentious probate map. As Briggs J (as he then was) stated:

> [W]ithout in any way detracting from the continuing authority of *Banks v Goodfellow*, it must be recognised that psychiatric medicine has come a long way since 1870 in recognising an ever widening range of circumstances now regarded as sufficient at least to give rise to a risk of mental disorder, sufficient to deprive a patient of the power of rational decision making, quite distinctly from old age and infirmity. The mental shock of witnessing an injury to a loved one is an example recognised by the law, and the affective disorder which may be caused by bereavement is an example recognised by psychiatrists, as both [experts] acknowledged. The latter described the symptomatic effect of bereavement as capable of being almost identical to that associated with severe depression. Accordingly, although neither I nor counsel has found any reported case dealing with the effect of bereavement on testamentary capacity, the *Banks v Goodfellow* test must be applied so as to accommodate this, among other factors capable of impairing testamentary capacity, in a way in which, perhaps, the court would have found difficult to recognise in the nineteenth century.

13.28 Briggs J encapsulated the main reason why affective disorder may impair testamentary capacity. He stated that the thrust of the *Banks v Goodfellow* test

> is primarily about the mental capacity to understand or comprehend... [whereas]... the evidence of the experts in the present case shows... that affective disorder such as depression, including that caused by bereavement, is more likely to affect powers of decision-making than comprehension. A person in that condition may have the capacity to understand what his property is, and even who his relatives and dependents are, without having the mental energy to make any decisions of his own about whom to benefit.

13.29 In 2013, in a similar case to *Key v Key* (*Turner v Phythian*)[21] the testatrix was found to have lacked capacity because she 'was suffering from an affective disorder brought

[19] *King v Hudson* [2009] NSWSC 1013.
[20] *Key v Key* [2010] EWHC 408 (Ch).
[21] *Turner v Phythian* [2013] EWHC 499 (Ch).

about by her deep grief at the death of her brother, combined with her continuing fragile mental state arising from her advanced age, her physical frailty, and her continuing grief for her husband.'

Manic states

Manic states as part of bipolar affective disorder also deprive a person of judgement and consideration. Testators would be impulsive and liable to bequeath their estate or substantial parts of it to people or organizations with no moral claim. However, a search of reported cases has not revealed any in which a will was challenged on the grounds of incapacity due to a manic illness. **13.30**

Perhaps the most important fact to note about affective disorders, be they on the depressed or manic side of normal, is that all are potentially treatable, and in the majority of cases remission and recovery can be expected. Wills, therefore, need *not* be made during episodes of illness, but should await recovery. **13.31**

Schizophrenia and Delusional Psychoses

One of the central issues in relation to testamentary capacity is that of 'insane delusion'. Delusions are very common in all types of schizophrenia and occur by definition in delusional psychoses. John Banks, in the legal world perhaps the most famous testator of all, probably suffered from paranoid schizophrenia, in modern terminology, which first became manifest at the age of 29 or 30: the year of his birth is uncertain, but likely either 1811 or 1812.[22] From the moment of his first confinement in a lunatic asylum he suffered from persecutory delusions, which became focused upon a Keswick grocer, Featherstone Alexander. Even after the latter died, Banks believed that he was pursued and molested by his malevolent spirit. John Banks' psychosis was later complicated by epilepsy, which did not appear until a few months before he gave instructions for his famous last will, in December 1863 when he was 51 or 52. As is well known, his will was upheld because his 'insane delusion [did] not influence his will in disposing of [his] property and bring about a disposal of it which, if [his] mind had been sound, would not have been made.' **13.32**

In the much more recent case of *Kostic v Chaplin*[23] the testator, Bronislav (Bané for short) Kostic, suffered from a delusional psychosis. The judge neatly summarized what he had to do as follows. **13.33**

> The main issue that I have to decide in this case is whether Bané had testamentary capacity to make the 1988 and 1989 Wills, it being common ground that from the

[22] D. Lush <http://www.step.org/banks-v-goodfellow-1870>.
[23] *Kostic v Chaplin* [2007] EWHC 2298 (Ch).

> mid-1980s until the end of his life he suffered from a serious and untreated mental illness which took the form of a delusional disorder. In particular, he believed that there was an international conspiracy of dark forces against him in which, at least, his wife, mother, and sister were implicated. The central question is whether Bané's delusions affected the dispositions of his estate in the 1989 Will, or (if it is invalid) the 1988 Will.

Kostic disinherited his son, Zoran, and intended to leave his fortune to the Conservative Party to set up a trust in honour of his father. The judge summarized his conclusion as follows.

> I am fully satisfied on the basis of all the evidence that Bané's decision to disinherit Zoran in the 1988 and 1989 Wills was heavily influenced by his delusions, and in particular by his belief that Zoran was implicated in the global conspiracy he saw around him. In the language of *Banks v Goodfellow*, his natural affection for Zoran had been poisoned by the disorder of his mind, and his insane delusions brought about a disposal of his property which would not have been made if he had been of sound mind.

13.34 Schizophrenic thought disorder, an impairment of logical thinking, was the central issue in the case of the *Vegetarian Society v Scott*.[24] The testator had a notebook in which he had written a variety of things over many years. The experts, instructed respectively by each side, agreed on the diagnosis of schizophrenia, and that the writings exhibited logical thought disorder. One of the experts considered that the logical thought disorder would have affected his capacity to give coherent instructions for a will; whereas the other expert's opinion was that there was evidence from letters he had written, and the statements of professionals with whom he had had business dealings, that he was capable of logical thinking for the purpose of goal-directed action, including when giving instructions for the disputed will. The will was upheld.

Personality Disorder

13.35 Whether personality disorder constitutes a disorder of the mind within the meaning of the *Banks v Goodfellow* judgment is itself a rather contentious matter. Just as psychopathy is the type of personality disorder that arouses debate about responsibility in criminal law, so it is paranoid personality disorder which features in contentious probate. The International Classification of Disease 10th revision (ICD-10) criteria for paranoid personality disorder are listed here.

> A paranoid personality disorder is characterized by:
> a. excessive sensitiveness to setbacks and rebuffs;
> b. tendency to bear grudges persistently, e.g. refusal to forgive insults and injuries or slights;

[24] *The Vegetarian Society and Anor v Scott* [2013] EWHC 4097 (Ch).

c. suspiciousness and a pervasive tendency to distort experience by misconstruing the neutral or friendly actions of others as hostile or contemptuous;
d. a combative and tenacious sense of personal rights out of keeping with the actual situation;
e. recurrent suspicions, without justification, regarding sexual fidelity of spouse or sexual partner;
f. tendency to experience excessive self-importance, manifest in a persistent self-referential attitude;
g. preoccupation with unsubstantiated 'conspiratorial' explanations of events both immediate to the patient and in the world at large.

Includes: expansive paranoid, fanatic, querulant, and sensitive paranoid personality (disorder).

Excludes: delusional disorder (F22), schizophrenia (F20).

Where paranoid personality disorder is concerned, the difficulty for courts is to differentiate between beliefs that are essentially overvalued ideas, i.e. false beliefs that are understandable within the context of an individual's personality, or whether they are delusions. The matter is complicated by the fact that some paranoid personalities may develop frank delusional beliefs. **13.36**

In the case of *Ritchie v Joslin*[25] the expert for the claimants was of the opinion that the testatrix 'was suffering from a paranoid personality disorder when she believed that her children were not helping her and that this poisoned her affections to the extent of preventing the exercise of her natural faculties.' The expert for the defendants was more reserved about whether she had a personality disorder but was more certain that she had no other mental disorder. The judge accepted the claimant's expert's view and the relevant section of the judgment reads as follows. **13.37**

> To my mind the evidence plainly points to the fact that Mary's motive in making the will was to cut out her children rather than to benefit NOS. This emerges clearly from the file notes. There was no rational reason for her to cut out all her children. Plainly therefore her affections to her children were poisoned. This, too, emerges from the file notes. I have set out the allegations above. In addition there are references to the children 'not deserving her money'. As set above the allegations she made about her children which she gave as a reason for cutting them out were untrue but were believed by Mary to be true. They were, in my view, delusions. Those beliefs did so poison her mind so as to cause her to cut her children out of her will. There was a strong moral obligation in all the circumstances of the case to leave the estate to the family. In my view she would not have cut out her family but for those beliefs. It follows in my view that Mary did not have testamentary capacity. I would revoke the grant of probate.

Purely from a psychiatric standpoint the psychiatrist among us is not convinced that this testatrix was deluded, but more of the opinion that she had a paranoid personality. The judicial decision was, therefore, that a personality disorder of extreme degree **13.38**

[25] *Ritchie & Ors v Joslin & Ors* [2009] EWHC 709 (Ch).

may amount to a disorder of mind that can lead to failure to satisfy the insane delusion limb of the *Banks v Goodfellow* test.

13.39 The same issues arose in a more recent Scottish case[26] where the decision went the other way to that in *Ritchie v Joslin*. The testator by all accounts was a truly unpleasant man, a sexual predator, paedophile, adulterer, and paranoid individual, to mention just a few of his bad traits, who disinherited his children. The judge made it clear that his personality was not sufficient to remove his testamentary capacity, stating

> The requirement for the pursuers [claimants] must therefore be to show that the testator's will and codicils were the result of thinking that was truly the result of mental disorder; mere antipathy towards his children, prejudice, intolerance or even caprice will not suffice.

13.40 The judge also understood that psychiatry differentiates between mental illness and personality disorder.

> The conclusions I feel compelled to draw from the evidence of 'sexual disinhibition' are not favourable to the testator's moral character. He seems to have been sexually predatory, selfish and careless for the feelings and wellbeing of others. That is however, irrelevant so far as the present action is concerned. Whilst the psychiatric experts refer to the behaviour they do not regard it as showing mental disorder. The behaviour described may be repugnant but it does not in my view shed light on the testator's capacity, or lack thereof, to dispose of his estate by testamentary disposition... The other aspects of the testator's behaviour which the pursuers seek to characterize as delusional are, in my view, equally problematic. Distrust as to his first wife's sexual fidelity or the paternity of his sons is capable, as all the expert psychiatrists spoke to, of being construed as delusional ideation. It has not however been proven to my satisfaction that such thinking was necessarily delusional... I am not satisfied that the pursuers have established that there were periods when the testator's paranoid personality disorder was of such delusional intensity as to deprive him of testamentary capacity. Whilst the testator was, on the basis of all the evidence I have heard, clearly a driven man and capable of ruthless and even harsh behaviour at times, close examination of the evidence does not suggest that his behaviour was the result of delusional thoughts. This of itself is sufficient to dispose of the issue in the case in the favour of the defenders [defendants].

13.41 In the even more recent case of *Bray v Pearce*[27] the court accepted that the testatrix had a paranoid personality disorder and had also developed a paranoid psychosis, referred to as paraphrenia.[28] The judge ruled that both conditions were responsible for her disinheriting her nephew in favour of her one-time window cleaner. He stated:

> Even for a curmudgeonly old lady with strong views and a habit, it seems, of changing her wills, the Deceased's exclusion of Mr Bray (and indeed any other family member

[26] *Stewart & Ors v Franks & Ors* [2013] ScotCS CSOH_63.

[27] *Bray v Pearce* [2014] Chancery Division Case No: HC12D04569, not otherwise reported.

[28] A now outdated term for schizophrenia coming on in later life.

> or charity) as a beneficiary, in favour of Mr Pearce, might well be explained as resulting at least in part from paranoid or schizoid-like delusions. For this purpose I would regard both her paranoid personality disorder and her paraphrenia as constituting testamentary incapacity.

In summary, where personality disorder is concerned, it seems that there are three broad conclusions. First, where the beliefs and actions of a testator are determined as manifestations solely of his personality, it is unlikely that he will be found to lack capacity. Second, where it becomes difficult to determine whether his beliefs are manifestations of his personality or of delusions, his capacity is called into question: but there is insufficient case law to predict what the decision of a court might be. Third, where a testator with a paranoid personality has developed clearly recognizable delusional beliefs, the decision whether those delusions determined his testamentary dispositions is easier for a court to decide vis à vis the *Banks v Goodfellow* test. **13.42**

14

THE VALUE OF STANDARDIZED COGNITIVE AND OTHER TESTS IN CONTENTIOUS PROBATE

In contentious probate the parties tend to grab at cognitive test results like shipwrecked passengers from the *Titanic* scrambling to get into a lifeboat. Lawyers, medical experts, and, dare one say it, judges may also seek refuge there. Without wishing to take this metaphor too far, we should say that not all cognitive tests are seaworthy enough for the particular conditions, and some are little better than flotsam. In this chapter we shall look at some of the tests that are encountered most frequently in probate cases, and try to assess their value in this context. **14.01**

Before we do this it might be helpful to define who carries out these tests. First, there are psychiatrists and psychologists. The essential difference between the two is that the former are qualified medical practitioners with postgraduate training in psychological medicine. The latter have university degrees in psychology with a postgraduate training and qualification in clinical psychology. Each of these two professions has sub-specialists in areas that may touch upon contentious probate. **14.02**

As the majority of cases of disputed wills have elderly testators with dementia or depression at their core, old age psychiatrists, sometimes called psychogeriatricians, are the medical experts most frequently called upon. Neuropsychiatrists specialize **14.03** in mental disorders of adulthood in which there is a known or presumed brain lesion: for example, a brain tumour or traumatic brain injury. They also deal with cases of dementia that develop before old age. Geriatricians, also known as physicians in old age medicine or elderly care, have a wide experience of dementia, albeit in the context of physical illness, and may also use cognitive tests to assess mental capacity.

14.04 Clinical psychologists are trained and experienced in detailed psychological testing. As we shall see later in this chapter, the majority of testators in contentious probate cases are tested by doctors using only screening tests. Unfortunately, few testators are subject to detailed psychological testing of individual higher cerebral functions. Those who are may have been assessed by general clinical psychologists, by clinical psychologists attached to old age psychiatry services, or by specialist neuropsychologists who, like their counterparts neuropsychiatrists, specialize in cases where there is a known or presumed brain lesion.

14.05 Some of the tests described below are also administered by other healthcare workers, notably GPs, mental illness nurses, occupational therapists, and physiotherapists.

Cognitive Tests

14.06 The *Collins English Dictionary* defines cognition as '(Psychology) the mental act or process by which knowledge is acquired, including perception, intuition, and reasoning the knowledge that results from such an act or process.' Cognitive tests set out to evaluate some of the individual abilities that we have discussed in the preceding two chapters. This is important because they vary not only in whether they test a particular function at all, but also how well they assess the functions that they do set out to test. We shall discuss the following tests:

i. The Mini Mental State Examination (MMSE);
ii. The Montreal Cognitive Assessment (MoCA);
iii. The Abbreviated Mental Test Score;
iv. The Addenbrooke's Cognitive Examination—Revised (ACE-R);
v. Clock-drawing tests and the GPCog (General Practitioner assessment of Cognition) Test;
vi. The Informant Questionnaire on Cognitive Decline in the Elderly (IQCODE);
vii. The Bristol Activities of Daily Living Scale (BADLS), and the Barthel Index.

14.07 These have been chosen because of the relative frequency of their use in contentious probate cases, and not because they are necessarily better than other tests. Uncommonly, we have encountered detailed testing by a neuropsychologist, and in such cases it may be necessary for lawyers to seek clarification on the results from an expert.

The Mini Mental State Examination (MMSE)

This test is the most commonly used in clinical practice and, therefore, the most frequently seen in contentious probate. It consists of a series of questions that test orientation, episodic memory, concentration, language comprehension, writing, and copying a diagram. The questions are merely a collection of those that clinicians have asked at the bedside for decades, but were gathered into a questionnaire to screen medical patients for dementia at Johns Hopkins Hospital,[1] Baltimore, USA. We should have wished to reproduce the MMSE here, not least to show that there is no mystique about it. However, in spite of the fact that it was freely available and used free of charge between 1975 and 2010, within the last five years the authors sold the copyright to a company called Psychological Assessment Resources (PAR) which has forbidden all reproduction of it, and seeks as far as it can to exert its copyright for profit. This caused outrage in the medical profession which was reflected in an editorial in the world's leading medical journal.[2] Not only is it absurd to take out copyright on questions that long antedate the MMSE, but the questionnaire itself, is readily to be found on the Internet by a Google search, and readers are encouraged to look there. **14.08**

The MMSE was not alone in the 1970s. There were several similar screening questionnaires devised in the UK and widely used. Most of these have been superseded by the MMSE, largely because of American domination of the regulations for clinical trials and the need to make the latter internationally comparable. Of the British questionnaires it is worth mentioning the Mental Test Score[3] because it has been abbreviated and is discussed in detail below. **14.09**

The everyday purpose of *screening* tests is to select those people who need full investigation of suspected dementia. It is both to the credit and discredit of the MMSE that it has come to be used not only as a screening test, but as a measure of severity and, when repeated at intervals, as a measure of the rate of decline in dementia: credit because it is simple and convenient to use with the minimum of training. Credit, too, because it has been of some value in research, e.g. in clinical trials as mentioned above. **14.10**

In contentious probate the value of the MMSE is far less clear-cut and, because so often there are few 'hard' data for courts to consider, there is a risk of it being **14.11**

[1] M. F. Folstein, S. E. Folstein, and P. R. McHugh (1975) '"Mini-mental state": A practical method for grading the cognitive state of patients for the clinician'. *Journal of Psychiatric Research* 12 (3): 189–98.

[2] J. C. Newman and R. Feldman (2011). 'Copyright and open access at the bedside'. *N Engl J Med* 365: 2447–9.

[3] H. M. Hodkinson (1972). 'Evaluation of a mental test score for assessment of mental impairment in the elderly'. *Age and Ageing* 1: 233–8.

overvalued. First of all, the MMSE is heavily weighted towards memory items, and barely, if at all, tests executive function. Second, it is more valid in dementia due to Alzheimer's disease than with other dementias, especially frontal and subcortical (Parkinson's and DLB). Third, whilst it has some value in estimating the degree of severity in groups of patients, e.g. for research or audit, in any one individual a single score may under- or overestimate severity. Fourth, other conditions, such as depression, may cause a falsely low score.

14.12 Bearing these caveats in mind, we can say that MMSE scores may be used as an approximate estimate of severity in individual patients *for whom there is enough other clinical evidence to confirm a diagnosis of dementia*, especially Alzheimer's disease. The ranges of generally accepted scores are shown in Table 14.1.

14.13 The values in Table 14.1 should not be taken to conclude that a score of 25–30 indicates normality, for the MMSE is subject to *ceiling and floor effects*. Ceiling effect means that scores at the higher end of the range do not adequately discriminate between different levels of cognitive ability. Equivalently a floor effect means that scores at the lower end do not discriminate adequately between highly impaired cases. In contentious probate the floor effect of the MMSE is less important, since it is unlikely that anyone scoring lower than 10/30 would have testamentary capacity. The ceiling effect has more potential importance, since it cannot be assumed that someone scoring between 25 and 30 was not demented. We have certainly seen cases scoring within this range who have had scores on the ACE-R (see below), for example, that fall well within the dementia range.

14.14 The ceiling effect in the MMSE brings out the point that what psychiatrists call *premorbid ability* (the patient's ability before becoming ill) can affect test results. All psychological tests are supposed to control for premorbid ability, but this is not always achieved. Highly intelligent individuals with underlying or developing dementia can score within so-called normal ranges. Some of the tasks in the tests may have been too difficult for a premorbid person: the classic example being subtraction of serial sevens from one hundred in the MMSE. The authors recognized this by giving the alternative task of spelling 'world' backwards. However, if the patient was only semi-literate before developing dementia, this

Table 14.1 Ranges of MMSE scores vis à vis notional severity

MMSE Score out of 30	Severity
24–20	Mild
20–15	Mild to moderate
15–10	Moderate to severe
10 and below	Severe

test, too, may be beyond his means. On the other hand, if a patient was known to be particularly good at mental arithmetic before he became ill, and does poorly on the serial sevens task, the test yields useful information on cognitive deterioration. The lesson from all this is that a diagnosis of dementia depends not simply on a cognitive test result, but demands a detailed history of the patient from a reliable informant.

The Montreal Cognitive Assessment (MoCA)

The MoCA[4] (pronounced 'mocker') which is also scored out of 30, is currently **14.15**
well on the way to replacing the MMSE in clinical practice, for two reasons. First, although the clinician who devised it owns the copyright, he makes it freely available for non-commercial clinical and academic purposes.[5] Second, it has advantages over the MMSE in testing a wider variety of abilities, including executive function. It can be found easily on the Internet.[6] This is not to say that it is without the limitations of a good screening test, but it is already appearing in more contentious probate cases. The MoCA contains most of the important elements of the MMSE but executive function is tested with a trail-making and a clock-drawing test. The trail-making test is shown in Figure 14.1.

Comparisons of the MoCA with the MMSE have come out in favour of the former. **14.16**
The sensitivity of the MoCA, a technical statistical measure of the true positive rate for diagnosis of mild cognitive impairment (MCI), was found to be superior to the MMSE in a set of memory clinic patients.[7] In a series of patients with Parkinson's disease (PD) the MMSE showed a marked ceiling effect in comparison to the MoCA.[8] In summary, there have now been several research papers which have shown the superiority of the MoCA over the MMSE as a screening test for MCI and dementia in a variety of clinical situations.

As yet there are no ranges of MoCA scores that reflect severity equivalent to those for **14.17**
the MMSE shown in Table 14.1. The authors of the test have put it forward only as a screening test and have proposed that a score of 26 and above is normal, i.e. does not require further assessment of possible cognitive impairment.

---

[4] Z. S. Nasreddine et al. (2005). 'The Montreal Cognitive Assessment, MoCA: a brief screening tool for mild cognitive impairment'. *J.Am. Geriatr.Soc.* 53(4) 695–9.

[5] <http://www.mocatest.org/permission.asp>.

[6] <http://www.gesundheit.belgien.be/internet2Prd/groups/public/@public/@dg1/@acutecare/documents/ie2divers/19074274.pdf>.

[7] T. Smith, N. Gildeh, and C. Holmes (2007). 'The Montreal Cognitive Assessment: validity and utility in a memory clinic setting'. *The Canadian Journal of Psychiatry* 52 (5).

[8] C. Zadikoff (2008). 'A comparison of the mini mental state exam to the Montreal cognitive assessment in identifying cognitive deficits in Parkinson's disease'. *Movement Disorders* 23 (2) 297–9.

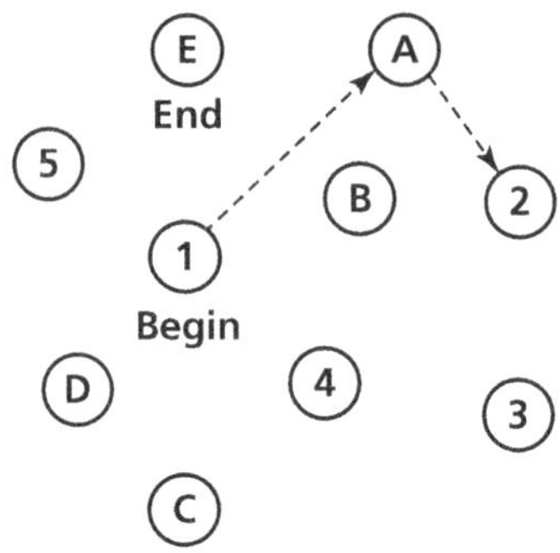

Figure 14.1 Trail-making test from the MoCA.

The instruction is: 'Draw a line going from a number to a letter in ascending order. So begin here [point to 1] and draw a line to A, then to 2 and so on. And end here [point to E].'

Scoring: allocate 1 point if the subject successfully draws the following pattern: 1–A–2–B–3– C–4–D–5–E without drawing any lines that cross. Any error that is not immediately self-corrected earns no point.

The Abbreviated Mental Test Score (AMTS)

14.18 The AMTS crops up frequently in contentious probate cases but is often mislabelled, especially by GPs, as the 'mini-mental test'. It was devised by Hodkinson (reference at footnote 3) who found that the abbreviated version of the Mental Test Score was just as discriminating as the long version.[9] Table 14.2 shows the test.

Table 14.2 The Abbreviated Mental Test Score (AMTS)

Age
Time (to the nearest hour)
Give the address '42 West Street' and ask the patient to repeat it to ensure it has been heard correctly. Ask for it to be repeated at the end of the test.
Current year
Name of the place (e.g. name of the hospital)
Recognition of two persons (doctor, nurse, etc.)
Date of birth
Year of First World War[10]
Name of present monarch
Count backwards from 20 to 1

[9] At the time Hodkinson was a practising physician for the elderly. He went on to become professor of geriatrics at University College Hospital, London, from which post he retired in order to train as a barrister. At the time of writing he practises as a distinguished expert in contentious probate. See, for example *Ashkettle v Gwinnett* [2013] EWHC 2125 (Ch).

[10] For the present generation of older people the date of the Second World War is often asked.

As can be seen, the AMTS is simple and thus easy to administer. Many accident and emergency departments in the UK have the test printed on admission forms used by doctors and nurses. Unfortunately, all too often the form is not filled in. Geriatricians, other physicians, occupational therapists, and physiotherapists use it during hospital admissions, whilst it is also commonly used by GPs. **14.19**

Because the AMTS is often used in the context of acute hospital admissions it may not be of value in discriminating delirium from dementia. But if there is good evidence that the patient is not delirious, a score of seven or below gives a fair indication of the need to investigate whether or not the patient has dementia: the lower the score, the stronger the indication. **14.20**

The Addenbrooke's Cognitive Examination—Revised (ACE-R)

Professor John Hodges developed the test, but has had to revise it to ACE-III because ACE-R contains within it the MMSE and PAR have insisted on exerting their copyright. However, in current contentious probate cases in which the ACE appears it is the version with the MMSE. This has had the fortuitous advantage of revealing the limitations of the MMSE, as we shall see. **14.21**

The ACE sets out systematically to test a series of functions: attention, memory, fluency, language, and visuospatial ability. Within these areas executive function is tested because integrated psychological planning is required. The total score is out of 100, and for the ACE-R the sensitivity and specificity have been calculated on samples of patients and controls. Sensitivity, as already mentioned, is a measure of the true positive rate. Specificity is a measure of the true negative rate. For the ACE-R a cut-off score of less than 88 gives a 94 per cent sensitivity and 89 per cent specificity. This means that 94 out of 100 cases scoring below 88 are likely to have dementia; whereas 11 out of 100 may get a false positive rating of dementia. If the cut-off score is reduced to less than 82, the sensitivity is 84 per cent and the specificity is 100 per cent, which means that 16 out of 100 cases of dementia could be missed, but none is likely to be given a wrong diagnosis of dementia. Of all the tests mentioned in this chapter the ACE yields the most valid results for the assessment of dementia in contentious probate cases. **14.22**

In our experience several cases with ACE-R scores have given interesting results. Here are two examples. A patient of 79 who suffered brain damage after an operation scored 60/100 on the ACE-R but 25/30 on the MMSE. Almost exactly four years later he scored 61/100 on the ACE and 23/30 on the MMSE. Other tests administered confirmed marked executive impairment. As the claimant in the legal action he was contending that his cognitive impairment was due to the operation; whereas the hospital trust was proposing that he had a progressive dementia, i.e. Alzheimer's disease, which **14.23** was precipitated by the complications of the operation. The marked impairment on the ACE-R which remained the same over four years supported the patient's case.

14.24 In a testamentary capacity case, an 81-year old-woman was admitted to hospital with a cardiac illness. The AMTS was 10/10, i.e. completely normal. Over the next few weeks, following a minor stroke, she developed a depressive psychosis that was completely missed by the attending physicians. They appreciated that she was anxious, but failed to grasp why. After the minor stroke the physiotherapist administered the ACE-R, and she scored 73/100 and 25/30 on the MMSE. Six weeks later the physiotherapist again administered the ACE-R and the patient scored 25/67, meaning that she was so inaccessible that she could not complete all the questions. The MMSE was 15/27. The patient was written off as demented and eventually died without her treatable illness ever being diagnosed. The salutary lesson here is that a severe depressive illness can show up as a *pseudo-dementia* on cognitive testing.

Clock-Drawing Tests and the GPCog Test

14.25 In essence, all that the patient is asked to do is to draw a clock and set the hands at a specified time: usually after the hour mark so that one of the hands has to be slightly off a number. A clock-drawing test is part of the MoCA, but there is a variety of different codified versions of the test.[11] This is not the place to argue the relative merits

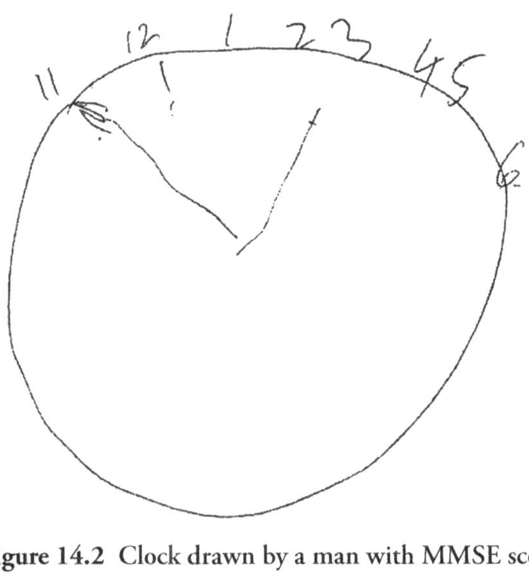

Figure 14.2 Clock drawn by a man with MMSE score of 18/30.

[11] See for example <http://aging.ufl.edu/files/2012/05/clockanalysis.pdf>.

of the various methods, but simply to emphasize that this very simple test can give a good indication of executive and visuo-spatial function in dementia.

Figure 14.2 shows a clock-drawing test done by a highly intelligent, self-made **14.26**
wealthy testator, who on the same day scored 18/30 on the MMSE, i.e. in the purportedly mild to moderate range of severity, and is an example of how potentially misleading the MMSE can be.

Clock drawing can also be used to assess the progress of dementia. Figure 14.3a **14.27**
shows an essentially normal clock drawn by a senior university academic with early Alzheimer's dementia who had some definite cognitive impairment but scored 28/30 on the MMSE, a clear example of the ceiling effect. The patient was asked to set the hands at 1.45. Although the end result was correct, the patient had great difficulty in setting the hands correctly and took a long time to do it.

Figure 14.3b shows an attempt by the same patient exactly four years later. He **14.28**
was asked to draw a clock, and he drew a circle and left it at that. He was then asked to put the numbers in, and he put marks at the quarter points. As he could not put in the numbers, he was asked where the 12 goes, and he wrote 12 at the half-hour mark. Finally, he was asked to set the hands at 1.45, and he wrote 45 at the 15-minute mark. At this stage his MMSE was below 10.

The GPCog test[12] was developed as a simple screening test for general practitioners. **14.29**
Anyone can try it at the URL given in reference 12. The test has the advantage of

Figure 14.3a Normal clock drawn with difficulty.

[12] <http://www.gpcog.com.au/>.

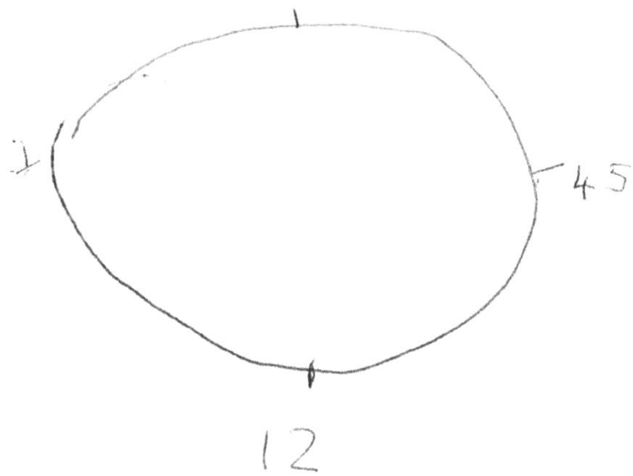

Figure 14.3b Clock by the same patient exactly four years later.

extreme simplicity and includes a clock-drawing test. In our opinion, for that reason, it is better than the AMTS in the GP setting. If informants are available, there is also a part of the test designed for them and similar to the IQCODE described in the next section.

The Informant Questionnaire on Cognitive Decline in the Elderly (IQCODE)

14.30 In medicine the patient's history is of paramount importance. It is a sad fact of high-tech modern Western medicine, with such diagnostic aids as MRI and CT scanners, that this principle has been weakened, and is not practised with the rigour it once was. Today's graduating doctors would find it difficult to practise in a country where no high-tech assistance is available. In dementia the history is every bit as important, and usually more important, than cognitive tests. The IQCODE was developed by Professor Anthony Jorm in Australia.[13] As with the Mental Test Score the original was a long questionnaire, but its authors abbreviated it and have shown that the shorter version has robust validity. Someone who is close to the patient, preferably a spouse or other person who knows him well is asked 'Now we want you to remember what your friend or relative was like ten years ago and to compare it with what he/she is like now. Ten years ago was 20—.' There follow sixteen questions which are shown in Table 14.3.

[13] A. F. Jorm (2004) *International Psychogeriatrics* 16:3, 1–19.

Table 14.3 Questions of the short IQCODE.

		1	2	3	4	5
1	Remembering things about family and friends, e.g. occupations, birthdays, addresses	Much improved	A bit improved	Not much change	A bit worse	Much worse
2	Remembering things that have happened recently	Much improved	A bit improved	Not much change	A bit worse	Much worse
3	Recalling conversations a few days later	Much improved	A bit improved	Not much change	A bit worse	Much worse
4	Remembering his/her address and telephone number	Much improved	A bit improved	Not much change	A bit worse	Much worse
5	Remembering what day and month it is	Much improved	A bit improved	Not much change	A bit worse	Much worse
6	Remembering where things are usually kept	Much improved	A bit improved	Not much change	A bit worse	Much worse
7	Remembering where to find things that have been put in a different place from usual	Much improved	A bit improved	Not much change	A bit worse	Much worse
8	Knowing how to work familiar machines around the house	Much improved	A bit improved	Not much change	A bit worse	Much worse
9	Learning how to use a new gadget or machine around the house	Much improved	A bit improved	Not much change	A bit worse	Much worse
10	Learning new things in general	Much improved	A bit improved	Not much change	A bit worse	Much worse
11	Following a story in a book or on TV	Much improved	A bit improved	Not much change	A bit worse	Much worse
12	Making decisions on everyday matters	Much improved	A bit improved	Not much change	A bit worse	Much worse
13	Handling money for shopping	Much improved	A bit improved	Not much change	A bit worse	Much worse
14	Handling financial matters, e.g. the pension, dealing with the bank	Much improved	A bit improved	Not much change	A bit worse	Much worse
15	Handling other everyday arithmetic problems, e.g. knowing how much food to buy, knowing how long between visits from family and friends	Much improved	A bit improved	Not much change	A bit worse	Much worse
16	Using his/her intelligence to understand what is going on and to reason things through	Much improved	A bit improved	Not much change	A bit worse	Much worse

14.32 The result is computed by adding up the individual scores and dividing the total by the number of questions asked. In a study comparing the IQCODE with the AMTS, and using a cut-off score of greater than 3.44 to indicate dementia, Harwood et al.[14] found that the IQCODE was superior to the AMTS in detecting cognitive impairment in a series of elderly medical inpatients. But both tests together were superior to one alone. The IQCODE clearly provides different information to that given by cognitive tests, but, as Jorm himself writes, in the paper quoted at footnote 13, 'because the IQCODE provides information complementary to brief cognitive tests, harnessing them together can improve screening accuracy.'

The Bristol Activities of Daily Living Scale (BADLS) and the Barthel Index

14.33 These two scales are measures of activities of daily living (ADL), such as washing, dressing, feeding, and mobility. The BADLS,[15] which is more comprehensive than the Barthel,[16] also contains questions on orientation in time and place. Both scales are essentially measures of physical capacity, but, together with specific cognitive tests, they may reflect cognitive function. For example, inability to dress or use the telephone could simply be due to physical impairment following a stroke; but in someone with Alzheimer's dementia and relatively little physical impairment, dyspraxia is the more likely cause. In summary, ADL scales may in some cases be indirect measures of cognitive failure.

[14] D. M. J. Harwood, T. Hope, and R. Jacoby (1997) 'Cognitive impairment in medical inpatients I: Screening for dementia—is history better than mental state?'. *Age and Ageing* 26 (1): 31–5.

[15] R. S. Bucks et al. (1996) 'Assessment of activities of daily living in dementia: development of the Bristol Activities of Daily Living scales'. *Age and Ageing* 25, 113–20.

Unlike all the other questionnaires and tests in this chapter, except the IQCODE, the BADLS scores 'the other way round', i.e. the higher the score. the greater the impairment.

[16] <http://www.dundee.ac.uk/medther/Stroke/Scales/barthel.htm>.

15

COMMUNICATING WITH CLIENTS

Indices of Suspicion

'He did not exhibit any signs of any mental condition.'

[A solicitor responding to a *Larke v Nugus* request.]

This and similar quotations, of which we have seen far too many, have coalesced into dark clouds of millions of pounds of costs for litigants, albeit with silver linings for lawyers and medical experts. So let us be clear here: **15.01**

Signs of mental illness are not always on show;
Solicitors are not trained to elicit signs of mental illness and are likely to detect it only when it is glaringly obvious;
There is evidence that solicitors are bad at detecting mental illness;
It can be difficult for psychiatrists to elicit evidence of mental illness, but they are at least trained to do so.

A seminal study by Robert Hunter, a senior solicitor, and Claire Royston, a senior consultant old age psychiatrist, has most unfortunately not been published in a peer-reviewed journal, but only indirectly on the Internet,[1] where a good description of it may be found. **15.02**

Part of the study is reproduced here. **15.03**

[1] <http://www.privateclientadviser.co.uk/news/legal-practice/solicitors-failing-judge-clients%E2%80%99-testamentary-capacity>.

In the study, 91 solicitors and 92 consultant psychiatrists were shown two short films portraying an elderly gentleman attending a solicitor to give instructions for his will. The films demonstrated two interview styles, essentially showing a good and a bad interview technique.

They were then asked to complete a short questionnaire with distracter questions and two key questions: did the client have a mental disorder? Did the client potentially lack the capacity to make a will?

The client, a late-middle-aged formerly successful businessman, was deliberately scripted and portrayed to have executive function deficits covered by a social veneer.

He discloses that he has had a stroke, but his social rapport and boardroom skills appear to have confused those watching the interviews. The extent of the client's impairments demonstrated in the film were such that there are sufficient 'clues' that he does have a mental disorder and that he would fail a test of his capacity to give instructions for a will.

When presented with the evidence from the good interview technique film, 60% of solicitors correctly recognized that the client had a mental disorder, compared to 84% of psychiatrists watching the same film.

The results from solicitors and psychiatrists watching the film where the bad interview techniques were employed were striking. Bad interviewing techniques resulted in only two per cent of solicitors recognizing that the client had a mental disorder, versus 73% of psychiatrists.

When asked about the client's testamentary capacity, 90% of solicitors came to the correct conclusion from the good film compared to 75% of psychiatrists. Again, the effect of the type of interviewing techniques was very evident; when solicitors watched the bad interview only 33% came to the correct conclusion—that the client potentially lacked testamentary capacity.

15.04 The Golden Rule advocates a medical opinion in all cases of elderly testators.[2] This is a simple solution, but it is not feasible in many, for a variety of reasons. Perhaps it is not always necessary to ask for a medical opinion when the solicitor has known his client for many years, detects no difference in him, and is asked to make a new and uncontroversial will. Nevertheless, it might also be wise for a will draftsman's default position at the start to be one of *suspicion*, and work to allay it, for, in the words of the Chinese writer Lu Xun (1881–1936), 'To be suspicious is not a fault. To be suspicious all the time without coming to a conclusion is the defect.'

15.05 There are a number of clues that should make one entertain the possibility of an underlying mental disorder. Here is a list that could not possibly be exhaustive:

- Testator's appearance unkempt, dirty, smelly;
- Testator unsure if he has made a previous will;
- Testator does not know where his previous will is kept;

[2] See Chapter 6.

- Testator cannot remember what the provisions of previous wills were;[3]
- Testator cannot recall names of parents, siblings, or descendants;
- Testator cannot recall or work out the ages of his children;[4]
- Testator is being looked after by a carer, be it a relative or a paid carer;
- Testator recently bereaved;
- Testator gives a *potentially paranoid*[5] reason for disinheriting a previous beneficiary;
- Testator tries to insist that the main beneficiary is present during instructions;
- Testator changes his mind frequently over the process of giving instructions and does not recall what previous instructions were;
- Someone other than the testator communicates with the solicitor, especially in writing;
- Previous beneficiaries are disinherited;
- Children are disinherited;
- Beneficiary is a new or relatively new acquaintance;
- Beneficiary is a much younger non-relative of the opposite sex;
- Beneficiary is a carer.

It can be seen that some of this list overlaps with the list of red flags for undue influence discussed in Chapter 13. But, as undue influence is difficult to plead, the alternatives pleas of lack of capacity and want of knowledge and approval may well emerge from some of the elements on this list. **15.06**

Difficulty may arise when a will draftsman tries to recommend a medical opinion. Some testators become affronted; others object to paying yet more money. Perhaps they will be persuaded by the argument that too much of their hard-earned wealth may go to lawyers and doctors if the will is challenged. A specialist will certainly charge for an opinion, but a GP may not always do so. However, as we have repeatedly stressed, it is not good enough simply to tell the testator to go and get an opinion from his GP. The will draftsman must himself properly instruct the GP as we have outlined below and elsewhere in this book.[6] **15.07**

Unlike Napoleonic law, English law upholds freedom of testation. However, if children are disinherited, the testator can leave a legacy of bitterness that plunges his family into irretrievable discord. Testators may not want to be told this, but if the will draftsman exercises his judgement with care, it can sometimes be wise to do so. If the testator will not veer from his path, he might, in the course of discussions with the **15.08**

[3] See 2.29.

[4] Many of us cannot say our children's ages straight out, but we can usually work them out with reference to the present year and events such as marriage. This question sometimes reveals that a testator does not know the present year.

[5] e.g. a son has allegedly tried to get some of the testator's money, or move him out of his house and put him in a home.

[6] See Chapter 6.

will draftsman, reveal evidence of paranoid thinking that warrants further investigation by a medical practitioner.

Instructing Experts

15.09 We have already discussed instructing medical practitioners on giving an opinion on testamentary capacity. But it is well to remind solicitors that only that small body of experienced medical experts in contentious probate are guaranteed to know the legal test. In publishing their article 'How to assess capacity to make a will' in the British Medical Journal,[7] Jacoby and Steer hoped that more GPs would become aware of the legal test for testamentary capacity and be willing to undertake assessments, but the hope has not been realized. It can, therefore, be safely said that advising a client to get their GP to witness their will may be ill advice for the following reasons. First, the GP is unlikely to be competent to assess capacity; second, the GP might unwittingly witness the will without making any attempt to assess capacity (we have seen this), and thus put himself in an awkward position if the will is challenged later; third, solicitors often fail to chase up the advice to see if it was carried out. We advise here that a GP is potentially able to assess testamentary capacity, but has to be properly instructed with the legal tests, and be given information on the client's assets and who the potential beneficiaries might be. The article by Jacoby and Steer is readily available to download (<http://www.ncbi.nlm.nih.gov/pmc/articles/PMC1925203/>), and could be included with instructions. If a specialist doctor is asked to make the assessment, e.g. a psychiatrist or geriatrician, they, too, may need to be instructed in exactly the same way. We give a specimen Golden Rule instruction letter in Appendix 3.

Talking to the Testator

Where?

15.10 Old age psychiatrists generally prefer to see patients in their own homes. We may reasonably substitute client for patient here. The client feels more relaxed and less intimidated in his own environment. The will draftsman is able to pick up all sorts of clues that would not be available in his office. For example, is there evidence of squalor? Does the client or the house smell unclean? Has the client remembered that the will draftsman is visiting? Are there empty bottles of alcohol around the place? Are neighbours needed to let the will draftsman in? Having listed some of the

[7] R. Jacoby and P. Steer [2007] *British Medical Journal* 335; 155–7.

benefits of taking instructions in the client's home, we accept, of course, that this is not necessary or desirable with everyone, and the office has to be an alternative.

We have already discussed deathbed wills in Chapter 7 at 7.15, mentioning that hospital staff are not permitted to witness wills. Unfortunately, in our experience, a few nurses and junior doctors unwittingly agree to act as witnesses, but they should not be asked to do so. This is because it is feared that they will be taken in some way to have attested the patient's capacity to execute the will. Nurses and resident doctors are not trained to assess testamentary capacity. In many hospitals, if there is no one else to witness the will, a member of the managerial staff, usually from the Patient Services Department, may agree to be a witness. **15.11**

How?

If the testator asks for a beneficiary to be present during instructions, we strongly advise that the request be declined. It may be necessary to explain to him that this is simply against solicitors' good practice, and might increase the chances of the will being challenged later. As mentioned in the list above, insistence on a beneficiary being present should turn on a red light of suspicion that capacity might be impaired. **15.12**

We have already emphasized the point that solicitors are neither equipped to, nor good at, detecting mental disorder. We therefore advise taking care not to be deceived by a good social façade. Many people with moderately severe dementia maintain very good social skills that mask underlying cognitive deficits. Solicitors can make the problem worse by asking closed-ended questions or questions expecting the answer yes or no. Open-ended questions are much more likely to reveal whether the testator understands what the issues are, and whether he has sufficient cognitive function to answer them. For example, the question 'do you own your own house?' may be less informative than 'what property do you own?'. If the will draftsman has given the client a series of written questions about his family and the extent of his property, it is wise to check who has answered them. It may be obvious that the responses are written in a different hand or typed on a computer. If it is the latter, the will draftsman might ask if the testator has a computer and filled in the questionnaire himself. If someone else has done it, a way of detecting possible memory impairment is to ask the testator to give the information verbally to the will draftsman, who now has the probably correct answers in front of him. **15.13**

It is worth adding that written questions do not always get the right answers unless the person answering understands the reason for them. Inability to understand them may, of course be due to dementia, but not necessarily so, as many, especially older, people without cognitive impairment have difficulty with questionnaires. **15.14**

Simple, jargon-free questions, whether written or verbal, are the best. If the client appears not to understand, the question should be rephrased rather than repeated. **15.15**

However, the will draftsman who has read this book will be aware that difficulty in understanding might be due to receptive dysphasia.

15.16 Another way in which solicitors might be deceived into thinking that there is no cognitive impairment is if the client can talk readily about the past, in order to avoid the present, because he has less difficulty in retrieving information from long-term store, than putting new information into memory. For example, a man was able to recount in detail about pre-flight procedures for aircrew whilst being unaware of the current time, day, week, or year. Yet another pitfall is the confabulating client (see Chapter 12). It might well be impossible for a will draftsman to detect confabulation, but if facts can be checked with an independent informant, so much the better.

15.17 Doctors testing episodic memory often ask patients to give some item from the recent news. The patient who replies 'I don't take any notice of that sort of thing' is usually trying to conceal memory impairment. Solicitors will probably not be asking clients that question in particular, but if they receive that response to a question which one would expect them to know, the same phenomenon of concealing memory impairment is probably at work. Another clinical question that illustrates a point will draftsmen could well note, is the one to which the questioner, himself, does not know the answer. An example is the inexperienced doctor who asks 'what did you have for breakfast this morning?'. Unless the doctor knows, which is unlikely, the question is worthless. For will draftsmen this situation may be more complex because it might be difficult to find out what the correct answer is. But the principle of not asking questions to which there is no way of knowing the answer is still valid.

15.18 In Chapter 2 we have already indicated that an elderly or frail testator's mental state may fluctuate, and he can have 'good days and bad days'. If this might be the case, it is a good idea to ask a relative or carer if they have noticed fluctuation and, if so, when might be the best time to take instructions. We have encountered the case of a woman who was due to be assessed by an old age psychiatrist early one afternoon. The doctor was held up by both emergency work and traffic, and did not arrive until the evening. She was curt, abrupt and hurried with the patient who had been anxious enough waiting for the doctor to arrive at her home, and she performed worse on cognitive testing than she did at other times. Of themselves, good days and bad days are not indicators of capacity or lack of it, which is of course a separate issue. In other words, a person showing good days and bad days may or may not have capacity. As Strauss J stated in *Simon v Byford*[8]

> In my view, the key to the dispute of fact is Professor Howard's evidence that once capacity is lost it is lost, but that the patient's mental state may be further adversely affected by other factors at some times. This explains the 'good days' and 'bad days'

[8] *Simon v Byford* [2013] EWHC 1490 (Ch).

> observed by Martin, both in Mrs Simon and in his mother-in-law. Therefore, it is not so surprising that Mrs Simon was at times unable to recollect that David was dead, perhaps because of distress or tiredness, and at other times, as some of the evidence shows, well able to recall it.

The moral of the tale is that the testator should, where possible, give instructions for and execute the will on a *good day*.

Bad Notes, Good Notes

The importance of keeping good notes cannot be overemphasized. *In Key v Key*[9] the solicitor who drew up the disputed will was heavily criticized by the judge for his notes which were extraordinarily sketchy and written on the back of an envelope. This plea to keep good notes applies just as much to doctors as it does to solicitors. Stories can often cement principles in the memory, which is our reason for telling the following one that occurred many years ago. A man sued a general practice for the loss of part of a finger. He had gone to one of the partners in the practice with an infection under a fingernail. The GP prescribed an antibiotic and advised the patient to call back after three days if it was not better. The patient re-attended three days later and saw another partner in the practice who agreed that the finger was not better, and prescribed another antibiotic, advising the patient to return in three days if the finger was still no better. Three days later the patient saw a third partner who realized that the finger was much worse, and sent the patient off to the local hospital where part of the finger had to be amputated. The doctors' defence insurance society sought the advice of medical experts who all agreed that the doctors had *not* been negligent, but a settlement had to be made because the doctors' notes were unsatisfactory to say the least. The first note read 'finger buggered'. The second note read 'finger still buggered'. And the third note read 'finger really buggered now. Off to hospital'. In our experience of contentious probate cases solicitors' and doctors' notes vary very widely in quality. It should be obvious to both professions that poor notes lay one open to serious peril under cross-examination and when the judge gives his decision. **15.19**

So, what are good notes? If they are handwritten and could one day be produced in evidence, they must above all be readable. Since many of us may have handwriting that is difficult to read, especially when having to take notes and communicate with a client at the same time, rough notes are acceptable provided a full typed attendance note is produced within 24 hours. **15.20**

The notes should begin with the date and time of attendance and who was present. What should be in the attendance note? Any observations about the testator's **15.21**

[9] *Key v Key* [2010] EWHC 408 (Ch).

appearance and behaviour could be useful if the will is challenged, but we urge will draftsmen not to make the mistake of writing something along the lines of the quotation at the head of this chapter. Remember that some Horace Rumpole is patiently waiting in his chambers for the day when he can ask 'do you have training and experience in assessing mental conditions?'. The following extract from one of our file notes is acceptable because no diagnostic opinion on mental disorder is being expressed:

> [S]he presented as a very cheerful and friendly lady. She welcomed me with coffee and was happy to talk with me. Her talk was normal and coherent. Her mood seemed normal. She was well orientated in time and place. She was able to give me an account of her past history which was consistent with the one her son gave me on the telephone. I did not detect any significant problem with her short-term memory in our conversation together. She was able to tell me all her activities over the next week.

Of course, if some abnormality of speech and behaviour is observed, it should be recorded, in a neutral way.

15.22 Once the potential testator has indicated what he wants to do with his estate, why not pose what could be termed *Banks v Goodfellow* questions? Lest the testator thinks he is being taken for a fool, it is wise to explain that one is required to ask these questions to minimize the risk of the will being challenged later. Doctors often have to explain to their patients that some of their questions may seem absurdly simple, to which the great majority do not object. When the few do object, it is almost invariably because they fear that their cognitive impairment is about to be exposed. If this happens in the solicitor–client situation it should switch on another red light of suspicion. Most clients, like most patients, will readily accept being asked 'Please explain to me what you understand by a will.' The answer should be recorded verbatim. Similarly, all answers to what might be termed *Banks v Goodfellow* questions should be recorded verbatim. Where questions asked and answers given are written down, the effect as evidence in court is very impressive and cogent, as exemplified in *d'Apice v Gutkovich*.[10]

15.23 Clearly, solicitors cannot be expected to decide either who has a moral claim on the estate, or whether a person is being included or excluded from a will because of *insane delusion*. But asking the testator to list the names of siblings, offspring, offspring-in-law, and grandchildren is a basis for arousing or allaying suspicion. If a testator cannot name his first-degree relatives, this is prima facie evidence of memory impairment, and ought to lead to a medical assessment.

15.24 Reasons for excluding previous beneficiaries need to be carefully explored. These might be perfectly innocent and reasonable, but if allegations are made about a

[10] *d'Apice v Gutkovich—Estate of Abraham* (No. 2) [2010] NSWSC 1333.

previous beneficiary, suspicions could be aroused. For example, we have seen several cases where an offspring or other close person has been excluded 'because they don't visit me anymore.' When the will is challenged, evidence emerges that the excluded beneficiary did indeed visit, and the allegations were made either because episodic memory was severely impaired, or the testator had been sequestered by the main beneficiary who was preventing visits.[11]

In summary, this chapter, first, urges will draftsmen always to be on their guard and **15.25**
not to draw conclusions about capacity just because the testator appears *normal*, whatever that word means. Second, good attendance notes are mandatory and save later embarrassment. Third, when a medical opinion is required, the doctor must be properly instructed and the report chased up. Fourth, bear in mind that what the testator says might not necessarily be the truth, not because he is mendacious, but because he has cognitive impairment.

[11] *Catling v Catling* [2014] EWHC 180 (Ch).

APPENDICES

APPENDIX 1

Will Draftsman's Observation Sheet on Testamentary Capacity

1. Meeting	
Venue	
Date/time	
Client	
Who requested the meeting?	
Anyone else present, with the client?	
Why were they present?	
Advice given about the presence of others?	
Relationship of others present with client or intended beneficiary?	
2. Recent events	
Are you aware of any matters that have given rise to doubts as to his/her capacity in the past?	
Are you aware of any medical or legal opinions in the past as to his/her capacity?	
Are you aware of any medications, such as painkillers, which may act to deprive him/her of capacity?	
Has his/her medical history been disclosed to you?	
Has his/her doctor disclosed information to you regarding capacity?	
If necessary, would he/she accept the need for and submit to a medical examination specifically for testamentary capacity?	

3. **How did the client present himself/herself?**	
Was his/her manner consistent with any previous contact?	
Dress normal or unusual?	
Sober?	
Voice slurred?	
Attention span?	
Speech coherent and rational?	
Was his/her manner unusual (agitated/distracted)?	
If there has been previous contact, was he/she aware of it or did he recognize who you were?	
Was he/she aware of why you were there?	
Was he/she aware of how your meeting was arranged?	

4. **Communication**	
Was communication easy?	
Did he/she readily understand what was said and reply coherently?	
Did he/she refer to notes made before the meeting?	
If so, were those his/her own notes or had they been written or dictated by someone else?	

5. ***Banks v Goodfellow***	
The client needs to understand that he is making a will, and that it will have the effect of carrying out his wishes on his death.	
Does he/she understand that the will will take effect on death and not before?	
Has he/she understanding of the normal foreseeable consequences and implications (in layman's terms) of not making a will?	

Does he/she understand the nature of a will is such that the dispositions can be altered at any time before his/her death?	
Does he/she understand that if there is already a will then it will be replaced by the proposed new will?	
If he/she is replacing a previous will, does he/she understand why it is being changed and what the changes will be?	
Is he/she aware of the need for an executor and able to select one (or more if appropriate)?	
Is his/her choice of executor rational and practical?	
Can he/she identify who will inherit under the will?	
Does he/she know the property and interest in it that the beneficiaries should receive?	
Does he/she understand the meaning and purpose of any conditions he/she attaches to the gift?	
Does he/she understand that if he/she disposes of any parts of the estate during his/her lifetime this will affect the gifts in the will?	
Does he/she understand that any beneficiary might die before him/her?	
He/she must know the extent of his property and what it consists of	
Does he/she have an understanding in broad terms of the extent and value of his/her estate?	
Does he/she understand the extent of his/her liabilities and the liability of the estate to settle them?	

<table>
<tr><td>Does he/she have an understanding of the devolution of any jointly owned property?
(In practice this is usually an understanding reached after the appropriate advice from the draftsman.)</td><td></td></tr>
<tr><td>Does he/she have an understanding of the devolution of assets that pass on death, but not as part of the free estate?
(In practice this is usually an understanding reached after the appropriate advice from the draftsman.)</td><td></td></tr>
<tr><td colspan="2">He/she must be able to recall those who have claims on him/her and understand the nature of those claims, so that he/she can both include and exclude beneficiaries from the will.</td></tr>
<tr><td>Does he/she exhibit the normal understanding and perceptions of those close to him/her (whether relations or not) and the usual gifts that a testator would make to such persons?</td><td></td></tr>
<tr><td>Is the benefit proposed for any of the persons disproportionate (big or small) and if it is can he/she give a rational explanation for it?</td><td></td></tr>
<tr><td>If he/she is ignoring any of this category of person, does he/she understand why this is being done, and can he/she give a reasoned decision?</td><td></td></tr>
<tr><td>Can he/she understand the relative merits of those for whom he/she would normally be expected to make provision and be able to take into account need, disability, age, etc?</td><td></td></tr>
<tr><td>Is he/she aware of the relative extent to which he/she may already have made provision for any of those who could be considered to have claims on him/her?</td><td></td></tr>
</table>

Does he/she exhibit any disorder or delusion that influences or prevents the exercise of his/her natural faculties?	
Have any of the questions above in section [5] revealed any information as to delusions?	
6. Tests of capacity	
Did you administer any formal test of capacity?	
If so, what was it and what were the results?	
Did you use check questions during the meeting? And what were the results?	
7. Undue influence	
Would you consider the client to be vulnerable to undue influence?	
Does anything in the discussion raise suspicions of undue influence in your mind?	
Is there anything in the proposed gifts in the will (or disclosed lifetime gifts) that gives rise to concern about undue influence?	
8. Further observations	
Did the client exhibit any problems with memory, particularly short-term? (Record examples.)	
Was the client able to remember information discussed during the meeting, at the end?	
Did the client take notes during the meeting and, as far as you could see, were they rational?	
Was the client distracted by trivialities at the expense of understanding important issues?	
Was the client drowsy during the meeting?	

Did the client have reasonable awareness of current events and show capacity for rational conversation?	
Did the client understand the relationships between different members of his/her family?	
Did the client exhibit any delusional or obsessive behaviour or opinions during the meeting?	

APPENDIX 2

Annotated Specimen File Note

First Note: 1 March 2014, 12.30pm

> There is often no evidence of consideration of capacity in a file note. There is no right or wrong length for a file note to be—it needs to be sufficiently long to address the relevant capacity issue and show the manner in which the issue was approached. In the case of *Wharton v Bancroft* [2012] EWHC 91 (Ch), where the will preparer correctly anticipated a dispute, his file note was 5 ½ pages long.

Attending: Mrs Agnes Smith (accompanied by her daughter, Sally)—50 minutes in my office.

> There is no 'correct' time to spend with a client to be able to reach a conclusion about capacity. Obviously if the time is short then the will preparer will be open to an allegation that insufficient time was taken. In this example the will preparer has not met the testatrix before and so needs to be satisfied about instructions and satisfied about capacity. In the case of *Re Stolkin deceased* [2013] EWHC 1140 (Ch), a will preparer took instructions and arranged for a will to be executed all within 20 minutes—the will was found to be valid but this period of time would be regarded as dangerously short.

1. Sally Jones, *nee* Smith is a longstanding client of this firm—one of my colleagues dealt with her divorce. Last week she came to meet me. She said that her mother (Agnes) lives with her. Agnes is 82. She has asked me to prepare a will for Agnes. She brought in an undated typed note setting out her mother's wishes. The document was typed by Sally but signed by Agnes.

> This is not an uncommon situation. There may be good reasons why a helpful relative would want to type out instructions to help an elderly testatrix—this is precisely what happened in *Feltham v Freer Bouskell* [2013] EWHC 1952 (Ch). There the trial judge found that there was nothing inappropriate—but the will preparer will want to be alert to ensure that there is no undue influence and that instructions are freely given.

2. The note showed that Agnes wanted to leave two-thirds of her estate to Sally and one-third to her other daughter, Emma. Last week Sally told me that Agnes has three children, namely herself, Emma, and John. John lives in Scotland and he rarely has any contact with Agnes. Emma lives about ten miles away and often comes to visit Agnes at home and takes her out from time to time. Emma is married and works full time. Sally told me that she is divorced. Agnes was married but her husband died six years ago.

> Sometimes a testator may be brought to the office soon after the death of a partner. The practitioner will be alert to look for signs of depression or affective disorder which may affect the judgement of the testatrix—see *Key v Key* [2010] EWHC 407 (Ch) where a will was made eight days after the death of the testator's wife of 65 years.

3. Agnes has found it difficult to live on her own and sold her home to then live with Sally. Agnes now has approximately £550,000 saved in various investments. Sally told me that her mother is becoming more forgetful.

> Will preparers will give credit to Sally for mentioning the fact that her mother is becoming more forgetful and alerting the will preparer to the issue of capacity. Some beneficiaries will choose to keep issues of forgetfulness from the will preparer.

4. I am aware of the test of capacity in *Banks v Goodfellow*. I am aware of the test of capacity set out in the Mental Capacity Act 2005. I am aware of the assumption of capacity contained within Section 1 of the Act but I approach this matter with an open mind. I will need to be satisfied that Agnes has capacity to make her will.

> Of course there is no reason to state in a file note that the will preparer is aware of the test of capacity in *Banks v Goodfellow* and the test of capacity set out in the Mental Capacity Act. This is a clear message to those who may wish to challenge a will. This file note would be disclosed pursuant to *Larke v Nugus* and it tells the reader straight away that there has been a robust assessment from someone who knows what they are doing, making the will much more difficult to challenge; *Hawes v Burgess* [2013] EWCA Civ 74.

5. Sally accompanied her mother into my office.

> There is nothing untoward about Sally bringing her mother into the office—a testator will often want help and advice from a close member of the family.
>
> It is important to ensure that Agnes is relaxed and in a comfortable environment, particularly when meeting a will preparer for the first time.
>
> What is essential is that the will preparer does not seek to carry out a capacity assessment or investigate possible undue influence with Sally present.
>
> The file note must record the point at which Sally left the room and any contribution she makes while in the room.

She introduced Agnes to me and repeated that she believes that her mother wants to make a will. Agnes was smartly dressed in a tweed suit with pearls. I complimented her on her appearance and she said she chose it especially as it was not every day that she sees a solicitor to make a will.

> This statement is beyond mere social rapport. It demonstrates a planning capability on the part of Agnes—an indicator of capacity—and starts to demonstrate an indication of the first part of the *Banks v Goodfellow* test, i.e. what it means to make a will.

She presented as a frail lady and walked with the aid of a stick. She made appropriate eye contact with me and greeted me with a smile and a 'hello'. Having given her my name at the start of the meeting she used it correctly throughout.

> The will preparer will not presume a lack of capacity simply by the way Agnes presents. On the other hand inappropriate dressing, dirty clothes, an inability to dress, a lack of eye contact, and a low mood may be evidence of mental disorder. Reflecting the presentation of the individual in a file note is important.

We had a general chat, during which she told me that this was the first time she had been out for over a week because of the dreadful weather recently.

General casual chat can be used to put Agnes at ease and this is important. The will preparer will however be asking subtle questions to make a preliminary informal assessment as to capacity.

The observation on the weather, if correct, helps establish memory.

I asked how she travelled here today, she replied that Sally had brought her in her car and parked in the car park round the corner.

Being unaware or vague about how she had got to the office would have raised concerns about short-term memory.

6. I asked her if I could see her without Sally being present so that I know that her instructions are freely given. Agnes told me that she would rather Sally stayed since 'she knows all my business'. I told her that unfortunately I have to see her without a beneficiary being present—otherwise it would be much more difficult to establish that the will was valid. Agnes agreed and Sally left the room.

It is common for an elderly testator to want a relative to stay with them whilst instructions are given. Whilst ultimately the decision is for the client, the will preparer needs to be strong here. The weight given to an assessment of capacity with a beneficiary present in the room will be greatly reduced—hence the explanation to be given. Recording this exchange with the client is important.

7. I tried to put Agnes at ease. I asked her what her occupation used to be. She told me she was a school cook. I asked her when she retired but she was not sure. I asked her if she was married. She said that she was happily married to John but he died a while back. She could not tell me exactly the date of his death.

Again the will preparer is looking for evidence of capacity in an informal way. The vagueness as to when she retired and when her husband died may well be explicable but it is important to note it. Not being able say when he died could be tackled by asking her when she was married and for how long. An inability to recall this would give rise to concern.

8. I asked her why she wants to make a will and she said that she wants to make sure things will be 'done right' when she has gone.

The will preparer is here going to address the three primary tests of the *Banks v Goodfellow*—knowledge about what a will means, value of the estate, and consideration of moral claims. The will preparer will look to ask an open question 'why she wants to make a will' and will want to record the words used by Agnes. In the interests of brevity this part of the file note is curtailed. In reality more enquiry and explanation would be made and recorded here.

9. I then turned to her assets. She told me that Sally looks after everything and that Sally knows what the assets are—Sally will 'sort everything out'. I pressed her further. She said that most of her money is in the building society. She cannot remember the name of the building society but knows that it is the one 'just around the corner'. The staff are always so nice to her there.

It is not uncommon that a person might not remember such a name (given name changes in recent years). The fact that it is round the corner and the staff know her shows, if true, that she has recall of where the account is.

She did not really know how much money she has so I tried a different approach. I ask her how she came to have money in a building society account. She explained that she found life a bit of a struggle after her husband died and she sold their home three years ago to go and live with Sally. She recalled that her house sold for about £600,000, so she thinks that that is how much she must have. She does not spend much nowadays. She no longer drives.

> It is common for an elderly testator not to know how much money they have—but these questions need to be answered. The answers could be evidence of lack of capacity so this issue needs to be explored. The discrepancy between her figure and Sally's needs to be considered.

I asked about her income. She identified that she had a state pension and that it was paid monthly into her building society account together with a widow's pension from her husband's work for the local council. She paid the widow's pension to Sally to help with the household bills and used the council pension for her spending money.

> This is helpful as there is an awareness of what income she has to support herself, where it is from, and how it is used.

I asked if she paid any other money to Sally and she said she thought that she had paid some to Sally to clear the mortgage when she moved in so that Sally wouldn't have to worry about the mortgage, but she couldn't remember how much.

> This could be a concern. Her vagueness might be reasonable by the passage of time. Could there be issues of undue influence? On the other hand it could be reasonable. This issue must be discussed further.

I asked Agnes if she had made a will before. She said that she cannot remember but that she 'might have done'. She cannot remember what was in any previous will she made or where it is.

> The will preparer needs to be careful about the answer to the question about previous wills. If Agnes says that she had not made an earlier will and it is proved after her death that she had, this will be seized upon by a claimant as evidence of forgetfulness which tends to prove a lack of capacity. If a testatrix says that she has not made a will before, the will preparer might want to question this with Sally. By saying that she does not know, it is at least an honest answer and again alerts the will preparer to capacity issues. Although *Simon v Byford* [2013] EWHC 1490 (Ch) found that the capacity test in *Banks v Goodfellow* did not require a testatrix to know about the terms of a previous will when making a subsequent will, establishing what her understanding is helps both the will preparer and exhibits the amount of knowledge that she has.

10. I asked her what she wants to happen to her money after she has died. She says that Sally has been very good to her but struggles with money. Sally is not well off and has to be careful with money; she has a part-time job. Emma has 'married well' and is doing very well. She says that John lives 'somewhere up North' and that she has not seen him for some time.

> Answers given by any testator need to be treated with caution when they apparently do not know this information about a child. Agnes could have seen or even stayed with John recently and simply saying that he lives 'somewhere up North' or that she has not seen him for some time may again be evidence of serious memory impairment. This is an area that the will preparer could look to cross check when Sally returns to the room, without initially revealing what he has been told.

He had a good job anyway and he is wealthy in his own right. She does not want to leave him anything.

> The will preparer has here looked to satisfy the third limb of the *Banks v Goodfellow* test. Agnes has given an apparently rational explanation, but it is one that needs to be treated with care. How does he know he has a good job and is wealthy?
>
> Dementia can take different forms with different causes. Frontal lobe damage can arise through physical injury or mental decline. It can be difficult to detect. Frontal lobe damage often affects judgement or the quality of understanding to make decisions. Sufferers can appear to score highly on MMSE tests and respond well to questions. Doing *The Times* crossword every day would not be an indicator of capacity to make a will. Practitioners will need to be alert to this possibility and this is another reason why specialist medical evidence may be needed. A decision that may appear to be rational may in fact not be rational or may be based on delusions (see Chapter 14).

She told me that she wants to leave Sally two-thirds of her estate and one-third to Emma—with nothing for John. The questions of funeral instructions and gifts of jewellery or other personal items were discussed, but nothing was required in the will as she said that 'the girls know what she wants'. I asked her who she wants to deal with her financial affairs after she passes away and she tells me that as Sally knows most about her money she should do this.

11. I showed her the note that was typed earlier by Sally. She tells me that she does not remember signing a note but agrees that this is her signature.

I ask her if she takes any prescription medicines—she says she does but cannot remember what tablets she takes. I tell her about the 'Golden Rule' and what this means to her if her will was challenged, but she says she does not want to see any doctor before making her will.

> The will preparer would really want to make further enquiries here—perhaps with consent from Agnes—with Sally. Remember the will preparer will only see a partial picture. Agnes may have been referred by her GP to a psychiatrist precisely because of memory problems. There may already have been assessments of capacity carried out by medical practitioners which lie buried in her GP records, waiting to be disclosed when a probate dispute arises.
>
> Care should be taken with someone who simply cannot pronounce the name of her medicines—description of what she takes might be given instead.

There are various features that put me on alert as to whether or not Agnes has capacity to make a will. Amongst other things, as can be seen, she has forgotten her husband's date of death, she has forgotten the name of her building society, she was not able to volunteer immediately the value of her estate, and she does not know if she has made a will before.

> Here it can be useful to summarize the points for and against capacity in order to support the conclusion that she had sufficient capacity and why a will could be prepared.

12. Sally returned to the room (at my request) and she asked Agnes if things had gone OK. Agnes said yes and told her of the terms of the will, including that Sally was to be the executor.

> There is no harm in a mother telling a child this but is worth recording as it does show that Agnes's short-term memory functioned sufficiently.

During the conversation I asked Sally whether she had seen her brother recently. She said no and that his apparent indifference to the family had upset all three of them. Once he had qualified as a solicitor he became 'too grand' for them and seemed rather embarrassed about his origins.

> This is all useful, but the amount of contact needs to be explored—telephone calls, letters, birthday/Christmas cards and presents, etc. The omission of a child is not merely an issue for capacity. This interviewer should be considering the extent to which it is reasonable to raise the issue of the I(PFD)A 1975.

13. I am satisfied that Agnes has capacity to make a will. She has correctly satisfied me according to the terms of the *Banks v Goodfellow* test. In making this judgement I note that both the terms of the will and the assets in the estate are quite simple.

> The last sentence is added to show that the interviewer is aware that the simplicity of will assets and family circumstances had required a slightly lower level of capacity than would otherwise be the case.

Second Note: 8 March 2014

1. I have prepared the will in line with the note given by Sally and arranged with Agnes that she would come to the office today to sign it. As before, she was accompanied by Sally who volunteered to wait in our reception area until matters were dealt with.

> That Sally volunteered to stay outside is worth recording. If Sally had only reluctantly agreed to stay outside that also would have been worth recording. Doing this voluntarily helps indicate a lack of pressure on her mother.

2. Agnes clearly remembered our meeting last week and addressed me by name. I read through the relatively short will one clause at a time. When doing so, I explained the main features.
   - By making the will she revokes (or cancels) any earlier wills.
   - After she has died, Sally will deal with the administration of her estate; collecting in her money, paying her debts, and sharing out what is left with Emma.
   - Two-thirds of what is left after the payment of her debts and costs is to go to Sally, and one-third to Emma, and nothing will go to John.

I asked Agnes if this is what she wanted—and she confirmed that it was. Miss Anne Smith (receptionist) then came into the room. Agnes signed the will and I signed as the first witness and Anne as the second witness.

APPENDIX 3

Specimen 'Golden Rule' Letter to a Medical Practitioner Requesting an Opinion on Testamentary Capacity *Prior to Execution of a Will*

Dear Dr [___]

Re My client/Your patient Mr Albert Smith of [address & DOB].

I represent your patient Mr Smith. I am currently advising him on the preparation of a new will. I would be grateful if you would let me know if you would be willing and able to provide me with a report as to whether or not you believe your patient has the mental capacity to make a will. I confirm that I shall, of course, pay your reasonable fee for attending Mr Smith and for the preparation of your report. I should be grateful if you would please let me have an estimate of your costs. Given the urgency that the law attaches to a will for an ill or elderly client I should be grateful if you would also telephone me with your answer. I am sorry to burden you with the length of this letter but it is essential that I set out the relevant legal issues.

Time is of the Essence

The making of a will is an important issue for Mr Smith and, because of his age, the law obliges me to deal with his will more quickly than might otherwise be the case for a younger person.[1] The financial implications of failing to produce a will quickly, if Mr Smith had capacity, can be substantial.

To meet this obligation, I would expect you to be able to see Mr Smith and provide me with a report within the next two weeks. If you are not likely to be able to meet this time limit then please telephone me straightaway.

The Legal Tests

The test for testamentary capacity is commonly broken down into four elements—this is called the '*Banks v Goodfellow* test'. It is essential that Mr Smith must:

1. be capable of understanding the nature of his act and its effect i.e. that by making this will he is giving away his property upon his death to persons of his choice; and
2. be capable of understanding the nature and extent of the property of which he is disposing. This does not require an exact understanding but a broad appreciation of his assets and a reasonable estimate of their value. To assist you I attach details of his assets; and
3. appreciate the claims to which he ought to give effect. This is to say be able to recognize those who through natural ties of love and affection he would normally make provision for. To assist you I send you a family tree; and

[1] There is no doubt that time is of the essence in connection with the preparation of a will—time becomes even more important the older a testator becomes—in the case of *Feltham v Freer Bouskell* [2013] EWCH 1952 it was found that a delay of five weeks was too long. To save time it is recommended that the will draftsman should contact the GP practice by telephone to indicate if they would be willing to provide a report within the relevant time limit in the first instance—some GPs are reluctant to provide this type of report.

4. have no disorder of his mind that shall poison his affections nor have delusions that affect the terms of his will.

The relevant sections of the Mental Capacity Act 2005 might usefully be considered (there is considerable overlap with the components above). The main points to note are as follows.

1. A person must be assumed to have capacity unless it can be established that he lacks capacity.
2. A person lacks capacity if at the material time he is unable to make a decision for himself in relation to the matter because of an impairment of, or disturbance in the functioning of, the mind or brain.
3. A person is unable to make a decision for himself if he is unable to:
    a. understand the information relevant to the decision;
    b. retain that information;
    c. use or weigh that information as part of the process of making the decision; or
    d. communicate his decision (whether by talking, using sign language, or any other means).

The law upholds the right of elderly people to leave their property as they choose—even if their mental faculties have declined considerably—provided that decline does not fall below the threshold set out above.[2]

Other Matters

An individual suffering from mild to moderate cognitive impairment may still have capacity to make a will, even if testamentary capacity is open to some doubt. You will appreciate that you are being instructed to advise as it is my view that there may be some doubt about Mr Smith's capacity to make a will. [*Here the writer may give a short summary of his concerns about the testator.*]

The test of capacity to make a will is assessed in an individual in the light of his particular circumstances. Thus, a testator with a high-value, complex estate and a complex will would be likely to require a higher capacity to execute the will than an individual with a modest-value estate and a simple will.

Balance of Probabilities

You must form your view as to capacity on the balance of probabilities. You need not be satisfied beyond reasonable doubt.[3]

The Assets of Mr Smith

[*Here list the assets of Mr Smith and indicate whether his estate is straightforward or complex—and given a general indication as the likely realisable value.*][4]

Expected Beneficiaries

[*Here identify those persons who may regard themselves as potentially entitled to benefit from the estate of Mr Smith.*[5] *Indicate which of those individuals are to be included and which are to be excluded—together with reasons given to the will draftsman. It would be helpful to include a family tree.*]

---

[2] This is a quotation from the first instance case of *Simon v Byford* [2013] EWCH 1490 and it is an important point to make to avoid misunderstanding.

[3] See *Perrins v Holland* [2009] EWCH 1945.

[4] It is only a general indication as to the assets of Mr Smith that needs to be provided—a precise valuation of shares or building society accounts, etc. need not be provided.

[5] A family tree is helpful to help the medical practitioner to understand the nature of the family relationships. If the will draftsman is aware of a reason why a particular family member is to have a

Previous Wills

Despite enquiries, I am informed that there are no previous wills.

[*Alternatively*] I have discovered that a previous will was made some years ago. A copy of the previous will is enclosed. Mr Smith may demonstrate to you a reason for the changes made between the last will and the proposed will.

The Proposed Will

The proposed will is enclosed. I have taken instructions from Mr Smith with regard to this will and this reflects his instructions to me. [*Insert summary, e.g.:*] You will see that it is a relatively straightforward document and makes provision for three children, A, B, and C, but excludes child D, on the grounds that Mr Smith tells me he rarely sees D and their personal relationship is said to have broken down.

It would help me considerably if you would agree to act as one of the witnesses to the will in the event that Mr Smith does have the requisite capacity to sign it.[6] The legal guidance to will draftsmen is, for wills for elderly clients, that a medical practitioner should be present to witness the execution of the will if this is practicable without giving rise to undue delay [*We recommend that this paragraph is optional, in case the GP might be put off by the prospect of too much work.*]

I should be grateful if you would be so kind as to acknowledge receipt of this letter and let me know if you would be willing to prepare a report and act as a witness to the will—if so, presuming that Mr Smith does have capacity, please return the executed will together with your fee note and a brief report as to capacity—this report will be retained with my will file and will be relied upon as evidence as to capacity in the event that the will of Mr Smith is challenged after his death.

Your Report

Please let me have a brief report dealing with your findings and conclusions as to capacity to make this will. Please address the following when writing the report.

- It should contain details of your professional qualifications and your experience of dealing with assessments of capacity;
- It should state the length of time that Mr Smith has been your patient;
- If you carry out any commonly administered tests of cognitive function please include the score and a copy of the test score sheet.
- Please add any other comments which tend to indicate either capacity or lack of capacity, together with your own reasons for forming a view as to why Mr Smith does, or does not, have capacity to make this will.
- Wherever possible please refer to actual words used by, or explanations given by, Mr Smith.

If you require any further information, assistance, or guidance please do not hesitate to contact me.

I look forward to hearing from you.

Yours sincerely,

---

share enhanced or reduced it would be helpful to explain this in the letter of instruction. Likewise if there are family friends or partners who may have had an expectation to be included as a beneficiary then an explanation about their position should be tendered.

[6] The Golden Rule anticipates that a will should be witnessed by a medical practitioner—this could be particularly important in a case of fluctuating capacity.

APPENDIX 4

The Letter of Instruction

Specimen Letter of Instruction to Psychiatrist

Dear Dr [___]
Re Medico-Legal Report Albert Smith
Formerly of:
Date of birth:
Date of death:

I represent Emma Smith—one of the daughters of Albert Smith who died on the 10 August 2014. Albert Smith made a will on 3 February 2012 ('the 2012 will'). There is now a dispute as to the validity of that will. The 2012 will is challenged by Michael Smith who claims that a will made on 1 July 2010 (the 2010 will) is valid. Michael Smith is excluded under the 2012 will but is included in the 2010 will. I need your assistance to help the court to determine which will is valid—in particular Michael Smith asserts that Albert did not have capacity to make a will either at the time he gave instructions for, or when he executed the 2012 will. Legal proceedings have not yet been started but a formal letter of claim has been received and a formal response has been sent.

Background to the Case

[*A general short introduction to the issues in the case may help set the scene for the medical expert—perhaps briefly describe the background of the case and the particular issues involved.*]

The Legal Tests

The test for testamentary capacity is commonly broken down into four elements—this is called the '*Banks v Goodfellow* test'. It is essential that Mr Smith must:

1. be capable of understanding the nature of his act and its effect, i.e. that by making this will he is giving away his property to persons of his choice upon his death; and
2. be capable of understanding the nature and extent of the property of which he is disposing. This does not require an exact understanding but a broad appreciation of his assets and a reasonable estimate of their value. To assist you I attach details of his assets; and
3. appreciate the claims to which he ought to give effect. This is to say be able to recognize those who through natural ties of love and affection he would normally make provision for. To assist you I send you a family tree; and
4. not suffer from disorder of his mind sufficient to poison his affections.

The relevant sections of the Mental Capacity Act 2005 are also to be taken into consideration; however there is considerable overlap with the components above. The main points to note are as follows.

1. A person must be assumed to have capacity unless it can be established that he lacks capacity.
2. A person lacks capacity if at the material time he is unable to make a decision for himself in relation to the matter because of an impairment of, or disturbance in the functioning of, the mind or brain.

3. A person is unable to make a decision for himself if he is unable to:
   a. understand the information relevant to the decision;
   b. retain that information;
   c. to use or weigh that information as part of the process of making the decision; or
   d. to communicate his decision (whether by talking, using sign language, or any other means).

The test of capacity to make a will is not monolithic—i.e. it is tailored to the task in hand. A testator with a high-value, complex estate and a complex will would be likely to require a higher capacity to execute the will than an individual with a modest-value estate and a simple will.

Balance of Probabilities

You must form your view as to capacity on the balance of probabilities. You need not be satisfied beyond reasonable doubt.[1]

The assets of Mr Smith at the time he gave instructions for the Will

[*Here give a general indication as to the assets of Mr Smith to give the expert an indication whether the estate is straightforward or complex and give a general indication as to the likely realisable value. It may be worth simply noting whether the value of the assets have changed between date of instruction and date of death so that the expert can appreciate the degree of responsibility which is attached to this case.*][2]

Expected Beneficiaries

[*Here identify those persons who may regard themselves as potentially entitled to benefit from the estate of Mr Smith. Indicate which of those individuals are to be included and which are to be excluded—together with reasons given to the will draftsman. It would be helpful to include a family tree.*][3]

The 2012 Will

You will see from the copy of the 2012 Will enclosed that it is a relatively short and straightforward document. Emma Smith is appointed executrix and sole beneficiary of the estate. [*Alternatively if the estate assets are substantial and the Will is complex then a comment should be made here.*]

Your Role

I am sure that you will be familiar with Part 35 of the Civil Procedure Rules together with the supporting Practice Direction. It is essential to me that your report complies with the requirements of Part 35. If you require any guidance or assistance from me with regard to the preparation of your report then please do not hesitate to contact me. I am sure that you will appreciate that it is your duty to help the Court on matters within your expertise and that this duty overrides any obligation to me or my client (CPR 35.3).

---

[1] See *Re Perrins deceased, Perrins v Holland* [2009] EWCH 1945; [2009] WTLR 1387 Ch D.

[2] It is only a general indication as to the assets of Mr Smith that needs to be provided—a precise valuation of shares or building society accounts etc need not be provided.

[3] A family tree is helpful to help the medical practitioner to understand the nature of the family relationships. If the will draftsman is aware of a reason why a particular family member is to have a share enhanced or reduced it would be helpful to explain this in the letter of instruction. Likewise if there are family friends or partners who may have had an expectation to be included as a beneficiary then an explanation about their position should be tendered.

The Relevant Issues

[*Here set out in brief the position of each party—why is it said that the deceased did not have capacity to make a will and what is the claimant's response? Draw the attention of the expert to the quality of the notes/assessment of capacity made by the will preparer at the time the will was prepared and to relevant medical records or lay evidence. It may be appropriate to ask the expert first to determine whether there is a 'real doubt' about capacity—establishing 'real doubt' may put the burden of proving the validity of the will on the propounder.*]

You will see that I have deliberately sent you witness statements. I believe that the witness statements are essential to help you to understand the facts and the background of the case. If you seek to rely on witness statements then I know that you will defer to the court on findings of fact. Simply because a statement is made in a witness statement it does not necessarily mean that it is true if disputed by the other side.

Enclosures

I take this opportunity to enclose:-

1. The 2012 will
2. The 2010 will
3. A *Larke v Nugus* letter
4. A *Larke v Nugus* response
5. The will preparer's file of papers [*if relevant or significant*]
6. Relevant witness statements from either side to the extent that they have been disclosed
7. The letter of claim
8. The letter of response
9. GP records [*these will be inevitable in virtually every case*]
10. Hospital records
11. Care home daily diary entries
12. A family tree.

Your Report

Please let me have your report dealing with your conclusions as to the capacity of Mr Smith to make a will at the time he gave instructions for, and executed, his will in 2012. You will see that I have paginated the GP, hospital, and care-home records. If you rely on any particular document as being relevant to your conclusions then please identify the document not only by the date but also by reference to the page number.

Please insert a formal statement in your report acknowledging your overriding duty to the court and not to the parties who have engaged you. Please also insert at the end of your report before your signature the following statement of truth.

> 'I confirm that I have made clear which facts and matters referred to in this report are within my own knowledge and which are not. Those that are within my own knowledge I confirm to be true. The opinions I have expressed represent my true and complete professional opinions on the matters to which they refer.'

I hope to receive your report within the next eight weeks. If this is not going to be possible then please let me know now. Please acknowledge receipt of these papers.

If you require any further information, assistance, or guidance then please do not hesitate to contact me.

Yours sincerely,

APPENDIX 5

Banks v Goodfellow

The Court of Queen's Bench
6th July 1870
(hearings January 11th and May 13th 1870)
An appeal from a jury trial before Brett J at Cumberland Spring Assizes 1869
The Court:
Cockburn CJ; Blackburn, Mellor, and Hannen JJ
----------oOo----------

COCKBURN, CJ (on behalf of the court):

This is an action brought by the plaintiff, as heir at law of John Banks, to try the validity of a will made by the latter in favour of one Margaret Goodfellow; of whom, she having died since the decease of the testator, the defendant is the heir. The question in issue at the trial was the capacity of the testator to make a will.

Instructions for the will, taken by the attorney who prepared it, were signed by the testator and attested by witnesses in his presence, on the 2nd of December, 1863; the will, formally prepared from such instructions, was duly executed on the 28th of the same month. The question is, whether on both or either of those days the testator was of sound mind, so as to be capable of making a will.

It is a fact beyond dispute that the testator, John Banks, had at former times been of unsound mind. He had been confined, as far back as the year 1841, in the county lunatic asylum; discharged, after a time, from the asylum, he remained subject to certain fixed delusions. He had conceived a violent aversion towards a man named Featherstone Alexander, and notwithstanding the death of the latter some years ago, he continued to believe that this man still pursued and molested him; and the mere mention of Featherstone Alexander's name was sufficient to throw him into a state of violent excitement. He frequently believed that he was pursued and molested by devils or evil spirits, whom he believed to be visibly present. Besides these delusions, which were spoken to by two witnesses whose evidence was above suspicion, the one a medical man who attended him from 1856 to the end of 1862, the other the clergyman of the parish in which the testator resided, there was a body of evidence which, if believed, was strong to establish a case of general insanity. The jury, however, found in favour of the will, and therefore must have believed this evidence to be greatly exaggerated, or must have come to the conclusion that the will was made during a lucid interval.

From September, 1863, he had a succession of epileptic fits, and a blister was applied to his head, and the medical man who attended him throughout this period deposed that his mental power, such as it was, suffered from the fits, and that he considered him insane, and incapable of transacting business during the whole time.

On the other hand, it appeared that the testator managed his own money affairs (which, however, were on a limited scale), and was careful of his money. According to the evidence of a witness named Tolson, who had acted as his agent in receiving the rents of some cottage property at Keswick, amounting to about 80*l* a year, the testator had not only always shewed himself capable of transacting business with him, but had also on the last occasion of Tolson's coming to pay the rents, suggested to him to take a lease of the cottages in question, so as to relieve him (the testator) from all risk or trouble in the matter. He had also desired Tolson, when he came to pay over the next half-year's rents, to bring with him a Mr Ansell, an attorney of Keswick, as he wanted to see him about making a will. On the 2nd of December, 1863, Tolson went to Arkleby, where the testator lived, taking Ansell with him. On their arrival, the testator, according to the statement of Ansell and Tolson, told Ansell he wished to make his will. He fetched from his room a will which he had made in 1838, in favour of his sister, who had since died, and said he wished to give all his property to his niece, Margaret Goodfellow, in the same way. On Mr Ansell asking who should be the executors, the testator turned to his niece, who was present, and asked who she thought should be executors; whereupon she desired that Tolson should be one, and asked who should be the other, when the name of the other executor, Thirlwall, was suggested by a person present, and assented to by the testator. The instructions thus received by Ansell were put down by him on paper, and having been read over to the testator, were, by the desire of Ansell, signed by him, and his signature was formally attested by two witnesses, so as to make the paper a sufficient and valid will, although it was intended that a more formal document should afterwards be prepared and executed; the reason given by Ansell for such signing and attestation of the instructions being, that he always pursued this course when his clients lived at a distance from him, and time would be required between the taking the instructions and the final completion of the will. The distance between Keswick and Arkleby is about twenty miles, and the road was said to be bad.

After the matter of the will had been disposed of, a conversation took place concerning the proposed lease to Tolson. The testator calculated the amount of the rents, and finding that they came to 80*l*, offered Tolson a lease of the cottages for seven years, at a rent of 76*l* a year. This being agreed to by Tolson, Ansell was instructed to prepare a lease on these terms; and the instructions, having been reduced to writing, were signed by the testator and Tolson. After this, Tolson proceeded to settle with the testator for the rents received by him, which amounted to 40*l*. 7*s*. 4*d*. Of this Tolson produced 29*l* in cash, and offered his cheque for the remainder, but the testator observed that a cheque would be of no use to him, as there was no bank near, and desired Tolson to pay the balance into a bank at Keswick, at which the testator had an account. After this, a conversation ensued with a Mrs Routledge, at whose house the testator lodged, as to the amount which he should pay her weekly for his board and lodging combined, which, if truly reported, tended strongly to shew that he was then capable of managing his affairs.

On the 28th of December Tolson took over the will and lease, which had been prepared by Ansell, to the testator, who, having read them two or three times, said they were all right, after which both instruments were executed by him, and the will was duly attested.

The testator lived till July, 1865. His niece, Margaret Goodfellow, survived him, but died in 1867, under age and unmarried. She was his heir at law. He had other nephews and nieces, to whom he is said to have been attached. The effect of the will, if valid, is, that the property goes to the defendant, who is no relation in blood to the testator, as the heir at law of Margaret Goodfellow, instead of to any relative of the testator. This possible consequence of Margaret Goodfellow dying without issue and intestate, does not, however, appear to have presented itself to the mind of any of the parties at the time of making the will.

Upon this evidence, the learned judge left it to the jury to say, '*whether, on the 2nd of December, 1863, or on the 28th of December, 1863, or on both, the testator was capable of having such a knowledge and appreciation of facts, and was so far master of his intentions, free from delusions, as would enable him to have a will of his own in the disposition of his property, and act upon it*'; the learned judge telling the jury that '*the mere fact of his being able to recollect things, or to converse rationally on some subjects, or to manage some business, would not be sufficient to shew he was sane; while, on the other hand, slowness, feebleness, and eccentricities would not be sufficient to shew he was insane*'; with the further direction that '*the whole burden of shewing that the testator was fit at the time was on the defendant*'. The jury returned a verdict for the defendant, saying that they found that the will '*was a good and valid will.*'

The present rule was applied for and obtained on two grounds: first, that the judge misdirected the jury; second, that the verdict was against the weight of the evidence. The alleged misdirection is that the learned judge, in leaving to the jury the question whether at the time of making the will the testator was free from delusions, did not proceed to tell them that though the delusions, under which the testator had undoubtedly before laboured, might not have been present to his mind at the time of making the will, yet, if they were latent in his mind, so that, if the subject had been touched upon, the delusions would have recurred, he was of unsound mind and therefore incapable of making a will.

We must take it, for the present purpose, as a fact, that the testator, though generally of weak intellect, was able to manage his own affairs, and, apart from the delusions under which he laboured, was, at all events at the time of executing one or both of the testamentary instruments in question, of sufficient testamentary capacity. We must also take it that no delusion manifested itself at the time of making the will. On the other hand, there is ample proof that the delusions existed in the interval between the making of the will and the death of the testator, as they had done before; and it is therefore quite possible that these delusions may have remained, at the time of making the will, uncured and latent in the testator's mind, and capable of being evoked and reproduced at any moment, if anything had occurred to lead his thoughts to the subject.

The inquiry not having been directed to this point, it is quite possible that all that the jury meant in finding in the affirmative of the question whether the testator was '*free from delusions*' at the time of making his will, was that the delusions were not present to his consciousness, not that they were eradicated from his mind; and that if the question had been specifically put to them whether the delusions still remained latent in the testator's mind, and his mind was to the extent of these delusions unsound, they would have found in the affirmative.

It therefore becomes necessary to consider how far such a degree of unsoundness of mind as is involved in the delusions under which this testator laboured would be fatal to testamentary capacity; in other words, whether delusions arising from mental disease, but not calculated to prevent the exercise of the faculties essential to the making of a will, or to interfere with the consideration of the matters which should be weighed and taken into account on such an occasion, and which delusions had in point of fact no influence whatever on the testamentary disposition in question, are sufficient to deprive a testator of testamentary capacity and to invalidate a will.

We must assume, for the present purpose, that the testator laboured under the insane delusions ascribed to him; but, on the other hand, that these delusions had not, nor were calculated to have, any influence on him in the disposal of his property; and that, irrespective of these delusions, the state of his mental faculties was such as to render him capable of making a will. For, whatever may have been the evidence as to general insanity, the verdict of the jury, which there was ample evidence to support, and in which the learned judge who presided at the trial states that he concurs, establishes that at the time of making the will, irrespectively of the delusions referred to, the testator was sufficiently in possession of his faculties.

The question whether partial unsoundness, not affecting the general faculties, and not operating on the mind of a testator in regard to the particular testamentary disposition, will be sufficient to deprive a person of the power of disposing of his property, presents itself here for judicial decision, so far as we are aware, for the first time. It is true that, in the case of *Waring v Waring* 6 Moo. P. C. 841, the Judicial Committee of the Privy Council, and, in the more recent case of *Smith v Tebbitt* Law Rep 1 P & M 398 Lord Penzance, in the Court of Probate, have laid down a doctrine, according to which any degree of mental unsoundness, however slight, and however unconnected with the testamentary disposition in question, must be held fatal to the capacity of a testator. But in both these cases, as we shall presently shew, the wide doctrine embraced in the judgment was wholly unnecessary to the decision, and we therefore feel ourselves warranted, and indeed bound, to consider the question as one not concluded by authority, and on which we are called upon to form our own judgment. The question is one of equal importance and difficulty, and we have given it our best consideration.

The text-writers throw no light upon the point. They content themselves with stating in general terms that to be capable of making a will a man must be of sound disposing mind and memory, and that persons non compotes cannot make a will; but they are silent as to the degree of mental disturbance which will amount to a want of disposing mind and memory. The cases prior to *Waring v Waring*, in which the law on the subject of mental unsoundness, as affecting the capacity to make a will, has come into question, are by no means numerous. It may be as well to pass them in review.

In *Combe's Case* Moore 759: s.c. 8 Vin Abr 43, No. 22 it is said to have been agreed by the judges, '*that sane memory for the making of a will is not always where the party can in some things answer with sense, but he ought to have judgment to discern and to be of perfect memory, otherwise the will is void.*' So, again, in the *Marquis of Winchester's Case* 6 Rep.23, '*By the law, it is not sufficient that the testator be of memory, when he makes the will, to answer familiar and usual questions, but he ought to have a disposing memory, so as to be able to make a disposition of his estate with understanding and reason.*' In the case of *Greenwood v Greenwood* 3 Curt App. xxx, an action brought to recover estates under a will, the validity of which was disputed, the principal indication of insanity relied on being a strange aversion on the part of the testator towards his only brother, his heir at law, and a groundless suspicion of the latter having attempted to poison him, Lord Kenyon, in charging the jury, said: '*I take it a mind and memory competent to dispose of property, when it is a little explained, perhaps may stand thus: having that degree of recollection about him that would enable him to look about the property he had to dispose of, and the persons to whom he wished to dispose of it. If he had a power of summoning up his mind, so as to know what his property was, and who those persons were that then were the objects of his bounty, then he was competent to make his will.*' In other cases, such as the well-known case of *Dew v Clark* (3 Add.79): Haggard's Report of Judgment p 19, the insane delusion had a direct bearing on the provisions of the will. In such cases, the delusion being once proved, and its connection with the will being manifest, there could be no difficulty in setting aside the will. Cases of this description afford little or no assistance towards the solution of the question before us. Again, other cases occurring prior to the case of *Waring v Waring*, such as *The Attorney General v Parnther* (3 Bro. C. C. 441) and *Cartwright v Cartwright* (1 Phillim. 90, 100), had reference to the effect to be given to a lucid interval at the time of making the will, rather than to the degree of mental unsoundness which would constitute testamentary incapacity. The judgment in the latter case is, however, not unworthy of attention. The case was a remarkable one, from the fact that the will had been made by a person actually confined in a lunatic asylum, and who was undoubtedly insane both before and after the making of the will; nevertheless it was upheld. Sir William Wynne, the then Judge of the Prerogative Court of Canterbury, in giving judgment, uses language tending strongly to shew that, in his opinion, the rationality of the act done affords an effectual test of the mental capacity of the party doing it. He says: '*I think the strongest and best proof that can arise as to a lucid interval is that which arises from the act itself: that I look upon as the thing to be first examined, and if it can be proved and established that it is a rational act rationally done, the whole case is proved. What can you do more to establish the act? Because, suppose you are able to shew that the party did that which appears to be a rational act, and it is his own act entirely, nothing is left to presumption in order to prove a lucid interval. Here is a rational act rationally done. In my apprehension, where you are able completely to establish that, the law does not require you to go further, and the citation from Swinburne (Swinburne, part ii s.3) states it to be so. The manner he has laid it down is (it is in the part (2) in which he treats of what persons may make a will): "If a lunatic person, or one that is beside himself at some times, but not continually, make his testament, and it is not known whether the same were made while he was of sound mind and memory or no, then, in case the testament be so conceived as thereby no argument of phrensy or folly can be gathered, it is to be presumed that the same was made during the time of his calm and clear intermissions; and so the testament shall be adjudged good, yea, although it cannot be proved that the testator useth to have any clear and quiet intermissions at all, yet, nevertheless, I suppose that if the testament be wisely and orderly framed, the same ought to be accepted for a lawful testament.*"'

'*Unquestionably*,' Sir William Wynne continues, '*there must be a complete and absolute proof the party who had so framed it did it without any assistance. If the fact be so that he has done as rational an act as can be, without any assistance from another person, what there is more to be proved, I don't know, unless the gentlemen could prove by any authority, or law, what the length of the lucid interval is to be, whether an hour, a day, or a month. I know no such law as that. All that is wanting is, that it should be of sufficient length to do the rational act intended. I look upon it, if you are able to establish the fact that the act done is perfectly proper, and that the party who is alleged to have done it was free from the disorder at the time, that is completely sufficient.*'

Without going to the length of adopting to its full extent what is here said as to the effect of the rational character of the will, or at all saying that effect can be given to the rationality of the disposition beyond, that which is due to it as evidence of the sanity of the testator, we advert to this case and the judgment of Sir William Wynne as shewing that a more indulgent view of the effect of insanity, as affecting testamentary incapacity, was then taken than has latterly prevailed.

We come now to the case of *Waring v Waring* (since followed by that of *Smith v Tebbitt*) in which the doctrine now contended for on behalf of the plaintiff was for the first time laid down. It may be shortly stated thus: To constitute testamentary capacity, soundness of mind is indispensably necessary. But the mind, though it has various faculties, is one and indivisible. If it is disordered in any one of these faculties, if it labours under any delusion arising from such disorder, though its other faculties and functions may remain undisturbed, it cannot be said to be sound. Such a mind is unsound, and testamentary incapacity is the necessary consequence.

As has already been observed, neither in *Waring v Waring* nor in *Smith v Tebbitt*, was the doctrine thus laid down in any degree necessary to the decision. Both these were cases of general, not of partial, insanity; in both the delusions were multifarious, and of the wildest and most irrational character, abundantly indicating that the mind was diseased throughout. In both there was an insane suspicion or dislike of persons who should have been objects of affection; and, what is still more important, in both it was palpable that the delusions must have influenced the testamentary disposition impugned. In both these cases, therefore, there existed ample grounds for setting aside the will without resorting to the doctrine in question. Unable to concur in it, we have felt at liberty to consider for ourselves the principle properly applicable to such a case as the present. We do not think it necessary to consider the position assumed in *Waring v Waring*, that the mind is one and indivisible, or to discuss the subject as matter of metaphysical or psychological inquiry. It is not given to man to fathom the mystery of the human intelligence, or to ascertain the constitution of our sentient and intellectual being. But whatever may be its essence, everyone must be conscious that the faculties and functions of the mind are various and distinct, as are the powers and functions of our physical organization. The senses, the instincts, the affections, the passions, the moral qualities, the will, perception, thought, reason, imagination, memory, are so many distinct faculties or functions of the mind. The pathology of mental disease and the experience of insanity in its various forms teach us that while, on the one hand, all the faculties, moral and intellectual, may be involved in one common ruin, as in the case of the raving maniac, in other instances one or more only of these faculties or functions may be disordered, while the rest are left unimpaired and undisturbed—that while the mind may be overpowered by delusions which utterly demoralize it and unfit it for the perception of the true nature of surrounding things, or for the discharge of the common obligations of life, there often are, on the other hand, delusions, which, though the offspring of mental disease and so far constituting insanity, yet leave the individual in all other respects rational, and capable of transacting the ordinary affairs and fulfilling the duties and obligations incidental to the various relations of life. No doubt when delusions exist which have no foundation in reality, and spring only from a diseased and morbid condition of the mind, to that extent the mind must necessarily be taken to be unsound; just as the body, if any of its parts or functions is affected by local disease, may be said to be unsound, though all its other members may be healthy, and their powers or functions unimpaired. But the question still remains, whether such partial unsoundness of the mind, if it leaves the affections, the moral sense, and the general power of the understanding unaffected, and is wholly unconnected with the testamentary disposition, should have the effect of taking away the testamentary capacity.

We readily concede that where a delusion has had, as in the case of *Dew v Clark*, or is calculated to have had, an influence on the testamentary disposition, it must be held to be fatal to its validity. Thus if, as occurs in a common form of monomania, a man is under a delusion that he is the object of persecution or attack, and makes a will in which he excludes a child for whom he ought to have provided; though he may not have adverted to that child as one of his supposed enemies, it would be but reasonable to infer that the insane condition had influenced him in the disposal of his property. But, in the case we are dealing with, the delusion must be taken neither to have had any influence on the provisions of the will, nor to have been capable of having any; and the question is, whether a delusion, thus wholly innocuous in its results as regards the disposition of the will, is to be held to have the effect of destroying the capacity to make one.

The state of our own authorities being such as we have shown, we have turned to the jurisprudence of other countries, as on a matter of common juridical interest, to see whether we could there find any assistance towards the solution of the question. We have, however, derived but little advantage from the inquiry. The Roman law, the great storehouse of juridical science, is as vague and general on the subject as our own. The madman (*furiosus*), and the person of defective intelligence (*mente captus*), are declared incapable of making a testament; but as to what shall constitute madness or defectiveness of intelligence, sufficient to prevent the exercise of the testamentary right, the authorities are silent. The continental codes are equally general in their terms, simply providing either that persons must be of sound mind to make a will, or that persons of unsound mind shall be disabled from doing so. The older writers appear not to have been alive to the distinction between total and partial unsoundness as affecting testamentary capacity. In recent times, however, the question has been mooted by eminent and distinguished jurists, but unfortunately with a marked discordance of opinion. M. Troplong, in his well-known work, '*Le Droit Civil Expliqué*' (Commentaire sur le donations entre vifs et testaments, tom. ii 451–7), and M. Sacase, in a treatise entitled '*La Folie considérée dans ses rapports avec la Capacite Civilé*' (p. 16), have adopted the doctrine of the unity and indivisibility of the mind, and the consequent unsoundness of the whole if insane delusion anywhere exist. Writers equally entitled to respect have maintained the contrary view. Legrand du Saulle, in a very able work, entitled *La Folie 'Devant les Tribunaux'* (p. 146) contends that '*hallucinations are not a sufficient obstacle to the power of making a will, if they have exercised no influence on the conduct of the testator, have not altered his natural affections, or prevented the fulfilment of his social and domestic duties; while, on the other hand, the will of a person affected by insane delusion ought not to be admitted if he has disinherited his family without cause, or looked on his relations as enemies, or accused them of seeking to poison him, or the like. In all such cases, where the delusion exercises a fatal influence on the acts of the person affected, the condition of the testamentary power fails: the will of the party is no longer under the guidance of reason, it becomes the creature of the insane delusion.*' M. Demolombe, in his great work, the *Cours de Code Napoleon* (Traité des donations entre vifs et testaments Liv. iii tit. 2 ch. ii), M. Castlenau, in his treatise, '*Sur l'Interdiction des Aliénés*', and Hoffbauer, in his remarkable work on Medical Jurisprudence relating to Insanity, have maintained the doctrine that monomania, or partial insanity, not affecting the testamentary disposition, does not take away the testamentary capacity. Mazzoni, in a recent work, entitled '*Istituzioni di diritto civile Italiano*' (Liv. iii tit. 2, s 3), lays it down that '*monomania is not an unsoundness of mind which absolutely and necessarily takes away testamentary capacity, as the monomaniac may have the perfect exercise of his faculties in respect of all subjects beyond the sphere of the partial derangement.*'

None of these writers, however, have gone very deeply into the subject, or considered it with reference to the principles on which mental alienation should be held to form a ground for taking away testamentary capacity. The older jurists were content to say that an insane person was incapable of making a testament, because he has no mind, '*quia mente caret*', as it is said in the *Institutes* (Instit. Lib. II. Tit. 12, 1); or because he could not have a will, and therefore was incapable of declaring his ultimate will as to the disposal of his property—positions obviously unsatisfactory when the fact becomes recognized that a man may labour under harmless delusions, which leave the other faculties of his mind unaffected, and leave him free to make a disposition of his property uninfluenced by their existence. In our day the doctrine has sprung up of the unity and indivisibility of the mind, but the ground on which insanity should cause incapacity appears to have been overlooked in the reasoning on which it is founded. It is important to recall it.

The law of every civilized people concedes to the owner of property the right of determining by his last will, either in whole or in part, to whom the effects which he leaves behind him shall pass. Yet it is clear that, though the law leaves to the owner of property absolute freedom in this ultimate disposal of that of which he is thus enabled to dispose, a moral responsibility of no ordinary importance attaches to the exercise of the right thus given. The instincts and affections of mankind, in the vast majority of instances, will lead men to make provision for those who are the nearest to them in kindred and who in life have been the objects of their affection. Independently of any law, a man on the point of leaving the world would naturally distribute among his children or nearest relatives the property which he possessed. The same motives will influence him in the exercise of the right *of* disposal when secured to him by law. Hence arises a reasonable and well warranted expectation on the part of a man's kindred surviving him, that on his death his effects shall become theirs, instead of being given to strangers. To disappoint the expectation thus created and to disregard the claims of kindred to the inheritance is to shock the common sentiments of mankind, and to violate what all men concur in deeming an obligation of the moral law. It cannot be supposed that, in giving the power of testamentary disposition, the law has been framed in disregard of these considerations. On the contrary, had they stood alone, it is probable that the power of testamentary disposition would have been withheld, and that the distribution of property after the owner's death would have been uniformly regulated by the law itself. But there are other considerations which turn the scale in favour of the testamentary power. Among those who, as a man's nearest relatives, would be entitled to share the fortune he leaves behind him, some may be better provided for than others; some may be more deserving than others; some from age, or sex, or physical infirmity, may stand in greater need of assistance. Friendship and tried attachment, or faithful service, may have claims that ought not to be disregarded. In the power of rewarding dutiful and meritorious conduct, paternal authority finds a useful auxiliary; age secures the respect and attentions which are one of its chief consolations. As was truly said by Chancellor Kent, in *Van Alst v Hunter* (5 Johnson NY Ch Rep at p 150), '*It is one of the painful consequences of extreme old age that it ceases to excite interest, and is apt to be left solitary and neglected. The control which the law still gives to a man over the disposal of his property is one of the most efficient means which he has in protracted life to command the attentions due to his infirmities.*' For these reasons the power of disposing of property in anticipation of death has ever been regarded as one of the most valuable of the rights incidental to property, while there can be no doubt that it operates as a useful incentive to industry in the acquisition of wealth, and to thrift and frugality in the enjoyment of it. The law of every country has therefore conceded to the owner of property the right of disposing by will either of the whole, or, at all events, of a portion, of that which he possesses. The Roman law, and that of the Continental nations which have followed it, have secured to the relations of a deceased person in the ascending and descending line a fixed portion of the inheritance. The English law leaves everything to the unfettered discretion of the testator, on the assumption that, though in some instances, caprice, or passion, or the power of new ties, or artful contrivance, or sinister influence, may lead to the neglect of claims that ought to be attended to, yet, the instincts, affections, and common sentiments of mankind may be safely trusted to secure, on the whole, a better disposition of the property of the dead, and one more accurately adjusted to the requirements of each particular case, than could be obtained through a distribution prescribed by the stereotyped and inflexible rules of a general law.

It is unnecessary to consider whether the principle of the foreign law or that of our own is the wiser. It is obvious, in either case, that to the due exercise of a power thus involving moral responsibility, the possession of the intellectual and moral faculties common to our nature should be insisted on as an indispensable condition. It is essential to the exercise of such a power that a testator shall understand the nature of the act and its effects; shall understand the extent of the property of which he is disposing; shall be able to comprehend and appreciate the claims to which he ought to give effect; and, with a view to the latter object, that no disorder of the mind shall poison his affections, pervert his sense of right, or prevent the exercise of his natural faculties—that no insane delusion shall influence his will in disposing of his property and bring about a disposal of it which, if the mind had been sound, would not have been made.

Here, then, we have the measure of the degree of mental power which should be insisted on. If the human instincts and affections, or the moral sense, become perverted by mental disease; if insane suspicion, or aversion, take the place of natural affection; if reason and judgment are lost, and the mind becomes a prey to insane delusions calculated to interfere with and disturb its functions, and to lead to a testamentary disposition due only to their baneful influence—in such a case it is obvious that the condition of the testamentary power fails, and that a will made under such circumstances ought not to stand. But what if the mind, though possessing sufficient power, undisturbed by frenzy or delusion, to take into account all the considerations necessary to the proper making of a will, should be subject to some delusion, but such delusion neither exercises nor is calculated to exercise any influence on the particular disposition, and a rational and proper will is the result; ought we, in such case, to deny to the testator the capacity to dispose of his property by will? It must be borne in mind that the absolute and uncontrolled power of testamentary disposition conceded by the law is founded on the assumption that a rational will is a better disposition than any that can be made by the law itself. If therefore, though mental disease may exist, it presents itself in such a degree and form as not to interfere with the capacity to make a rational disposal of property, why, it may be asked, should it be held to take away the right? It cannot be the object of the legislator to aggravate an affliction in itself so great by the deprivation of a right the value of which is universally felt and acknowledged. If it be conceded, as we think it must be, that the only legitimate or rational ground for denying testamentary capacity to persons of unsound mind is the inability to take into account and give due effect to the considerations which ought to be present to the mind of a testator in making his will, and to influence his decision as to the disposal of his property, it follows that a degree or form of unsoundness which neither disturbs the exercise of the faculties necessary for such an act, nor is capable of influencing the result, ought not to take away the power of making a will, or place a person so circumstanced in a less advantageous position than others with regard to this right.

It may be here not unimportant to advert to the law relating to unsoundness of mind arising from another cause—namely, from want of intelligence occasioned by defective organization, or by supervening physical infirmity or the decay of advancing age, as distinguished from mental derangement, such defect of intelligence being equally a cause of incapacity. In these cases it is admitted on all hands that though the mental power may be reduced below the ordinary standard, yet if there be sufficient intelligence to understand and appreciate the testamentary act in its different bearings, the power to make a will remains. It is enough if, to use the words of Sir Edward Williams, in his work on Executors, '*the mental faculties retain sufficient strength fully to comprehend the testamentary act about to be done*' (*Williams on Executors* 6th ed. Vol. 1 p. 37, n. x). '*Non sani tantum*,' says Voet in his *Commentary on the Pandects* (Lib. 28, tit. I, s. 36), founding himself on the language of the Code, Book 6, tit. 23, 1.15, '*sed et in agone mortis positi, seminece ac balbutiente lingua voluntatem prornentes, recte testamenta condunt, si modo mente adhuc valeant*.'

This part of the law has been extremely well treated in more than one case in the American Courts.

In the case of *Harrison v Rowan* (3 Washington, at p. 585; referred to in *Sloan v Maxwell*, 2 H. W. Green (New Jersey Ch. Rep.) at p. 570), in the United States Circuit Court for the district of New Jersey, the law was thus laid down by the presiding judge: '*As to the testator's capacity, he must, in the language of the law, have a sound and disposing mind and memory. In other words, he ought to be capable of making his will with an understanding of the nature of the business in which he is engaged, a recollection of the property he means to dispose of, of the persons who are the objects of his bounty, and the manner in which it is to be distributed between them. It is not necessary that he should view his will with the eye of a lawyer, and comprehend its provisions in their legal form. It is sufficient if he has such a mind and memory as will enable him to understand the elements of which it is composed, and the disposition of his property in its simple forms. In deciding upon the capacity of the testator to make his will, it is the soundness of the mind, and not the particular state of the bodily health, that is to be attended to; the latter may be in a state of extreme imbecility, and yet he may possess sufficient understanding to direct how his property shall be disposed of; his capacity may be perfect to dispose of his property by will, and yet very inadequate to the management of other business, as, for instance, to make contracts for the purchase or sale of property. For, most men, at different periods of their lives, have meditated upon the subject of the disposition of their property by will, and when called upon to have their intentions committed to writing, they find much less difficulty in declaring their intentions than they could in comprehending business in some measure new.*'

In the case of *Den v Vancleve* (12 Southard at p. 660) the law was thus stated: '*By the terms "a sound and disposing mind and memory" it has not been understood that a testator must possess these qualities of the mind in the highest degree; otherwise, very few could make testaments at all; neither has it been understood that he must possess them in as great a degree as he may have formerly done; for even this would disable most men in the decline of life; the mind may have been in some degree debilitated, the memory may have become in some degree enfeebled; and yet there may be enough left clearly to discern and discreetly to judge, of all those things, and all those circumstances, which enter into the nature of a rational, fair, and just testament. But if they have so far failed as that these cannot be discerned and judged of, then he cannot be said to be of sound and disposing mind and memory.*'

In the subsequent case of *Stevens v Vancleve* (4 Washington at p. 267) it is said: '*The testator must, in the language of the law, be possessed of sound and disposing mind and memory. He must have memory; a man in whom the faculty is totally extinguished cannot be said to possess understanding to any degree whatever, or for any purpose. But his memory may be very imperfect; it may be greatly impaired by age or disease; he may not be able at all times to recollect the names, the persons, or the families of those with whom he had been intimately acquainted; may at times ask idle questions, and repeat those which had before been asked and answered, and yet his understanding may be sufficiently sound for many of the ordinary transactions of life. He may not have sufficient strength of memory and vigour of intellect to make and to digest all the parts of a contract, and yet be competent to direct the distribution of his property by will. This is a subject which he may possibly have often thought of, and there is probably no person who has not arranged such a disposition in his mind before he committed it to writing. The question is not so much what was the degree of memory possessed by the testator? as this: Had he a disposing memory? was he capable of recollecting the property he was about to bequeath; the manner of distributing it; and the objects of his bounty? To sum up the whole in the most simple and intelligible form, were his mind and memory sufficiently sound to enable him to know and to understand the business in which he was engaged at the time he executed his will?*'

This view of the law is fully adopted by the Court in the case of *Sloan v Maxwell* (2 H W Green (N J Chan. R) 563), and is there stated to have been approved by Chancellor Vroom in a case as to the will of Tace Wallace, which, however, is not reported. It appears to have had the sanction of Chancellor Kent, in the case of *Van AM v Hunter* (5 Johnson N Y Ch Rep at 159), already referred to.

In a case of *Harwood v Bolter* (3 Moo PC 282), before the Judicial Committee of the Privy Council, in which case a will had been executed by a testator on his deathbed, in favour of a second wife, to the exclusion of the other members of his family, he being in a state of weakened and impaired capacity from disease producing torpor of the brain, and rendering his mind incapable of exertion unless roused, Erskine, J, delivered the judgment of the Court in these terms: (3 Moo P C at 291) '*Their Lordships are of opinion that, in order to constitute a sound disposing mind, a testator must not only be able to understand that he is by his will giving the whole of his property to one object of his regard, but he must also have capacity to comprehend the extent of his property, and the nature of the claims of others, whom by his will he is excluding from all participation in that property; and that the protection of the law is in no cases more needed than it is in those where the mind has been too much enfeebled to comprehend more objects than one; and more especially, when that one object may be so forced upon the attention of the invalid as to shut out all others that might require consideration. And, therefore, the question which their Lordships propose to decide in this case is, not whether Mr Baker knew, when he executed this will, that he was giving all his property to his wife, and excluding all his other relations from any share in it, but whether he was at that time capable of recollecting who those relations were, of understanding their respective claims upon his regard and bounty, and of deliberately forming an intelligent purpose of excluding them from any share of his property. If he had not the capacity required, the propriety of the disposition made by the will is a matter of no importance. If he had it, the injustice of the exclusion would not affect the validity of the disposition, though the justice or injustice of the disposition might cast down some light upon the question as to his capacity.*'

From this language it is to be inferred that the standard of capacity in cases of impaired mental power is, to use the words of the judgment, the capacity on the part of the testator to comprehend the extent of the property to be disposed of, and the nature of the claims of those he is excluding. Why should not this standard be also applicable to mental unsoundness produced by mental disease?

It may be said that the analogy between the two cases is imperfect; that there is an essential difference between unsoundness of mind arising from congenital defect, or supervening infirmity, and the perversion of thought and feeling produced by mental disease, the latter being far more likely to give rise to an inofficious will than the mere deficiency of mental power. This is, no doubt, true, but it becomes immaterial on the hypothesis that the disorder of the mind has left the faculties, on which the proper exercise of the testamentary power depends, unaffected, and that a rational will, uninfluenced by the mental disorder, has been the result.

It is said, indeed, by those who insist that any degree of unsoundness should suffice to take away testamentary capacity, that where insane delusion has shewn itself, it is always possible, and indeed may be assumed to be probable, that a greater degree of mental unsoundness exists than has actually become manifest. But this view, which is by no means universally admitted, is unsupported by proof, and must be looked upon as matter of speculative opinion. It seems unreasonable to deny testamentary capacity on the speculative possibility of unsoundness which has failed to display itself, and which, if existing in a latent and undiscovered form, would be little likely to have any influence on the disposition of the will. No doubt, where the fact that the testator has been subject to any insane delusion is established, a will should be regarded with great distrust, and every presumption should in the first instance be made against it. Where insane delusion has once been shewn to have existed, it may be difficult to say whether the mental disorder may not possibly have extended beyond the particular form or instance in which it has manifested itself. It may be equally difficult to say how far the delusion may not have influenced the testator in the particular disposal of his property. And the presumption against a will made under such circumstances becomes additionally strong where the will is, to use the term of the civilians, an inofficious one, that is to say, one in which natural affection and the claims of near relationship have been disregarded. But where in the result a jury are satisfied that the delusion has not affected the general faculties of the mind, and can have had no effect upon the will, we see no sufficient reason why the testator should be held to have lost his right to make a will, or why a will made under such circumstances should not be upheld. Such an inquiry may involve, it is true, considerable difficulty, and require much nicety of discrimination, but we see no reason to think that it is beyond the power of judicial investigation and decision, or may not be disposed of by a jury directed and guided by a judge. In the case before us, two delusions disturbed the mind of the testator; the one that he was pursued by spirits, the other that a man long since dead came personally to molest him. Neither of these delusions—the dead man not having been in any way connected with him—had, or could have had, any influence upon him in disposing of his property. The will, though in one sense an idle one, inasmuch as the object of his bounty was his heir at law, and therefore would have taken the property without its being devised to her, was yet rational in this, that it was made in favour of a niece, who lived with him, and who was the object of his affection and regard. And we must take it on the finding of the jury that irrespectively of the question of these dormant delusions, the testator was in possession of his faculties when the will was executed.

Under these circumstances, we see no ground for holding the will to be invalid. If, indeed, it had been possible to connect the dispositions of the will with the delusions of the testator, the form in which the case was left to the jury might have been open to exception. It may be, as was contended on the part of the plaintiff, that in a case of unsoundness, founded on delusion, but which delusion was not manifested at the time of making the will, it is a question for the jury whether the delusion was not latent in the mind of the testator. But, then, for the reasons we have given in the course of this judgment, we are of opinion that a jury should be told, in such a case, that the existence of a delusion, compatible with the retention of the general powers and faculties of the mind, will not be sufficient to overthrow the will, unless it were such as was calculated to influence the testator in making it.

This, in effect, disposes of the question of misdirection. As, for the reasons we have given, we are of opinion that if the testator was, at the time of making the will, of capacity to make a will as defined by the learned judge, the existence of mental disease, if latent, so as to leave him free from the consciousness and influence of delusion, there having been a total absence of all connection between the delusion and the will, would not overthrow the will, it follows that there can have been, practically speaking, no misdirection in not leaving the question of latent delusion to the jury. Where delusions are of such a nature as is calculated to influence the testator in making the particular disposition, as was the case in *Waring v Waring* (G Moo. P. C. 341), and in *Smith v Tebbitt* (Law Rep. 1 P. & M. 398), a jury would not in general be justified in coming to the conclusion that the delusion, still existing, was latent at the time, so as to leave the testator free from any influence arising from it; but in the present case the disposition was quite unconnected with the delusions, and consequently there is no reason to suppose that the omission to call the attention of the jury to this specifically can have affected the verdict. Looking to the evidence given on the trial, and to the verdict of the jury, it appears to us that if this case were submitted to another jury, whatever they might find as to the existence of latent delusion, their decision must be in favour of the will as to the absence of all connection between the delusions and the disposition made by the testator. It would, consequently, be worse than useless to put the parties to the expense of a new trial, when in our judgment the only proper or possible result must be a second verdict establishing the will.

Counsel:
Manisty, Q. C., Aspinall, Q. C., and *Kemplay,* for the plaintiff.
Holker, Q. C., and *C. Hutton,* for the defendant.
Attorney for plaintiff: J. G. Waugh.
Attorneys for defendant: Nethersole and Speechley.

INDEX